INTERPRETING ISAIAH

INTERPRETING ISAIAH

Issues and Approaches

Edited by
David G. Firth *and*
H. G. M. Williamson

APOLLOS

IVP Academic
An imprint of InterVarsity Press
Downers Grove, Illinois

APOLLOS (an imprint of Inter-Varsity Press, England)   InterVarsity Press, USA
Norton Street, Nottingham NG7 3HR   P.O. Box 1400, Downers Grove, IL 60515-1426
Website: www.ivpbooks.com   World Wide Web: www.ivpress.com
Email: ivp@ivpbooks.com   Email: email@ivpress.com

UK ISBN 978-1-84474-382-7
USA ISBN 978-0-8308-3703-8

Set in Monotype Garamond 11/13pt
Typeset in Great Britain by Servis Filmsetting Ltd, Stockport, Cheshire
Printed and bound in Great Britain by 4edge Ltd

British Library Cataloguing in Publication Data

A catalogue record for this book is available from the British Library.

Library of Congress Cataloging-in-Publication Data

Interpreting Isaiah: issues and approaches / edited by David G. Firth
and H. G. M. Williamson.
        p. cm.
    Includes bibliographical references and indexes.
    ISBN 978-0-8308-3703-8 (US: pbk.: alk. paper)—ISBN
    978-1-84474-382-7 (UK: pbk.: alk. paper)
    1. Bible. O.T. Isaiah—Criticism, interpretation, etc.   I. Firth,
    David G. II. Williamson, H. G. M. (Hugh Godfrey Maturin), 1947-
    BS1515.52.I58 2009

    224'.106—dc22

                                                                2009013292

P   19   18   17   16   15   14   13   12   11   10   9   8   7   6   5   4   3   2   1
Y   25   24   23   22   21   20   19   18   17   16   15   14   13   12   11   10   09

CONTENTS

CONTRIBUTORS

John Goldingay is David Allan Hubbard Professor of Old Testament at Fuller Theological Seminary, Pasadena. He is the author of commentaries on Isaiah, Psalms and Daniel, and of an Old Testament Theology.

Philip S. Johnston is Senior Tutor in Old Testament at Wycliffe Hall, Oxford. He has co-authored a book of Hebrew vocabulary analysis (*Les Psaumes*) and studied the Old Testament portrayal of death and afterlife in *Shades of Sheol*. He is also co-editor of *Interpreting the Psalms*.

Nathan MacDonald is Lecturer in Old Testament at the University of St Andrews, Scotland, and leader of the Sofja-Kovalevskaja research team at Georg-August Universität Göttingen, Germany. He is the author and editor of five books including *Deuteronomy and the Meaning of 'Monotheism'* and *Not Bread Alone*.

David J. Reimer is Senior Lecturer in Biblical Studies at the University of Edinburgh, with a particular interest in Old Testament theology and ethics.

Richard L. Schultz is the Carl Armerding and Hudson T. Armerding Professor of Biblical Studies at Wheaton College in Wheaton, Illinois, having previously taught in Giessen, Germany. He is author of *The Search for Quotation:*

Verbal Parallels in the Prophets, which reflects his long-term interest in the book of Isaiah and in inner-biblical interpretation.

S. D. (Fanie) Snyman is professor of Old Testament Studies at the University of the Free State in South Africa. He completed his doctoral dissertation on the book of Malachi and has published numerous articles in journals. He has also co-authored a number of books in Afrikaans.

Jacob Stromberg has taught Hebrew and Old Testament at Oxford University and Duke Divinity School. In 2008 he completed his doctorate at Oxford on the post-exilic formation of Isaiah. His dissertation will be published shortly. He is also writing an introduction to Isaiah.

Dwight Swanson is Senior Lecturer in Biblical Studies at Nazarene Theological College, Manchester. His academic focus is on Qumran. He is author of *The Temple Scroll and the Bible* and is researching the use of the Bible in the Dead Sea Scrolls.

Torsten Uhlig did his undergraduate studies at the University of Leipzig and wrote his PhD thesis, 'The Theme of Hardening in the Book of Isaiah', at the University of Gloucestershire. He works as a pastor in the Evangelical Lutheran Church of Saxony in Germany.

Rikk E. Watts is Professor of New Testament at Regent College, Vancouver. He has written *Isaiah's New Exodus in Mark*, a commentary on the Old Testament in Mark and a range of articles on Isaiah and the use of the Old Testament in the New Testament.

Paul D. Wegner is Professor of Old Testament at Phoenix Seminary, Phoenix, Arizona. He is author of *The Journey from Texts to Translations*, *A Student's Guide to Textual Criticism of the Bible* and *Using Hebrew in Ministry*.

H. G. M. Williamson is Regius Professor of Hebrew in the University of Oxford. In addition to commentaries on Chronicles and Ezra-Nehemiah, he has published widely on Isaiah, including *The Book Called Isaiah* and *Isaiah 1 – 5*.

Lindsay Wilson is Vice Principal and Lecturer in Old Testament at Ridley Melbourne Mission and Ministry College, Melbourne, Australia. He has written *Joseph Wise and Otherwise*, and has just completed a commentary on *Job* in the Two Horizons series.

ABBREVIATIONS

1QIsa^a	Isaiah^a, Cave 1, Qumran
1QIsa^b	Isaiah^b, Cave 1, Qumran
3QpIsa	Pesher Isaiah, Cave 3, Qumran
4QcryptA	Words of the Maskil to All Sons of Dawn, Cave 4, Qumran
4QDeut^q	Deuteronomy^q, Cave 4, Qumran
4QIsa^a	Isaiah^a, Cave 4, Qumran
4QIsa^b	Isaiah^b, Cave 4, Qumran
4QIsa^c	Isaiah^c, Cave 4, Qumran
4QIsa^d	Isaiah^d, Cave 4, Qumran
4QIsa^e	Isaiah^e, Cave 4, Qumran
4QIsa^f	Isaiah^f, Cave 4, Qumran
4QIsa^g	Isaiah^g, Cave 4, Qumran
4QIsa^h	Isaiah^h, Cave 4, Qumran
4QIsaⁱ	Isaiahⁱ, Cave 4, Qumran
4QIsa^j	Isaiah^j, Cave 4, Qumran
4QIsa^k	Isaiah^k, Cave 4, Qumran
4QIsa^l	Isaiah^l, Cave 4, Qumran
4QIsa^m	Isaiah^m, Cave 4, Qumran
4QIsaⁿ	Isaiahⁿ, Cave 4, Qumran
4QIsa^o	Isaiah^o, Cave 4, Qumran
4QIsa^p	Isaiah^p, Cave 4, Qumran

4QIsa^q	Isaiah^q, Cave 4, Qumran

4QIsa^q   Isaiah^q, Cave 4, Qumran
4QIsa^r   Isaiah^r, Cave 4, Qumran
4QpapIsa^p   Papyrus Isaiah^p, Cave 4, Qumran
4Qpap pIsa^c Papyrus Pesher Isaiah^c, Cave 4, Qumran
4QpIsa^a   Pesher Isaiah^a, Cave 4, Qumran
4QpIsa^b   Pesher Isaiah^b, Cave 4, Qumran
4QpIsa^c   Pesher Isaiah^c, Cave 4, Qumran
4QpIsa^d   Pesher Isaiah^d, Cave 4, Qumran
4QpIsa^e   Pesher Isaiah^e, Cave 4, Qumran
5QIsa   Isaiah, Cave 5, Qumran
11QPs^a   Psalms^a, Cave 11, Qumran
Mur Isa   Dead Sea Scroll fragment with parts of Isaiah 1:4–14
AB   Anchor Bible
ABD   *Anchor Bible Dictionary*, ed. D. N. Freedman, 6 vols. (New York: Doubleday, 1992)
ACCS   Ancient Christian Commentary on Scripture
AHw   *Akkadisches Handwörterbuch*, W. F. von Soden, 3 vols. (Wiesbaden: Harrossowitz, 1965–81)
AnBib   Analecta biblica
ANET   *Ancient Near Eastern Texts Relating to the Old Testament*, ed. J. B. Pritchard, 3rd ed. (Princeton: Princeton University Press, 1969)
ATANT   Abhandlungen zur Theologie des Alten und Neuen Testaments
BBB   Bonner Biblische Beiträge
BBET   Beiträge zur biblischen Exegese und Theologie
BBR   *Bulletin for Biblical Research*
BCSBS   *Bulletin of the Canadian Society of Biblical Studies*
BDB   F. Brown, S. R. Driver and C. A. Briggs, *A Hebrew and English Lexicon of the Old Testament* (Oxford: Clarendon, 1907; repr. Peabody: Hendrickson, 2005)
BETL   Bibliotheca ephemeridum theologicarum lovaniensium
BEvT   Beiträge zur evangelischen Theologie
BHK   *Biblia Hebraica*, ed. R. Kittel, 16th ed. (Stuttgart: Würtemburgische Bibelanstalt, 1973)
BHS   *Biblia Hebraica Stuttgartensia*, ed. K. Elliger and W. Rudolph (Stuttgart: Deutsche Bibelstiftung, 1983)
Bib   *Biblica*
BIS   Biblical Interpretation Series
BN   *Biblische Notizen*

BSac	*Bibliotheca sacra*
BWANT	Beiträge zur Wissenschaft vom Alten und Neuen Testament
BZAW	Beihefte zur Zeitschrift für die alttestamentliche Wissenschaft
c.	circa
CBQ	*Catholic Biblical Quarterly*
CBQMS	Catholic Biblical Quarterly Monograph Series
CC	Continental Commentaries
ConBOT	Coniectanea biblica: Old Testament Series
COut	Commentaar op het Oude Testament
CR:BS	*Currents in Research: Biblical Studies*
DCH	*Dictionary of Classical Hebrew*, ed. D. J. A. Clines, 6 vols. (Sheffield: Sheffield Phoenix, 1993–2008)
DDD	*Dictionary of Deities and Demons in the Bible*, ed. K. van der Toorn, B. Becking and P. W. van der Horst, 2nd ed. (Leiden: Brill; Grand Rapids: Eerdmans, 1999)
DJD	Discoveries in the Judaean Desert
DSB	The Daily Study Bible Series
DSD	*Dead Sea Discoveries*
EBib	*Etudes bibliques*
EdF	Erträge der Forschung
ErIsr	*Eretz-Israel*
ESV	English Standard Version
ET	English translation
EVV	English versions
FAT	Forschungen zum Alten Testament
FB	Forschung zur Bibel
FOTL	Forms of the Old Testament Literature
FRLANT	Forschungen zur Religion und Literatur des Alten und Neuen Testaments
GHAT	Göttinger Handkommentar zum Alten Testament
GKC	*Gesenius' Hebrew Grammar*, ed. E. Kautzsch, rev. and tr. A. E. Cowley (Oxford: Clarendon, 1910)
HALOT	L. Koehler and W. Baumgartner, *The Hebrew and Aramaic Lexicon of the Old Testament*, tr. and ed. under the supervision of M. E. J. Richardson, 5 vols. (Leiden: Brill, 1994–2000)
HBS	Herders biblische Studien
HBT	*Horizons in Biblical Theology*
HCOT	Historical Commentary on the Old Testament
Heb.	Hebrew
HTKAT	Herders Theologischer Kommentar zum Alten Testament

HTR	*Harvard Theological Review*
ICC	International Critical Commentary
IDBSup	*Interpreter's Dictionary of the Bible: Supplementary Volume*, ed. C. Krim (Nashville: Abingdon, 1976)
impf.	imperfect
Int	*Interpretation*
ITC	International Theological Commentary
JAOS	*Journal of the American Oriental Society*
JBL	*Journal of Biblical Literature*
JDDS	Jian Dao Dissertation Series
JHI	*Journal of the History of Ideas*
JNES	*Journal of Near Eastern Studies*
JSNTSup	Journal for the Study of the New Testament, Supplement Series
JSOT	*Journal for the Study of the Old Testament*
JSOTSup	Journal for the Study of the Old Testament, Supplement Series
JSS	*Journal of Semitic Studies*
JSSM	Journal of Semitic Studies Monographs
JTS	*Journal of Theological Studies*
KHAT	Kurzer Hand-Commentar zum Alten Testament
LCBI	Literary Currents in Biblical Interpretation
LHB/OTS	Library of the Hebrew Bible / Old Testament Studies
LSTS	Library of Second Temple Studies
LXX	Septuagint
MS(S)	Manuscript(s)
MT	Masoretic Text
Mus. Inv.	Museum Inventory (Rockefeller Museum)
NASB	New American Standard Bible
NCB	New Century Bible
NCBC	New Century Bible Commentary
NEB	New English Bible
NET	New English Translation
NIB	*The New Interpreter's Bible*, ed. L. E. Keck, 12 vols. (Nashville: Abingdon, 1993–2002)
NIBCOT	New International Biblical Commentary on the Old Testament
NICOT	New International Commentary on the Old Testament
NIDOTTE	*New International Dictionary of Old Testament Theology and Exegesis*, ed. W. A. VanGemeren, 5 vols. (Carlisle: Paternoster; Grand Rapids: Zondervan, 1996)

NIV	New International Version
NJB	New Jerusalem Bible
NJPS	New Jewish Publication Society Tanakh
NovTSup	Novum Testamentum Supplements
NRSV	New Revised Standard Version
NT	New Testament
NTS	*New Testament Studies*
OBT	Overtures to Biblical Theology
Or	*Orientalia* (NS)
OT	Old Testament
OTG	Old Testament Guides
OTL	Old Testament Library
OTS	Old Testament Studies
OTWSA	Ou-Testamentiese Werkgemeenskap in Suid Afrika
PAM	Palestine Archaeological Museum
part.	participle
PBM	Paternoster Biblical Monographs
PIBA	*Proceedings of the Irish Biblical Association*
pl.	plural
POut	De Prediking van het Oude Testament
PRSt	*Perspectives in Religious Studies*
PSB	*Princeton Seminary Bulletin*
Q	Qere (the Hebrew text to be read out)
RevQ	*Revue de Qumran*
RSV	Revised Standard Version
SAA	State Archives of Assyria
SBL	Society of Biblical Literature
SBLDS	Society of Biblical Literature Dissertation Series
SBLSymS	Society of Biblical Literature Symposium Series
SBLWAW	Society of Biblical Literature Writings from the Ancient World
SBS	Stuttgarter Bibelstudien
SBT	Studies in Biblical Theology
SEÅ	*Svensk exegetisk årsbok*
sg.	singular
SJT	*Scottish Journal of Theology*
SNTSMS	Society for New Testament Studies Monograph Series
SO	Symbolae osloenses
SOTSMS	Society for Old Testament Studies Monograph Series
ST	*Studia theologica*

STDJ	Studies on the Texts of the Desert of Judah
Syr	Syriac
TB	Theologische Bücherei: Neudrucke und Berichte aus dem 20. Jahrhundert
TDOT	*Theological Dictionary of the Old Testament*, ed. G. J. Botterweck, H. Ringgren and H.-J. Fabry, 15 vols. (Grand Rapids: Eerdmans, 1974–2006)
Tg(s)	Targum(s)
TGUOS	Transactions of the Glasgow University Oriental Society
TNIV	Today's New International Version
TynBul	*Tyndale Bulletin*
Vg	Vulgate
VT	*Vetus Testamentum*
VTSup	Supplements to Vetus Testamentum
WBC	Word Biblical Commmentary
WMANT	Wissenschaftliche Monographien zum Alten und Neuen Testament
WUNT	Wissenschaftliche Untersuchungen zum Neuen Testament
ZAW	*Zeitschrift für die alttestamentliche Wissenschaft*
ZBK	Zürcher Bibelkommentare

INTRODUCTION

David G. Firth and H. G. M. Williamson

The book of Isaiah is perhaps the best-known prophetic book of the Hebrew Scriptures. Its historic importance is evident from its prominence at Qumran and in the New Testament, and it has continued to stimulate reflection and discussion by faithful Jewish and Christian believers ever since. Though at times those discussions have seemed more like a battle to be fought over the book's interpretation than something which promotes God's reign, we should at least recognize that this shows that the interpretation of Isaiah has been seen as a matter of the utmost importance. It is a text to be weighed, on which to meditate and pray, and through which to explore the ways in which God works. It is a text that has been understood as formative to the identity of the people of God.

However, study of Isaiah is in the midst of a period of great change. A generation ago the dominant tendency was either to study Isaiah as containing three distinct works whose internal relationships were limited or to expend considerable effort in demonstrating that Isaiah of Jerusalem was the author of the whole book in the eighth century BC. One could say that in either case, the focus was author-centred, with the question being whether one dealt with one, two or three authors (and perhaps a few redactors as well). Although the arguments were not static, the leading questions were largely formulated in the nineteenth century. It would be wrong to say that these questions are no longer important, but they now seek a place on the scholarly agenda alongside many others. In particular, a great deal of work is now being done on the ways in which the book of Isaiah is shaped and how its component parts relate to one another, so that text-centred questions have now come to the fore. Scholars are thus interested in asking about the purposes behind the shape of the book and how the various component parts engage with one another as well as exploring the insights opened up by increased awareness of the ways in which Hebrew poetry, and prophetic literature in particular, seeks to communicate. In addition, we are increasingly aware that the interpretation of texts is not a neutral process, and that the questions we ask may be generated by interpreters themselves, so that another significant body of research is concerned with reader-centred matters. Feminist and liberationist concerns have been prominent, though any approach to Isaiah that starts with present-day concerns can properly be considered here.

The study of Isaiah is changing and therefore books about Isaiah also need to change. While many excellent resources are available, they tend to fall into two categories. Many are introductions aimed at beginning students, which attempt to provide an overview of scholarship on Isaiah. Others contain various highly learned articles, often focusing on the minutiae that contribute to the goals of scholarship. But there is less literature that bridges the gap between the two, building on introductory work and helping readers to take the next steps in the study of Isaiah. This book, like its companion volume on Psalms,[1] helps to meet that need, assuming some foundational knowledge gained elsewhere and guiding readers through current issues and approaches.

The chapters within this book fall into three basic groups. The first of these (by H. G. M. Williamson) presents an overview of current scholarly approaches to the book of Isaiah, creating a context for the various discussions that follow. The second group then examines a range of themes within Isaiah and approaches to it, including both specific issues and more general matters relevant to the book as a whole. The reception of the book at Qumran and in the New Testament is also considered here. The third group offers three exegetical explorations of Isaiah so that the discussion of approaches to the book is earthed in specific exegetical work. A range of different approaches to the book of Isaiah is thus modelled.

As with the volume on Psalms, this book was produced by a collaborative effort. The various chapters have been written by members and guests of the Tyndale Fellowship Old Testament Study Group. Draft chapters were

---

1. P. S. Johnston and D. G. Firth (eds.), *Interpreting the Psalms: Issues and Approaches* (Leicester: Apollos; Downers Grove: IVP, 2005).

circulated electronically and then discussed at the conference in July 2008 (in Cambridge, England), with beneficial interaction among contributors and other participants. We were thus able to draw on the skills of a community of scholars committed to the work being done here, and questions and comments from many participants have in some way helped shape the final presentation of the chapters. At the same time, we have sought to reflect the diversity of the Tyndale Fellowship in the chapters themselves, so that, although all the contributors are united in their commitment to the authority of Scripture and the importance of faithful interpretation, we have consciously sought to include a range of different approaches to Isaiah reflecting different perspectives on the author, the text or the reader. This is particularly evident in the exegetical papers that reflect this diversity in their understanding of the nature of exegesis as well as the formation of the book of Isaiah, but it is also apparent in the essays that discuss different issues. This diversity is also evident in the contributors themselves – some are renowned scholars whose work on Isaiah is well known, while others have only recently completed their doctoral studies. Allowing space for such diversity is important if we are truly to appreciate the range of approaches to Isaiah currently available. It is thus not our purpose to offer an overview that resolves all the critical questions about Isaiah and allows only one approach to the book. Rather, we want to take seriously the fact that there is a range of issues and approaches, and that we learn most about Isaiah when we allow a dialogue in which they can be heard, though here a dialogue shaped by committed Christian faith.

The editors would like to thank all the contributors for their happy acceptance of suggested changes, some substantial, in order to keep to strict word limits and to fulfil the book's aims.

PART 1: ORIENTATION

1. RECENT ISSUES IN THE STUDY OF ISAIAH

H. G. M. Williamson

The most noteworthy development in study of the book of Isaiah over the past two decades or so has been the rediscovery of the book's unity. Prior to that, it was normal for commentaries to be written by different authors on different sections of the book, and for textbooks on prophecy to have separate (and separated) chapters on Isaiah of Jerusalem, 'Deutero-Isaiah', and so on. Nowadays, as we shall see, the picture looks very different.

This does not in the least mean, however, that scholars have reverted to a view that the book was all written by a single individual. While that position is still defended from time to time, it is more normal for a view of overall literary unity to be held in conjunction with a (sometimes quite radical) analysis of the history of the book's growth over two or more centuries with many hands contributing to it. Indeed, there are those who would now question whether, for instance, we should still think of a single author as being responsible for the bulk of chapters 40–55 (Deutero-Isaiah) or whether we should not rather envisage these chapters as the product of incremental growth by a larger number of writers.

'Unity' can be variously understood. I attempted to give some account of how it developed and was understood in the first chapter of a monograph published in 1994[1] and the variety of opinion has certainly not diminished

1. *The Book Called Isaiah: Deutero-Isaiah's Role in Composition and Redaction* (Oxford:

since. That will nevertheless provide a reasonable starting date for this further progress report. In line with these recent developments, I shall start with issues relating to the book as a whole before then proceeding to touch on a few of the major issues relevant to the various major sections of the book taken on their own.

Reception history

Following the loosening generally of the total dominance of historical-critical research in biblical research, the way that a book like Isaiah has been received by the church, the synagogue or culture in general has been a focus for renewed attention. The reception of Isaiah in the ancient translations of the Bible, such as the Septuagint, in the Dead Sea Scrolls and in the New Testament is treated elsewhere in this volume and has continued as a lively subject of research. Beyond that, however, we may note that, following the pioneering work of Sawyer,[2] which is rather an eclectic mix of subjects, there are single-authored studies of Isaiah by Blenkinsopp[3] (on the ancient world) and Childs[4] (surveying

---

Footnote 1 (*continued*)

> Clarendon, 1994). Other surveys from around that same period include M. A. Sweeney, 'The Book of Isaiah in Recent Research', *CR:BS* 1 (1993), pp. 141–162; M. E. Tate, 'The Book of Isaiah in Recent Study', in J. W. Watts and P. R. House (eds.), *Forming Prophetic Literature: Essays on Isaiah and the Twelve in Honor of John D. W. Watts*, JSOTSup 235 (Sheffield: Sheffield Academic Press, 1996), pp. 22–56; and several of the chapters in R. F. Melugin and M. A. Sweeney (eds.), *New Visions of Isaiah*, JSOTSup 214 (Sheffield: Sheffield Academic Press, 1996); e.g. R. Rendtorff, 'The Book of Isaiah: A Complex Unity', on pp. 32–49.

2. J. F. A. Sawyer, *The Fifth Gospel: Isaiah in the History of Christianity* (Cambridge: Cambridge University Press, 1996). Sawyer is scheduled to publish the Isaiah volume in the relatively new Blackwell Bible Commentary series, which focuses on reception history.

3. J. Blenkinsopp, *Opening the Sealed Book: Interpretations of the Book of Isaiah in Late Antiquity* (Grand Rapids: Eerdmans, 2006). German is able to distinguish rather better than English between *Rezeptionsgeschichte* (the history of the text's reception) and *Wirkungsgeschichte* (the history of its later impact); Blenkinsopp's volume falls more under the second category.

4. B. S. Childs, *The Struggle to Understand Isaiah as Christian Scripture* (Grand Rapids: Eerdmans, 2004).

some of the great commentators through the ages) as well as a useful collection of essays arising from the work of one of the SBL seminars.[5]

Students who are interested in this topic are being increasingly aided by the provision of translations of works that they might otherwise find difficult to access. The *Dead Sea Scrolls Bible*[6] supplies a translation of the great Isaiah scroll, with differences from the received Hebrew text picked out in italics and with readings from the many other (fragmentary) scrolls of Isaiah indicated in the footnotes. In addition English translations of the Septuagint and Targum have long been available. Most recently, extracts from a number of patristic commentaries have been published in two series, one on selected chapters[7] and the other on the whole book.[8] The chief difference between these two works is that Wilken focuses on considerably longer extracts from a more circumscribed list of writers while McKinion and Elliott have generally very short extracts drawn from a much wider range of writers and genres. Now that there is a modern critical edition of the major medieval Jewish commentaries available,[9] an English translation is a major desideratum (at present, there is only an 1873 translation of Ibn Ezra).

The book as a unity

Themes

As indicated above, 'unity' is something of a slippery concept. This can be most clearly seen from the different ways in which scholars now approach the task of studying a major theme in the book as a whole. Does unity mean that we can now engage in fully synchronic study, reading the book without regard to the hypothetical history of its growth, or should it be read sequentially,

---

5. C. M. McGinnis and P. K. Tull (eds.), *'As Those Who Are Taught': The Interpretation of Isaiah from the LXX to the SBL*, SBLSymS 27 (Atlanta: SBL, 2006).

6. Edited by M. Abegg et al. (Edinburgh: T. & T. Clark, 1999).

7. R. L. Wilken, *Isaiah, Interpreted by Early Christian and Medieval Commentators*, The Church's Bible (Grand Rapids: Eerdmans, 2007). It is worth noting that this volume also includes a translation of the LXX of Isaiah by M. Silva (his contribution to the forthcoming *New English Translation of the Septuagint*).

8. S. A. McKinion (ed.), *Isaiah 1–39*, ACCS (Downers Grove: IVP, 2004); M. W. Elliott (ed.), *Isaiah 40–66*, ACCS (Downers Grove: IVP, 2007).

9. M. Cohen (ed.), *Mikra'ot Gedolot 'Haketer': Isaiah* (Ramat Gan: Bar Ilan University, 1996).

much in the way that we read a modern book, or should we still adhere to a diachronic approach, analysing how one part builds upon another, while doing more justice to the book's unity than was previously the case by acknowledging that one part of the book has been consciously influenced by another?

A case can be made for all three of these approaches, and certainly all are well represented in modern studies. The 'sequential' view was initially urged most forcefully by Darr,[10] who took the family (introduced already in the second verse of the book) as an appropriate theme against which to test her method. Her lead is explicitly cited in the more recent work of Gray on what some might consider the more central theme of social justice,[11] though in fact he restricts the main focus of his study to chapters 1 and 58, albeit read sequentially. Although not, perhaps, using exactly this label, several studies of other themes by a variety of scholars effectively treat the text in the same way in that they work through the book in order, allowing the picture of their particular theme to build up sequentially as they go along, for instance on Torah,[12] sickness and healing,[13] light,[14] righteousness[15] and allusions to the Nathan oracle, with its wordplay on house/dynasty.[16]

Probably still the more common approach, however, is to take a topic and study it in each of the major sections of the book and then see what happens

10. K. P. Darr, *Isaiah's Vision and the Family of God*, LCBI (Louisville: Westminster John Knox, 1994).

11. M. Gray, *Rhetoric and Social Justice in Isaiah*, LHB/OTS 432 (New York: T. & T. Clark, 2006); see esp. pp. 56–58.

12. I. Fischer, *Tora für Israel – Tora für die Völker: Das Konzept des Jesajabuches*, SBS 164 (Stuttgart: Katholisches Bibelwerk, 1995); M. A. Sweeney, 'The Book of Isaiah as Prophetic Torah', in Melugin and Sweeney, *New Visions*, pp. 50–67.

13. Z. Kustár, *'Durch seine Wunden sind wir geheilt': Eine Untersuchung zur Metaphorik von Israels Krankheit und Heilung im Jesajabuch*, BWANT 154 (Stuttgart: Kohlhammer, 2002). It should be noted, however, that Kustár's aim in this sequential reading is to arrive at rigorously diachronic conclusions relating to the book's growth and redaction.

14. R. E. Clements, 'A Light to the Nations: A Central Theme of the Book of Isaiah', in Watts and House, *Forming*, pp. 57–69.

15. R. Rendtorff, 'Isaiah 56:1 as a Key to the Formation of the Book of Isaiah', in *Canon and Theology: Overtures to an Old Testament Theology* (Edinburgh: T. & T. Clark, 1994), pp. 181–189.

16. D. Janthial, *L'oracle de Nathan et l'unité du livre d'Isaïe*, BZAW 343 (Berlin: de Gruyter, 2004).

when they are all put together. This has the advantage of retaining a diachronic dimension to the study (how a theme may have developed through time as opposed to within the present literary arrangement of the text), but of course it is subject to the objection that the historical growth of the text is not an assured result but subject to informed hypothesis. While this latter point may be granted, the objection should nevertheless not be overplayed, since it is often possible to make a good case for the influence of one passage on another, so that it is possible to reach a greater degree of agreement on relative chronology than absolute, and that is sufficient for this purpose.

This, at any rate, is the approach I took in my study of messiah and servant in the book,[17] both attempting to show how the different circumstances in the pre-exilic and exilic periods resulted in different presentations of the royal agent whom God required to bring in his unchanging purpose of just rule and how in the final part of the book there is a tendency to draw these different elements together into a composite presentation. Other studies that follow this general approach include Leclerc on justice (so making a nice contrast with Gray, as noted above),[18] and Ma on the Spirit.[19]

Finally, there are those who attempt to study some theme or other in Isaiah without regard to any sort of diachronic concern. Their reasons for doing so may vary: some are ideologically committed to this approach out of a particular understanding of literary theory,[20] others for so-called 'canonical' considerations, while others may simply have concluded that the results of diachronic research are so insecure that it is better to proceed without attending to them. As an example of this third approach could be mentioned Davies's study of ethics in Isaiah,[21] of the second the 'canonical' analysis of the messianic

---

17. *Variations on a Theme: King, Messiah and Servant in the Book of Isaiah* (Carlisle: Paternoster, 1998). For a similar approach on a different theme see my essay '"From One Degree of Glory to Another": Themes and Theology in Isaiah', in E. Ball (ed.), *In Search of True Wisdom: Essays in Old Testament Interpretation in Honour of Ronald E. Clements*, JSOTSup 300 (Sheffield: Sheffield Academic Press, 1999), pp. 174–195.

18. T. L. Leclerc, *Yahweh Is Exalted in Justice: Solidarity and Conflict in Isaiah* (Minneapolis: Fortress, 2001).

19. W. Ma, *Until the Spirit Comes: The Spirit of God in the Book of Isaiah*, JSOTSup 271 (Sheffield: Sheffield Academic Press, 1999).

20. In the case of M. Goulder, however, this should be termed a liturgical rather than a literary theory; see his *Isaiah as Liturgy*, SOTSMS (Aldershot: Ashgate, 2004).

21. A. Davies, *Double Standards in Isaiah: Re-evaluating Prophetic Ethics and Divine Justice*, BIS 46 (Leiden: Brill, 2000); see esp. pp. 5–8. Davies's work may be instructively

theme by Heskett (which thus forms a good illustrative point of comparison and contrast with my own study mentioned earlier),[22] and of the first Laato's study of the Zion theme.[23]

Despite the variety of approaches that this section of our survey has revealed, the most remarkable fact to appreciate is that so many studies are being undertaken in the first place. It is clear that the return to the study of Isaiah as a whole is proving fruitful for theological research, and it is probable that the appearance of such studies will continue for some time to come. It should not be forgotten, however, that a significant catalyst for the development of this approach in the first place was the application of a rigorous form of redaction criticism, and so it is appropriate that we should give some attention to this next.

Redaction criticism

As used in modern biblical studies, redaction criticism is somewhat variously understood. At the heart of the matter, however, is a concern to understand how earlier written materials were shaped into the books which we now have, a process that in theory might include the joining of previously separate materials (as in the compilation of a historical work), the reordering of material in the process of so doing, and the changing or shaping of the earlier materials to make them fit better with the purpose of the new work which then emerges (both processes to be seen at work in the formation of Chronicles by comparison with Samuel and Kings, for instance). Even when not so labelled, this approach to biblical literature in fact has a very long history.

A complication in more recent times has come about through the identification of what in German is known as *Fortschreibung*, for which there is really no satisfactory English equivalent.[24] It refers to the phenomenon whereby

---

Footnote 21 *(continued)*

compared with the somewhat more diachronic approach adopted by J. Barton, 'Ethics in the Book of Isaiah', in C. C. Broyles and C. A. Evans (eds.), *Writing and Reading the Scroll of Isaiah: Studies of an Interpretive Tradition*, VTSup 70.1–2 (Leiden: Brill, 1997), pp. 67–77.

22. R. Heskett, *Messianism within the Scriptural Scroll of Isaiah*, LHB/OTS 456 (New York: T. & T. Clark, 2007).

23. A. Laato, *'About Zion I Will Not Be Silent': The Book of Isaiah as an Ideological Unity*, ConBOT 44 (Stockholm: Almqvist & Wiksell, 1998).

24. My colleague John Barton suggests 'supplementation'; one might also consider 'extension' or 'continuation', but none is fully satisfactory.

a scribe or editor picks up on an element in a text and adds something to it, often with a catchword to make the join. The addition may typically reapply the original saying to a new context or comment on it in some way. Isaiah 5:30 is a clear example, where the image of the lion growling over its prey (spoken of the Assyrian army in the previous verses) is reapplied in a more cosmic or universal manner.[25] In the study of the book of Isaiah, however, this term is now sometimes being developed to explain much larger sections of the work, including much or even all of the second main part.

In terms of the development of the book as a whole, there are two basic understandings currently under discussion, though of course there are many varieties within these two main groupings.[26] One, which is probably the majority opinion, is associated especially with the work of the late O. H. Steck and his pupils, though others have adopted a similar position, either independently or in conscious development of his view. The key elements of this opinion are first that the core of Isaiah 40 – 55 was first composed as a separate work, with allusions from time to time to work of the earlier prophet Isaiah just as there are clearly allusions to Jeremiah, Lamentations and other parts of the biblical literature as it then existed. Secondly, this material both grew in itself and came to be joined to the earlier material from Isaiah in an overall redaction of the whole, a clear indication of which in its earliest form may be seen in the similarities between Isaiah 11:11–16, 27:12–13 and 62:10–12. A consequence of this approach is that we should certainly abandon any reference to Trito-Isaiah as an individual, since the material in chapters 56–66 is to be regarded as the product of a varied accumulation of material by processes of both *Fortschreibung* and redaction.[27] Even more radically, there are voices raised to

---

25. For the details see my commentary *A Critical and Exegetical Commentary on Isaiah 1–27*. Vol. 1: *Commentary on Isaiah 1–5*, ICC (London: T. & T. Clark, 2006), pp. 408–410.

26. For a much fuller, valuable survey of research on all this see P. Höffken, *Jesaja: Der Stand der theologischen Diskussion* (Darmstadt: Wissenschaftliche Buchgesellschaft, 2004).

27. The majority of O. H. Steck's earlier numerous articles on these matters have been conveniently gathered in two volumes: *Studien zu Tritojesaja*, BZAW 203 (Berlin: de Gruyter, 1991); and *Gottesknecht und Zion: Gesammelte Aufsätze zu Deuterojesaja*, FAT 4 (Tübingen: Mohr Siebeck, 1992). A more recent drawing together of some of the major conclusions may be found in 'Autor und/oder Redaktor in Jesaja 56–66', in Broyles and Evans, *Writing and Reading*, pp. 219–259; see too *Bereitete Heimkehr: Jesaja 35 als redaktionelle Brücke zwischen dem Ersten und dem Zweiten Jesaja*, SBS 121 (Stuttgart: Katholisches Bibelwerk, 1985).

query whether we need even talk any more of Deutero-Isaiah, for much the same reasons.[28]

The other main approach to the book (which I favour) takes the view that there never were two separate works to be joined redactionally as a second stage. Rather, an early form of the work (which had no doubt itself been subject to some development, arguably in the reign of Josiah,[29] and more certainly in the exilic period, as a reflection on the fall of Jerusalem[30]) was taken up by the late exilic prophet whom we call Deutero-Isaiah, who both added his own material to it to address the radically different circumstances of his own day[31] and shaped the earlier material in such a way as to prepare for his new announcement of salvation. That, at any rate, was the view I sought to defend in my 1994 monograph, and, although some modifications should no doubt be entered as a result of more recent work and criticisms, its basic premise seems to me still defensible and to have the advantage that the 'unity' of the book is more organic and less the result of the simple juxtaposing of previously unrelated blocks of material.[32]

---

28. See R. J. Coggins, 'Do We Still Need Deutero-Isaiah?', *JSOT* 81 (1998), pp. 77–92.

29. H. Barth, *Die Jesaja-Worte in der Josiazeit: Israel und Assur als Thema einer produktiven Neuinterpretation der Jesajaüberlieferung*, WMANT 48 (Neukirchen-Vluyn: Neukirchener Verlag, 1977); J. Vermeylen, *Du prophète Isaïe à l'apocalyptique: Isaïe, I – XXXV, miroir d'un demi-millénaire d'expérience religieuse en Israël*, 2 vols. (Paris: Gabalda, 1977–8); M. A. Sweeney, *King Josiah of Judah: The Lost Messiah of Israel* (Oxford: Oxford University Press, 2001).

30. Cf. R. E. Clements, 'The Prophecies of Isaiah and the Fall of Jerusalem in 587 B.C.', *VT* 30 (1980), pp. 421–436.

31. See e.g. R. Albertz, 'Das Deuterojesaja-Buch als Fortschreibung der Jesaja-Prophetie', in E. Blum et al. (eds.), *Die Hebräische Bibel und ihre zweifache Nachgeschichte: Festschrift für Rolf Rendtorff zum 65. Geburtstag* (Neukirchen-Vluyn: Neukirchener Verlag, 1990), pp. 241–256, though I do not myself regard this as an appropriate use of the description *Fortschreibung*.

32. Support for the view that Deutero-Isaiah was especially indebted to the first part of the book, even while allowing that there are also references to other biblical works, comes from the detailed and methodologically self-conscious analysis of R. Nurmela, *The Mouth of the Lord Has Spoken: Inner-Biblical Allusions in Second and Third Isaiah*, Studies in Judaism (Lanham: University Press of America, 2006). His results call for modification of the contrary claims of B. D. Sommer, *A Prophet Reads Scripture: Allusion in Isaiah 40–66* (Stanford: Stanford University, 1998); and P. T. Willey, *Remember the Former Things: The Recollection of Previous Texts in Second Isaiah*, SBLDS 161 (Atlanta: Scholars Press, 1997).

Most recently, Jake Stromberg has argued convincingly in his doctoral thesis, soon to be published, that a comparable process is to be seen in the drawing together of the final part of the work. He finds evidence in chapters 65–66 of awareness of the whole of the earlier part of the book and also of redactional intervention at certain key turning points in 1–55, such as the end of chapter 1, by the same hand. On such a view, I should judge that Isaiah 40 – 55, with its message of salvation or 'comfort' after judgment, lies at the heart of the book: chapters 1–39 broadly lead up to it, and chapters 56–66 derive from it in terms of application; and this overall shape of the work is to be seen as reflected also at a number of key turning points throughout the work.[33]

While these two main approaches to the composition history of the book as a whole differ markedly from each other, they are nevertheless mostly united against earlier studies by the direction of travel that is now commonly adopted. As regards the first part of the book, it was normal for monographs and commentaries in the past to start by isolating those passages thought to be 'authentic' to the eighth-century prophet, to give them most attention and then to treat more lightly the rest of the material as 'secondary additions'. Nowadays redaction critics nearly always work the other way round, seeking first to arrive at an understanding of the text as it currently exists (synchronic analysis) and then working back from that to the more hypothetical earlier stages (diachronic analysis).[34] Of course, even with regard to the finished form of the text there are many different understandings, not least with regard to the appropriate method to arrive at a 'final-form' reading; how much more, then, may one expect the analysis of the previous history of the text to differ from one scholar to another. But this cannot shroud the very marked change in approach from earlier years and the extent to which redaction critics of differing opinions agree among themselves about this as the proper starting point.

It is sometimes objected that such studies cannot therefore be of much value because they frequently disagree so much with one another. While the variety

---

33. A similar conclusion was drawn in a provisional manner at the end of one of the early programmatic studies in the new phase of research on Isaiah by R. Rendtorff, now available in an English translation as 'The Composition of the Book of Isaiah', in *Canon and Theology*, pp. 146–169.

34. A prominent example of this is the extensive study by U. Berges, *Das Buch Jesajas: Komposition und Endgestalt*, HBS 16 (Freiburg: Herder, 1998). For some remarks of my own see 'Synchronic and Diachronic in Isaian Perspective', in J. C. de Moor (ed.), *Synchronic or Diachronic? A Debate on Method in Old Testament Exegesis*, OTS 34 (Leiden: Brill, 1995), pp. 211–226.

of hypotheses cannot be gainsaid, it would be foolish to ignore the very considerable gains that these selfsame studies have brought about. Redaction criticism starts from detailed observations about the text itself and it advances hypotheses to explain those observations. Those fundamental data, too long ignored or overlooked in the study of the several parts of the book in isolation, will not go away and the outcome has been a richer appreciation of the deep texture of Isaiah as a book than had previously been appreciated. No doubt scholars will continue to debate for many years to come the relative merits of the different hypotheses that seek to explain how this all came about, but it seems unlikely that they will ever again do so in the fragmented way that dominated so much of the twentieth century, at least until its closing decade or two.

Isaiah 1 – 39

Having discussed some of the major issues in research relating to the book as a whole, I turn now to consider some of the points that arise in relation to one or other of the three main parts of the book on their own. Some of these certainly look rather different in the light of the issues we have discussed so far, but they are nevertheless most conveniently ordered according to the traditional divisions. It goes without saying that there is space here to touch on only a few of the most significant of the many publications on Isaiah that continue to pour out from the academic and religious publishing houses. I shall address the three main parts of the book in order.

The person of the prophet

The most dramatic development in the study of the first part of the book of Isaiah in recent years concerns the changing perception of the person of the historical prophet himself. In the past there was a general presumption that he preached judgment, and debate focused on the extent to which he also proclaimed a message of hope, whether in the shorter or the longer term. This debate largely concerned, as may be imagined, the 'authenticity' of passages such as 1:21–26, 9:1–6 and 11:1–5, and those who took a positive view on the matter sometimes also used that conclusion to argue for a positive interpretation of the arguably ambiguous Immanuel prophecy as well. The nature of the arguments was set out with exceptional and helpful clarity in John Barton's Old Testament Guide to Isaiah 1 – 39.[35]

---

35. J. Barton, *Isaiah 1–39*, OTG (Sheffield, Sheffield Academic Press, 1995), pp. 64–82.

More recently, however, a radically different understanding has begun to find favour. It is based mainly on two considerations: the nature of prophecy elsewhere in the ancient Near East at that time and an even more radical literary-critical analysis of the relevant chapters than had prevailed previously.

The study of prophecy in the heartland of the Neo-Assyrian Empire has become a popular subject of research since the publication of an accessible edition by Parpola[36] and the subsequent studies and translations by such scholars as Weippert and especially Nissinen.[37] These have now been applied to our understanding of Isaiah in an impressive and important study by M. de Jong.[38] The upshot of his analysis is that what may be recovered of the historical Isaiah shows him closely to have resembled prophets elsewhere in the ancient Near East. His oracles relate to particular historical circumstances, and are strongly supportive of the king. Only much later did the tradition of Isaiah as a preacher of judgment develop.

In order to maintain this position, of course, de Jong has to engage in some quite radical literary-critical surgery, and in this he is not unlike a slightly earlier study by Becker.[39] In order to illustrate the kinds of issues at stake, we may conveniently take chapters 6–8, the so-called Isaiah Memoir. Nobody could read Isaiah 6 as it now stands and suppose that Isaiah was a prophet of weal! The hardening saying in verses 9–10 is as negative as it could possibly be, and even if (as I am inclined to believe) verses 12–13 are part of an exilic redaction, verse 11 is still sufficient to make quite clear that Isaiah foresaw the advent of a major destruction. In the following chapters, therefore, although Isaiah may have initially promised Ahaz deliverance from the Syro-Ephraimite threat, Ahaz's rejection of his message leads clearly enough to an anticipation that judgment at the hand of the Assyrians will follow.

Becker and de Jong see things quite differently, however. Although they

---

36. S. Parpola, *Assyrian Prophecies*, SAA 9 (Helsinki: Helsinki University, 1997).

37. E.g. M. Nissinen, with contributions by C. L. Seow and R. K. Ritner, *Prophets and Prophecy in the Ancient Near East*, SBLWAW 12 (Atlanta: SBL, 2003); M. Weippert's many studies, scattered in journals and collected volumes, are too numerous to list here, but as a fairly recent example one might consult his review article of Parpola's edition in *Or* 71 (2002), pp. 1–54.

38. M. de Jong, *Isaiah among the Ancient Near Eastern Prophets: A Comparative Study of the Earliest Stages of the Isaiah Tradition and the Neo-Assyrian Prophecies*, VTSup 117 (Leiden: Brill, 2007).

39. U. Becker, *Jesaja – von der Botschaft zum Buch*, FRLANT 178 (Göttingen: Vandenhoeck & Ruprecht, 1997).

do not agree completely in their analyses, the main consideration is that the ministry of the historical Isaiah must be confined to the first-person material in these chapters, and furthermore they argue that the account of Isaiah's call originally ended at 6:8 ('here am I; send me'), whereupon we jump to the next first-person passage, namely 8:1–4, where the defeat of the invading northern coalition is clearly anticipated. Becker's views have already stimulated some lively debate,[40] and it may be anticipated that de Jong's fine study will only add to that. It may also be added in passing that Blenkinsopp has studied the three extended prose passages in which Isaiah plays a role (Isa. 7, 20 and 36 – 39) and found that they share certain stylistic features in common which may be broadly labelled as Deuteronomic, while the portrayal of Isaiah that they present seems to be at some variance from the picture one might develop on the basis of the verse oracles taken alone.[41]

The Isaiah Memoir

It is clear that one important element in all this discussion is the status of the so-called Isaiah Memoir in chapters 6–8 (or 9:6), long considered a cornerstone in the recovery of the historical course of the first part of Isaiah's ministry. It seems to tell of his call, followed by an account of his activity during the Syro-Ephraimite crisis, concluding with his withdrawal (for a time at least) from public life because of the rejection of his message. In its classic form these chapters were considered to have been the first part of the book written and so a secure starting point for the composition history of the book as well as for the reconstruction of Isaiah's life and work.

With allowance made for the likelihood that some elements within these chapters may have been added later (e.g. 7:18–25 and 8:19–23), there are those

---

40. See esp. M. Köckert, U. Becker and J. Barthel, 'Das Problem des historischen Jesaja', in I. Fischer, K. Schmid and H. G. M. Williamson (eds.), *Prophetie in Israel*, Altes Testament und Moderne 112 (Münster: LIT, 2003), pp. 105–135 (see too the instructive article by R. G. Kratz on pp. 1–22). In this debate Köckert outlines the four main portrayals of the historical Isaiah that have been canvassed in recent scholarship, Becker defends the position in his monograph already discussed, and Barthel responds with a slightly less radical presentation, largely adumbrated in his detailed and fine monograph *Prophetenwort und Geschichte: Die Jesajaüberlieferung in Jes 6–8 und 28–31*, FAT 19 (Tübingen: Mohr Siebeck, 1997).

41. J. Blenkinsopp, 'The Prophetic Biography of Isaiah', in E. Blum (ed.), *Mincha: Festgabe für Rolf Rendtorff zum 75. Geburtstag* (Neukirchen-Vluyn: Neukirchener Verlag, 2000), pp. 13–26.

such as Clements who continue to uphold the basic theory.[42] Others, however, have raised questions which, if justified, suggest that the Memoir hypothesis is not the most satisfactory way to account for these chapters.[43] The main consideration concerns chapter 7. On the one hand this is in the third person, whereas chapters 6 and 8 are in the first person, so that the theory has to postulate quite gratuitously that chapter 7 was altered in the course of later transmission – something for which there is neither evidence nor reason. On the other hand, there are so many points of similarity between chapter 7 and the Hezekiah narratives in 36–39[44] that it is difficult not to suppose that they were composed in association with each other, the one to illustrate the nature of a faithless king and the other that of a faithful king. It follows from both these observations that chapter 7 owes its position to later redactional activity, not to original continuous composition, and on this there is now a good measure of agreement.[45] At the most, therefore, the Memoir hypothesis can apply only to (parts of) chapters 6 and 8, but in that case it has become so removed from the hypothesis as originally formulated and generally understood that it no longer seems worthwhile clinging to it. It may be considered to detract attention from the possibility of other and more satisfactory explanations of the material.

Isaiah 24 – 27

Among the many other topics of recent discussion in connection with Isaiah 1 – 39, the four chapters often designated the 'Isaiah Apocalypse' have generated more than their fair share of literature. Few parts of Isaiah have benefited more from the more recent shifts in the interpretation of the book as a whole than this one.

---

42. R. E. Clements, 'The Prophet as an Author: The Case of the Isaiah Memoir', in E. Ben Zvi and M. H. Floyd (eds.), *Writings and Speech in Israelite and Ancient Near Eastern Prophecy*, SBLSS 10 (Atlanta: SBL, 2000), pp. 89–101. See too (though very differently) T. Wagner, *Gottes Herrschaft: Eine Analyse der Denkschrift (6,1–9,6)*, VTSup 108 (Leiden: Brill, 2006).

43. E.g. S. A. Irvine, *Isaiah, Ahaz, and the Syro-Ephraimitic Crisis*, SBLDS 123 (Atlanta: Scholars Press, 1990), esp. pp. 120–131; Williamson, *Variations*, pp. 73–101; B. S. Childs, *Isaiah*, OTL (Louisville: Westminster John Knox, 2001), pp. 42–44.

44. See (among many others) E. W. Conrad, *Reading Isaiah*, OBT (Minneapolis: Fortress, 1991), pp. 34–51.

45. Note e.g. that there is a substantial measure of agreement on this matter between Becker and Barthel (see above, n. 40), despite the many other major differences between them.

Until comparatively recently, these chapters were usually regarded as a late and somewhat isolated insertion into their present setting, divorced from their immediate context and unrelated to the wider book as a whole. Interest in them was restricted to what they could tell us about the development from prophecy to apocalyptic, and much ink was spilt in trying to tie down possible historical references such as the identity of the anonymous city which features so frequently throughout these chapters.

It is surprising that nobody seemed at that time to have bothered to ask why this material was added just here. Given the basic paradigm about the book's growth bequeathed to us by Duhm, it might have been expected that it would come at the end of the book, given the view of most scholars that the material is uniformly quite late. I have long thought (though I have no direct evidence to support this) that part of the reason must have been that during those decades the various sections of the book were so firmly regarded as having been written in isolation from one another that the oddity of the present arrangement never even occurred to most commentators.

Concern for the overall shape of the book in more recent research together with the development of more literary methods such as intertextuality and the appreciation of the role of metaphor has transformed this rather barren picture.[46] From this there has emerged an understanding that the author of this material worked intensively with a detailed awareness of previous literature on which he drew extensively but which he turned in a universalizing direction. The chapters thus come to take their natural place following the series of oracles against the nations in chapters 13–23, transforming their historically bound sayings into a presentation of universal and timeless application. It can at least be seen to make good sense in general terms in its present setting,

---

46. Some of the major studies from the period covered by this survey include H. J. Bosman and H. van Groll (eds.), *Studies in Isaiah 24–27: The Isaiah Workshop – De Jesaja Werkplaats*, OTS 43 (Leiden: Brill, 2000); B. Doyle, *The Apocalypse of Isaiah Metaphorically Speaking: A Study of the Use, Function and Significance of Metaphors in Isaiah 24–27*, BETL 151 (Leuven: University Press and Peeters, 2000); R. Scholl, *Die Elenden in Gottes Thronrat: Stilistisch-kompositorische Untersuchungen zu Jesaja 24–27*, BZAW 274 (Berlin: de Gruyter, 2000); D. C. Polaski, *Authorizing an End: The Isaiah Apocalypse and Intertextuality*, BIS 50 (Leiden: Brill, 2001); S. A. Nitsche, *Jesaja 24–27: ein dramatischer Text*, BWANT 166 (Stuttgart: Kohlhammer, 2006); J. T. Hibbard, *Intertextuality in Isaiah 24–27*, FAT 2nd Series 16 (Tübingen: Mohr Siebeck, 2006). Note should also be made here of the commentary by W. A. M. Beuken, *Jesaja 13–27*, HTKAT (Freiburg: Herder, 2007).

though research will need to continue to elucidate some of its obscure and enigmatic features.

Isaiah 40 – 55

A significant gulf has opened up in recent years between German and Anglo-Saxon scholarship with regard to 'Deutero-Isaiah'. On the whole, works in English have continued the earlier standard line of treating these chapters as a more or less coherent unit. Of course, some continue to isolate the four so-called servant songs as a separate layer, others the satirical anti-idol passages, and the odd verse here and there might be treated as a later gloss. But in striking contrast with the position in chapters 1–39, these chapters are regarded as mostly deriving from a single author.[47] Within this circle of scholarship, therefore, interest in composition has tended to focus on how the smaller units as isolated by form criticism have been combined into larger, meaningful wholes, a form of rhetorical criticism.

In German-language scholarship, however, the picture looks very different. Here a whole series of monographs have argued for various elaborate schemes of literary-critical division, dividing the chapters into a number of layers, based mainly on what are thought to be irreconcilable points of tension in the text. Again some of these are the familiar ones already mentioned, but these works generally go a great deal further in treating even the apparently core material as highly fragmented.

Perhaps a little glibly, I was able to write in 1994 that these various studies came to such varying conclusions that it was not possible to engage with them in detail; no general consensus position had emerged with which one might attempt some interaction (though I did venture some remarks in dialogue with one of the more moderate proponents of this newer approach, H.-J. Hermisson). Already there were some who were addressing themselves to a discussion of the problems of method that the discussion had thrown up,[48]

---

47. See e.g. most of the recent major commentaries, such as J. L. Koole, *Isaiah III*, HCOT, 2 vols. (Kampen: Kok Pharos, 1997; Leuven: Peeters, 1998); J. Blenkinsopp, *Isaiah 40–55: A New Translation with Introduction and Commentary*, AB 19A (New York: Doubleday, 2002); J. Goldingay and D. Payne, *A Critical and Exegetical Commentary on Isaiah 40–55*, ICC, 2 vols. (London: T. & T. Clark International, 2006).

48. J. Werlitz, *Redaktion und Komposition: Zur Rückfrage hinter die Endgestalt von Jesaja 40–55*, BBB 122 (Berlin: Philo, 1999).

and now most recently Albertz, a scholar of generally moderate opinion, has sought to draw out the general underlying direction which these multifarious studies have in common.[49] How far he will have succeeded remains to be seen, but the very fact that he has been able to make this attempt indicates that this newer approach can no longer be ignored. The next step, which has not yet been seriously addressed, so far as I am aware, is to examine what difference such a view would have for exegesis. If the consensus based on the previous work of C. Westermann and others no longer obtains, those with more theological interests will need to consider its implications.

A further complicating factor for this latter enterprise is the doubt that has been cast on the historical location of Deutero-Isaiah. Although Duhm himself and some of the other earlier pioneers were quite divided on this issue, certainly by the middle of the last century the overwhelming preponderance of opinion was that the prophet delivered his message in Babylon shortly before the fall of the Neo-Babylonian Empire to Cyrus the Persian. In this setting the proclamation of deliverance and the need to encourage faith among the despondent exilic community seemed to make excellent sense.

This consensus has been challenged in recent years above all by Hans Bartsad, though a number of others are now starting to rally to his cause. In a series of studies Barstad has sought step by step to undermine the pillars on which the previous consensus relied, whether explicitly or by way of presupposition. It is a mistake, he argues, to interpret Deutero-Isaiah's journey metaphors as referring to a literal return from Babylon to Jerusalem as if it were a second exodus; there are no Babylonian loan-words or other esoteric knowledge of Babylonian matters that might betray the author's location; there was quite sufficient economic and cultural life in Judah which survived the fall of Jerusalem to admit the possibility of high-quality literary activity there during the exilic period; and so on.[50]

Putting these two recent developments together could lead to a very different approach to this section of the book from that with which most of

---

49. R. Albertz, *Israel in Exile: The History and Literature of the Sixth Century B.C.E.*, Studies in Biblical Literature 3 (Atlanta: SBL, 2003).

50. H. Barstad, *A Way in the Wilderness: The 'Second Exodus' in the Message of Second Isaiah*, JSSM 12 (Manchester: University of Manchester, 1989); *The Myth of the Empty Land: A Study in the History and Archaeology of Judah during the 'Exilic' Period*, SO 28 (Oslo: Scandinavian University Press, 1996); *The Babylonian Captivity of the Book of Isaiah: 'Exilic' Judah and the Provenance of Isaiah 40–55* (Oslo: Novus, 1997).

us are familiar. Far from being the work of an individual ministering to his dispirited compatriots in Babylon, these chapters might be seen rather as a series of ongoing reflections within the temple/Zion tradition (which Isaiah himself knew well, of course) on the future of the community as a centre for the regathering of the dispersed in every nation (not just Babylon) in the new period of salvation and restoration.[51] Alternatively, others will find a Babylonian Deutero-Isaiah confined more to the underlying text in chapters 40–48, with 49–55 perhaps orientated more towards the Judean community of the early return, whether by the same prophet or by others in the same tradition.

Time will tell, of course, and as yet the foundations for such a reinterpretation are only the view of a small minority. But the very possibility serves the important purpose of reminding us to what extent our exegesis is tied to our understanding of the setting of the material under consideration. It only goes to show how important the questions of so-called 'introduction' are for the whole way in which we interpret and apply the biblical message. The suggestion that there can be reliable theological exegesis without bothering with such concerns seems to be belied by this Isaianic example.

Isaiah 56 – 66

In some important respects the previous consensus about some major aspects of the composition of the last main part of the book still holds. The dense web of citations from, and allusions to, earlier parts of the book (esp. chs. 40–55) as well as within these chapters themselves is evident, and this allows scholars to build up patterns of dependence that allow for somewhat more secure diachronic conclusions than elsewhere.[52] (We have already noted the important part that all this plays in theories about the redaction of the book of Isaiah as a whole.) With the exception of his understanding of 63:1–6, Smith's presentation of this method and its results makes for an exceptionally

---

51. For an earlier discussion tending in this direction with relation to the unity of the book as a whole see G. I. Davies, 'The Destiny of the Nations in the Book of Isaiah', in J. Vermeylen (ed.), *The Book of Isaiah*, BETL 131 (Leuven: University Press and Peeters, 1989), pp. 93–120.

52. See esp. W. Lau, *Schriftgelehrte Prophetie in Jes 56–66: Eine Untersuchung zu den literarischen Bezügen in den letzten elf Kapiteln des Jesajabuches*, BZAW 225 (Berlin: de Gruyter, 1994).

clear statement of the case in its simplest form,[53] namely that chapters 60–62 were written first and in closest relationship to the world of 40–55, while the remaining material was built up subsequently in an envelope style around this core in order to answer some of the problems that the apparent non-fulfilment of the promises had raised. The opening and closing paragraphs of the section as a whole are clearly paralleled, the remainder of 65–66 answers the main elements in the pre-existing lament recorded in 63:7 – 64:11,[54] and so on.

Smith himself sees effectively only two hands at work in all this (minor additions apart), while others inevitably find the whole process to be more complex, but in this case the variations do not appear to make a great deal of practical difference to the task of interpretation. It has become an accepted general approach to study the development of a theme from the central core to the later dependent material – of the temple,[55] for instance, or of the watchman theme[56] or the nature of the community.[57] Alongside this, interest in what these chapters may reveal about the development of the post-exilic community has not abated. The older view of Hanson, who found here and elsewhere evidence of an increasingly sharp division between what he called visionary and hierocratic groups,[58] while still attractive in many respects, has not won support in its detailed suggestions. Nevertheless, he has stimulated a range of alternative studies that attempt to identify the social or religious circles or sects which may lie behind the obviously polemical rhetoric of much of this material as well as to trace the way in which they identify themselves

---

53. P. A. Smith, *Rhetoric and Redaction in Trito-Isaiah: The Structure, Growth and Authorship of Isaiah 56–66*, VTSup 62 (Leiden: Brill, 1995).

54. Contrast, however, J. Goldenstein, *Das Gebet der Gottesknechte: Jesaja 63,7 – 64, 11 im Jesajabuch*, WMANT 92 (Neukirchen-Vluyn: Neukirchener Verlag, 2001), who represents the alternative view that this prayer is late.

55. See J. Middlemas, 'Divine Reversal and the Role of the Temple in Trito-Isaiah', in J. Day (ed.), *Temple and Worship in Biblical Israel*, LHB/OTS 422 (London: T. & T. Clark, 2005).

56. L.-S. Tiemeyer, 'The Watchman Metaphor in Isaiah lvi–lxvi', *VT* 55 (2005), pp. 378–400.

57. L. Ruszkowski, *Volk und Gemeinde im Wandel: Eine Untersuchung zu Jesaja 56–66*, FRLANT 191 (Göttingen: Vandenhoeck & Ruprecht, 2000).

58. P. D. Hanson, *The Dawn of Apocalyptic* (Philadelphia: Fortress, 1975). In a number of respects Hanson took forward the extremely influential work of O. Plöger, *Theocracy and Eschatology* (Oxford: Blackwell, 1968 [German original, 1959]).

with relation to earlier figures in the Isaiah tradition, such as the servant.[59] Given the way that study of all aspects of the post-exilic Persian period has blossomed of late, it may be anticipated that this will remain a particular focus of research for some time to come.[60]

© H. G. M. Williamson, 2009

---

59. E.g. B. Schramm, *The Opponents of Third Isaiah: Reconstructing the Cultic History of the Restoration*, JSOTSup 193 (Sheffield: Sheffield Academic Press, 1995); L.-S. Tiemeyer, *Priestly Rites and Prophetic Rage: Post-Exilic Prophetic Critique of the Priesthood*, FAT 2nd Series 19 (Tübingen: Mohr Siebeck, 2006). In his commentary Blenkinsopp gathers together the fruits of a number of his previous articles on this topic, as well as including a very valuable survey of research in his introduction; see J. Blenkinsopp, *Isaiah 56–66: A New Translation with Introduction and Commentary*, AB 19B (New York: Doubleday, 2003).

60. For orientation see L. L. Grabbe, *A History of the Jews and Judaism in the Second Temple Period*. Vol. 1: *Yehud: A History of the Persian Province of Judah*, LSTS 47 (London: T. & T. Clark International, 2004), esp. pp. 90–94 and 256–261.

PART 2: THEMES, THEOLOGY AND TEXT

2. MONOTHEISM AND ISAIAH

Nathan MacDonald

This chapter concerns two apparently straightforward matters, monotheism and Isaiah, which are in fact complicated and contested. That this is the case with Isaiah is well known. The issue here might be summarized as the differences between Isaiah the book and Isaiah the prophet. The pre-critical assumption was that there was a straightforward correspondence between book and prophet. The book of Isaiah, all sixty-six chapters of it, was the product of a prophetic figure living in Judah at the end of the eighth century BC. Each of the prophets was an almost isolated recipient of divine revelation who recorded what he heard and saw, which was then immediately received as an inspired writing. The development of historical-critical approaches swept away this simplistic picture, reaching a high point of sorts with Duhm's positing of three major stages in the composition of Isaiah. The division of the book into sections attributed to Isaiah of Jerusalem (1–39), Second or Deutero-Isaiah (40–55) and Third or Trito-Isaiah (56–66) was never more than a heuristic device, though, a brief summary of a reality that was in many ways far more complex. Developments in redaction criticism have increasingly exposed the complex redactional history of the book and shown that the earlier critical division of the book still held to a view of the prophets (in this instance the three Isaiahs) as relatively independent figures. The result has been a greater awareness of the book's compositional complexity but also of its unity.[1]

---

1. See, among others, H. G. M. Williamson, *The Book Called Isaiah: Deutero-Isaiah's Role in Composition and Redaction* (Oxford: Clarendon, 1994).

Monotheism is a no less complicated matter. The conceptuality originates as a means of religious classification. Its analytical power stems from its reification of religious belief and practice to a single belief relating to the number of deities held to exist. It has a long history of usage within Old Testament studies particularly as a means of plotting developments within the history of Israelite religion. There has been controversy over the point at which monotheism became a characteristic of Israelite belief. In the middle part of the twentieth century many held that Israel's commitment to the first commandment was the animating element of Israelite religion from a very early stage. It led inexorably to distinctive religious expressions that set Israel apart from the polytheism of her ancient Near Eastern neighbours. This portrayal of Israelite religious history has largely disintegrated since the 1980s, with most scholars holding that Israel exhibited fairly typical religious beliefs and practices for the ancient Near East, though with perhaps a tendency towards a smaller pantheon and, among some groups, a YHWH monolatry. The appearance of an exclusive monotheism was a development of the latter that took place only in the exilic and post-exilic period.[2] More recently I and others introduced a different set of issues, not concerning the development of monotheism within Israel, but the conceptuality of monotheism. That monotheism is not an unproblematic category has long been recognized, as a result of which a related set of words has been developed to handle its perceived deficiencies, such as monolatry, henotheism and so forth.[3] Yet larger problems arise from the tendency to work with an assumption about what monotheism is and what it logically entails. In a discussion of the book of Ezekiel, John Barton helpfully describes the nature of the problem: 'We partly misread Ezekiel if we think it is about monotheism or divine omnipotence in our sense; yet the distorting lens through which we read the book is itself partly a result of the book's existence and contents.'[4] This hermeneutical problem confronts us

---

2.   See R. K. Gnuse, *No Other Gods: Emergent Monotheism in Israel*, JSOTSup 241 (Sheffield: Sheffield Academic Press, 1997). Gnuse gives detailed attention to the important shift in the debate about monotheism that took place in the 1980s and early 1990s. Since 1997 there have been a number of important monographs and essays.

3.   For a discussion of these words see my *Deuteronomy and the Meaning of 'Monotheism'*, FAT 2.1 (Tübingen: Mohr Siebeck, 2003), pp. 53–54.

4.   J. Barton, 'The Messiah in Old Testament Theology', in J. Day (ed.), *King and Messiah in Israel and the Ancient Near East*, JSOTSup 270 (London: Sheffield Academic Press, 1998), pp. 365–379; here p. 371.

with every biblical book that is thought to articulate monotheism. What is required according to Barton is

> a critical analysis of the reception history of biblical texts, but one which compares that history carefully both with the original meaning of the texts and with the theological doctrine that has both resulted from and been read back into the texts in question.[5]

It was precisely this sort of task that I undertook in my *Deuteronomy and the Meaning of 'Monotheism'*. Mark Smith in his *Origins of Biblical Monotheism* recognized the same problem in a different manner.[6] Smith rightly questions whether we know what a 'god' was in the ancient world. Only after he has addressed this foundational issue can Smith return to the question of how Israelite monotheism emerged in the ancient Near East.

Most recent work on monotheism and Isaiah has assumed a relatively uncomplicated critical account of Isaiah and monotheism. Second Isaiah, understood as Isaiah 40 – 55, is recognized as an early, if not the earliest, proponent of a full monotheism. That this is the case is demonstrated not only by unambiguous monotheistic formulae, but by the presence of other ideas consequent upon monotheism. These include YHWH's complete mastery of nature and history, derision of cultic images, and a generous universalism. Such accounts of Second Isaiah's monotheism can be found in the essays by Hans Wildberger and more recently Hywel Clifford.[7]

Distinctive in their own ways, the essays by Clifford and Wildberger nevertheless operate with a similar account of Second Isaiah's monotheism, which

---

5. Ibid., p. 371. See also Ulrich Mauser, who writes, 'it is my thesis that the Biblical insistence on the oneness of God is so different from the monotheistic consciousness of our time that the almost universal procedure of reading the Bible through the spectacles of a modern monotheist must result in a serious misreading of its message' ('One God Alone: A Pillar of Biblical Theology', *PSB* 12 [1991], pp. 255–265; here p. 257).

6. M. S. Smith, *The Origins of Biblical Monotheism: Israel's Polytheistic Background and the Ugaritic Texts* (New York: Oxford University Press, 2001).

7. H. Wildberger, 'Der Monotheismus Deuterojesajas', in H. Donner, R. Hanhart and R. Smend (eds.), *Beiträge zur alttestamentlichen Theologie* (Göttingen: Vandenhoeck & Ruprecht, 1977), pp. 506–530; H. Clifford, 'Deutero-Isaiah and Monotheism', in J. Day (ed.), *Prophecy and the Prophets in Ancient Israel: Proceedings of the Oxford Old Testament Seminar* (London: T. & T. Clark International, forthcoming). I am grateful to Dr Clifford for providing me with a copy of his chapter prior to publication.

can justly be taken to represent the consensus within Old Testament studies. Yet, as I have begun to indicate, this account deserves to be problematized in significant ways. First, any modern treatment of Second Isaiah's monotheism is surely going to have to take into consideration the compositional complexity of the book of Isaiah and the possibility that Second Isaiah was composed as a continuation of a revised First Isaiah. We cannot simply work with the monotheism of Isaiah 40 – 55 (or more accurately Isa. 40 – 48), piling up reification upon reification. If we have learned anything from redaction criticism since the 1960s it is that we must attend both to the material composed by the biblical writers and how they worked with earlier materials; or, at least, that is the case, if we wish to go on speaking about 'Second Isaiah' in good conscience.

Secondly, we must give attention to the rhetorical and occasional nature of Second Isaiah's work. Too often Second Isaiah is treated as an exercise in systematic theology – albeit with a nod to its late exilic context. Mark Smith points us in the right direction by describing Second Isaiah as a new stage in religious rhetoric, rather than a new stage in religion.[8] The occasional nature is important too, for what is presented falls far short of a comprehensive picture of YHWH, Israel or the expectations upon them. Temple and sacrifice, for example, are barely mentioned (Isa. 43:22–24; 44:28). The prophet, promising imminent salvation, offers comfort and encouragement to an exiled people. Elevating it may be, but it is a message that is narrowly conceived, and understandably so. Nevertheless, we should not ignore the hints to realities presupposed for (the monotheism of) Second Isaiah. Though sometimes overlooked by those who argue for Second Isaiah's universalism, this is a message that will lead to Judah, more specifically Jerusalem. In addition, there is a *tôrâ* associated with YHWH and his chosen servant. Second Isaiah's monotheism may be less bare than it often appears. Cultic realities may be presupposed, rather than explicitly articulated.

Thirdly, I wonder at the tendency to view Second Isaiah as the climax of the development of Israelite monotheism, the quintessence of Israelite monotheism even. One must surely be perturbed by the accounts of Israelite monotheism that end abruptly and without explanation with the anonymous exilic prophet. Rather overlooked is Fritz Stolz's perceptive insight in giving over sixteen pages of his *Introduction to Biblical Monotheism* to a chapter entitled 'The Reworking of the Concept of God in the Post-exilic Period'.[9] Equally

---

8. Smith, *Origins*, p. 193. Smith's book gives considerable attention to the rhetoric of monotheism.

9. F. Stolz, *Einführung in den biblischen Monotheismus* (Darmstadt: Wissenschaftliche Buchgesellschaft, 1996), pp. 187–202.

suggestive is Mark Smith's brief consideration of 'the formation of monotheistic theologies' in the post-exilic period, where he gives attention to the Priestly writer, wisdom literature and apocalyptic material.[10] Along the same lines and more directly related to Isaiah are the recent comments by Klaus Koch:

> The Deutero-Isaianic chapters do not mark the end of Israel's road to monotheism. There was an extended sequel in the following centuries. Isaiah 56–66, nowadays often called Trito-Isaiah, is to a great extent a commentary and reinterpretation of chs. 40–55 originating in post-exilic times. At the turn of the era the communities of 'the new covenant' at Qumran and in the New Testament had recourse to these chapters for the legitimation of their self-understanding.[11]

Koch's comments are rather compressed and seem primarily concerned with the reapplication of Isaianic material, but the first sentence merits sustained reflection. One implication as Koch rightly recognizes is that an essay on monotheism in Isaiah cannot satisfy itself with Second Isaiah's words in Isaiah 40 – 55, or even the prophet's role in composing and redacting materials in Isaiah 1 – 39; it must also include the so-called Third Isaiah (Isa. 56 – 66).

In my view, then, a new approach to monotheism and Isaiah needs to be undertaken. Contra Clifford it is not enough to repristinate an older consensus, enriching it with parallels to early Greek philosophical developments. Rather, a careful re-examination of the whole book in all its redactional complexity is needed that gives careful attention to both the beliefs *and* practices[12] that stem from Israel's appropriate recognition of her God as unique. Such a task is, of course, far beyond that which can be undertaken in a brief chapter. Consequently I can offer only brief probes of some critical issues. I will begin by examining Isaiah 40 – 48 and offering some critical reflections on the monotheism in those chapters, before turning wider afield in Isaiah.

---

10. Smith, *Origins*, pp. 167–178.

11. K. Koch, 'Ugaritic Polytheism and Hebrew Monotheism in Isaiah 40–55', in R. P. Gordon (ed.), *The God of Israel*, University of Cambridge Oriental Publications 64 (Cambridge: Cambridge University Press, 2007), pp. 205–228.

12. Thus answering Moberly's call for a 'thick description' of monotheism. See R. W. L. Moberly, 'How Appropriate Is "Monotheism" as a Category for Biblical Interpretation?', in L. T. Stuckenbruck and W. E. S. North (eds.), *Early Jewish and Christian Monotheism*, JSNTSup 263 (London: T. & T. Clark International, 2004), pp. 216–234; here p. 233. Cf. my attempt to analyse the monotheism of Deuteronomy (MacDonald, *Deuteronomy*).

Throughout the chapter it is necessary to bear in mind that I use the terms First, Second and Third Isaiah, as well as monotheism, as scholarly shorthands. As we have already seen, the meaning of these terms is not self-evident and the reader should bear in mind at all points the complexity that surrounds these matters.

Monotheism and Isaiah 40 – 48

Clifford's recent essay offers a defence of what he justifiably sees as the consensus view on Second Isaiah and its monotheism. In Second Isaiah we have the clearest evidence of the emergence of an absolute monotheism towards the end of the exile. Idol satire plays a central role, for this sees other gods satirized as nothing more than human creations. YHWH, by contrast, is the creator of all. This creative power is seen not only in the founding of the cosmos, but also in the formation of history. YHWH's unique power in this sphere is seen through predictive prophecy. With this power in history YHWH brings weal and woe. According to Clifford, YHWH's creative power, his sovereignty over history, and his ability to prophesy provide the 'bases for monotheism'. These beliefs give rise to a monotheistic rhetoric that exhibits itself in exclusionary formulae as well as the traditional incomparability formulae that we find at earlier points in Israel's history.[13] Monotheistic rhetoric is also displayed in the appropriation of various divine names and epithets. Second Isaiah's monotheism results in a number of consequences. First, we have what is usually described as universalism, though Clifford avoids this term. He is right to do so, for, as Levenson has argued, its meaning is not transparent and can be used in a variety of ways. Nevertheless, Clifford finds in Second Isaiah what we might call a strong universalism: 'one religion for one world under one God'.[14] Secondly, Clifford discerns a systematizing potential, by which he means Second Isaiah's theology has 'unity and consistency'.

Second Isaiah's monotheistic affirmations

Clifford's description of Second Isaiah's monotheism provides a useful foil, for I wish to offer an alternative account that differs in a number of respects. In providing this alternative account, however, we must remember that the

---

13. For an earlier discussion of incomparability formulae see C. J. Labuschagne, *The Incomparability of Yahweh in the Old Testament* (Leiden: Brill, 1966).

14. Clifford, 'Deutero-Isaiah'.

perceived centrality of monotheism in these chapters very much reflects viewing them through modern lenses. Albani rightly warns that 'it is necessary once again to remember that the establishing of monotheism is not portrayed as the central claim of the Deutero-Isaiainic proclamation'.[15] Perhaps the exilic prophet *is* the purveyor of monotheism, heir to centuries of development within Israelite religion, but he did not see himself as such and we are wise to be mindful of it.

A natural place to begin in examining monotheism in the book of Isaiah is Second Isaiah's affirmations about YHWH. Certainly the prophet offers strong claims for the uniqueness of YHWH, for which there already seems to have existed a vivid tradition. He deploys the incomparability formulae to demonstrate that YHWH is not simply a god among the gods. The formulae of self-predication 'I am he' and 'I am YHWH' seem consciously to echo the exodus story with its idea of YHWH's triumph over foreign powers and deities. YHWH also lays claim to the divine title, El.[16] Second Isaiah's distinctive use suggests that YHWH has exclusive claim to a title that evokes supremacy in a West Semitic context.[17] The claim to uniqueness is demonstrated forcefully in the fulfilment of predicative prophecy.

Does Second Isaiah go beyond this traditional affirmation of uniqueness in his statements that 'there is no other' (Isa. 45:5–6, 14, 18, 21–22; 46:9)? Many scholars believe that, under the unique pressure of accounting for YHWH's actions in the Babylonian exile, the anonymous prophet moves beyond an affirmation of uniqueness to a denial of the ontological existence of other deities. With Second Isaiah, Israel makes the breakthrough to monotheism. However, the matter is not as straightforward as the standard accounts suggest.

---

15. M. Albani, 'Deuterojesaja Monotheismus und der babylonische Religionskonflikt Nabonids', in M. Oeming and K. Schmid (eds.), *Der eine Gott und die Götter: Polytheismus und Monotheismus im antiken Israel*, ATANT 82 (Zurich: Theologischer Verlag, 2003), pp. 171–201; here p. 172.

16. The reference does not seem to be to the West Semitic deity El.

17. For the distinctive use of El in Second Isaiah see R. Rendtorff, *''El* als israelitische Gottesbezeichnung. Mit einem Appendix: Beobachtungen zum Gebrauch von *hā'ĕlōhîm'*, *ZAW* 106 (1994), pp. 4–21; here p. 12. Koch observes of 45:20–22, 'In the Hebrew text Yahweh is characterized as *elohim* as well as *el*. Both nouns are commonly translated "god", but in these chapters *el* seems to have the connotation 'highest god', as formerly at Ugarit, whereas *elohim* signifies every supposed divine being' (Koch, 'Ugaritic Polytheism', p. 218).

First, we should observe that the statement 'there is no other' is usually appended to formulae of self-predication, 'I am YHWH' or 'I am El'. As I have already indicated, these seem to be claiming that YHWH is unique. They have a parallel in Deuteronomy, where the statement 'there is no other' is prefixed with 'YHWH is God' (Deut. 4:35, 39). In the book of Deuteronomy many gods are mentioned, but only YHWH is '*the* God' (to provide a very literal translation). Thus the statement 'there is no other' may do no more than affirm the uniqueness of YHWH negatively. There is no other deity that belongs to this category. Even if this argument were not to prove persuasive, we must observe, secondly, the rhetorical nature of Second Isaiah's message. The difficulties are especially apparent when we observe that Queen Babylon makes a similar claim to YHWH in Isaiah 47: 'I am, and there is no other.'[18] What kind of ontological claim would this be? Thirdly, it has often been observed that in the middle part of the first millennium Assyrian and Babylonian worshippers were apt to describe their deities in exclusive terms. This rhetorical affectiveness is described by Hartmann as 'henolatry'. The worshipper describes the deity being petitioned as without rival, yet this can exist alongside a flourishing polytheism.[19] The rhetoric of Second Isaiah could function in a similar way.

It is not surprising, then, that there has always existed a minority of scholars who have dissented from the idea that Second Isaiah proclaims monotheism. Thus, in his work on *Second Isaiah's Message*, de Boer writes:

> The depiction of the virgin Babylonit in xlvii who says: no one besides me, is a good illustration of the meaning of the expression. She does not mean to say that she is the only woman, but that she is unique. Each other town is of a minor class compared to Babel. Likewise YHWH is not saying that he is the only god, but he is

---

18. Queen Babylon's claim does not exactly correspond to any of YHWH's assertions, but the vocabulary is common to both. Blenkinsopp observes the similarities and argues that 'this claim [by Queen Babylon] . . . is borrowed by the prophet as one of several similar expressions about the incomparability and uniqueness of Yahweh (45:5–6, 18, 22; 46:9)' (J. Blenkinsopp, *Isaiah 40–55*, AB 19 [New York: Doubleday, 2000], p. 282).

19. B. Hartmann, 'Monotheismus in Mesopotamien?', in O. Keel (ed.), *Monotheismus im Alten Israel und seiner Umwelt*, Biblische Beiträge 14 (Fribourg: Schweizerisches Katholisches Bibelwerk, 1980), pp. 50–81; H. Vorländer, 'Der Monotheismus Israels als Antwort auf die Krise des Exils', in B. Lang (ed.), *Der einzige Gott* (Munich: Kösel, 1981), pp. 84–113.

proclaiming his unique strength. No one besides me means: I have no competitor, no rival.[20]

Writing at about the same time, James Barr is similarly sceptical about the claims made for Second Isaiah:

> It may also be asked whether the question of mere existence is as important as has been commonly held for those later texts such as Deutero-Isaiah which are supposed to maintain the fullest type of monotheism. When we read in Ps. 14:1 *'amar nabbal be-libbo 'en 'elohim* [the fool has said in his heart there is no god], we are commonly agreed that the foolish man is no absolute atheist asserting the abstract non-existence of God; he is denying his significance, refusing to reckon with God. Is it not possible to understand in much the same way those places where Deutero-Isaiah uses the same negative particle? . . . [I]t is doubtful whether Deutero-Isaiah really represents a culmination of Israelite monotheism in which the powerlessness of other gods is absolutized into their non-existence.[21]

In a similar vein, John Collins has more recently suggested that Second Isaiah is about power, not ontology, while Christopher Seitz speaks about a 'henotheism of a particularly potent stripe'.[22]

Such views recognize that these monotheistic statements aim not at an ontology for its own sake, but YHWH's power to act for his people. In particular it is noteworthy that a number of these monotheistic statements climax with a soteriological claim: 'Besides me there is no saviour' (43:11); 'there is no one who can deliver from my hand' (43:13); 'there is no other rock' (44:8; cf. Deut. 32); 'a righteous God and a Saviour; there is no one besides me' (45:21); 'turn to me and be saved, all the ends of the earth! For I am God, and there is no other' (45:22).[23] The idols of the nations and Queen Babylon, in contrast, are unable to save themselves or others (44:9–20; 47:8–11). These monotheistic

---

20. P. A. H. de Boer, *Second Isaiah's Message*, OTS 11 (Leiden: Brill, 1956), p. 47.

21. J. Barr, 'The Problem of Israelite Monotheism', TGUOS 17 (1957–8), pp. 52–62; here pp. 53–55.

22. J. J. Collins in 'Audience Questions', in H. Shanks and J. Meinhardt (eds.), *Aspects of Monotheism: How God Is One* (Washington, DC: Biblical Archaeology Society, 1997), pp. 107–120; here p. 116; C. R. Seitz, 'The Divine Name in Scripture', in *Word Without End: The Old Testament as Abiding Theological Witness* (Grand Rapids: Eerdmans, 1998), pp. 251–262; here p. 255.

23. All Bible translations in this chapter are my own.

statements must not be isolated from the overall thrust of Second Isaiah's message that YHWH has come to act decisively. He will bring justice and righteousness to Israel and the nations by means of Cyrus, bringing down the mighty and strengthening the faint (chs. 40–41).

YHWH's monotheistic claims are based on his ability to prophesy the future. This is also true of Queen Babylon's claims to divinity, which are based on her magical powers (47:10). This claim to be the unique deity is only secondarily related to YHWH's control over creation and historical events. That is, it is this power that ensures that when YHWH speaks about the future, he speaks truly. In this way I agree with Stuhlmueller that Second Isaiah 'never argued from the basis of Yahweh Creator'.[24] It is misleading to speak, as Klaus Koch does, of a 'cosmological proof'.[25] The importance of prophetic fulfilment provides an interesting overlap between the prophet's vocation and the divine activity.

The affirmations about YHWH in Second Isaiah do not necessarily correspond to our assumptions about monotheism.[26] There are difficulties in confidently identifying the implications of Second Isaiah's rhetoric. Consequently, as we have seen, there is disagreement about the meaning of Second Isaiah's affirmations. Clifford concedes as much by shifting the argument about monotheism from Second Isaiah's exclusionary formulae to the idol polemic.[27]

Second Isaiah's idol polemic

According to Clifford, Second Isaiah's idol satire is of central significance to his monotheism. All gods are equated with idols, which are nothing but human creations. The prophet witnesses to a rigorous process of de-deification. As Clifford himself recognizes, a prior question is whether the idol polemic is part of the original Second Isaiah or the result of later redaction, as some have suggested. Even granting this I wonder whether the common understanding of the idol polemic properly appreciates what the prophet seeks to achieve in these polemics. In this respect I find suggestive the work by Knut Holter on the idol fabrication passages in Second Isaiah. Holter argues that the contrast the prophet wishes to draw is not, as often understood, between YHWH and

---

24. C. Stuhlmueller, *Creative Redemption in Deutero-Isaiah*, AnBib 43 (Rome: Biblical Institute, 1970), p. 168.

25. Koch, 'Ugaritic Polytheism', pp. 219–222.

26. On assumptions about 'monotheism' see MacDonald, *Deuteronomy*.

27. Indeed, Clifford argues that if, as some suggest, the idol polemic belongs to a later redactional layer, monotheism may not have been achieved until a post-exilic redaction of Isaiah (Clifford, 'Deutero-Isaiah').

the idols, but between YHWH and the idol-makers.[28] Developing Holter's idea, it seems to me that simultaneously a contrast is drawn between the Babylonian idols and Israel.[29]

The contrast between the Babylonian idols and Israel is expressed in a number of ways. First, while the idols are chosen and created by the idol-makers, Israel is the choice and creation of YHWH. In the process of making an idol, the idol-makers are said to 'select' some wood (40:20), a word that is used elsewhere by the prophet of Israel's election. The process of making the idol is described in great detail in Isaiah 44:9–20, which is the most extended polemic against the idol-makers. Isaiah mocks those who make, from the same piece of wood, an idol and a fire. In the verses that follow the words used for the creation of the idol are also used of Israel. In the act of new creation, YHWH has *formed* Israel (vv. 21, 23); he is the one who has *done* a marvellous act of redemption (v. 23). The act of recreation and redemption indicates a second element of contrast, one with an ironic twist. The idol-makers take a tree and form a dead idol that cannot see or hear; YHWH takes dead Israel, who cannot see or hear, and forms new life. The lifelessness of idols is a well-known topos in idol polemics. The prophet utilizes it in 44:9: 'their witnesses neither see nor know', but only as a foil to denounce the idol-makers for their senselessness (v. 18). Elsewhere in Isaiah, however, it is not the nations that are deaf and blind, but Israel (42:16–20; 43:8; cf. 6:9–10).[30] It is only with YHWH's words to the prophet that Israel can now see, so that she cannot give the credit to her idols (48:5–11). In no place is this comparison of Israel and the Babylonian idols sharper than in chapter 46. In a vivid image the prophet contrasts the Babylonians carrying their idols into captivity, with YHWH who carries his people. Thirdly, the reason why Israel has had her eyes and ears opened is so that she can serve YHWH. While the idol-makers cry to their gods, 'you are my god' (44:17), YHWH says to Israel 'you are my servant' (44:21). The task of the servant is to recognize YHWH's deeds and testify to them. The idols of the nations are witnesses that cannot see or know (44:9), but Israel is to be a trustworthy witness to YHWH's acts (43:10, 12).

---

28. K. Holter, *Second Isaiah's Idol Fabrication Passages*, BBET 28 (Frankfurt am Main: Peter Lang, 1995).

29. N. MacDonald, 'Aniconism in the Old Testament', in R. P. Gordon (ed.), *The God of Israel*, University of Cambridge Oriental Publications 64 (Cambridge: Cambridge University Press, 2007), pp. 20–34; esp. 29–31.

30. Cf. G. K. Beale, 'Isaiah vi 9–13: A Retributive Taunt Against Idolatry', *VT* 41 (1991), pp. 257–278.

The prophecies in Isaiah 40 – 48 contain a contrast primarily between YHWH and the Babylonians. The polemic is aimed against the idol-makers, not the Babylonian pantheon. Thus it is consistently the nations that are called to trial by YHWH in these chapters, not their gods. It is not necessary to exclude the existence of a comparison between YHWH and the Babylonian gods, but Second Isaiah is primarily concerned to create a comparison of the latter and Israel, the servant of YHWH. Both are blind, dumb and powerless. In this comparison ontology is not the issue.

Second Isaiah's universalism

The difficulties in interpreting Second Isaiah and its rhetoric are particularly apparent when we come to the thorny question of universalism. Clifford is not alone in discerning a strong universalism, but he does so by ignoring the numerous scholars who wish to emphasize Second Isaiah's particularism. The language of universalism and particularism is rather unfortunate. It can encourage a two-dimensional approach and a tendency towards polarization. In fact justice needs to be done to the centrality of Israel and Jerusalem in the divine plan and the role of the nations. Kaminsky and Stewart seek to capture this when they observe that 'the prophet evokes a type of universalism, but one that maintains and even deepens Israel's particularistic election'.[31] It is Israel that will be the light to the nations (42:6; 49:6), and bring the justice of YHWH's *tôrâ* (42:4; 51:4). The vision of Second Isaiah accords well with Isaiah 2:1–4, where the nations stream to Jerusalem in order to learn *tôrâ*.[32] At the centre of YHWH's instituted order is his servant Israel. It is to her that splendour and salvation come (46:13). As a result the nations will come to Israel in humility and subservience (45:14; 49:7; and infamously 49:23). This is a universal recognition of the glory of Israel's God, rather than all nations partaking on equal terms in the worship of YHWH.

The importance of Jerusalem and the land in Second Isaiah is too often overlooked. This is especially the case when Isaiah 40 – 55 is seen as part of a monotheistic redefinition of Israelite identity stemming from the trauma of the exile. Reshaping did take place but its character is different from what is sometimes suggested. Mark Smith, for example, draws attention to 'the loss of monarchy and land as defining marks of Judean identity' that 'issued in a

---

31. J. Kaminsky and A. Stewart, 'God of All the World: Universalism and Developing Monotheism in Isaiah 40–66', *HTR* 99 (2006), pp. 139–163; here p. 162.

32. For the relationship of this passage to Deutero-Isaiah see Williamson, *Book Called Isaiah*, pp. 144–154.

probing search for a reworked identity'. Second Isaiah elevates YHWH because of the failure of political boundaries and institutions. Israel's God and the text he gives Israel become central in this new religious identity. Indeed, Smith even ventures 'we might say that text substitutes for land'.[33] Clearly, this 'loss of monarchy and land' is complete in Smith's view. Yet this portrayal is difficult to square with the centrality of return to the land in Second Isaiah's message and with what we know about Second Temple Judaism. Land and the temple are certainly reconfigured in the post-exilic period, but neither is erased. Arguably the exile could be seen as making these realities even more important than they formerly were. Many of the most important texts about land in the Old Testament originate from times when its loss had to be contemplated.

In my view, summarizing Isaiah's message about Israel and the nations with the epigram 'one religion for one world under one God' is to distort seriously the prophet's message. It fails to do justice to Barton's plea that we carefully attend to the differences between the original meaning of the text and its reception. The difficulties arise because there is an allusiveness to Second Isaiah's rhetoric that will allow Isaiah 40 – 55 to be read in different ways in new contexts. This is most obviously the case in later Christian inter-pretations, where the church's inclusion of Gentile converts reflects a careful attentiveness by early Christians to the Old Testament's statements about the nations. Nevertheless, such moves may already be presaged on the level of the whole book of Isaiah. As Kaminsky and Stewart rightly observe, there is 'a greater receptivity to the inclusion of some Gentiles within the elect group [as] appears even within the late texts of Third Isaiah in chapters 56 and 66'.[34] We should note, though, that even this selective inclusion of some Gentile converts falls a long way short of Clifford's 'one religion for one world'.

Monotheism and the rest of Isaiah

In our discussion of Second Isaiah's universalism we have begun to step beyond the narrow confines of Isaiah 40 – 48, or even Isaiah 40 – 55, and to notice the relevance of texts elsewhere in the book of Isaiah. As already indi-cated it will not be possible to make more than a few suggestive probes of the

---

33. Smith, *Origins*, pp. 193–194. Clifford offers a similar reification of Israelite monotheism in his elevation of 'international' to characterize Deutero-Isaiah's message, understating the centrality of Israel and the land in chs. 40–55.

34. Kaminsky and Stewart, 'God of All the World', p. 162.

way in which themes from Isaiah 40 – 48 find echo elsewhere in the book of
Isaiah. A complete study would need to work with a detailed account of the
redaction of the book, and it is not possible to do so within a short compass.
Nevertheless, utilizing the same headings as we have already used I shall seek
to examine monotheism elsewhere in the book of Isaiah. I shall observe some
interesting patterns but leave a comprehensive account for another occasion.

Isaiah's monotheistic affirmations

The monotheistic affirmations that are so marked a feature of the rhetoric of
Isaiah 40 – 48 are absent from the rest of the book. This includes the parts traditionally designated as First Isaiah and Third Isaiah, but also the second half
of Second Isaiah. The rest of Isaiah makes few explicit references to other
gods. The striking exception to these observations is the narrative concerning
Hezekiah (Isaiah 36 – 39), which now functions as a bridge between First and
Second Isaiah. The Rabshakeh boasts about his conquests and the failure of
other deities to deliver the nations he has conquered (36:13–20). In response
Hezekiah utters a prayer that echoes many themes from Second Isaiah, albeit
expressed in novel ways (37:16–20).[35] Hezekiah confesses that YHWH alone is
God (hā'ĕlōhîm) and that he is YHWH alone.[36] The defeat of other nations is recognized, but the gods of the nations that Rabshakeh has destroyed were only
idols. Hezekiah pleads with YHWH to save Jerusalem so that the nations will
acknowledge YHWH. The overlap with some of the themes we have identified
in Second Isaiah is apparent. There is less of an overlap to First Isaiah, with
the exception of referring to YHWH as 'Lord of Hosts' and the idols as 'the
work of human hands' (37:19).[37] The response to this prayer is also notable.
The oracle Isaiah delivers has typical themes in common with First Isaiah,
most especially the theme of YHWH's exaltation at the expense of all others,
including Sennacherib (37:22–29).[38]

---

35. Seitz notes the lack of precise parallels with Second Isaiah (C. R. Seitz, *Zion's Final
    Destiny: The Development of the Book of Isaiah* [Minneapolis: Fortress, 1991], pp.
    83–86).
36. Isa. 37:20 reads, 'you are YHWH alone'. It is common to insert 'God' with the
    synoptic parallel in 2 Kgs 19:19; 1QIsa^a and LXX. The present text would provide
    an interesting parallel to 43:11; 45:5–6, 18.
37. Williamson, *Book Called Isaiah*, pp. 192, 196.
38. The influence of Deutero-Isaiah has often been identified in this oracle, but see
    now ibid., pp. 194–196. The appearance of Isaianic themes does not represent a
    judgment about authorship.

The relationship between Hezekiah's prayer and Isaiah's oracle makes for a suggestive lexicon between First and Second Isaiah. In other words, First Isaiah's emphasis on the exaltation of YHWH corresponds to Second Isaiah's monotheistic affirmations. As is well known, the loftiness of Israel's God is an important aspect of First Isaiah's presentation of YHWH. In the account of his call, Isaiah describes YHWH's sitting on a throne that is 'high and lifted up' (6:1). As Williamson observes, 'the description of God in Isa. 6:1 has exerted an influence on the whole of the Isaianic tradition'.[39] It is noteworthy, however, that Isaiah 40 – 55 does not speak of YHWH's being lifted up and exalted in the way that First Isaiah, or even Third Isaiah (57:15), does. Nevertheless these chapters are suffused with the theme of YHWH's exaltation, albeit expressed in different terms: those of a monotheistic rhetoric.

Does my suggested correspondence between First Isaiah's presentation of YHWH's exaltation and Second Isaiah's monotheistic affirmations shed any additional light on how monotheism might be reflected in the first half of Isaiah? It seems significant that one of the most sustained reflections on the exaltation of YHWH in chapter 2 includes an idol polemic. Idols do not avail the Judeans. As YHWH is exalted, they are thrown into the depths by their frustrated creators (2:20). Yet, as I suggested was the case in Second Isaiah, the book's polemic is more often aimed at human beings than at their images of worship. Indeed, we may observe that other gods are rarely mentioned in First Isaiah.

In this respect the description of Babylon in Isaiah 14 is characteristic. Heavenly and political language overlap as Babylon's attempt to seize divine prerogatives is described. The King of Babylon has designs upon being El Elyon, God Most High (14:14). Nevertheless, like all other kings who have aspired to this position he finds himself cast into the underworld. Isaiah's oracle is rightly compared by Seitz to Psalm 82; there also divine and political language overlaps so that it is unclear whether it is rulers or gods who are being threatened with mortality.[40] The overlap between the gods and earthly rulers is also apparent in the Isaianic Apocalypse (Isa. 24 – 27). The eschatological exaltation of YHWH on Mount Zion will see both the heavenly host and the kings of earth punished (24:21). This sees the former powers dethroned, those who formerly ruled over the Judeans. But are the 'other lords' of 26:14 deities or human rulers? In Isaiah 1 – 39, then, gods and kings have in common an insatiable desire for power and status which they have used to lord it over Judah

---

39. Ibid., p. 40.

40. C. R. Seitz, *Isaiah 1–39*, Interpretation (Louisville: John Knox, 1993), p. 135.

and Jerusalem. The prophet unmasks this and prophesies their ruin. Second Isaiah continues this theme with its portrayal of Babylon's divine pretensions and the contrast it draws between YHWH and the human idol-makers.

In contrast to the humiliation of all powers, earthly or cosmic, is the exaltation of YHWH. According to 2:11 he alone will be exalted, a theme developed in 12:4 and 33:5, 10. The exaltation of YHWH forms a counterpoint to the oppression that has marked the self-exaltation of human beings, for YHWH is exalted in righteousness. This is developed in 5:14–16, where the contrasting human examples are the Jerusalem aristocracy:

> Therefore Sheol has enlarged its appetite,
>   and opened its mouth without measure;
> her nobility and her multitude go down,
>   her revellers and all who exult in her.
> Humanity is bowed down, mankind is brought low,
>   and the eyes of the haughty are humbled.
> But the Lord of hosts is exalted by justice,
>   and the Holy El shows himself holy by righteousness.[41]

These verses are significant for a couple of reasons. First, there is the confluence of the themes of exaltation, holiness and justice-righteousness. All three will recur in modified form in Isaiah's commissioning (Isa. 6). The relationship of YHWH's exaltation to his holiness is significant. Probably under the influence of Isaiah 6 the theme of YHWH's exaltation has become a significant element in the book's unity across its different parts. The same is true, with some qualifications, for the title 'Holy One of Israel';[42] according to 5:16 exaltation and holiness are corollaries of one another. Second, the attribution of justice and righteousness is striking. It has usually been thought that the attributes are rightly divine, such that the divine justice and righteousness are

---

41. NRSV's 'the nobility of Jerusalem and her multitude go down' (v. 14) is better as an interpretation than a translation.

42. For those qualifications see the nuanced article by H. G. M. Williamson: 'Isaiah and the Holy One of Israel', in A. Rapoport-Albert and G. Greenberg (eds.), *Biblical Hebrew, Biblical Texts: Essays in Memory of Michael P. Weitzman*, JSOTSup 333 (Sheffield: Sheffield Academic Press, 2001), pp. 22–38. Williamson observes that the title 'Holy One of Israel', while originating with Isaiah of Jerusalem, is particularly characteristic of Second Isaiah, but is much less common, sometimes absent, in later texts (Isa. 24 – 27; 34 – 35; 55 – 66).

seen in the judgment of the haughty. Moberly has, however, argued that justice and righteousness are usually human attributes in Isaiah, and the purpose of the passage is didactic. True exaltation, the kind characteristic of YHWH, is expressed primarily in certain moral practices rather than the ways usually considered as evidence of status by human beings.[43] Moberly's point is well made. In First Isaiah YHWH's exaltation and his character is contrasted with the exaltation that human beings attain which leads to the oppression of God's people. With First Isaiah acting as a prelude to Second Isaiah, these ideas have an important effect on the message of the anonymous prophet. The God of Isaiah 40 – 55, who is unique and above everything else, is portrayed acting out of his own righteousness for the sake of salvation, and in opposition to the oppression of the captives by Babylon. The monotheism of Second Isaiah is soteriologically, not ontologically, orientated.[44]

Isaiah's idol polemic

We have already observed that Hezekiah's prayer refers to 'the work of human hands' (37:19). The gods of the other nations prove futile and unworthy of the title. The similarities to Second Isaiah are apparent, though the vocabulary is different, as Williamson observes.[45] The expression 'the work of human hands' or similar occurs elsewhere in Isaiah 1 – 39: 2:8, 31:7; cf. 17:8. It draws attention not only to the powerlessness of idols, but also to the human role in production. Idols are a futile attempt to control human destiny when YHWH determines the course of affairs.

It is striking that, as we have seen with Second Isaiah, the description of the idol is easily exchangeable with the description of Israel. The 'work of human hands' is the idols, but YHWH also has a work. The 'work of his hands' can be used of his people (19:25; 29:23; cf. 17:7; 29:16). Thus, as in Second Isaiah, the comparison to be made is that between YHWH and the idol-makers, and not between YHWH and the idols.

---

43. R. W. L. Moberly, 'Whose Justice? Whose Righteousness? The Interpretation of Isaiah V 16', *VT* 51 (2001), pp. 55–68. See the further discussion in H. G. M. Williamson, *Isaiah 1–5*, ICC (London: T. & T. Clark International, 2006), pp. 375–376.

44. In passing over to Third Isaiah a further transformation takes place. The emphasis on YHWH's exaltation remains, but the appeal to do justice and righteousness apparent in First Isaiah reappears sharpened by an eschatological context.

45. Williamson, *Book Called Isaiah*, p. 196.

Isaiah's universalism

In the book of Isaiah the place of the nations has an important role. This has already been shown in detail by Graham Davies in a chapter entitled 'The Destiny of the Nations in the Book of Isaiah'. Davies demonstrates that the nations are a concern across every part of Isaiah and such material contributes to our sense of the unity of the book.[46] Since Davies has completed such a detailed study on the subject there is no need to replicate his work. Instead I wish to draw attention to a number of features in the book's portrayal of Israel and the nations.

First, the book's reflections upon the nations clearly stem from throughout its history of composition. The eighth-century Isaiah of Jerusalem is portrayed prophesying during significant political crises (the Syro-Ephraimite war, the invasion of Sennacherib) when the relationship between the Israelite nations and with surrounding enemy nations was deeply pressing. Some of the latest material in the book, such as Third Isaiah and the Isaiah Apocalypse, address the future of the nations in general. Clearly, one of the book of Isaiah's distinctive contributions is its detailed reflections upon Israel and the nations.

Secondly, in the final form of the book the judgement of the nations has been retained, but subordinated to a hopeful future where the nations gather to Jerusalem to learn and worship (Isa. 2:1–4; 66:18–25).[47] We should not assume, however, that the history of the book's development maps in any simple way on to a spectrum between particularism and universalism, as though the book moves from a narrow particularism to an all-embracing universalism. The history of the book's composition, and the development of Israelite religion in general, is far more complex. To speak of particularism making way to universalism is to offer an algebraic solution when only calculus will do.

Thirdly, although the book envisages other nations sharing Israel's blessing – often in surprising ways that go some way beyond what we have seen in Second Isaiah – this is never done in a way that evacuates Israel's election of meaning. A few examples will illustrate. In 2:2–4 the nations are portrayed learning from YHWH. This is achieved through pilgrimage to Zion, where justice and *tôrâ* are dispensed. In chapter 19 the Assyrians and Egyptians become worshippers of YHWH, being numbered among his people (vv. 18–25). Yet even in this remarkable vision Israel remains 'a blessing in the midst of the

46. G. I. Davies, 'The Destiny of the Nations in the Book of Isaiah', in J. Vermeylen (ed.), *The Book of Isaiah / Le Livre de Isaïe: Les oracles et leurs relectures. Unité et complexité de l'ouvrage*, BETL 81 (Leuven: Peeters, 1989), pp. 93–120.

47. Ibid., pp. 93–95.

earth' and YHWH's 'heritage'. The Isaianic apocalypse depicts an eschatological meal with all the nations gathered, no longer suffering death (25:6–8). The location of this meal must not be forgotten, for it is Zion. It is from here that YHWH will reign and display his glory (24:21–23). Finally, the gathering of all nations to recognize YHWH in 66:18–25 is a gathering to worship in *Jerusalem*. It is integral to this section that this gathering is a result of the return of the scattered remnant of Israel to Jerusalem.[48]

Conclusion

Neither Isaiah nor monotheism is a simple reality. Scholarship since the 1800s has recognized this with Isaiah, less so with monotheism. Our examination of monotheism in Isaiah has shown the extent to which certain themes pervade the whole book: the uniqueness of YHWH, the futility of idolatry, and the destiny of the nations. There can, nevertheless, be important differences between the ways these themes are developed. This was most apparent with 'universalism'. In the light of this we may need to give more careful attention to the differences and commonalities that monotheistic theologies exhibit in Isaiah and elsewhere in the Old Testament.

© Nathan MacDonald, 2009

---

48. Kaminsky and Stewart, 'God of All the World', p. 160.

3. TOO HARD TO UNDERSTAND? THE MOTIF OF HARDENING IN ISAIAH

Torsten Uhlig

In Isaiah 6:9–10 the prophet Isaiah is sent to make his audience 'too hard to understand'. However, it seems as if this idiom itself is too hard to understand! This article seeks to illumine some aspects of Isaiah's mission that some have labelled 'the motif of hardening'. Furthermore, it will outline the use of this theme in other passages, noting its overall contribution to the theology of the book of Isaiah (Isa.).[1]

---

1. Some other studies of the motif of hardening include K. T. Aitken, 'Hearing and Seeing: Metamorphoses of a Motif in Isaiah 1–39', in P. R. Davies and D. J. A. Clines (eds.), *Among the Prophets: Language, Image and Structure in the Prophetic Writings*, JSOTSup 144 (Sheffield: Sheffield Academic Press, 1993), pp. 12–41; G. K. Beale, 'Isaiah VI 9–13: A Retributive Taunt Against Idolatry', *VT* 41 (1991), pp. 257–278; C. A. Evans, *To See and Not Perceive: Isaiah 6.9–10 in Early Jewish and Christian Interpretation*, JSOTSup 64 (Sheffield: Sheffield Academic Press, 1989); J. L. McLaughlin, 'There Hearts *Were* Hardened: The Use of Isaiah 6,9–10 in the Book of Isaiah', *Bib* 75 (1994), pp. 1–25; G. D. Robinson, 'The Motif of Deafness and Blindness in Isaiah 6:9–10: A Contextual, Literary, and Theological Analysis', *BBR* 8 (1998), pp. 167–188, and those studies mentioned further below.

Noting the occurrence of the motif of hardening in Isaiah

Where the Old Testament describes people as unable to change their mind, intentions or perception, it speaks of their 'hardness' (of heart). Sometimes people put themselves into this state of hardness (see the warning in Ps. 95:8; then also Deut. 15:7; 2 Chr. 36:13); sometimes it is said that they are hardened by YHWH (Deut. 2:30; Josh. 11:20). The call of the prophet Isaiah (Isa. 6) is one of the most perplexing passages in the Old Testament in this respect. His task is what many would regard as the total opposite of a prophet's mission:

> Go, and say to this people:
>
> 'Keep on hearing, but do not understand;
> keep on seeing, but do not perceive.'
> Make the heart of this people dull,
>   and their ears heavy,
>   and blind their eyes;
> lest they see with their eyes,
>   and hear with their ears,
> and understand with their hearts,
>   and turn and be healed.
> (Isa. 6:9–10 ESV)

The prophet Isaiah is to achieve among his audience a state in which they are unable to repent. This strange call has come to be known as the commission of 'hardening': the prophet Isaiah has to 'harden' his audience through his ministry. But clearly this commission involves additional aspects. It is not simply the hardness of hearts that is in view, but the perception (seeing and hearing) and the understanding of the audience that Isaiah is to affect. It is this combination of aspects which some have called the 'motif of hardening'.

Furthermore, when we read on in Isaiah, we become aware that this motif is not restricted only to Isaiah 6. Terms of perception and understanding, like 'to see', 'to hear', 'eyes', 'ears', 'blind', 'deaf', 'to understand', 'to recognize', 'understanding', 'knowledge' and so on occur elsewhere in the book. Among the passages that take up the motif of hardening of Isaiah 6 are Isaiah 1:2–3; 11:2, 9; 29:9–10, 17–24; 30:30; 32:1–4; 35:5; 40:21, 28; 41:20; 42:18–25; 43:8–13; 44:9–20; 46:12–13; 48:1–11; 50:4–11; 52:13 – 53:12; 55:1–5; 56:9 – 57:2; 58:3; 59:1, 8–12; 63:7 – 64:12 (63:17). As the motif of hardening runs through major parts of Isaiah, we need to take all these passages into account when we examine the use of the motif of hardening in the book of Isaiah and consider its contribution to the theology of Isaiah. However, Isaiah 6 remains our central focus. As we turn our attention to some of its characteristics, we will note some key elements of the interpretation of hardening.

Interpreting the motif of hardening in Isaiah 6

There are five features of Isaiah 6 that can guide us in our interpretation of hardening in Isaiah. They encompass (1) the structure of Isaiah 6, (2) the vision of Isaiah, (3) his reaction to this vision, (4) the circumstances of his sending and (5) the arrangement of Isaiah's call in Isaiah 6:9–10.

The structure of Isaiah 6 and the call to harden as the goal of the vision

When we look at the structure of Isaiah 6, the call of Isaiah to harden the people (vv. 9–10) emerges as the goal of the whole passage. Verses 1–11 can be seen as two parallel scenes, each being introduced by a verb of perception with Isaiah as the subject and YHWH as the object ('I saw the Lord', v. 1 // 'and I heard the voice of the Lord', v. 8). This is followed by the description of Isaiah's reaction ('and I said', vv. 5, 8), and a response to Isaiah ('then one of the seraphim flew', v. 6 // 'and he said', v. 9). The response to Isaiah in the second scene prompts another reaction from Isaiah (v. 11).[2]

That the call to harden the people in verses 9–10 is the goal of the whole passage can also be seen in its funnel-like structure: the verbs that introduce each scene ('to see', v. 1; 'to hear', v. 8) occur together in the call of Isaiah (vv. 9–10). One can say both scenes flow together in Isaiah's call. Isaiah 6 indicates through its structure that the whole vision leads to the call of Isaiah to harden the people.

The vision of Isaiah

The fact that the whole vision of Isaiah leads to the call of hardening is amplified by several other features. What Isaiah sees evokes the impression of an impending judgment of YHWH: the intrusion of the seraphim into the realm of YHWH's court makes his presence more threatening. The seraphim are most probably winged serpents that pose serious danger in the desert (cf. Num.

---

2. This structure of Isa. 6 emerges when one looks at the Heb. verb forms. On the additional element in the first scene (v. 4: the shaking of the pivots and the filling with smoke) see below.

21:6, Isa. 14:29, 30:6, where the same term is used for 'snake').[3] In so far as these creatures have been included in the sphere of the universal king YHWH, his presence no longer protects, but itself becomes a threat. This impression is further strengthened by a new development in the vision. After the seraphim utter their doxology, the pivots of the thresholds tremble and the whole building begins to fill with smoke (v. 4). Many interpreters see traits of an epiphany in this description,[4] but it seems more likely that the trembling and the filling with smoke indicate the hiding of YHWH is an aspect of his judgment.[5]

If read this way, Isaiah's reaction (v. 5) is unsurprising: he fears for his life. For our interpretation of hardening, however, it is how Isaiah explains his fear of death that is of particular interest.

Isaiah's reaction to the vision of judgment

Corresponding to the three holies of the seraphim, the prophet Isaiah gives three reasons why he fears for his life ('woe is me'): he is lost, he is a man of unclean lips and lives among a people of unclean lips, and his eyes have seen the king, YHWH Sabaoth.

The mentioning of 'unclean lips' is noteworthy in two respects. First, the term 'unclean, impure' in verse 5 is often used in cultic contexts. But there are some cases where this term is related to unjust behaviour in society (cf. Hos. 5:1, 3; 6:10; Mic. 2:10).[6] Once this is realized, the striking correspondences

---

3. Cf. T. N. D. Mettinger, 'Seraphim', *DDD*, pp. 742–743; and O. Keel, *Jahwe-Visionen und Siegelkunst: Eine neue Deutung der Majestätsschilderungen in Jes 6, Ez 1 und 10 und Sach 4. Mit einem Beitrag von A. Gutbub über die vier Winde in Ägypten*, SBS 84.85 (Stuttgart: Katholisches Bibelwerk, 1977), pp. 70–115, who presents seals that have been found in the territory of eighth-century BC Judah and that show serpentine figures (Egyptian Uraei).

4. Cf. J. Blenkinsopp, *Isaiah 1–39: A New Translation with Introduction and Commentary*, AB 19 (New York: Doubleday, 2000), pp. 225–226.

5. This has been argued in F. Hartenstein's detailed study. In respect to the interpretation of the shaking pivots of the thresholds (v. 4a), Hartenstein draws on a range of biblical and Near Eastern texts to argue that v. 4 is about the hiding of YHWH who remains present in his judgment of the people. See F. Hartenstein, *Die Unzugänglichkeit Gottes im Heiligtum: Jesaja 6 und der Wohnort JHWHs in der Jerusalemer Kulttradition*, WMANT 75 (Neukirchen-Vluyn: Neukirchener Verlag, 1997).

6. For more detailed discussions of the ethical implications of 'unclean' in some passages in the OT cf. e.g. D. P. Wright, 'Unclean and Clean (OT)', *ABD* 6:729–741;

with Psalm 15, and particularly Psalm 24,[7] suggest a combination of ethical issues with being present in the sanctuary in Isaiah 6.[8] Secondly, in so far as 'lips' are crucially related to communication and speech, two passages in the immediate literary context have to be considered: in Isaiah 3:8–10, verse 8b reads, 'their tongue [here a different Heb. term is used] and deeds are against YHWH, to defy (the eyes of)[9] his glory'.[10] Thus communication and YHWH's 'glory' occur together here as in Isaiah 6:3, 5. Then, according to verse 9, the people communicate ('they proclaim') their sins like Sodom, which ends in the same 'Alas' cry as in Isaiah 6:5. Additionally, the lines in Isaiah 5:18–20 are noteworthy. Here the 'Woe' of a dirge applies to those who mock YHWH and his plan (v. 19). By this means they increase their sins, and this *communicative* act is described figuratively as 'ropes of *deceit*' (v. 18). This culminates in the depiction of total perversion of communication: evil is said to be good and good is turned into evil (5:20). Taking this literary context into account, it appears that Isaiah fears for his life because of the misguided communication among his people. He finds himself confronted with the holy YHWH while he is aware of his own condition: he is part of a society where perversion of communication plays an important part in the disturbed (religious, social and political) order. Even more, Isaiah states that his 'unclean lips' have become a characteristic of his (and his people's) being and nature: He does not say 'because I have unclean lips' but 'because I am a man of unclean lips'. The 'unclean lips' qualify his nature and so Isaiah fears for his life as his whole being cannot stand the confrontation with the holy YHWH.

The assertion 'for my eyes have seen the king YHWH Sabaoth' fits into this whole train of thought. Although there are passages in the Old Testament that speak about the danger or impossibility of seeing YHWH and living, this

---

Footnote 6 (*continued*)

G. J. Wenham, 'Purity', in J. Barton (ed.), *The Biblical World*, 2 vols. (London: Routledge, 2002), 2:380–381, 391–392.

7. Cf. H. Wildberger, *Isaiah 1–12: A Commentary*, CC (Minneapolis: Fortress, 1991), p. 268.

8. Cf. similarly J. F. A. Sawyer, *Isaiah Volume 1*, DSB (Louisville; London: Westminster John Knox, 1984), pp. 70–71; Wildberger, *Isaiah 1–12*, p. 268, and G. Y. Glazov, *The Bridling of the Tongue and the Opening of the Mouth in Biblical Prophecy*, JSOTSup 311 (Sheffield: Sheffield Academic Press, 2001), pp. 122–123.

9. See Wildberger, *Isaiah 1–12*, p. 125, on this awkward phrase.

10. Unless stated otherwise, all translations (and italics in Bible quotations) are my own.

does not necessarily form the background for Isaiah's cry. Another strand of passages refer to the wish of seeing YHWH (cf. Pss 11:7; 17:15; 27:4, 13; 42:2–3; 63:3; 84:11–13). These are often related to the image of YHWH as a king who is to implement righteousness. In these contexts, where the righteous seeks help from YHWH against the unjust, seeing YHWH means being in the sphere of his justice.[11] But if seeing the king YHWH includes the connotations that YHWH, the righteous king, saves the righteous by overcoming (judging) the unjust,[12] then the reaction (and explanation) of Isaiah is all the more remarkable: Isaiah is aware of his participation in the perverted communication/injustices; so when he sees King YHWH, he must regard him as the one who is to judge him. He is in sheer terror, 'for I am lost'.[13] In sum, Isaiah expresses his fear of being lost because as one participating in the unjust communicative processes of his people he is confronted with the holy king YHWH who is to implement justice and righteousness by judgment (cf. Isa. 5:1–7).

The circumstances of the sending of Isaiah

If one compares Isaiah's call with other prophets, then it is interesting to see that Isaiah volunteers for this ministry while many other prophets hesitate. Some interpreters have pointed to the similarities with 1 Kings 22 and argued that Isaiah 6 is a different form of a call narrative or a commission for a

---

11. Cf. M. S. Smith, '"Seeing God" in the Psalms: The Background of the Beatific Vision in the Hebrew Bible', *CBQ* 50 (1988), pp. 171–183; and B. Janowski, *Konfliktgespräche mit Gott: Eine Anthropologie der Psalmen* (Neukirchen-Vluyn: Neukirchener Verlag, 2003), pp. 90–97. See there also the comments on Exod. 24:10 and further literature.

12. Cf. Janowski, *Konfliktgespräche*, pp. 147–151.

13. The Heb. phrase here translated 'for I am lost' is disputed. Some opt for an ambiguity in Isa. 6:5 between 'for I am lost' and 'for I must be silent'; thus e.g. J. J. M. Roberts, 'Double Entendre in First Isaiah', *CBQ* 54 (1992), pp. 44–46. Others maintain the meaning 'to be silent, must be silent': e.g. O. Kaiser, *Isaiah 1–12*, OTL (London: SCM, 1983), pp. 117, 128, n. 60; Glazov, *Bridling*, pp. 134–149. But against these proposals one must admit that Isaiah does speak in v. 5! This, taken with the interpretation of the whole reaction of Isaiah in its immediate literary context, makes the interpretation 'for I am lost' the most plausible. For this meaning of the term see Isa. 15:1; Jer. 47:5; Hos. 4:6; 10:7; Pss 30:13; 49:13; thus also e.g. R. E. Clements, *Isaiah 1–39*, NCB (Grand Rapids: Eerdmans; London: Marshall, Morgan & Scott, 1980), p. 75; J. N. Oswalt, *The Book of Isaiah Chapters 1–39*, NICOT (Grand Rapids: Eerdmans, 1986), p. 171, n. 5.

limited time. But that Isaiah voluntarily takes up the prophetic ministry can be better explained from within Isaiah 6 and a noteworthy structural feature. The sequence of both scenes in Isaiah 6:1–11 of 'perception of YHWH' (v. 1 // v. 8), 'Isaiah's reaction' (v. 5 // v. 8) and 'response to Isaiah' (vv. 6–7 // vv. 9–10) is 'disturbed' by an additional element in the first scene: in verse 4 the pivots of the thresholds tremble and the temple is filling with smoke. There is no correspondence to this element in the second scene. In the first scene Isaiah is confronted with the hiding YHWH (v. 4) and fears for his life. But one of the seraphim comes to him with a burning coal and purifies his lips. It burns away Isaiah's sins; one could say Isaiah suffers judgment already but in such a way that he is not eliminated. Once he has experienced the purifying judgment, he can hear YHWH. And now – *after* the judgment – there is nothing that stands between him and YHWH. But, at the same time, the people with whom he had formerly identified himself (v. 5) have now become 'this people'. The element that showed the hiding of YHWH from his people (v. 4) is lacking in the second scene. YHWH is not hidden for Isaiah, as he can (now) understand YHWH. But Isaiah is now in this role to hide YHWH from 'this people' by delivering the hardening message. That is why Isaiah can volunteer but has to deliver such a devastating message. Isaiah speaks from beyond the judgment that the people yet await.

This leaves us with the question of how Isaiah is to achieve his call of hardening.

The arrangement of the call of Isaiah

For our analysis of hardening in Isaiah 6, we need to recognize the differentiation between the literal imperatives in verse 9 and the figurative imperatives in verse 10a. The imperative in verse 9, 'Go, and say to this people', expresses what Isaiah is actually to do. He is called to go to the people and speak to them. The included quotation introduces and summarizes his proclamation; the imperatives to hear and see serve as an attention marker that introduces the prophetic speech and create the expectation that there is more to come. As such it epitomizes the whole proclamation of Isaiah. The addition of the consequences (that they will not perceive and understand)[14] gives it at the same time the character of a summary. These literal imperatives are complemented by the figurative imperatives in verse 10. They cannot be put into real action; they indicate the effects that Isaiah's proclamation will have. But these verses

---

14. I translate the quotation as 'Hear indeed and you will not perceive; see indeed and you will not understand.'

and imperatives belong closely together: it is through his actual proclamation to 'this people' that Isaiah will fulfil the figurative imperatives of 'making fat, hard' and 'smearing over'. The differentiation within this relationship in verses 9–10 serves an important function: it dissociates the effect of Isaiah's proclamation (v. 10) from the content of the message and Isaiah's own intention (v. 9). Whatever he says or wants to say, like the quotation in verse 9, the effect will be the hardening of his audience (thus v. 10). This is determined by the universal king, YHWH Sabaoth.

As regards the fulfilment of this call, the book of Isaiah never actually reports how Isaiah went to the people and delivered this message. But at least for the readers and hearers of the book it is through Isaiah 6 itself that the call of verses 9–10 is fulfilled. As an account in the first person singular, it is Isaiah himself who tells his readers and hearers that he is called to harden them.

After we have noted several features of Isaiah 6 and their contribution to our interpretation of hardening, we can now summarize some of the central aspects of hardening. Hardening is a part of the impending judgment of YHWH that is indicated in Isaiah 6 by the hiding of YHWH. The mention of the 'unclean lips' by the prophet Isaiah evokes those passages in the literary context that speak of the perverted communication among the people and between the people and YHWH (cf. Isa. 3:8–9; 5:18–20; additionally see e.g. Isa. 28:15 [17]; 29:20–21; 30:12; 32:5–6). After Isaiah himself experienced the purifying judgment of his unclean lips (vv. 6–7), he is sent to 'this people', who still have unclean lips, to harden them. Thus hardening appears as the specific judgment on the perverted communication. This is to make the people's communication impossible because of its total deviation from the principles of righteousness. As judgment comes upon the people because of the lack of righteousness in general (cf. Isa. 5:1–7 and its specification in Isa. 5:8–30), so hardening is part of this as the specific judgment of unjust communication.

This interpretation of hardening as the consequence from perverted communication receives support from three passages discussed below in relation to the reversal of hardening: In Isaiah 50 the servant has a

> tongue of those who are taught,
> that I may know how to sustain with a word
>   him who is weary.
> (Isa. 50:4 ESV)

For the purpose of proper and comforting communication his ear is awakened. The importance of proper communication is then resumed in Isaiah

53:9, where it is said that the one through whom the 'we' have been able to change their mind (Isa. 53:4–5) has not deceived ('there was no deceit in his mouth', v. 9). Finally, acknowledging misguided communication (Isa. 59:13) is part of the prayer in Isaiah 59:9–15a, which the hardened (cf. Isa. 59:8, 10) speak in repentance. These passages strengthen the view that hardening is the specific judgment on unjust communication as part of the general judgment that YHWH brings upon the people of Judah and Jerusalem.

Finally, hardening appears as a communicative act. YHWH calls the prophet Isaiah to preach to the people and determines that the effect of his message will be the people's inability to perceive and understand (hardening of ears, eyes and hearts). Having noted the central aspects of the motif of hardening in Isaiah 6, we will now see how this motif is used elsewhere in Isaiah and what it contributes to the book of Isaiah's theology.

The use of the motif of hardening and its contribution to the theology of Isaiah

How one relates the various parts of the book with their different theological ideas and assumed historical background on the one hand and the noticeable themes and phrases that run through the whole book on the other is a central issue in the interpretation of Isaiah. The motif of hardening has been identified as one of these themes that appear throughout Isaiah and therefore contribute to its unity.[15] But a closer look at some of the passages dealing with the motif of hardening shows that the occurrence of this motif does not level the differences within the individual parts of Isaiah. The motif of hardening in Isaiah contributes to the unity as well as the differentiation within the book.

---

15. See the groundbreaking article of R. E. Clements, 'The Unity of the Book of Isaiah', *Int* 36 (1982), pp. 117–129; additionally his 'Beyond Tradition-History: Deutero-Isaianic Development of First Isaiah's Themes', *JSOT* 31 (1985), pp. 101–104; H. G. M. Williamson, *The Book Called Isaiah: Deutero-Isaiah's Role in Composition and Redaction* (Oxford: Clarendon, 1994), pp. 46–51. In his chapter 'Patterns in the Prophetic Canon: Healing the Blind and the Lame', in G. M. Tucker, D. L. Petersen and R. R. Wilson (eds.), *Canon, Theology, and Old Testament Interpretation: Essays in Honor of Brevard S. Childs* (Philadelphia: Fortress, 1988), pp. 189–200, Clements points to the tradition-historical development of the theme from the metaphorical to the literal blindness and deafness in Isaiah.

The use of the motif of hardening in further passages of Isaiah 1 – 39

We have seen that the call of Isaiah to harden the people is part of the general judgment that YHWH is going to bring over them. Because of the lack of justice and righteousness in their political (Isa. 3:12, 13–15), social (Isa. 3:13–15; 5:7–8, 23) and religious realms (Isa. 3:8; 5:12, 18–19, 24), YHWH has to implement these through judgment (cf. Isa. 5:1–7). Hardening is the judgment specifically with respect to the lack of righteousness in the area of communication. This perspective of YHWH's impending judgment is central in Isaiah 1 – 39, and the motif of hardening fits into this perspective: YHWH's intention to harden the people so that they do not see, hear or understand recurs clearly in Isaiah 29:9–10.[16] Interestingly, dishonest communication plays an important role (cf. Isa. 29:13) also in this context.

But Isaiah 1 – 39 is not restricted to the proclamation of near judgment. Several passages formulate the perspective that after the purifying judgment a time of new righteousness will come (cf. Isa.1:24–27; Isaiah has already experienced this purifying judgment in 6:7–8, so he speaks to his people from beyond the purifying judgment before it comes upon them). The motif of hardening is used in the same way: after it is said that YHWH hardens his people in the present (Isa. 29:9–10), the prophet Isaiah looks forward to when the imperceptiveness and ignorance of YHWH's people will be overcome (Isa. 29:17–24; see also Isa. 35:5). Thus the motif of hardening is used in Isaiah 1 – 39 in the same way as judgment in general in these chapters. Hardening is brought upon the audience of Isaiah as the specific judgment upon unjust communication just as judgment comes because of the lack of righteousness in the political, social and religious realms. After the purifying judgment, the people of YHWH will live as a new society in accordance with justice and righteousness, and the overcoming of hardening will be part of this renewal. Thus the motif of hardening plays quite an important role within this outline in Isaiah 1 – 39, and this is highlighted by the fact that the 'vision of Isaiah' starts with a notion of the people's ignorance (Isa. 1:2–3) – a central aspect of the motif of hardening.

---

16. The terms 'the prophets' and 'the seers' in Isa. 29:10 are often regarded as later additions. If we read further in this chapter we can note that the issue of seeing, hearing and understanding concerns primarily the whole people (cf. Isa. 29:18, 24). The effect of the additional mention of the prophets and the seers may therefore not be a restriction of hardening to them but an increase of hardening – even to the prophets and seers.

The use of the hardening motif in Isaiah 40 – 55

However one sees the issues of date and authorship in Isaiah, there is no doubt that the outlook and message changes in chapter 40. Judgment has taken place and yet its effects remain until the present (cf. Isa. 40:2 and the way Isa. 40:8 takes up Isa. 28:1). The concern of YHWH is now to comfort 'my people' (Isa. 40:1). For that purpose YHWH wants to call a prophet despite the latter's hesitation due to the people's desolate situation (Isa. 40:6–7). This call is formulated with several references to Isaiah's call (Isa. 6).[17] These correspondences indicate that the following message should be read together with the proclamation of Isaiah and that the need of this new call has its roots in the 'vision of Isaiah' (Isa. 1 – 39). This has a lot to do with the motif of hardening as its use in Isaiah 40 – 66 suggests.

Isaiah 40 – 55, unlike Isaiah 56 – 66 (see below), presumably addresses the exiles in Babylon around the time when the Persian king Cyrus appears (cf. Isa. 45:1–7; 48:20–21). The motif of hardening is interrelated with several crucial themes and issues that address this situation.

For example, this is the case in those passages that use the motif of hardening in characterizing the exiles: Isaiah 42:18–25 describes the blindness, deafness and ignorance of the addressees. And it associates this with the theme of the servant: being imperceptive and ignorant and in prison, the exiles cannot fulfil their commission as the servant of YHWH (Isa. 42:1–9). In Isaiah 46:12–13 the hardness of the exiles is related to their unrighteousness: they are called 'hard of heart' and 'far from righteousness'. This characterization reaches a climax in Isaiah 48:1–11, where several other important themes related to the motif of hardening are found. Isaiah 48:1 states again that Jacob-Israel does not relate to YHWH in righteousness. The following verses substantiate this claim in associating two other fundamental themes of Isaiah 40 – 55 with the motif of hardening (the theme of predicting the 'former – the latter – the new things' and the sinfulness of Jacob-Israel).

Besides hardness, the other central aspect of how Isaiah 40 – 55 describes the audience's present condition can be characterized as sinful. Up to Isaiah 48:1–11 this notion occurs in Isaiah 43:16–28 and Isaiah 46:8–11. Interestingly, these passages are structurally related to passages characterizing the exiles as hardened: Isaiah 43:16–28 parallels Isaiah 42:18–25, and Isaiah 46:8–11 precedes Isaiah 46:12–13. In Isaiah 48:8 sinfulness is finally brought into a

---

17. Cf. Williamson, *Book*, pp. 37–38; B. S. Childs, *Isaiah: A Commentary*, OTL (Louisville: Westminster John Knox, 2000), pp. 295–297; C. R. Seitz, 'The Book of Isaiah 40–66: Introduction, Commentary, and Reflections', in *NIB* 6:334–336.

relationship with the assertion of the people's hardness: the eyes of the people have not been opened; they have not heard nor known because they are sinners from before birth. Thus the hardness of the addressees is explained by ('for') their nature, which is treacherous and sinful ('that from before birth you were called a rebel' ESV).

The theme of YHWH's predictions is equally applied to the people's hardness in Isaiah 48:6–8, and it shows a particular temporal perspective: because of their hardness 'from of old', YHWH now has to announce the new thing. There are several passages in which the argument is used that YHWH announced the 'former things' in order to show his superiority and uniqueness (see e.g. Isa. 41:21–28). Given the 'former things I declared *of old*' (Isa. 48:3 ESV) refers to the proclamation of Isaiah; that is, Isaiah 1 – 39 (cf. Isa. 13:17),[18] which is about to be realized in the present (Isa. 41:21–28), then the statement 'from *of old* your ear has not been opened' (Isa. 48:8 ESV) means as follows: since the time of the proclamation of Isaiah your ear has not been able to hear. This presupposes a considerable time since the prophet Isaiah has proclaimed and started to harden the people (here: closed the eyes). The addressees can recognize the validity of this statement only when 'the former things' proclaimed by Isaiah have passed for them.

Isaiah 48:1–11, with its use of the motif of hardening, stands at a crucial point in Isaiah 40 – 55. The main traits of the characterization of the addressees are combined here before the 'new things' are finally revealed (Isa. 48:16b: 'And now the Lord GOD has sent me, and his Spirit' ESV) and the addressees can be summoned to flee from Babel (Isa. 48:20–21). In this context, Isaiah 48:1–11 serves to clarify and insist that when the exiles leave Babel, they also have to leave their Babel-likeness,[19] which in the case of Jacob-Israel consists of hardness and sinfulness. We will see below, in respect to Isaiah 50 and Isaiah 52:13 – 53:12, why it is so important for those who are hardened and sinners to leave Babylon with 'the new thing', that is, under the leadership of the servant (cf. Isa. 48:16b, 20–21; 49:7–12).

The motif of hardening appears also in contexts that deal with the relationship between Jacob-Israel and the nations. Appointed as YHWH's witnesses before the nations (Isa. 43:8–13), Jacob-Israel will fulfil their call as YHWH's servant (Isa. 42:1–9), although they are imperceptive and ignorant (Isa. 42:18–25). The consequence will be the overcoming of their hardness (Isa. 43:10).

---

18. Cf. B. S. Childs, *Introduction to the Old Testament as Christian Scripture* (Philadelphia: Fortress, 1979), pp. 328–330.

19. Note the correspondences between Isa. 47 and 48:1–11.

Looking at the broader context,[20] we can realize that the motif of hardening equates and separates the exiles in Babylon from the other nations: both are witnesses to their gods (Isa. 43:8–13 // Isa. 44:6–20), like the idol-worshipping nations Jacob-Israel are hardened, too (Isa. 43:8 // Isa. 44:9, 18–20), but the outlook is different: there is a chance that the hardness of the servant Jacob-Israel can be overcome when they fulfil their appointment as the witness of YHWH ('You are my witnesses [. . .] that you may *know* and believe me and *understand* that I am he', Isa. 43:10 ESV).

At several points we have already touched the theme of the 'servant' in relation to the motif of hardening. It is of particular importance as regards the overcoming of hardening. One central passage in this respect is Isaiah 50. This is yet another passage after Isaiah 49:1–12 dealing with the individual servant.[21] Terminology related to the motif of hardening occurs in Isaiah 50:4–5, 10. But further issues need to be taken into account to get a more comprehensive idea of how hardening is addressed in this passage.

Many commentators interpret Isaiah 50:4–5 in the context of the 'third servant Song' (vv. 4–9) and see in these verses a description of the equipment of the servant for his prophetic task. But it is more than just a general statement. As the one whose ears have been opened by YHWH (Isa. 50:5), the servant contrasts with the state of the addressees in this respect (Isa. 48:8). Moreover, these phrases appear as exact antonyms to the phrase 'make their ears heavy' (Isa. 6:10). Thus the servant says that YHWH has started to overcome the restrictions on perception he inaugurated through Isaiah (Isa. 6:9–10). This is further emphasized by the phrase 'he awakens my ear' (Isa. 50:4 ESV). What YHWH has done with the servant goes beyond the general equipment of a prophet. In the person and ministry of the servant, he has started to reverse the hardening. This reversal can also be seen in the contrast between the people in Isaiah 8:11 – 9:6 and Isaiah 30:8–14 on the one hand and the servant in Isaiah 50:4–5 and how the exiles can now react to this on the other.[22] Thus, in contrast to the hardening of Isaiah's audience (Isa. 8:11 – 9:6; Isa. 30:8–14) and the condition of the addressees of Isaiah 40 – 66 (Isa.

---

20. Isa. 43:8–13 and 44:6–20 correspond to each other in the parallel panels of speech: Isa. 42:18 – 43:15 // 43:16 – 44:22 with the introduction being Isa. 42:14–17 and the concluding hymn being Isa. 44:23.

21. With H. G. M. Williamson, *Variations on a Theme: King, Messiah and Servant in the Book of Isaiah* (Carlisle: Paternoster, 1998), I see the people Jacob-Israel as the servant in Isa. 42:1–9, while in Isa. 49:1–12 an individual servant is commissioned.

22. Cf. Williamson, *Book*, pp. 73, 106–109.

42:18–25; Isa. 48:1–11), hardening as the inability to perceive and understand is overcome in the person and ministry of the servant. He is able to hear.

We have noted above already that this is closely associated with proper communication: the servant has 'a tongue of those who have been instructed' in order 'to know how to sustain the weary with a word' (v. 4). His acts of communication are meant to be good for his audience. He is to 'sustain the weary', to build them up, to encourage them through communication. The servant achieves a total reversal even in respect to communication. In Isaiah 6 we found that Isaiah's commission to harden the people was presented as YHWH's judgment as a consequence of the perverted communication of his people ('a people of unclean lips', Isa. 6:5), whose *tongue* and deeds are against YHWH' (Isa. 3:8). With the servant, not only has the overcoming of hardening begun, but he also restores communication.

There are three further passages of importance regarding the motif of hardening in Isaiah 40 – 55, namely 51:1–8, 52:13 – 53:12 and ch. 55. As regards hardening in Isaiah 51:1–8, there is a noteworthy development within the passage. Right at its beginning, the addressees are called those 'who pursue righteousness' (Isa. 51:1 ESV). The introduction of the final part (51:7–8),[23] however, designates them as 'those who know righteousness, the people who have my instruction in your hearts' (v. 7). These new designations reflect the speech to which they are called to listen (cf. Isa. 51:4–6). In listening to the servant in Isaiah 51:1–8[24] their unrighteousness and hardness (Isa. 46:12–13; 48:1–11) is overcome: they finally 'know righteousness'.

Thus the overcoming of hardening inaugurated with the servant (Isa. 50:4–5) is also possible for the audience of Isaiah 40 – 55. They are called to perceive, to listen and see (Isa. 51:1–2, 4, 6–7), and this leads to knowledge and a change of heart (v. 7). The contrast with Isaiah 6:9–10 could not be starker.

Isaiah 52:13 – 53:12 is of interest for our discussion in two respects. First, it deals with a problem closely related to the hardening of the people – their sinfulness (cf. Isa. 48:8). It refers in this respect again to the individual servant. In Isaiah 50 the overcoming of hardening is inaugurated with the servant. Now in Isaiah 52:13 – 53:12 the problem of the people's sins is also resolved with reference to the servant: he has died for them, their transgressions were laid upon him so that the people can have peace and be healed (cf. Isa. 53:4–6). Thus what was

---

23. Isa. 51:1–8 consists of three sections (vv. 1–3, 4–6, 7–8). They are introduced by imperatives, of which the first and third are identical and the second is a close formulation.

24. It seems to me that the servant speaks not only in Isa. 50:4–9 but also in 51:1–8.

combined as two central problems of the people Jacob-Israel in Isaiah 48:1–11 is resolved through the servant; he is the 'new thing' announced in Isaiah 48:16b, with whom the people are to flee from Babel (Isa. 48:20–21; 49:7–12), and by listening to his voice, their hardness can be overcome (Isa. 50:10).

Secondly, the motif of hardening is present in Isaiah 52:13 – 53:12 in the content and the function of the speech of the 'we'. Its content shows that the 'we' expresses the right *insight* on the significance of the servant for them.[25] They agree with YHWH in their view of the servant.[26] But this insight is the result of a change of mind: there had been a time when they did not esteem the servant and regarded him as stricken by God (Isa. 53:3–4). This change of view parallels the change from those who are hardened and far from righteousness, to those who 'know righteousness' (Isa. 51:7). Thus the speech of the 'we' in Isaiah 53:1–10 verifies the announcement or claim of Isaiah 51:7 that the addressees know righteousness. Isaiah 51:7 is true in so far as the addressees identify themselves with the 'we' of Isaiah 53:1–10. Those who join the speech of Isaiah 53:1–10 emerge as those whose hardness has been overcome. The function of this is to give a testimony before the 'many nations' and 'many kings', 'for that which has not been *told* them they *see*, and that which they have not *heard* they *understand* (Isa. 52:14–15 ESV). In doing so, the 'we' fulfils a twofold commission. As Isaiah 48:20–21 summoned the exiles to flee from Babylon and to declare with a shout of joy that 'YHWH has redeemed his servant Israel', so the exiles who go out from Babel (Isa. 52:11–12) fulfil this appeal by declaring the words of Isaiah 53:1–10. And as the people are appointed as YHWH's witness before the nations (Isa. 43:10), the 'we' fulfils this commission when they give the testimony of Isaiah 53:1–10 before 'many nations' and 'many kings' (Isa. 52:13–15). Their hardness has been overcome: they have fulfilled their role as witnesses and can realize that they know indeed and believe in YHWH and know his identity (cf. Isa. 43:10). Thus the relationship to the nations is addressed here again and this passage also clarifies how the exiles are to go out from Babylon.

Finally, we turn to the motif of hardening found in the concluding unit of Isaiah 40 – 55. In Isaiah 54 – 55 we find the main message of Isaiah 40 – 55 in a nutshell: it announces to the city Zion (Isa. 54) that she will be fully restored, with her husband coming back to her (cf. vv. 4–10) and her children filling her walls (cf. vv. 1–3, 13, 17). It also summons the exiles once more to come and return to YHWH (Isa. 55). Once the overcoming of hardening is confirmed in Isaiah 52:13 –

---

25. The 'we' speak in Isa. 53:1–10 while YHWH speaks in 52:13–15 and 53:11–12.

26. Cf. Isa. 53:11b (YHWH) // 53:4a ('we'); Isa. 53:12b (YHWH) // 53:5a, 6b ('we').

53:12, the exiles can again be summoned like Isaiah's audience: 'listen to me' (the appeal in Isa. 55:2b is identical with Isa. 6:9 in Heb.). But as they return home, this call results not in their hardness but in their delight (Isa. 55:2b–3a): while Isaiah 'made fat the heart' (Isa. 6:10) of his audience through these summons to listen (and see), the final call of the addressees to listen will result in their soul having 'delight in fat' (thus verbally Isa. 55:2b) and their 'soul will live' (Isa. 55:3a). Now they can open wide their ear (Isa. 55:3a). Again, this is associated with their role as YHWH's witnesses, as the transference of the Davidic covenant particularly includes their witness before the nations (Isa. 55:3b–5).[27]

In sum Isaiah 51:7 claims that the hardness of the exiles is overcome in so far as they listen to the voice of the servant (Isa. 50:10). The truth of this claim, however, has to be confirmed by the exiles themselves. Only when they join in the testimony about the servant (Isa. 53:1–10) on their return (Isa. 52:11–12; cf. 55:2b–5) will they emerge as those whose hardness has been overcome and whose sins have been forgiven. Then they will fulfil their appointment as YHWH's witnesses before nations and kings (cf. Isa. 52:15 – 53:1) that they themselves do indeed believe in YHWH and know his identity (cf. Isa. 43:10). When they 'come' (Isa. 55:1) like this, they will listen and live (cf. Isa. 55:2b–3) and take on the role of David as witnesses before the nations (Isa. 55:3–5). Then their return will be a real transformation, one that accompanies the transformation of creation as well (Isa. 55:12–13). Having looked at these passages, we can realize just how interrelated the motif of hardening is with other crucial themes in Isaiah 40 – 55.

The use of the motif of hardening in Isaiah 56 – 66

Due to limited space, we can only note that the use of the motif of hardening in Isaiah 56 – 66 fits into the widespread perception of Isaiah 56 – 66 in relation to Isaiah 40 – 55. While Isaiah 40 – 55 proclaims unconditional salvation for the exiles, Isaiah 56 – 66 connects salvation with social behaviour (cf. esp. Isa. 58); while Isaiah 40 – 55 gives the impression that salvation is dawning, Isaiah 56 – 66 questions the time when YHWH will bring salvation and righteousness about.

In Isaiah 56:9 – 57:2 the motif of hardening is used to reveal the incompetence and failures of the leaders in Judah, who appear to be like the leaders of Isaiah's time (cf. Isa. 29:9–10).

---

27. See more detail on this in e.g. R. J. Clifford, *Fair Spoken and Persuading: An Interpretation of Second Isaiah* (New York: Paulist, 1984), pp. 188–194; Williamson, *Variations*, pp. 118–120.

The whole unit Isaiah 58 – 59 leads to the confession of sin in Isaiah 59:9–15a, where the whole people relate their unjust behaviour to aspects of the motif of hardening (cf. Isa. 59:10, 12). But since the task of the prophet (Isa. 58:1) is successfully fulfilled in this confession (cf. 59:12), one can say that the hardening of the people is overcome.[28]

Thus, as in Isaiah 40 – 55, the people are characterized as hardened, on the one hand (Isa. 56:9 – 57:2; 57:14), but on the other hand, their hardness can be overcome (Isa. 57:14; 59:8–12). In contrast to Isaiah 40 – 55, the motif of hardening is related not only to the relationship between the people and YHWH but also to the interactions among the people, that is, to their social life (thus esp. Isa. 58 – 59). While the majority of interpreters ascribe this difference to the later date presupposed in Isaiah 56 – 66, when the returned exiles had to cope with the disappointed promises of Isaiah 40 – 55, I see rather two different addressees in Isaiah 40 – 55 and Isaiah 56–66: Isaiah 40 – 55 may address the exiles in Babylon in order to call them back to Judah, while Isaiah 56 – 66 addresses those who have remained in Judah during that time. In this case both addressees are characterized simultaneously as hardened (Isa. 42:18–25, 48:1–11 in respect to the exiles; Isa. 56:9 – 57:2, 59:8–12 in respect to those in Judah) and have the opportunity to overcome this hardness (Isa. 50, 51:1–8, 52:13 – 53:12 for the exiles; Isa. 57:14, 58:1, 59:8–12 for those in Judah).

The final passage that takes up the motif of hardening is the communal lament in Isaiah 63:7 – 64:12 (cf. Isa. 63:17; 64:1–4). Where the final issues are addressed and the future is at stake for the people of YHWH, the motif of hardening plays an important part. A separation among the people comes to the fore after the lament (cf. Isa. 65:9–12; 66:5). It seems that the communal lament, and consequently the motif of hardening as part of it, has to do with this separation. YHWH answers the prayer by saying that only those who 'tremble at his word' are his servants and people (cf. Isa. 66:2, 5).

The motif of hardening and the expectation of a saviour

We have looked at several passages in different parts of Isaiah to see how the motif of hardening is used and contributes to the theology of Isaiah. Finally, we may attend to the connection of this motif with the so-called 'messianic prophecies', an aspect of great interest in the interpretation of

---

28. This interpretation is based on the way Isa. 57:14 refers to 8:14, which cannot be further substantiated here.

Isaiah.[29] Despite the amount of literature on this topic it has remained widely unnoticed that the motif of hardening occurs in some of these passages too.[30]

There are passages in Isaiah that announce future salvation (primarily for the people of Judah and Jerusalem), which is mediated through a person. In Isaiah 1 – 39 this person is described as a king (cf. Isa. 7:10–17[?]; 9:1–7; 11:1–9; 16:3–5; 32:1–4). Two of these passages announce the contrast of hardening as an effect of this king's rule. Isaiah 11:2, 9 comments that the Spirit of YHWH will rest upon this king, 'the Spirit of wisdom and *understanding* [. . .], the Spirit of *knowledge* and the fear of YHWH'. The effect of his rule will be that nobody will hurt or destroy 'in all my holy mountain; for the earth shall be full of the *knowledge* of YHWH'. This predicted king has knowledge and understanding in contrast to the people of Isaiah. And this belongs together with his rule in righteousness (Isa. 11:4–5). The same applies to the prediction of a king in Isaiah 32:1–4. Here again it is said that the king will reign in righteousness together with the princes. And the effect of that will be the opposite of the call of Isaiah:

> Then the *eyes* of those who *see* will *not be closed*,
>   and the *ears* of those who *hear* will *give attention*.
> The heart of the hasty will understand and know,
>   and the tongue of the stammerers will hasten to speak distinctly.
>
> (Isa. 32:3–4 ESV)

Here the motifs of eyes/seeing, ears/hearing, heart/understanding and knowing recur just as in Isaiah 6:10, but now with the opposite effect. Interestingly, the aspect of communication also recurs here, which we have found to be the central issue of hardening. With the reign of this king, communication shall be both possible and proper.[31]

---

29. Cf. e.g. D. Schibler, 'Messianism and Messianic Prophecy in Isaiah 1–12 and 28–33', in P. E. Satterthwaite, R. S. Hess and G. J. Wenham (eds.), *The Lord's Anointed: Interpretation of Old Testament Messianic Texts* (Carlisle: Paternoster; Grand Rapids: Baker, 1995), pp. 87–104; G. Hugenberger, 'The Servant of the Lord in the "Servant Songs" of Isaiah', ibid., pp. 105–140; R. L. Schultz, 'The King in the Book of Isaiah', ibid., pp. 141–165; and Williamson, *Variations*.

30. But see Schultz, 'King', p. 156.

31. This proper communication as an aim of the rule of the promised king is further highlighted by Isa. 32:5–8. What this passage speaks about is the opposite of 5:20.

Several passages in Isaiah 40 – 55 speak of the mediation of salvation through a certain person. But here it is the vague 'servant' that is to accomplish the promised salvation. And the motif of hardening occurs also in some of these passages. It is the mission of the servant in Isaiah 42:7 to open the eyes of the blind. But as the servant Israel is blind, deaf and ignorant himself (see the discussion on Isa. 42:18–25 above) he can testify for YHWH's uniqueness only among the (deaf, blind, ignorant) nations (cf. Isa. 44:6–20) as a witness to YHWH (Isa. 43:8–10). The servant Israel testifies as a witness to what the individual servant (Isa. 49:1–12) has done. The individual servant appears as someone who has experienced the opposite of hardening in order to achieve his mission: his ear is awakened and opened so that he can sustain the weary (Isa. 50:4–5; see on this passage above). As those who listen to the voice of this servant (Isa. 50:10) a group is speaking about the servant and the change of mind they have experienced (see on Isa. 52:13 – 53:12). By this means they fulfil their role as witnesses to YHWH before the many nations and kings so that

> that which has not been told them they see,
>> and that which they have not heard they understand.
>
> (Isa. 52:15 ESV)

Thus, however one sees the relationship between the promised king in Isaiah 1 – 39 and the servant in Isaiah 40 – 55, in each case, the motif of hardening plays an important part.

This outline has shown that the motif of hardening occurs in many passages in Isaiah. It is related to central themes and contributes to the specific message of the different parts of Isaiah 1 – 39, 40 – 55 and 56 – 66. Furthermore, it seems that the motif of hardening contributes to the unity of the book of Isaiah as much as it contributes to the specific outlook of individual parts. This comes to the fore especially in respect to the connection between 'hardening' and 'communication/righteousness': the lack of righteousness and proper communication causes judgment and hardening in Isaiah 1 – 39 and the outlook to the future in righteousness includes the reversal of hardening. The proclamation of salvation and righteousness in Isaiah 40 – 55 is associated with the overcoming of hardening. Finally, the inclusion of the social aspect of

---

Footnote 31 (*continued*)

This latter passage seemed to be a central reason for Isaiah's designation of the people as 'of unclean lips'.

righteousness in Isaiah 56 – 66 is correlated with the motif of hardening, in so far as those who lack social behaviour are characterized as hardened.

The effect of the motif of hardening: What does the 'motif of hardening' do?

The motif of hardening is not only puzzling when it comes to understanding it; one can also ask why it was included in this book. What should it have achieved for those who read or heard this book?

Some interpreters would argue that the strange call of Isaiah (Isa. 6:9–10) served to *explain* why his message had not been heard among the people. The experience of the prophet's rejection led to a retrojection into his call. This explanation was seen as necessary either for Isaiah's supposed pupils (thus the interpretation of Isa. 8:16)[32] or for the time of exile, when the people wondered why this had come upon them.[33]

Others argue that the motif of hardening is ironic. It serves to encourage the readers/hearers of Isaiah to listen, hear and believe so that what is presented ironically in Isaiah's call does not happen to them.

Laato argues that the motif of hardening contributes to the different periods that Isaiah envisages. In Isaiah 1 – 39 it is linked to the remnant theology, according to which most people are hardened during the purifying judgment of the Assyrian invasion, until only a remnant remains (referring to Isa. 6:11–12). Isaiah 40 – 55 presents a programme of salvation; it is part of the salvation of the exodus that the eyes of the blind can see and the ears of the deaf can hear. The use of the motif of hardening in Isaiah 56 – 66, however, explains why the programme of salvation of Isaiah 40 – 55 did not come to pass after the return from the Babylonian exile.[34]

For Conrad the motif of hardening serves to differentiate between 'the vision of Isaiah' in Isaiah 6 – 39 and the proclamation to the 'implied audience'

---

32. Cf. e.g. Clements, *Isaiah 1–39*, p. 77; Blenkinsopp, *Isaiah 1–39*; with a different nuance Williamson, *Book*, p. 106, n. 34.

33. Cf. e.g. Kaiser, *Isaiah 1–12*, pp. 118–121, 132; R. Coggins, 'Isaiah', in J. Barton and J. Muddiman (eds.), *The Oxford Bible Commentary* (Oxford: Oxford University Press, 2001), p. 444.

34. Cf. A. Laato, *'About Zion I Will Not Be Silent': The Book of Isaiah as an Ideological Unity*, ConBOT 44 (Stockholm: Almqvist & Wiksell, 1998), pp. 76, 80, 85, 96–97, 102, 140, 186–187.

in Isaiah 1 – 5; 40 – 66: while the audience of Isaiah's day was hardened and his message was sealed, the 'implied audience' are the people of the predicted 'in that day', who can both read and understand Isaiah's vision.[35]

Some observations in Isaiah may indicate that the motif of hardening served as more than just an explanation or theological concept. It may even be linked to the pragmatics of the prophetic scroll. The effect of the motif of hardening could be distributed according to the different proclamations of Isaiah (Isa. 1 – 39) and the other prophet (Isa. 40 – 66). The prophet Isaiah is called to harden his audience (Isa. 6:9–10), which comes to the readers/hearers of the whole scroll as a direct speech of Isaiah (in first person singular).

One feature in this respect is the ambiguous duration of Isaiah's hardening message (Isa. 6:11–13). There are several times in Isaiah 1 – 39 when the judgment even of the tenth could be potentially over. And yet reading further, the message of Isaiah continues to harden its audience (cf. Isa. 29:9–10). And with the inscription of his message (Isa. 30:9), this can even outlast the life of Isaiah: even in the time of Hezekiah, judgment is still to come (thus Isa. 39). It seems that this hardening message has lasted until the audience of Isaiah 40 – 55, and Isaiah 56 – 66 is addressed in their specific situation. They are always addressed directly, even when the issue is their present condition of hardness (cf. Isa. 42:18–25; 48:1–11; 56:7 – 57:2). But now their hardness can be overcome, when they listen to the voice of the servant (Isa. 50:10) and the proclamation of the prophet (Isa. 57:14; 58:1 – 59:15a). The prophetic scroll even provides passages in which the addressees can identify with the overcoming of hardening: Isaiah 53:1–10; 59:9–15a. As the 'we' that have undergone a change of mind, they can finally see, hear and understand.

Thus, by means of hardening and its reversal, the prophetic book serves to form the new people of Judah and Jerusalem, depending on how they relate to the message of the whole book. The book of Isaiah not only speaks about the restoration of the people in the Babylonian exile *and* in Judah; it also enacts their restoration as the 'servants of the Lord', the children of Zion (Isa. 54:17; Isa. 65:13–16). This may also shed new light on the lament in Isaiah 63:17. Does this lament reveal those who remained hardened after the previous message? If so, this prayer would lead to the separation between those still hardened (Isa. 63:17) and those whose hardness has been overcome, as is apparent in Isaiah 65 – 66.

---

35. Cf. E. Conrad, *Reading Isaiah*, OBT 27 (Augsburg: Fortress, 1991), pp. 34–51, 117–143.

While some aspects related to the motif of hardening remain hard to understand, it has been the aim of this chapter to contribute to an intensified study of this challenging aspect of Isaiah and its theology.

4. ISAIAH AND POLITICS

David J. Reimer

Introduction

It was Aristotle who famously observed that 'a human being is by nature a political animal'. He preceded this, however, with the slightly less famous observation that political institutions, too, are part of the natural order.[1] To the reader of the Bible, Aristotle's claims are quite understandable. Human community was God's idea in the first place, and the means of organizing communal life (whether of the family, the city or the nation) unfolds throughout the Bible's stories of divine–human interaction. One can think quite naturally, then, of the Bible as a 'political document', although that phrase itself retains a degree of ambiguity.

Although there has always been and continues to be interest in the Bible's political dimensions, they can be easily overlooked in more 'traditional' modes

---

1. Debate continues about how best to translate and understand Aristotle's claim here: C. D. C. Reeve's translation runs, 'It is evident from these considerations, then, that a city-state (*polis*) is among the things that exist by nature, [and] that a human being is by nature a political animal (*Ho anthrōpos physei politikēn zōon*) . . .' (Aristotle, *Politics*, Bk. 1, ch. 2 [1253a], tr. and ed. C. D. C. Reeve [Indianapolis: Hackett, 1998], p. 4).

of Bible study. Part of the problem here is that once one embarks on 'political' explorations, everything seems 'political'! Thus Robert Carroll claimed that there is a 'political dimension in all literature' which 'every interpretation of the text' (and here he pointedly included the biblical prophets) ought to take into account.[2] But this is hardly satisfactory, since 'politics' becomes simply another term for 'social activity'. While the term may be used this way, it is not the most illuminating for studying the biblical text.

My purpose here is to explore ways in which the political dimensions of the book of Isaiah can be attended to and integrated with other elements of biblical interpretation, and that in a way which has more precise content than simply a registering of its 'political dimension' à la Carroll. To be sure, there are a number of prominent aspects of the book which give a prima facie appeal to such a project, even if the details of each are contested. For example, Isaiah is often associated with a 'Zion theology' which understands the prophet to have held that Jerusalem enjoyed the special protection of Yahweh.[3] This in turn is related to the deliverance of Jerusalem during the 'Assyrian crisis' associated with Sennacherib's campaigns around 700 BC.[4] Another focus of study has been the relationship of Isaiah's career and traditions to the so-called Syro-Ephraimite war, usually dated around 734–732, which drew Judah and its monarch into the arena of international conflict.[5] Further conflict with Assyria

---

2. R. P. Carroll, 'Prophecy and Society', in R. E. Clements (ed.), *The World of Ancient Israel: Sociological, Anthropological and Political Perspectives* (Cambridge: Cambridge University Press, 1989), p. 214 – a claim that requires some nuance. I will not pursue the 'political' dimension of Isaiah in this sense here.

3. G. von Rad, *Old Testament Theology*. Vol. 2: *The Theology of Israel's Prophetic Traditions*, tr. D. M. G. Stalker (New York: Harper & Row, 1965), pp. 155–169; J. T. Strong, 'Zion: Theology of', in *NIDOTTE* 4:1314–1321.

4. R. E. Clements, *Isaiah and the Deliverance of Jerusalem: A Study of the Interpretation of Prophecy in the Old Testament*, JSOTSup 13 (Sheffield: JSOT Press, 1980); P. E. Dion, 'Sennacherib's Expedition to Palestine', *BCSBS* 48 (1988), pp. 3–25.

5. M. E. W. Thompson, *Situation and Theology: Old Testament Interpretations of the Syro-Ephraimite War*, Prophets and Historians Series 1 (Sheffield: Almond, 1982); Y. Gitay, 'Isaiah and the Syro-Ephraimite War', in J. Vermeylen (ed.), *The Book of Isaiah / Le livre d'Isaïe: les oracles et leurs relectures, unité et complexité de l'ouvrage*, BETL 81 (Leuven: Peeters, 1989), pp. 217–230, discerns a theological dimension to Isaiah's politics; for a reassessment of the historical sources available see R. Tomes, 'The Reason for the Syro-Ephraimite War', *JSOT* 59 (1993), 55–71.

marks assessments of Hezekiah in Isaiah 36 – 39.[6] Progressing further into the book, the 'naming' of the Persian King Cyrus by Yahweh and his designation as 'his anointed' (Isa. 45:1) subjects Cyrus' imperial power to the God of Judah.[7] Isaiah 56 – 66 has fuelled a vigorous debate about the existence and nature of partisan politics in restoration Judah, especially associated with the work of Paul Hanson.[8] One could further point to a feature that the book of Isaiah shares with most other prophetic books in the Old Testament: collections of oracles against foreign nations found in Isaiah 13 – 23, 46 – 47, along with other references to foreign nations which also naturally have a political interest.[9] Obviously, there is plenty of interest for our theme – in fact, too much!

My approach, then, will be to look at three recent works which suggest different ways in which the connections between politics, theology and the Bible might be negotiated, each originating in a different area of academic discourse, each providing a distinct orientation to our exploration, and briefly examine a test case for each: (1) Perhaps most simply, politics is thought of as managing the social arrangements of power. As such, mechanics of government and the relationships of states come to the fore. Norman Gottwald's working definition of politics fits well with this set of expectations: 'politics will be viewed

---

Footnote 5 (*continued*)

    Both of these conflicts loom large in the only monograph I am aware of devoted to Isaiah's politics, W. Dietrich, *Jesaja und die Politik*, BEvT 74 (Munich: Chr. Kaiser, 1976), which is restricted in its analysis to selected texts in Isa. 1 – 39.

6. C. R. Seitz, *Zion's Final Destiny: The Development of the Book of Isaiah, A Reassessment of Isaiah 36–39* (Minneapolis: Fortress, 1991); J. M. Kennedy, 'Yahweh's Strongman? The Characterization of Hezekiah in the Book of Isaiah', *PRSt* 31 (2004), pp. 383–397; A. H. Konkel, 'The Sources of the Story of Hezekiah in the Book of Isaiah', *VT* 43 (1993), pp. 462–482.

7. An overview of interpretations is offered by L. S. Fried, 'Cyrus the Messiah? The Historical Background to Isaiah 45:1', *HTR* 95 (2002), pp. 373–393; see below for further on this text.

8. P. D. Hanson, *The Dawn of Apocalyptic: The Historical and Sociological Roots of Jewish Apocalyptic Eschatology* (Philadelphia: Fortress, 1979), pp. 32–208; see the assessment by H. G. M. Williamson, 'The Concept of Israel in Transition', in R. E. Clements (ed.), *The World of Ancient Israel: Sociological, Anthropological and Political Perspectives* (Cambridge: Cambridge University Press, 1989), pp. 141–161; esp. pp. 149–153.

9. G. I. Davies, 'The Destiny of the Nations in the Book of Isaiah', in Vermeylen, *Book of Isaiah*, pp. 93–120; J. Høgenhaven, 'The Prophet Isaiah and Judaean Foreign Policy under Ahaz and Hezekiah', *JNES* 49 (1990), pp. 351–354.

as the public exercise of power, coupled with the legitimation of its use, within a given social and territorial space'.[10] (2) With Thucydides' *Peloponnesian War* (fifth century BC) still a vital voice to students of political science, historical perspectives mesh readily with political philosophy. Peter Iver Kaufman's taxonomy of Christian political culture in the West provides a helpful framework for considering Israelite political culture as well.[11] Kaufman's historical study attends to one aspect of political life – the claim of the apologists of those in power that 'a community's politics must be ordered to a divine plan'.[12] (3) Such rhetoric points beyond itself to the realm of ethics. Here I draw on Oliver O'Donovan's study of political ethics, which opens with the assertion 'The authority of secular government resides in the practice of judgment.'[13] In each case an overview of the approach will be followed by case studies drawn from Isaiah. In conclusion, I will return to the case of Cyrus to see how these three approaches might bear on the reading of a single text.

Politics and power (Gottwald)

Gottwald is critical of 'traditional' approaches to the study of politics in the Bible and ancient Israel, not only for giving it short shrift, but for altogether ignoring it so often. When it does register with the interpreter, Gottwald claims it is frequently accompanied by a weakness of theoretical nuance on the political side.[14] This lack is compounded by a fixation on historical 'facts' that fails to value the 'specific texture of "biblical historiography"' that defies restriction to modern literary categories.[15] Thus, Gottwald argues:

> A more generous view of the value of biblical sources for understanding the politics
> within and behind the text must be accompanied by a clear distinction between the
> religion and politics of ancient Israel and the religious and political experiences and

---

10. N. K. Gottwald, *The Politics of Ancient Israel* (Louisville: Westminster John Knox, 2001), p. 7.

11. P. I. Kaufman, *Redeeming Politics* (Princeton: Princeton University Press, 1990).

12. Ibid., p. 5.

13. O. O'Donovan, *The Ways of Judgment* (Grand Rapids: Eerdmans, 2005), p. 3.

14. Gottwald, *Politics*, pp. 12–13.

15. Ibid., pp. 13–14. He calls it an 'excessive historical "factualism"' which can present either 'in its skeptical or credulous versions' (p. 14) – although surely this stark alternative requires nuance.

outlooks of subsequent Jewish and Christian traditions and their spillover into secular political discourse.[16]

It is possible that Gottwald here falls prey to a historical fixation of his own: as we will see with Kaufman's study, below, biblical (even scriptural) perspectives have left a deep and indelible impression on traditions of political philosophy in the West. The 'clear distinction' for which he calls may stand as a warning against a superficial appeal to the Bible to bolster a modern political agenda.[17]

As the quote in the introduction (above) demonstrates, Gottwald's study gives primacy to the concept of political power.[18] He further posits that the central focus of the 'formal study of politics' is 'on the political power network that exercises highest authority over the broadest jurisdiction'.[19] Inevitably, then, interest in the individual 'political animal' is subordinated to that of the 'network' or institutions that exercise power, that govern. Such networks, Gottwald argues, may be (1) disbursed or decentralized (that is, non-state entities) or (2) centralized and autonomous (thus forming a 'state'). They must be studied in their social context, and not simply be described by a catalogue of institutions or offices.[20] To pursue this goal, Gottwald follows three lines of

---

16. Ibid., p. 14. The language of 'within and behind the text' finds an echo in J. G. McConville's *God and Earthly Power: An Old Testament Political Theology, Genesis–Kings* (London: T. & T. Clark International, 2006), pp. 6–11, although this work of Gottwald's is (curiously!) absent from McConville's considerations. The two works make interesting conversation partners.

17. This chapter cannot follow this trajectory, but interested readers could explore the reception history of K. Whitelam's *The Invention of Ancient Israel: The Silencing of Palestinian History* (London: Routledge, 1996); cf. also M. Greenberg, 'On the Political Use of the Bible in Modern Israel: An Engaged Critique', in D. P. Wright, D. N. Freedman and A. Hurvitz (eds.), *Pomegranates and Golden Bells: Studies in Biblical, Jewish, and Near Eastern Ritual, Law, and Literature in Honor of Jacob Milgrom* (Winona Lake: Eisenbrauns, 1995), pp. 461–471.

18. A useful survey of the theme in the OT can be found in J. P. M. Walsh, S. J., *The Mighty from Their Thrones: Power in the Biblical Tradition*, OBT (Philadelphia: Fortress, 1987).

19. Gottwald, *Politics*, p. 9.

20. Ibid., pp. 8–10. On the latter point, understanding the structures of the network, its 'offices held and functions performed' (p. 10) retains a place in discerning the social outworking of the exercise of power. For monarchic Israel see N. S. Fox, *In the Service of the King: Officialdom in Ancient Israel and Judah*, Monographs of the Hebrew Union College 23 (Cincinnati: Hebrew Union College Press, 2000).

inquiry: a 'constructively critical' reading of the biblical text,[21] comparative and contextual perspectives from wider ancient Near Eastern societies, and political theory itself.

The three major sections of the book are then devoted to pursing these strands of investigation. The Bible's story from clan to colony is critically recounted, with a special focus on the 'centralized' politics of the monarchic state. This in turn is set within the wider 'matrix' of ancient Near Eastern polities, chiefly to east (Mesopotamia) and west (Egypt). The task of 'integration' comes in the exercise of 'critical imagination' that attends not only to the development of Israel and Judah's political culture, but also to the international relations ('foreign affairs') in which they were enmeshed. When it comes to filling out the politics of the two monarchies, Gottwald cannot help but attend to the offices and roles that made up the ruling elite – but not without further attention to how these functionaries were interconnected with the non-official members of the society.[22] Although prophets figure in Gottwald's discussion, two problems persist: (1) uncertainties surrounding their social location limits confidence in placing them in a network of political relationships and to ascertain who, if anyone, they spoke for; and (2) the editorial process Gottwald envisages surrounding their literary deposits renders uncertain their relationship with monarchic times and therefore its political culture. He is still prepared to characterize them as typically identifying and castigating political/economic and religious abuses.[23]

The passage that runs from Isaiah 9:8 to 10:4 [MT 9:7 – 10:4] illustrates well both the problems and the prospects that an analysis of the socially embedded politics of power can bring. The immediate context only enriches this picture as this passage follows on from one of the 'ideal king' texts in Isaiah (9:2–7 [MT 9:1–6]; this pericope will not be a focus of attention here). This is a difficult text to explore in brief: its critical problems are well known and sharply divide commentators, especially the placement of 10:1–4.[24] My purpose here

---

21. Gottwald, *Politics*, p. 29.

22. Ibid., pp. 227–235.

23. Ibid., pp. 234–235. Gottwald does not refer to two brief and dated, but fundamental, studies: E. Jenni, *Die Politischen Voraussagen der Propheten* (Zurich: Zwingli-Verlag, 1956); B. Albrektson, 'Prophecy and Politics in the Old Testament', in H. Biezais (ed.), *The Myth of the State* (Stockholm: Almqvist & Wiksell, 1972), pp. 45–56.

24. Both R. E. Clements, *Isaiah 1–39*, NCB (London: Marshall, Morgan & Scott, 1980), and J. Blenkinsopp, *Isaiah 1–39: A New Translation with Introduction and Commentary*, AB 19 (New York: Doubleday: 2000), relocate this entire pericope, joining it to the

is simply to illustrate how some of Gottwald's concerns surface in Isaiah. Taking the passage 'canonically', the 'refrains' of 'his hand is stretched out still' punctuate the passage at 9:12, 17, 21 [MT 9:11, 16, 20] and 10:4. Lack of a precise historical setting does nothing to impede the view that divine judgment is visited on Israel (9:8–12 [MT 9:7–11]), caught in a conflagration with Syria, the former alliance apparently now recoiling on Israel itself.

At this point, however, there is no reference to king or court. (We might expect one after the narratives of chs. 7–8.) Rather, 9:13–17 [MT 9:12–16] indict a cross-section of the ruling classes, 'those who led this people led them astray' (v. 16 NRSV [MT v. 15]), and pointedly the 'elder' and the 'prophet' (v. 15 [MT v. 14]). The consequence is the withdrawal of Yahweh's care of the vulnerable. Some sense of continuing exploitation by the rulers is implied in verses 19–20 [MT 18–19], and the state level is again in view with the civil strife in Samaria (v. 21 [MT v. 20]). In Childs's evocative phrase, this is 'the final descent into a moral and political abyss'.[25]

Continuing with the 'woe' of 10:1–4, one sees further into the mechanics of this socio-economic exploitation. There is fairly widespread agreement that here we see legislation manipulated by those privileged to manage these affairs. The second-person address makes clear that we have prophetic invective here, even without any editorial frame identifying the speaking voice. The absence of divine protection for the poor (9:17 [MT 9:16]) is here identified wholly with those who 'decree' and 'write', enjoying such control of resources that their own wealth is bolstered (v. 3b). Instead of legal protection, there has been legal exploitation. Only the intervention of the deity will bring punishment on those who are (temporarily) above the law (v. 4).

Politics and salvation (Kaufman)[26]

Gottwald's analysis found that the state's prosperity also benefited other propertied classes, and thus the state's success in consolidating its goals could

---

Footnote 24 (*continued*)

> treatment of ch. 5 in their commentaries. But such a move is resisted by H. G. M. Williamson, *A Critical and Exegetical Commentary on Isaiah 1–27*. Vol. 1: *Isaiah 1–5*, ICC (London: T. & T. Clark, 2006), p. 345. It is likewise treated as a whole by B. S. Childs, *Isaiah: A Commentary*, OTL (Louisville: Westminster John Knox, 2001).

25.   Childs, *Isaiah*, p. 86.

26.   This summary contains some overlap with my Jeremiah study, 'Emerging from

be advantageous to others.[27] With some extensions and qualifications such a scenario leads to Kaufman's study in *Redeeming Politics*.[28] Two aspects of his historically based taxonomy of political theology commend it for use here: (1) he eschews the sort of study which investigates the 'extent of government control and intervention' in church–state affairs,[29] conceding that disentangling those religious and political threads is now nearly impossible; (2) positively, he aims to investigate the 'salvation' of the community by means of the 'political idealizations, symbols and spells circulated to inspire loyalty, obedience and service', so that '[s]alvation . . . comes to depend on the perpetuation of the current distribution of political power or on citizens' support of some redistribution' (p. 5). His shorthand for this set of concepts is 'sociolatry'.

Kaufman sketches three strategies: the first, forged by the apologists of Constantine (Eusebius in particular), makes 'empire' the bearer of *divine* government – call this 'conquest'; the second, termed 'clerocracy', 'absorbed political office into the church's ministry' (p. 78), and is exemplified especially (and contentiously) through the medieval papacy and Calvin's Geneva; and the third represents an adjustment to the Constantinian model in the face of crisis by locating real governance in the hands of the Sovereign Lord, although this 'did not guarantee worshipers would be delivered from every misfortune' (p. 129). Here Augustine's reaction to Rome's downfall provides the primary vehicle for reflection. If the 'conquest' model is sustained by the claim for success, the 'crisis' model determines the adaptations necessary when the claim for success plainly cannot be made.

There is throughout Kaufman's study, then, implicit tension between rule and religion. The triumphalist 'conquest' model attempts to assert that social flourishing resides in the outworking of the conqueror's power. Yet 'crisis' requires the opposite rhetorical strategy: that the imperilled 'salvation' of the community requires not a new conqueror to restore divine order, but rather a reconfiguration of the political culture. The situation of political ('clerotocratic') 'conflict' strikes me as Janus-headed: in seeking to promote the claims of religious leadership against the secular order it both challenges the 'conqueror' and provides apologetic strategies in 'crisis'. What is common

Chaos', to appear in H. M. Barstad and R. G. Kratz (eds.), *Prophecy in the Book of Jeremiah*, BZAW (Berlin: de Gruyter, forthcoming).

27. Gottwald, *Politics*, p. 230.

28. See n. 11 above. The playful title points towards the political expression of communal salvation – i.e. politics that (are meant to) redeem.

29. Kaufman, *Redeeming Politics*, p. 3.

throughout is the conviction that church and state inevitably must deal with each other to achieve 'political redemption' or, as Kaufman puts it, 'what is central . . . is the patent assumption that salvation is corporate and, in some respects, political as well as eternal' (p. 5).

The political landscapes the reader of Isaiah traverses could offer glimpses of all of Kaufman's chief scenarios, and a number of variations. Perhaps the 'Constantian' or imperial aspect is the one most hidden from view – at least as positively promoted. Yet even here the euphoric, stepped climax to the oracle against Egypt in Isaiah 19 (esp. vv. 16–25) gives evidence that at least the possibility could be held out of a new world order shared by the once-conquerors and the once-conquered. But this remains more in the realm of utopian wish than political reality.[30]

Isaiah 59 provides an interesting case study to see Kaufman's 'sociolatry' at work, and that clearly in his third category of 'crisis'.[31] Although there has been debate over the unity of the passage,[32] even those who tend to view it as more fragmentary sense the echoes and discern the progression of thought from section to section. Seemingly responding to the teaching on fasting and sabbath observance (ch. 58), this passage falls into three broad sections. Verses 1–8 set out the community's failings, thus separating it from God, and destroying it from within. The community is addressed in the second person in verses 1–3 before the third person description of their crimes is enumerated in verses 4–8. In the second section, verses 9–15a, the community's voice is heard. Unexpectedly, given the catalogue of iniquity in the preceding section, it is a litany of woe, expressing the disorientation accompanying the anarchy of the absence of justice (vv. 9–11). Verse 12 makes direct confession of sin in the second person to Yahweh, while verses 13–15a continue the confession, now detailing the content of the community's crimes. The divine response is recounted in the third main section, verses 15b–20. With no communal source for justice, Yahweh intervenes – or readies himself to (vv. 15a–17), for at verse

---

30. For a helpful taxonomy of such hopes, see C. Bultmann, 'Friedensvisionen im Alten Testament und für Leser des Alten Testaments', in C. Bultmann, B. Kranemann and J. Rüpke (eds.), *Religion, Gewalt, Gewaltlosigkeit: Probleme – Positionen – Perspektiven* (Münster: Aschendorff, 2004), pp. 159–180, 288–290.

31. In addition to the commentaries see also the close study of D. Kendall, S. J., 'The Use of Mišpaṭ [*sic*] in Isaiah 59', *ZAW* 96 (1984), pp. 391–405.

32. E.g. R. N. Whybray, 'the chapter does not form a single unit' (*Isaiah 40–66*, NCB [London: Marshall, Morgan & Scott, 1975], p. 220); C. Westermann, 'It is plainly a unity' (*Isaiah 40–66: A Commentary*, OTL [Philadelphia: Westminster, 1969], p. 344).

18 the verbs shift from waw consecutive imperfects to simple future imperfects, the significance of which is still debated. But as Blenkinsopp points out,
'What is being said here is the simple but often overlooked point that salvation
and judgment are inseparable.'[33]

This passage is often read as a theological statement relating the community
to God. True, it does not bristle with terms for officials and the operations of
the state. However, what is at issue throughout is the ordering of the community's life with justice (*mišpāṭ*, vv. 8–9, 11, 14–15), righteousness (*ṣĕdāqâ*, vv. 9, 14,
16–17), and hope for salvation (*yĕšû'â*, vv. 11, 17; √*yš'*, vv. 1, 16), all of which
are absent as the passage begins, while hope for their reappearance emerges
only after the intervention of Yahweh following the community's confession.
So the reason for the theological reading is clear enough, but these same terms
evoke Kaufman's concept of 'political redemption'. Here the shifting voices
are illuminating. The accusations that begin the chapter (vv. 1–3) which have
the character of summary turn quickly to simple statements that expand this
nightmare of social reality: violence, perversion of justice, deceit, economic
deprivation and further violence. Verse 8 summarizes the complete bankruptcy
of moral, and legal, sense.

The recognition of the truth of this rhetorical onslaught occurs in the
second-person response to the accusations in verses 9–15a, admitting first to
the desolate state of social life (vv. 9–11), and then the straightforward confession (vv. 13–15a), negotiated around the brief but telling second-person
address directly to the Lord (v. 12). In terms of 'political redemption', verse
14b is significant: 'for truth stumbles in the public square' (NRSV). As some
commentators notice, what seems to be envisaged here is the judicial process
(although it remains implicit), a notion that would correspond directly to that
of verse 4, where the courts are undermined by all forms of dishonesty.

Kendall notes that God's action to intervene and restore is not described
as *mišpāṭ*, although he sees its content reflected in related vocabulary.[34] His
conclusion, on the variegated use of the term 'justice', demonstrates that the
realization of corporate salvation is both political and divine: 'for the prophet
… it implies judicial abuse (v. 4) … the people … know *mišpāṭ* [*sic*] as salvation
(vv. 9–11) and as a public duty in which they had failed (v. 14) … Yahweh …
reacts with a judgment which saves the innocent and punishes the guilty'.[35]

---

33. J. Blenkinsopp, *Isaiah 56–66: A New Translation with Introduction and Commentary*, AB
   19B (New York: Doubleday: 2003), p. 198.

34. Kendall, 'Use of Mišpaṭ', p. 404.

35. Ibid., pp. 404–405.

Politics and judgment (O'Donovan)

The trajectory from Kaufman's political soteriology to O'Donovan's political ethics takes one to a very different mode of discourse (from history to
'ethics'),[36] which nonetheless could be seen as concerned with a similar *telos*,
the intersection of political concepts and 'God's redemption of the world' (p.
ix). As noted above, O'Donovan asserts that '[t]he authority of secular government resides in the practice of judgment' (p. 3), and it is the latter phrase
that is successively explored and nuanced in the book's opening chapters.
Promoting 'judgment' as a fundamental role for government 'strips' it of
other loci for authority, especially sovereignty itself that remains in 'Israel's
God and his Christ' (p. 4). For O'Donovan, this expression is *fully* articulated
within the New Testament and the 'new terms' that appear 'in the wake of
Christ's ascension' (p. 5). In putting things this way, O'Donovan is careful to
register the way ancient Israel's government should be differentiated from his
claim, which he roots rather in Romans 13:4. On the other hand, one could
argue that Moses participates in (and at one point constitutes!) the 'government' of the people he leads, while David's personal covenant comes to him
as one who is king (p. 3). In any case, O'Donovan points out suggestive ways
in which 'judging' in the Old Testament points toward the political function
of rendering judgment.

   Although judgment is government's 'essential' task, other functions do not
simply disappear; rather, all are 're-conceived within this matrix and subject
to the discipline of enacting right against wrong' (p. 5). Likewise, by virtue of
this claim, 'political leaders are not simply denied their authority', but rather by
their judgments attest to the 'appearing grace of God' (p. 5). Again it seems to
me that this is already an Old Testament concept. In ancient Israel was it *ever*
'possible to think of political authority as sovereign' (p. 5)?

   In giving further content to the concept of 'political judgment' O'Donovan
defines it as '*an act of moral discrimination that pronounces upon a preceding act or
existing state of affairs to establish a new public context*' (p. 7; O'Donovan's italics),
and this is elaborated by means of four glosses: judgment (1) discriminates
morally (here Solomon's decision with the two women in 1 Kgs 3 is given as
example), (2) is reactive, (3) has public prospects which establish contexts and
(4) is public in agency and representation (pp. 7–10). Observing that human

---

36. It ought to be noted, however, that O'Donovan resists, even refutes, the
   maintenance of a distinction between 'political theology' and 'political ethics'
   (*Judgment*, pp. ix–x).

government falls short of a divine ideal, O'Donovan considers political judgment under the headings of 'truth' (to which points 1 and 2 above appear to correspond), and 'effective action' (which seems to bear a relation to points 3 and 4, above) (p. 16). *Truth* is framed by *law*, while it is implied that *effectiveness* is articulated by *legislation* (pp. 22–23). Private vengeance is taken as a test case, and again an Old Testament example is invoked. The cities of refuge are seen as an institution that performs the task of subordinating a merely personal grievance to an act of public justice (pp. 23–25). To be sure, such judgments do not have the finality of the judgments of God, and this again demonstrates something of the limitations with which the reflection on truth and action began (pp. 26–30).

Political judgment, then, also has the quality of binding the public to its decisions (p. 53), but it also defends freedom against wrong (pp. 57–58). Seen thus, political judgment 'is response to wrong as injury to the public good' (p. 59). Although judgment was seen to be *reactive* in its actions (O'Donovan is clear that it is not *initiating*), still this observation provides a prospective dimension to its results.

This is a rich and dense study, and this brief survey is only the beginning of an account of 'political judgment'. It is enough, however, to test this matrix of ideas against Isaiah; and since O'Donovan himself offers a number of examples drawn from Isaiah, this project is not so forced as the claim that political judgment is best seen from a post-Easter vantage point might suggest.

One brief passage immediately suggests itself.[37] Isaiah 11:1–5 stands among the 'messianic' passages in the first part of the book.[38] Immediate 'political' interest is piqued by the phrasing in verse 1: that 'there shall come forth a shoot from the stump of Jesse' (NRSV). Naturally, this has occasioned speculation about whether this is a means of by-passing David's line without abandoning his 'house' altogether. Such questions rightly deserve attention, but, following O'Donovan's focus on political judgment, shift interest slightly further down the text. After describing the spiritual equipping this figure will enjoy, something like a job description is offered:

He shall not *judge* (*špṭ*) by what his eyes see,
or decide by what his ears hear;

---

37. O'Donovan himself begins the book with an appeal to Isa. 16:5; 42:1, 4.

38. H. G. M. Williamson gives them as 7:14, 8:23b – 9:6 (EVV 9:1b–7), 11:1–9, 16:4b–5 and 32:1–5 in *Variations on a Theme: King, Messiah and Servant in the Book of Isaiah* (Carlisle: Paternoster, 1998), p. 30.

but with righteousness he shall *judge* (*špṭ*) the poor,
  and decide with equity for the meek of the earth;
he shall strike the earth with the rod of his mouth,
  and with the breath of his lips he shall kill the wicked.
(Isa. 11:3b–4 NRSV; my italics)

There must, of course, be a correlation between the 'charismatic endow-ment', detailed in the preceding verses,[39] and this unusual form of judging which would seem to preclude the need for evidence. Judicial functions were a traditional part of the royal role (as Absalom's infamous sigh of 2 Sam. 15:4 demonstrates), but one would expect a just judge to have open eyes and ears (cf. Isa. 6:10). A translation such as Blenkinsopp's ('He will not judge by appearances, he will not decide by hearsay', p. 262) obviates the need for further reflection, but it also removes the striking characterization of *this* judge's mode of operation. What we see is a form of judgment that carries with it some of the finality that O'Donovan recognized would be absent from secular political judgments. The divinely endowed Spirit enables this royal figure to discern between the 'poor and meek', while his pronouncements (v. 4b) eradicate the wicked from the earth. Here we see all the functions of truth-telling and effective action, which tick all of O'Donovan's boxes.[40] It suggests one need not wait for the New Testament for a clear articulation of the principle that 'the authority of secular government resides in the practice of judgment'.

Reading politically: Cyrus in Isaiah 44:24 – 45:7

Having sampled texts from the first and last major sections of the book, it remains to investigate a text drawn from chapters 40–55 that takes each of these three approaches. We shall see that it is not always possible – or neces-sarily desirable – to distinguish these levels consistently. One text stands out as a striking statement of theopolitical surprise: the identification of Cyrus as the 'anointed' (*māšîaḥ*) of the Lord in Isaiah 45:1, the second in a pair of direct references to Cyrus, the other immediately preceding in 44:28, where he

---

39. Ibid., p. 46, plus J. Blenkinsopp, *Isaiah 1–39*, p. 265.

40. I.e., as stated above, this judging (1) discriminates morally, (2) is reactive, (3) has public prospects which establish contexts, (4) is public in agency and representation.

is called 'my shepherd'.[41] These in turn stand in a wider framework of implicit references to the Persian king whose capture of Babylon would mark the end of the Judean exile.[42] Having an inherent political interest, the discovery of the so-called Cyrus Cylinder has both piqued and complicated assessment of the role of Cyrus in Isaiah 40 – 55.[43] Such attention is not a modern phenomenon, even if this articulation of it is: Xenophon's *Cyropaedia* (*The Education of Cyrus*) used Cyrus' career as a vehicle for political reflection, although his project holds puzzles of its own.[44] The trajectory from Cyrus even intersects with Machiavelli, who identified Cyrus as one of a string of divinely ordained 'princes' standing in succession to Moses, whose success Machiavelli thought was guaranteed by divine favour – an intriguing connection which crops up again below.[45]

---

41. A brief taxonomy of approaches to this text is provided by Fried, 'Cyrus the Messiah?', pp. 373–374.

42. Fried (ibid., p. 390) gives the 'undisputed' corpus of Cyrus texts as 41:1–4, 41:25–26, 44:24–28, 45:1–13, 46:8–11, 48:14–16a, although the boundaries of those core texts are variously defined; disputed texts include 42:1–9. A. Kuhrt offers a recent assessment of historical issues relating to Cyrus in 'Ancient Near Eastern History: The Case of Cyrus the Great of Persia', in H. G. M. Williamson (ed.), *Understanding the History of Ancient Israel* (Oxford: Oxford University Press for the British Academy, 2007), pp. 107–127; it extends and updates her earlier piece 'The Cyrus Cylinder and Achaemenid Imperial Policy', *JSOT* 25 (1983), pp. 83–97.

43. A translation of the Cyrus Cylinder is included as Text 1 in the Appendix to Kuhrt, 'Case of Cyrus', pp. 119–121. Her earlier article touches on the claims that this text represents the first statement of 'human rights' (ibid., p. 84), claims which continue to provoke controversy: see H. de Quetteville, 'Historians Debunk "Nonsense" of Cyrus the Great's Declaration of Human Rights', *Daily Telegraph*, 17 July 2008, 'News', p. 15 (online version available at www.Telegraph.co.uk <http://tinyurl.com/6qlfxe>, accessed 6 Oct. 2008).

44. E.g. J. Tatum, *Xenophon's Imperial Fiction: On the Education of Cyrus* (Princeton: Princeton University Press, 1989), and C. Nadon, *Xenophon's Prince: Republic and Empire in the Cyropaedia* (Berkeley: University of California Press, 2001), and their critical reception.

45. C. J. Nederman, 'Amazing Grace: Fortune, God, and Free Will in Machiavelli's Thought', *JHI* 60 (1999), pp. 617–638 (see esp. 630–632); Nederman argues that *grazia* (grace) is the intermediary between *virtù* and *Fortuna*; cf. N. Machiavelli, *The Prince*, chs. 6 and 25; also the brief presentation of Nederman's case in his article 'Niccolò Machiavelli', in E. N. Zalta (ed.), *The Stanford Encyclopedia of Philosophy*

Ideally, the wider corpus of Cyrus texts in Isaiah should be drawn into this analysis, but, space precluding this approach, the single pericope of 44:24 – 45:7 must suffice with only an occasional glance at other texts. Scholars generally agree that this unit consists of two complementary stanzas:[46] 44:24–28, which speaks *about* Cyrus, and 45:1–7, which speaks *to* him.[47] Along with the several echoes between the stanzas, the explicit naming of Cyrus in 44:28 and 45:1 (only here in Isaiah) forges an obvious connection between them.

The emphasis on the Lord's making (44:24–26a) and speaking (44:26b–28) gives way to the announcement of Cyrus' own actions in 45:1b–3, albeit in the form of a promise of the Lord's enabling actions on Cyrus' behalf. The triple announcement of the speaking God (*hā'ōmer*, 44:26b, 27–28) finds a parallel in the thrice-repeated self-identification 'I am the Lord' (45:5, 6b, 7b). The whole is bound together by the claim of the Lord to be 'maker of all things / doer of all these things' (44:24 // 45:7).[48] Before exploring the poem's political dimensions, it is first necessary to highlight a few of its relevant features.

The first stanza holds three particular puzzles: (1) Who is being addressed? (2) Who is the 'servant' of verse 26? (3) How should the final couplet of verse 28b be understood? (1) Yahweh's self-declaration of creativity and thus sovereignty is addressed in verse 24b only to 'you' (sg.), but the identity is not made explicit. If context is a reliable guide here, then 44:21–23 requires the addressee

---

Footnote 45 *(continued)*
    (autumn 2008 ed.) <http://plato.stanford.edu/archives/fall2008/entries/machiavelli/>, accessed 6 Oct. 2008.

46. An exception is R. G. Kratz, *Kyros im Deuterojesaja-Buch: Redaktionsgeschichtliche Untersuchungen zu Entstehung und Theologie von Jes 40–55*, FAT 1 (Tübingen: Mohr Siebeck, 1991), whose fine-grained analysis of 45:1–7 and accompanying disconnection of it from its immediate context has not been widely followed.

47. Cf. J. P. Fokkelman, 'The Cyrus Oracle (Isaiah 44,24–45,7) from the Perspectives of Syntax, Versification and Structure', in M. Vervenne and J. van Ruiten (eds.), *Studies in the Book of Isaiah, Festschrift W. A. M. Beuken*, BETL 132 (Leuven: Leuven University Press / Peeters, 1997), pp. 303–323 (see esp. pp. 319–320). The pericope's boundaries are not universally agreed, with 45:8 often canvassed as the concluding verse. My sense is that 45:8 forms an inclusio with 44:21–23, which together frame the two stanzas between them, so that 44:21–23 has a Janus-like function, looking both forward to 45:8 and back to 44:1–2.

48. Hebrew *'ōse(h) kōl* // *'ōśeh kol-'ēlle(h)*; cf. 'The two parts are . . . clamped together . . .' (J. Blenkinsopp, *Isaiah 40–55: A New Translation with Introduction and Commentary*, AB 19A [New York: Doubleday, 2002], p. 245).

to be 'Israel'. Likewise, 'your redeemer' (v. 24a, *gōʾălekā*) inclines many to see the birth of Israel here. At the same time, the lack of specific address implies a distance that creates space for the explicit turn to Cyrus in 45:1.[49] (2) It might be thought that the reference to the singular 'servant' in verse 26 is simply the 'servant' as the people of God (cf. 44:21; also 43:10 where the sg. 'my servant' stands in parallel to the pl. 'my witnesses'). However, the lack of specificity in address again raises some uncertainty: Might the 'servant' even be the prophet?[50] Or could the 'servant' even be Cyrus? The latter remains unlikely, although as the poem unfolds, the speaking role of Cyrus begins to grow. (3) This is seen especially in the final part of verse 28: often flattened in translation so that it joins the string of participles which precede, this line does not begin with *hāʾōmer*, '(he) who says', but rather with *wĕlēʾmōr* ('to say', or the like), the conjunction plus infinitive construct. As argued by Fokkelman, this infinitive ought to be given 'full function', so that this line spells out the purpose that Cyrus will carry out.[51] Thus the purpose Cyrus fulfils is 'to say of Jerusalem . . . and of the temple . . . ', the rebuilding of the city and the re-establishing of the temple echoing Yahweh's own speech of verse 26.

With the second stanza (45:1–7) there is greater clarity – at least, the address to Cyrus is explicit – and yet the interpretative problems deepen. Most importantly, (1) what freight of meaning is 'his anointed' (*mĕšîḥô*, v. 1a) meant to deliver? Consequently, (2) what to make of the parallels often pointed out between this passage and the Babylonian 'Cyrus Cylinder'?[52] And (3) what is the relationship of Cyrus to Yahweh? (1) As noted above (n. 42), Fried sketches a continuum of typical understandings of the designation of Cyrus by Yahweh as 'his anointed': from those (few) who, following Torrey,[53] believe

---

49. So too J. Goldingay and D. Payne, *A Critical and Exegetical Commentary on Isaiah 40–55*, 2 vols., ICC (London: T. & T. Clark, 2006), 2:8; cf. Baltzer, *Deutero-Isaiah: A Commentary on Isaiah 40–55*, Hermeneia (Minneapolis: Fortress, 2001), p. 212.

50. Thus a suggestion from H. G. M. Williamson, *The Book Called Isaiah: Deutero-Isaiah's Role in Composition and Redaction* (Oxford: Clarendon, 1994), pp. 51–52, building on a suggestion by R. E. Clements's connecting 44:25 and 6:11–12.

51. Fokkelman, 'Cyrus Oracle', pp. 311–312. Cf. also the NJPS, NJB, NET Bible, and NASB, Redivierte Lutherbibel, among others, all of which follow this reading.

52. See n. 41, above.

53. Torrey himself cites A. Kaminka's lead in excising 'Cyrus' from 45:1 as an interpolation: C. C. Torrey, 'Isaiah 41', *HTR* 44 (1951), p. 124. Torrey concludes, 'The twice-appearing name, "Cyrus," is a later insertion in the Hebrew text, and scholarly exegesis can make no use of it' (p. 136).

the references to Cyrus are secondary; to those who argue that the 'anointing' 'simply indicates a commission'; a third position sees Cyrus as central but still of temporary significance; while the final group 'admit[s] that the anointing . . . mean[s] the end of the Davidic monarchy'.[54] Fried intends to establish the final position as correct. The evidence she marshals is impressive, but not finally persuasive. In claiming that just like the Egyptian and Babylonian collaborators, so also 'Deutero-Isaiah handed over to Cyrus the royal Judean title of "YHWH's anointed," as well as the entire royal Judean court theology associated with it' (p. 390), she fails to reckon with the contours of Cyrus' commission, and those elements which remain exclusive to the 'servant'. Fried skews the reading of Cyrus, for example, in glossing 'Yahweh loves him' (48:14b) as being the Lord's 'beloved'. As Blenkinsopp rightly notes, 'the verb "love" . . . is, at any rate, more political than emotive'.[55] (2) A comparison with the Egyptian and Babylonian sources invoked by Fried with Isaiah 45:1–7 shows that the former pair exude praise for the actions of the Persian monarchs, while the latter lauds Yahweh alone, who consistently acts on behalf of Cyrus. The anointing of Cyrus, then, conveys that he was 'specially set aside for a divine commission';[56] it does not bring the entirety of 'royal Judean court theology' in its wake.

(3) This conclusion is reinforced when the relationship between Yahweh and Cyrus is examined. Gottwald is an example of those who have claimed that Cyrus' call implies an expectation by the prophet of 'Cyrus' conversion to Israel's God'.[57] Westermann, among others, points out that this passage (in vv. 4–5) 'is the express statement that this will not be true'.[58] Cyrus remains only a tool in the Lord's hand, no different than Assyria was before him (cf. Isa. 10:5). That one was an instrument for weal and the other for woe does not change the nature of their relationship with the sovereign Lord. Still, the trajectory through these verses remains significant: Cyrus' progress as he enjoys the

---

54. Fried, 'Cyrus the Messiah?', pp. 373–374.

55. Blenkinsopp, *Isaiah 40–55*, p. 294.

56. Childs, *Isaiah*, p. 353; cf. Williamson, *Variations*, pp. 5–6; J. Goldingay, *The Message of Isaiah 40–55: A Theological-Literary Commentary* (London: T. & T. Clark, 2005), p. 263.

57. Gottwald goes further, including the promotion of Jerusalem as the 'religious capital of the Persian empire'; Gottwald, *Politics*, p. 100; cf. N. K. Gottwald, *All the Kingdoms of the Earth: Israelite Prophecy and International Relations in the Ancient Near East* (New York: Harper & Row, 1964), p. 338.

58. Westermann, *Isaiah 40–66*, p. 161; cf. Blenkinsopp, *Isaiah 40–55*, p. 249.

Lord's favour (45:1–3) is initially for Israel's benefit (45:4), but ultimately for the reputation of the one true God (45:5–7). The net result accrues blessing not only to Israel, but to the whole created order (45:8).

Although Gottwald does not give a great deal of attention to prophets in his *Politics of Ancient Israel*, Cyrus is necessarily the focus of attention at several points. Under Persian hegemony, Judah was left in the context of a 'colonial political order' which had the effect of promoting an 'apolitical or transpolitical' 'Israel' at the state level; by contrast, local politics naturally flourished.[59] Although the suggestion of a prophetic expectation of Cyrus' conversion was rejected, his 'critical imagining' of Judahite politics in the Persian period remains intriguing.[60] Politically, this colonial situation sees a ruling elite beholden to the empire whose expectation was that the colony would be 'politically pacified and economically profitable', whereas the Judean hope was for greater autonomy and an improved local economy: 'Obviously, these two desiderata were not easily reconciled . . . ' (p. 239). While the benefits to Judah generally and Jerusalem in particular are clearly in evidence (especially 44:26–27; 45:4), the differentiation of Cyrus from the 'servant' contributes to the political dynamic sketched by Gottwald. There is no expectation that Cyrus' government displaces local authority; 'authority' remains in the hands of the 'servant'.[61] The trajectory runs the opposite direction: Cyrus' success results in the intersection of Israel and the nations on a universal scale. Such a scenario relativizes the 'colonial' outlook identified by Gottwald.

What of Kaufman's 'sociolotry' (the articulation of political symbols necessary to the 'salvation' of the community)? This interest overlaps with the preceding discussion. As seen above, the rhetorical strategy of the 'crisis' situation (for, as with Isa. 59, such is the setting here) calls for an adjustment to the prevailing political order, although this may be achieved in different ways.[62] Three strategies in this pericope promote such 'adjustments'. (1) Although Fried's argument that Judean royal theology had been delivered *in toto* to Cyrus was rejected, the prophet allows for a tacit assumption that no Davidic figure has been identified to accomplish the purpose of Yahweh. This necessarily qualifies the nature and role of the Davidic hope expressed elsewhere in

59. Gottwald, *Politics*, p. 156.

60. For the following, see ibid., pp. 238–240.

61. M. C. Lind, 'Monotheism, Power, and Justice: A Study in Isaiah 40–55', *CBQ* 46 (1984), pp. 440–446.

62. Kaufman, *Redeeming Politics*, p. 129.

Isaiah. (2) On the other hand, the emphatic – indeed complete – subjugation of the 'conquering' imperial power to Israel's God provides a different political calculation of the emperor's worth. As seen above, imperial power remains within the gift of Yahweh; it carries no finality of its own. (3) Cyrus' words and purpose (46:28b) were seen above to be fully congruent with Yahweh's words and will (46:26b). This, coupled with the almost passive role allotted to Cyrus in 45:2–3, has the effect of giving Cyrus a quasi-prophetic function. At any rate, he is rendered no normal military conqueror. As Millard Lind notes, kingship,

> which in the thought of the ancient Near East was the office of violent power politics through which the gods gave continuity to the community, was made subservient to Yahweh who gave continuity to his community not by power politics but by his creative power of word-event, of promise/threat-fulfillment.[63]

Finally, it might be thought that O'Dovovan's themes of judgment and government are not well represented in this passage. We do not see a political venture marked by a reactive exercise of moral discrimination,[64] and on Lind's reading, such authority remains with the servant in any case.[65] Should Blenkinsopp's suggestion (and he is not alone in making it) that the 'song' of 42:1–4 applies to Cyrus prove correct, there would be much more interest in 'judgment' in relation to him.[66] But there is a trajectory within the context that suggests this element is not absent from Cyrus' task in the prophet's thought. As noted above, verse 8 provides a trajectory from this Cyrus poem that is framed in terms of the conjunction of 'salvation and righteousness', that is, the re-establishment of a flourishing creation is a work in accord with a divine moral standard, not simply the outcome of a conquering power. These words find an echo in 45:13 that reasserts the role of Cyrus to act in 'righteousness': the city's rebuilding and the release of exiles is expressly not for Cyrus' personal gain. In these ways, Cyrus' political intervention into Judah's affairs at Yahweh's behest may be seen to be consonant with the exercise of 'judgment',

---

63. Lind, 'Monotheism', p. 439.

64. Cf. above, n. 40.

65. Lind writes, 'the politics of violent power falls short of fulfilling Yahweh's oath and purpose; only a new politics, disclosed in the work and the way of the servant, establishes and fulfills Yahweh's oath' ('Monotheism', p. 446).

66. Blenkinsopp, *Isaiah 40–55*, pp. 210–211; the number of those finding a reference to Cyrus 42:5–9 is greater.

although this facet remains muted, to be more fully realized by another, later figure.[67]

Conclusions

This study has only begun to explore what attending to the political aspects of Isaiah might look like. There are other political interests which other readers would find of greater interest than the ones registered here. Still, my hope is that a more politically engaged reading of Isaiah might emerge when accompanied by guides attuned to register political textures and trajectories in ways not often privileged by students of the Bible.

© David J. Reimer, 2009

---

67. Thus Jenni observes that '[a] glance at the rest of the words of the prophet with their extravagant hopes shows that that which was expected in the Cyrus Songs of the Persian king was only a beginning, just a part of the ultimate hope' (*Voraussagen der Propheten*, p. 101; my tr.); cf. Williamson, *Variations*, p. 176.

5. FAITH IN ISAIAH

Philip S. Johnston

Introduction

Faith in God is the central theme of the Bible, displayed in great variety and richness in the Hebrew Bible and the Christian New Testament. Not surprisingly, then, faith is the motivation of most people who read these texts, often appropriating relevant elements to their own very different contexts. Similarly, many scholars are drawn to biblical study by personal faith, and then specialize in it as a professional discipline alongside the continued practice of their faith. Meanwhile there are significant groups of general readers and scholars who do not profess faith, yet whose close study of these ancient texts contributes to a better understanding of them by all.

Given the above, it is somewhat surprising that the theme of faith receives so little attention in current Old Testament / Hebrew Bible studies. There are of course several important reasons for this:

1. The discipline of detailed critical engagement with the biblical text emerged in recent centuries in opposition to dominant ecclesiastical interpretations that were dogmatic in both senses, controlled by systematic theology and insistent on their sole rectitude. As such, critical scholarship has often been instinctively suspicious of faith and consequently of its biblical portrayal.
2. The Biblical Theology movement of the mid-twentieth century was seen

by many as an attempt to revive a fideist interpretation of the Hebrew
Bible. Since many scholars viewed this approach as unsuccessful,
the general connection between scholarship and faith, including the
scholarly study of faith, was again suspect.

3. Various Western cultural developments, prominent in the late twentieth
century, have reinforced this suspicion: religious plurality in society
generally; secularization of university departments of theology and
religious studies; postmodern distrust of authority claims; and the great
variety of hermeneutics from specific sociocultural perspectives.

Nevertheless, it is interesting to note a recrudescence of scholarly interest in
biblical faith perspectives,[1] not least concerning the book of Isaiah. There have
been several recent doctoral studies on aspects of faith in Isaiah 1 – 39;[2] there
have also been studies on faith in other sections of this rich and complex book,
but not (to my knowledge) any integrative study of the book as a whole.[3] This
chapter seeks to survey some of this literature and the different perspectives
on faith in the book's various sections.[4]

Before proceeding further, we must look more closely at the concept of
'faith', particularly as expressed in the Hebrew stems '*mn* and *bṭḥ*. Ward notes
that earlier word studies which sought to interpret '*mn* in terms of etymology or
an alleged fundamental meaning 'have now been rejected as untenable'; rather,
it is 'the mental act of being sure about something or someone'.[5] He expands
this as '(a) Believing a prophetic oracle or a report of a revelatory event; (b)

---

1. In a different vein but with similar interests note R. W. L. Moberly, *Prophecy and Discernment* (Cambridge: Cambridge University Press, 2006).

2. Notably G. C. I. Wong, 'The Nature of Faith in Isaiah of Jerusalem' (PhD diss., University of Cambridge, 1995); D. Bostock, *A Portrayal of Trust* (Milton Keynes: Paternoster, 2006); J. Dekker, *Zion's Rock-Solid Foundations: An Exegetical Study of the Zion Text in Isaiah 28:16*, OTS 54 (Leiden: Brill, 2007).

3. Such a study is suggested by the title of H. Hagelia, *Coram Deo: Spirituality in the Book of Isaiah, with Particular Attention to Faith in Isaiah*, ConBOT 49 (Stockholm: Almqvist & Wiksell, 2001). But the work consists mostly of statistical vocabulary analysis, with meagre results by the author's own admission; cf. H. G. M. Williamson, Review of H. Hagelia, *Coram Deo*, *JSOT* 99 (2002), pp. 77–78.

4. Cf. the similar approach on a different theme by J. Barton, 'Ethics in the Book of Isaiah', in C. C. Broyles and C. Evans (eds.), *Writing and Reading the Scroll of Isaiah*, VTSup 70 (Leiden: Brill, 1997), vol. 1, pp. 67–77.

5. J. M. Ward, 'Faith, Faithfulness in the OT', *IDBSup* (1976), pp. 329–332, quotations

Believing in a prophet as a generally reliable messenger of God; (c) Believing/
trusting in God's promises and his ability to fulfil them; (d) Believing that something involving God is or will be the case; (e) Believing God's commandments.'[6]
The first four of these are certainly relevant to the book of Isaiah.

Healey writes similarly, 'The prophetic message reflects not primarily an ethical
instruction, but rather a call to an ongoing relationship of trust.'[7] He continues:

> The opposite of faith in the prophets is not unbelief; it is apostasy, because the faith
> which is required is not an act of assent but a commitment to a tradition, to a body
> of received things. The prophetic faith is clearly based in the covenant, especially
> the Sinai covenant, and expresses itself in *acts* of fidelity, not in creedal formulas.[8]

His article's final part ('OT Faith in Holistic Perspective') has the subheadings
'Remembrance' and 'Faith Confronts Fear'. While neither section cites Isaiah,
both could easily do so: the first in relation to chapters 40–55 and the second
to the whole book, with faith confronting fear for Ahaz, Hezekiah, the exiles
and the rebuilding community.

Combining the two approaches gives a definition of faith as an ongoing
relationship of trust in God, his promises and his messengers. We note at the
outset that this definition neither prescribes nor precludes other activity on the
part of the faithful, whether social, political or military.

Isaiah 1 – 12

Isaiah 7:1–9
In this first section of Proto-Isaiah[9] our theme comes to prominence in
chapter 7, which in its present form relates exchanges between prophet and

---

Footnote 5 (*continued*)
> from p. 329. Ward highlights the book of Isaiah as one of three specific contexts
> he discusses (following the exodus tradition and Abraham).

6. Ibid., pp. 329–330, omitting biblical references.

7. J. P. Healey, 'Faith: Old Testament', *ABD* 2:744–749; quotation from p. 747, citing
the example of Isa. 7:9. His opening comment is less helpful: 'Faith is a peculiarly
Christian concept' (p. 744); but here (following Aquinas) he sees faith as intellectual
assent, albeit moved by divine grace.

8. Ibid., p. 747, emphasis original.

9. Here Proto-, Deutero- and Trito-Isaiah indicate sections of the book.

king, with various attached oracles. In the context of the Syro-Ephraimite invasion of Judah and siege of Jerusalem, YHWH sends Isaiah to Ahaz with a message of advice and reassurance (v. 4):[10] 'Take heed, be quiet, do not fear, and do not let your heart be faint because of these two smouldering stumps of firebrands', that is, the invading kings with their designated puppet-king for Jerusalem. This is followed by a poetic oracle (with prose insertion) ending in a famous wordplay (v. 9b):

> If you do not stand firm in faith,
>> you shall not stand at all.

Both these sentences merit discussion concerning their portrayal of faith.[11]

As Wong notes, the prophet's opening words 'Take heed, be quiet' are often interpreted as a command of passivity,[12] influencing in turn the reading of verse 9b. There are several arguments for this.[13] (1) The niphal imperative *hiššāmēr* ('Take heed') is followed elsewhere by what one should *not* do; for example, Exodus 34:12 ('Take care not to make a covenant'). While the command here in Isaiah 7:4 has no dependent clause, its general effect is to prohibit activity. (2) The next term reinforces this: *hašqēṭ*, 'be quiet'; that is, cease activity. (3) Passages elsewhere in Isaiah contrast faith in YHWH with employing human resources; for example, 30:15 and 31:1. (4) Passages elsewhere in the Old Testament make a similar contrast, notably before the Israelites cross the Reed Sea: 'The LORD will fight for you, and you have only to keep still' (*ḥrš*; Exod. 14:14); and when Jehoshaphat and Judah face an eastern coalition: 'This battle is not for you to fight; take your position, stand still, and see the victory of the LORD on your behalf' (2 Chr. 20:17). Würthwein and von Rad suggest that Isaiah's instruction to Ahaz reflects Israel's Holy War tradition of YHWH fighting for Israel.

However, Wong counters these arguments well: (1) While *hiššāmēr* is often

---

10. All quotations are from the NRSV, unless indicated otherwise.

11. Recent studies and pertinent issues are well summarized by G. C. I. Wong, 'Faith in the Present Form of Isaiah vii 1–17', *VT* 51 (2001), pp. 535–547; and Bostock, *Portrayal*.

12. So, among others, G. von Rad, *Old Testament Theology*, vol. 2 (London: SCM, 1965), pp. 160–161 (though without using this phrase, *pace* Wong, 'Faith . . . Isaiah vii', p. 536); O. Kaiser, *Isaiah 1–12* (London: SCM, 1983), p. 141.

13. Wong, 'Faith . . . Isaiah vii', pp. 536–540, gives these as three, but his first point merits subdivision.

followed by a prohibition, it can also be followed by a command to obedience (e.g. Exod. 23:21, 'Be attentive'). And if there is a negative connotation here in Isaiah 7:4, it remains unclear what is prohibited; for instance, there is no explicit condemnation of Ahaz's inspection of the water supply (v. 3). (2) The command *hašqēṭ* implies not passivity but calmness and composure. In Isaiah 57:20 and Jeremiah 49:23 'the same word is used in contrast to the anxiety and fear symbolised by a tossing sea. The point there is not the absence of activity, but the absence of anxiety.'[14] (3) Neither Isaiah 30:15 nor 31:1 denounces the use of human resources per se (see discussion below). (4) Other Old Testament passages may reflect different perspectives, and should not necessarily influence the interpretation of Isaiah 7.[15] In any case, many texts link faith in YHWH with active engagement in battle, not least some texts associated with Holy War traditions. In particular, Deuteronomy 20:2–4 (key for Würthwein) gives preparation for military activity, and includes the phrase 'do not lose heart, or be afraid', which is echoed in Isaiah 7:4. Thus Wong convincingly argues that the opening prophetic instruction does not prescribe passivity or prohibit defensive preparations.[16] Further, the prophet is not warning against alliance with the invading coalition (implausible) or with Assyria (ignored here, unlike 2 Kgs 16:7–9).

If not passivity, what then is the prophet advising here? In a situation of general fear (v. 3), he seeks to reassure the king that the current aggressors are spent forces who will not succeed (vv. 4b, 7). The following exchange reinforces this with a promised sign of divine presence (vv. 10–14).[17] As Wong concludes, 'At the very least, then, we can conclude that faith here involves trusting in the promise of Yhwh spoken through his prophet.'[18]

---

14. Ibid., p. 537. He also notes that the LXX uses the root *hesychazō*, which occurs in 1 Thess. 4:11 in connection with getting on with one's own business and work.

15. Wong expresses this more strongly (ibid., p. 538).

16. Logically, therefore, neither does *ta'ămínû* in v. 9b. Cf. Ward, 'Isaiah does not try to tell Ahaz what are the specific implications of this faith for political action . . .' ('Faith', p. 331). Bostock (*Portrayal*, p. 190) reaches a similar if more cautious conclusion: 'on the other hand, he does not advocate any concrete form of action except trusting in YHWH'.

17. With the added complication of a different aggressor, Assyria, in the next verses (15–17).

18. Wong, 'Faith . . . Isaiah vii', p. 542. He also notes several links with ch. 1 to suggest that faith involves justice and righteousness: 'wearing out' (*l'h*) in 7:13 and 1:14; *'mn* in 7:9 and 1:21, 26; hypocrisy of Ahaz and Jerusalemites. While this association may

The oracle in verses 7–9 which concludes this first exchange is markedly different, with its chiastic structure, poetic nature, prose interjection, and concluding plural verbs; so it may very well have a different origin. Nevertheless, in its current setting it obviously complements the preceding prophetic message, and should be interpreted together with it. The concluding aphorism consists of a clever wordplay of '*mn* in hiphil and niphal, which translators struggle to capture; NRSV gives:

> If you do not stand firm in faith,
>   you will not stand at all.[19]

The plural verbal forms, while indicative of redactional activity, have a relatively straightforward application to the royal house[20] and/or the equally fearful wider populace (v. 2).[21] Neither verb has a qualifying complement, which leads to some imprecision as to their meaning, particularly the first verb. By common consent, the lack of object makes this hiphil inner-transitive (being/becoming faithful/firm) rather than declarative (declaring to be faithful/firm).[22] Wildberger helpfully defines its meaning as 'have confidence, overcome all despondency, show steadfastness'; and he summarizes Isaiah's message to Ahaz as 'Take the prophetic word seriously!'[23]

---

    be true in the wider prophetic message, in Isaiah as elsewhere, Bostock rightly
    comments that these links 'seem rather tenuous' (*Portrayal*, p. 201).

19. Similarly NIV/TNIV, with addition of 'your' before 'faith'. ESV: 'If you are not firm
    in faith, / you will not be firm at all.' Cf. Luther's translation: 'Glaubt ihr nicht, so
    bleibt ihr nicht'; H. Wildberger, *Isaiah 1–12* (Minneapolis: Fortress, 1991), p. 302.
    LXX renders the second verb 'perceive'; similarly Vg and Syr; see Wildberger, ibid.,
    p. 285; Bostock, *Portrayal*, p. 194, n. 172, with further discussion.

20. Bostock, *Portrayal*, p. 195. D. Janthial, *L'oracle de Nathan et l'unité du livre d'Isaïe*,
    BZAW 343 (Berlin: de Gruyter, 2004), pp. 100–101, notes the echo of Nathan's
    oracle that the Davidic house would be 'made sure' ('*mn*, niphal); Janthial sees this
    oracle as a guiding thread (*fil rouge*) throughout Isaiah.

21. Kaiser, *Isaiah 1–12*, p. 94.

22. So Bostock, *Portrayal*, pp. 196–197, citing Wildberger, *Isaiah 1–12*. Also called
    inwardly transitive or internal hiphil (B. K. Waltke, M. O'Connor, *An Introduction
    to Biblical Hebrew Syntax* [Winona Lake: Eisenbrauns, 1990], p. 439).

23. Wildberger, *Isaiah 1–12*, pp. 303–304. Similarly Bostock, *Portrayal*, pp. 197–198: 'it
    is belief in YHWH or his word that [Isaiah] is expected to promote'.

Isaiah 8:16–18

These verses conclude the so-called *Denkschrift* of 6:1 – 8:18, covering Isaiah's call and his interaction with Ahaz during the crisis of the Syro-Ephraimite invasion. They are widely accepted as authentic to Isaiah, and usually taken to indicate a change in the nature of his prophetic role, whatever the precise meaning of the terms in verse 16 or the nature of the prophetic family as signs in verse 18. Concomitant with Isaiah's own implicit withdrawal from public ministry is YHWH's explicit withdrawal in 'hiding his face from the house of Jacob' (v. 17). Whether or not Isaiah includes himself among those from whom YHWH hides (and the text can be read both ways), he proclaims his own continued faith: 'I will wait for the LORD . . . and I will hope in him' (v. 17). This personal declaration thus complements the summons to faith addressed to royalty and populace in surrounding chapters (notably chs. 7 and 12).

Both verbs clearly express the concept of waiting in expectation. The second, *qwh*, is more common, and occurs frequently in Isaiah of those waiting for/on YHWH, as well as of the viticulturist/YHWH waiting for good grapes / justice.[24] The first, *ḥkh*, is less common, but similarly occurs in the book with reference to the faithful and YHWH.[25] These verbs have the same connotation of waiting in eagerness and hope elsewhere in the Old Testament, notably in the psalms and other prophets.[26] As Wildberger notes, 'Both verbs are very close to what Isaiah means when he uses *h'myn* (believe).'[27] So arguably where Isaiah's children are signs through their names, the prophet is a sign through his expectant faith.

Isaiah 12

The book of Isaiah contains many hymns or hymn fragments, especially in chapters 40–55, and frequently as section conclusions.[28] By common consent,

---

24. Humans: Isa. 25:9; 26:8; 33:2; 40:31; 49:23; 59:9, 11; 'coastlands': 51:5; 60:9; viticulturist/YHWH: 5:2, 4, 7.

25. Both applications in Isa. 30:18; also of the faithful in 64:4.

26. E.g. *qwh* frequently of faithful psalmists, sometimes of their enemies; *ḥkh* in Ps. 33:20 (parallels *bṭh*); Hab. 2:3; Zeph. 3:8.

27. Wildberger, *Isaiah 1–12*, p. 368.

28. Cf. the so-called 'eschatological hymns of praise' noted by C. Westermann, *Isaiah 40–66* (London: SCM, 1969), p. 102: '[40.9ff.], 42.10–13, 44.23, 45.8, 48.20f., 49.13, 52.9–10'; his 1964 article also lists 51:3(?), 54:1–2: so H. G. M. Williamson, *The Book Called Isaiah* (Oxford: Oxford University Press, 1994), p. 119, n. 8.

and whatever its origin,[29] chapter 12 fulfils this function as a conclusion to the first major section of the book, and thus implicitly expresses the praise of the faithful. Against a backdrop of societal and royal faithlessness, of prophetic call, challenge and withdrawal, of divine judgment by and on Assyria, and of the idyllic future, the surviving community will again acknowledge God's salvation and express their trust.

Chapter 12 has many features of the hymn psalms, but is set in an eschatological context by the repeated 'in that day' (vv. 1, 4).[30] Verse 1 proposes thanksgiving that YHWH has replaced anger with comfort. Verse 2 then indicates trust as the true response to divine salvation. The second half of verse 2 echoes Exodus 15:2 word for word (with the addition of *yhwh* after the distinctive *yāh*), thus paralleling this experience with that paradigmatic deliverance. Here the verb (*bṭḥ*) is used without complement, though the context leaves no room for doubt that the object of trust is YHWH himself. The concept is also absolute in that it is not complemented by a call to either activity or passivity. Trust is explicated simply as lack of fear. It leads to joy, praise and proclamation, but it is not linked to specific practical or ethical conduct.

Isaiah 13 – 27

Isaiah 13 – 23

This long, more international section of the book says much about judgment on many nations in chapters 13–23, and about cosmic judgment and personal/national deliverance in chapters 24–27. But it has only occasional glimpses of the expression of faith, and even fewer references to the vocabulary of faith. For the oracles against the foreign nations, at least, this is hardly surprising, since the emphasis here (as indeed in other prophetic books) is the condemnation and punishment of those who opposed YHWH or his people. Almost by definition such nations lacked faith, and oracles announcing their judgment do not refer to it. Nevertheless, there are a few glimpses, mostly in relation to the surviving Israelite/Judean people. These references stand out

---

29. E.g. Williamson (*Book*, pp. 118–125) attributes it largely to Deutero-Isaiah; B. S. Childs, *Isaiah*, OTL (London: SCM, 2001), pp. 108–111, accepts this, though adds that it must be interpreted in its canonical context.

30. The first occurrence introduces a singular voice and the second a plural address (already anticipated in v. 3).

from their context, and for this and other reasons are usually assigned to late redaction. But whatever their compositional origin, they have the canonical effect of illuminating the cascading waves of stern judgment with vivid shafts of hope.

Two such glimpses come in 16:4b–5 and 17:7–8. The first interrupts the diatribe against Moab with a brief vision of the Davidic king, re-established in *ḥeṣed* and *'ĕmet* (loyalty and truth), and ruling with *mišpāṭ* and *ṣedeq* (justice and righteousness). While this is linked here to the posited Judean subjugation of Moab (cf. 16:1), it is expressed in terms associated elsewhere with the re-establishment of a community faithful to Yhwh. The second comes in the enigmatic chapter 17 with its indistinct dual focus on Damascus and Israel, and predicts a future when Israelites[31] who have forgotten their God (v. 10; cf. v. 4) will look (searchingly)[32] to 'their maker . . . the Holy One of Israel' (v. 7). The descriptive terms for God and the contrast with the same gazing at man-made altars strongly implies a renewed trust in Yhwh.

Another, larger glimpse comes in chapter 19, in the remarkable portrayal of the worship of Yhwh extending from Israel in opposite directions to the two normally hostile 'superpowers', Egypt and Assyria. While parts of these several oracles may initially have envisaged a Jewish diaspora in Egypt (vv. 18–19), other parts imply the knowledge and worship of Yhwh by native Egyptians and Assyrians (vv. 21–25). This is more than the personal faith in adversity enjoined on Judeans by the prophet in chapters 1–12; it is a stunning picture of the nations coming to worship the God of Israel (cf. 2:3).

The final glimpse of faith in this section occurs in chapter 22, not in further general eschatological oracles but in the differing assessments of three individuals. One of these has busied himself improving the water supply but ignoring 'him who planned it long ago' (v. 11). While unnamed, the addressee strengthening the city against siege is clearly King Hezekiah (elsewhere supported by Isaiah). The second, roundly condemned as a self-serving disgrace, is the steward Shebna. He will be replaced by the third, Eliakim, who is contrastingly commended: Yhwh's servant, father of the people, controlling all access to the royal house, and responsible for everything (notwithstanding its eventual collapse). These three cameos of individuals whose trust in Yhwh is respectively limited, absent or strong are a good representation of the nation at large, even if issues of faith are not elaborated here.

---

31. Or perhaps humanity generally; the Heb. is simply *'ādām*.

32. nrsv's 'regard' is too weak for the first verb *š'h*, at least in current English usage.

Isaiah 24 – 27

This distinctive, proto-apocalyptic section of the book changes the focus further, with its global panoramas, temporal detachment and progressive eschatology. While these features may well imply late composition, the redactional placement of this section after the oracles against the nations serves to extend their theme of judgment to a global dimension, and to highlight the responses of faith which punctuate the cataclysmic desolation. Unlike chapters 13–23, where responses of faith are rare, here they are frequent, and the contrast with the surrounding doom is all the more vivid.

This response of faith is usually conveyed in hymnic style, notably in 24:14–16, 25:1–5 and 26:1–6.[33] The last of these echoes chapter 12 as a song of victory and trust,[34] and most noticeably in verses 3–4. Just as in 12:2 the acknowledgment of divine salvation leads to affirmation of personal trust, so here (despite significant textual difficulties)[35] the experience of victory and protection (v. 1) leads first to the affirmation of faithfulness and trust ('*mn*, *bṭḥ*), then to its command (vv. 2–4). And as elsewhere, there is an explicit link with righteousness (*ṣdq*, v. 2) and peace (*šālôm*, v. 3). Also, as in chapter 12, the faithfulness of some contrasts markedly with the faithlessness of others, here Moabites (25:10b–12) and the wicked (26:10).

The response to YHWH of waiting in expectation, linked elsewhere explicitly to faith, is also represented in this section. The cry of despair in 24:16b ('I pine away. Woe is me!') is followed by inexorable punishment (24:17–23), exultant praise (25:1–5), defeat of death and restoration of the people by YHWH, for which and for whom they have waited (*qwh*, twice, 25:9). Other aspects of faith are related in ensuing verses: despite unbelieving rulers (whose shades will not rise), the righteous 'acknowledge [YHWH's] name alone' and seek him in earnest prayer (26:13, 16), and as a result will celebrate resurrection (26:19).[36] Whether these two references to the defeat of death envisage national restoration to Jerusalem, as in the final verses of the section (27:12–13), or personal resurrection from the dead, they amply illustrate the theme of faith in times of extreme (if non-historicized) trial.

---

33. The issues of whether these should be described as hymns or hymnic fragments and if so their exact delineation are not immediately relevant.

34. So Childs, *Isaiah*, p. 190: the unit is portrayed like an eschatological song, but sung in Judah.

35. See e.g. H. Wildberger, *Isaiah 13–27* (Minneapolis: Fortress, 1997), pp. 542–543.

36. For exegesis of this difficult verse, as well as commentaries, see P. S. Johnston, *Shades of Sheol: Death and Afterlife in the Old Testament* (Leicester: Apollos, 2002), pp. 224–225.

Isaiah 28 – 35

The perspective given in chapters 7 and 36–39, linked to particular kings and events, is also reflected in this more anthological collection of oracles, as illustrated by several key verses.

Isaiah 28:16

Jaap Dekker has recently written a 400-page monograph on this one verse and attendant issues, notably its exegesis in context, the Zion tradition in Isaiah and the Old Testament in general, and its interpretation in later traditions. In sum, he argues that 'the stone . . . refers to the rock-solid foundation that YHWH has established in Zion', that is, 'his choice to dwell in/on Zion' (cf. 8:18).[37] The verse presents a positive contrast to the perversity displayed by those who are condemned in the surrounding verses.

The closing phrase of verse 16 is of particular interest here: 'One who trusts will not panic.' Dekker argues with good reason that, as in 7:9, the verb *'mn* means faith 'in an absolute sense', that is, faith in God generally rather than in any particular prophetic promise or theological perspective.

> Just as the 'faith statement' of 7:9 should be understood against the background of YHWH's salvific activity on behalf of the house of David, so the 'faith statement' of 28:16 acquires its expressiveness from the salvific activities of YHWH with respect to Zion.[38]

Dekker also plausibly defends the traditional interpretation of the final two words (*lo' yāḥîš*) as 'shall not hurry off' (contra LXX: 'shall not be ashamed') and referring 'to the search for refuge in Egypt and to a more general religious sense of inner conflict'.[39] However, one could go further and see this as echoing the repeated prophetic encouragement to rest and quietness (cf. 30:15; 32:17).

Isaiah 30:15

This verse comes in a series of oracles that warn against reliance on Egypt (30:1–7), record the rejection of YHWH and his prophets (30:8–14) and predict failure of reliance on military means (30:15–17). Most scholars accept that at least verses 9–17 originate from Isaiah of Jerusalem and reflect his

---

37. Dekker, *Zion's Rock-Solid Foundations*, p. 344.
38. Ibid, p. 141.
39. Ibid, p. 143.

perspective.[40] Verse 15 seems to advocate the return to YHWH and trust in him, in contrast to the reliance on horses as a means of escape. However, two key terms in this verse are hapax legomena, and some scholars have argued against their traditional interpretation, as follows:[41] (1) *šûbâ* should be derived not from *šûb* but rather *yšb*, to give 'sitting, stillness'. (2) *biṭḥâ* should be interpreted as 'calmness', given the use elsewhere of the root *bṭḥ* with prepositions. But Wildberger and Wong both defend the traditional interpretation at length and convincingly, arguing that *šûbâ* here does indicate a turning in trust.[42] Wildberger concludes:

> Isaiah expected a substantive change in diplomacy. That change would not simply be to do nothing, but it would be a political stance based on faith that could not adequately be described as 'anti-military.' His political program was that the leaders would get themselves away from interactions with the major powers, moving instead toward a way of acting that assumed an inner peace that could be given by faith alone.[43]

Isaiah 32:17

Chapter 32 is framed by two eschatological glimpses of righteous justice, the first (vv. 1–8) effected by king and princes, the second (vv. 15–20) by 'a spirit from on high' (15). The latter gives the strongest link yet between our current theme of calm and trust[44] and another great Isaianic theme, that of justice and righteousness.[45] Many scholars conclude that verses 15–20 are later than Isaiah of Jerusalem.[46] Nevertheless, the themes of verse 15 are similar to those of the prophet himself, not least that of peaceful trust.

---

40. So G. C. I. Wong, 'Faith and Works in Isaiah xxx 15', *VT* 47 (1997), pp. 236–246; here p. 236.

41. Variously Dahood, Høgenhaven, Huber and Gonçalves; so Wong, ibid., pp. 238–240.

42. H. Wildberger, *Isaiah 28–39*, tr. T. H. Trapp, CC (Minneapolis: Fortress, 2002); and Wong, 'Faith and Works'.

43. Wildberger, *Isaiah 28–39*, p. 161.

44. Ibid., p. 256, follows Duhm and others in querying *hašqēṭ*, since it is ignored by the LXX and the colon is too long.

45. There are some links elsewhere, though note comment above on the attempt by Wong ('Faith . . . Isaiah vii') to link chs. 1 and 7.

46. Cf. Wildberger, *Isaiah 28–39*, p. 259, 'Most unlike Isaiah is the expectation that the spirit will be poured out . . . Isaiah himself would have spoken about Yahweh himself coming down . . . ' Also Williamson by implication in *Book*, pp. 226, 238.

Isaiah 36 – 39

Faith in Yʜᴡʜ is a key theme in these chapters, with the frequent occurrence of *bṭḥ* (esp. in Assyrian taunts) and with the response of faith by Hezekiah and Isaiah. The root *bṭḥ* comes eight times as a verb and once as a complementary noun.[47] These chapters are of course closely paralleled in 2 Kings 18 – 20, where there is one further occurrence in the laudatory introduction to Hezekiah's reign (18:5). For several recent scholars, the fact that *bṭḥ* occurs frequently elsewhere in Isaiah but so rarely elsewhere in Genesis–Kings[48] suggests that these Hezekiah narratives originated not in the Deuteronomistic History but in the Isaiah corpus or independently.[49] There are also links with the theme of trust, whether appropriate (in Yʜᴡʜ) or inappropriate (in Egypt), in many of the Isaiah texts already discussed.[50] Thus chapters 1–35 give a prior theological context to the theme of trust in chapters 36–37 (unlike the setting in 2 Kings, which has only one prior reference, albeit to Hezekiah's trust).

The Rabshakeh ridicules Hezekiah's confidence (36:4), and questions him and the people for their trust: in Egypt and its horses (36:5–6, 9); in Yʜᴡʜ when his altars have been removed (36:7); and in Yʜᴡʜ when the city is doomed (36:15). The last taunt is then repeated in Hezekiah's prayer to Yʜᴡʜ (37:15).[51] By contrast, Hezekiah's prayer focuses on Yʜᴡʜ's kingship over all the earth, and Isaiah's response concludes with Yʜᴡʜ's promise 'I will defend this city to save it, for my own sake and for the sake of my servant David' (37:35).[52]

---

47. Isa. 36:4 (verb and noun), 5–6 (twice), 7, 9, 15; 37:10; paralleled in 2 Kgs 18:19 (verb and noun), 20–21 (twice), 22, 24, 30; 19:10. By contrast, *bṭḥ* occurs twelve times in chs. 1–35 and five times in chs. 40–66; see J. W. Olley, '"Trust in the Lord": Hezekiah, Kings and Isaiah', *TynBul* 50 (1999), pp. 66–69.

48. Only three times: Deut. 28:52; Judg. 9:26; 20:36. All these 'have similarities to the Hezekiah context' (Olley, 'Trust', p. 63).

49. So ibid., pp. 74–75, followed by Bostock, *Portrayal*, p. 174, citing variously Smelik, Seitz, Konkel. J. W. Groves, *Actualization and Interpretation in the Old Testament* (Atlanta: Scholars Press, 1987), pp. 197–198, lists many connections between 36 – 39 and earlier chapters, including reliance on Yʜᴡʜ rather than Egypt.

50. Olley, 'Trust', pp. 66–68; Bostock, *Portrayal*, pp. 174–175.

51. Olley, 'Trust', pp. 64–65, expands these three types of reliance to five, but his first and third relate to Egypt, and his fourth and fifth to Yʜᴡʜ (Hezekiah's role is really secondary).

52. As Olley, ibid, p. 65, notes, this is the 'first reference in the whole narrative to

The deliverance of Jerusalem in 701 has often been associated with the so-called doctrine of the inviolability of Zion, variously as a pre-existing view adopted by Isaiah, or one developed by him, or a later extrapolation from this event. Of the passages dealing with faith noted so far, only this narrative links trust in YHWH with the explicit promise of Jerusalem's preservation. This point alone lends credence to the detailed arguments of Olley and Wong that this was not an integral aspect of Isaiah's theology, even if it was a specific promise on this one crucial occasion.

Isaiah 40 – 55

With chapters 40–55 we come to a different prophetic voice, a different literary style and a different prospective audience. The overall message is clearly one of encouragement to renew trust in YHWH, yet the terms for trust discussed above are used rarely here. However, they are not entirely absent, and occur in two key texts.

Isaiah 43:10

Here the leitmotif of servant is joined with that of witness, but with a surprising outcome. Normally the role of a witness is to give testimony to a third party, as in the previous verse (43:9). There God ostensibly challenges 'the nations' and 'the peoples' to produce witnesses, to testify that some among them have foretold 'the former things' – clearly a rhetorical challenge, making the point that there were no foretellers, and so there can be no such witnesses. Here in verse 10 YHWH nominates his chosen servant Israel as his witness. But, contrary to expectation, this is not (or at least not explicitly) in order that they would testify that YHWH had foretold these former things (and indeed would bring them to pass). Instead it is that they themselves would 'know . . . believe . . . understand'. It may well be, as Ward suggests, that 'by serving God as witnesses – prophets, teachers, lawgivers – Israel herself comes to know and believe more fully'; that is, faith builds upon faith.[53] Such a process is not spelt out, yet the verse focuses on the transformation of the witness and ignores the content of the testimony. For Whybray, this is a key verse: '[Deutero-Isaiah] here states what is the real aim of this oracle and indeed of

---

Davidic kingship'. In Kings the promise is repeated in the ensuing episode of Hezekiah's healing (2 Kgs 20:6), but not in the Isaiah account (Isa. 38:6).

53. Ward, 'Faith', p. 330.

his whole work, that the *exiles*, his audience, should be convinced of Yahweh's power.'[54]

This is the only verse in Isaiah 40 – 55 which uses *'mn* (hiphil) for belief in YHWH, though it also occurs for hypothetical belief in a prophetic report (53:1).[55] Here it is the second of three verbs which together portray the desired response. Some commentators stress the development from one term to another; so Oswalt: 'synonymous parallelism does not imply a static relationship among the terms but a developing one'; others, their combined effect; so Westermann: 'These three verbs refer to one and the same process.'[56] The verbs are different syntactically, which tends to bring out their distinct nuances: *yd'* (know) has no complement, though probably assumes 'YHWH' rather than simply 'this'; *'mn* (believe) has *l* with pronominal suffix for YHWH;[57] *byn* (understand) has a subordinate clause introduced by *kî*. Nevertheless, the substantive point is that belief, or perhaps better here 'conviction', is focused on YHWH and is associated with knowing and understanding.

Isaiah 50:10

This coda or postscript to the third so-called servant song[58] contains the only use in Deutero-Isaiah of *bṭḥ* in a positive sense.[59] The syntax of the verse is ambiguous, in that the relative clause of the second bicolon ('who walks

---

54. R. N. Whybray, *Isaiah 40–66*, NCBC (London: Marshall, Morgan & Scott, 1975), p. 85; emphasis original.

55. *'mn* niphal occurs of YHWH (49:7) and his 'sure love for David' (55:3), and *'mn* qal of 'foster fathers' (49:23).

56. J. N. Oswalt, *The Book of Isaiah Chapters 40–66*, NICOT (Grand Rapids: Eerdmans, 1998), p. 147, referencing Calvin for Isa. 43:10 and Alter for parallelism; Westermann, *Isaiah 40–66*, p. 122.

57. *DCH* (1:316) overlooks this, including the verse under '1a . . . trust someone' rather than '1c . . . trust Y'. Both *l* and *b* are used before a personal object.

58. It is not necessary to discuss here the delineation of these 'songs' or the concept generally.

59. Elsewhere the verb occurs for trust in images (42:17) and wickedness (47:10), and the adverb for false security (*lābeṭaḥ*, 47:8). Cf. J. Goldingay, *The Message of Isaiah 40–55* (London: T. & T. Clark, 2005), p. 414, 'As Isa. 40–55 does not elsewhere refer to *yir'â* with the positive connotation of reverence rather than fear, so it does not elsewhere refer to trust in a positive way, only to mis-located trust: see 42.17; 47.8, 10. The collocation of the two here in v. 10 shows that there is no tension between reverence and trust . . .'

... no light') could possibly apply to the servant (*'abdî* immediately precedes *'ăšer*),[60] but more likely applies to those addressed ('Who among you ... ?').[61] Nevertheless, the third bicolon clearly envisages the addressee(s), and its imperfects are better translated as jussives ('let him trust ... and rely ... ').[62] This small ambiguity, however, makes no difference to the overall sense, since the question calls for imitators of YHWH's servant, and the trust enjoined should characterize servant and followers alike.

The servant's trust is amply demonstrated in the previous verses (4–9): he listens to YHWH,[63] is not rebellious, submits to insult and injury, knows (*yd'*) that he will be not shamed but vindicated, and affirms divine aid. And in verse 10 the servant's followers walk trustfully in darkness without light. This collocation of knowledge and trust is reminiscent of 43:10, though with a different focus. There the nation servant would know YHWH, here the apparently individual servant (however identified) knows future vindication. A further intriguing link appears in verse 9. The persecuted servant describes YHWH as 'my vindicator' (*maṣdîqî*) or 'the one who makes/declares me righteous'.[64] The servant is not described directly as 'righteous' (*ṣaddîq*, or showing *ṣedeq/ṣĕdāqâ*), but his assurance that YHWH will establish him as righteous implies a similar link between reliance on YHWH and appropriate behaviour. The difference with earlier texts is that in Proto-Isaiah such behaviour was generally public and proactive in bringing *ṣedeq* and *mišpāṭ* to others, whereas here it is more private and reactive in teaching and example.

While there are few explicit references to faith/trust in Deutero-Isaiah, they are nonetheless indicative of the section more generally. These chapters ostensibly address an exiled community,[65] and often portray it as enfeebled and dispirited, so their primary focus is that of comfort and reassurance followed by exhortation and challenge. There is a constant presentation of YHWH as powerful over all nations yet continually interested in his chosen people, and of the imminence of his instigating 'new things'. There is a repeated injunction

---

60. Oswalt, *Isaiah 40–66*, p. 327, n. 41, incorrectly attributes this view to J. D. W. Watts, *Isaiah 34–66*, WBC 25 (Waco: Word, 1987), RSV and NEB. RSV and NRSV are ambiguous; NEB follows the majority.

61. So most translations and commentators; e.g. Oswalt, *Isaiah 40–66*, p. 329.

62. So Westermann, *Isaiah 40–66*, p. 232 (unaffected by his reordering of 50:10 – 51:8); Oswalt, *Isaiah 40–66*, p. 328; Childs, *Isaiah*, p. 390.

63. Here *'ădōnāy yhwh*, usually 'Lord GOD' in English versions.

64. *mišpāṭ* occurs in the same verse, but of the servant's opponent as *ba'al mišpāṭî*.

65. Regardless of later addition and redaction.

not to fear, which is really the opposite of trust. And there are positive portrayals of servanthood to which the addressees should aspire. Faith and trust
may not be directly linked with righteousness and justice as earlier in the book,
but then an exiled community was not in a position to put these concepts into
practice in the sociopolitical sphere.

Isaiah 56 – 66

The final major section of the book of Isaiah presents another set of texts
with perspectives that are different again. Emmerson speaks of the 'insoluble
problems' and 'bewilderingly diverse content' of these chapters, and notes
that they 'have sometimes been regarded as little more than an appendix,
compiled from rather random material'.[66] Nevertheless, many now see in this
section a concentric or chiastic pattern centred on chapters 60–62, with broad
agreement on the general pattern if not the details or its compilation history.[67] Rather differently, Childs proposes a linear pattern with progression, and
speaks more confidently of intent: 'Above all, Third Isaiah serves consciously
to unite the major themes of both First and Second Isaiah into one literary
composition.'[68] However, few others are as confident of this.

What then of faith in Trito-Isaiah? The immediately striking feature is a
further progression in vocabulary from the other two sections. While Proto-
Isaiah has many relevant occurrences of *'mn* and *bṭḥ*, and Deutero-Isaiah has
a few significant ones, Trito-Isaiah has none. Nowhere in this section are
these roots used of the appropriate response to YHWH by those addressed.[69]
This may of course be fortuitous – the number of relevant occurrences of
these terms in the other sections (excluding *bṭḥ* in chs. 36–37) is relatively
low, so their absence here may not be statistically significant. But it remains
suggestive.

At the same time, there are several other important expressions for those
who exercise faith. They 'hold fast' (*ḥzq*, hiphil) to *mišpāṭ* and *ṣĕdāqâ* (56:2; cf.

---

66. G. I. Emmerson, *Isaiah 56–66*, OTG (Sheffield: Sheffield Academic Press, 1992),
    pp. 12–13.

67. E.g. Westermann, *Isaiah 40–66*, pp. 296–308; Emmerson, *Isaiah*, pp. 15–23; P. A.
    Smith, *Rhetoric and Redaction in Trito-Isaiah*, VTSup 62 (Leiden: Brill, 1995); J.
    Blenkinsopp, *Isaiah 56–66*, AB 19B (New York: Doubleday, 2003), pp. 38–40.

68. Childs, *Isaiah*, p. 447.

69. *Bṭḥ* occurs once negatively (59:4); *'mn* of nursing (60:4) and of God (65:16, twice).

v. 1), to YHWH's covenant (56:4, 6), and to YHWH himself (64:7; Heb. v. 6).[70]
They are righteous and devout (57:1), humble and contrite (57:18; 66:2),[71] and
tremble at YHWH's word (66:2, 5). Of these terms, only the verb *ḥzq* (hold
fast) connotes the same active faith as *'mn* and *bṭḥ*, and is linked like them to
mišpāṭ and *ṣĕdāqâ*. The other expressions describe the faithful aptly, but more
in terms of their personal disposition than their response to YHWH.

Overall this suggests that the oracles envisage a more passive, quietist
response. The awaiting of divine salvation and deliverance (*yĕšû'â*, *ṣĕdāqâ*)
recalls that enjoined on Ahaz (and later the exiles) and practised by Hezekiah,
but the focus on cult (e.g. ch. 56) and on personal disposition differs from the
sociopolitical expectations of earlier times.

Conclusion

Faith is certainly as central in the book of Isaiah as elsewhere in the Bible. The
context for faith changed considerably from monarchy to exile to restoration,
and those displaying or failing to display faith ranged from individuals like
prophet and monarch to world powers like Egypt and Assyria. Nevertheless,
there is a noticeable shift in the second half of the book to communal faith in
times of difficulty and doubt, and to faith evidenced in personal disposition as
much as, if not more than, in social action. This conclusion is hardly surprising, given the religious and political developments over the period.

This shift in emphasis enriches the canonical book as a resource for appropriation by later believers, since it presents paradigms of faith appropriate for
several different contexts. Wildberger fittingly concludes the preface to his
monumental study with the striking challenge of Isaiah 7:9b, preceded by the
sentence 'The central theme of Isaiah's proclamation is as timely today as it
was in the time of the prophet.'[72]

© Philip S. Johnston, 2009

---

70. Cf. *ḥzq* for faith earlier in Isa., 27:5, 'let [the vineyard] cling to me for protection';
    35:4, 'Say to those who are of a fearful heart, / "Be strong . . . "'
71. 57:1, *ṣaddîq* (twice) and *'anšê ḥesed šāpāl* and *dk'* (niphal); 66:2, *'ānî ûnĕkê rûaḥ*.
72. Wildberger, *Isaiah 1–12*, p. vii.

6. NATIONALISM AND UNIVERSALISM IN ISAIAH

Richard L. Schultz

And they shall declare my glory among the nations.

(Isa. 66:19 NRSV)

Introduction: nationalism and universalism as a theological problem in Isaiah

As the book of Isaiah nears the conclusion of its remarkable sweep of Israelite and redemptive history, the prophet speaks of a time in the future when Israelite survivors of divine judgment will be dispatched in all directions as far as the distant coastlands to declare the Lord's 'glory among the nations' (66:19).[1] According to Horst Dietrich Preuss, this is the 'only possible discussion of an active missionary involvement' in the Old Testament.[2] Constituting one of its major themes, references to Israel in its relationship to the nations are found throughout the book of Isaiah. This theme also presents one of the book's most complex theological problems, for

---

1. Unless stated otherwise, all translations are from the NIV.
2. H. D. Preuss, *Old Testament Theology*, vol. 2, tr. L. G. Perdue, OTL (Louisville: Westminster John Knox, 1996), p. 303.

the canonical bugle called 'Isaiah' gives an indistinct sound regarding the nations' role and future within the divine plan. Six distinct perspectives can be identified:[3] the nations as agents of God's judgment, as objects of divine wrath and judgment, as recipients of unmediated divine blessing and election, as witnesses to God's salvific and punitive actions, as facilitators and servants following Israel's post-exile restoration to Jerusalem, and as participants in the salvation and worship of the one true God mediated through and alongside Israel. In sum, some Isaianic texts are more nationalistic in focus while others are more universalistic, and these two polar emphases cannot easily be harmonized.

Methodology

Clarification of definition

Some studies view this theme politically, noting Isaiah's focus on Israel's present and future existence as a flourishing nation in the Promised Land and questioning whether the book refers to other nations only as they relate to that future. Most, however, have a primary religious interest,[4] analysing to what extent Isaiah envisions the nations as some day sharing in Israel's divinely bestowed spiritual blessings. Since Israel's political-economic circumstances are deeply entwined with its religious status and practices, in keeping with its covenantal commitments, it can be difficult to determine the precise import

---

3. Helpful summaries are offered by G. I. Davies, 'The Destiny of the Nations in the Book of Isaiah', in J. Vermeylen (ed.), *The Book of Isaiah*, BETL 81 (Louvain: Leuven University Press, 1989), pp. 93–120; H. F. van Rooy, 'The Nations in Isaiah: A Synchronic Survey', OTWSA 22–23 (1979–80), pp. 213–229; and J. N. Oswalt, 'The Nations in Isaiah: Friend or Foe; Servant or Partner', *BBR* 16 (2006), pp. 41–51.

4. As expressed e.g. in descriptions of worship, missionary outreach, the revelation of divine glory or 'light', assurances of deliverance or salvation, and the administration of justice. See esp. C. T. Begg, 'The Peoples and the Worship of Yahweh in the Book of Isaiah', in M. P. Graham et al. (eds.), *Worship and the Hebrew Bible: Essays in Honour of John T. Willis*, JSOTSup 284 (Sheffield: Sheffield Academic Press, 1999), pp. 35–55; and R. E. Clements, 'A Light to the Nations: A Central Theme of the Book of Isaiah', in P. R. House and J. W. Watts (eds.), *Forming Prophetic Literature: Essays on Isaiah and the Twelve in Honor of John D. W. Watts*, JSOTSup 235 (Sheffield: Sheffield Academic Press, 1996), pp. 57–69.

of various, often poetic and metaphorically formulated, prophetic promises and threats.[5] Furthermore, the Hebrew semantic field of 'salvation' includes deliverance 'from every type of danger and distress, physical, spiritual and psychological'.[6] Accordingly, in the following analysis, I am looking for textual evidence of *relational, attitudinal, and moral-behavioural transformation* displayed by Israel, the nations or both groups viewed together.

Approaches to nationalism and universalism in Isaiah

Before offering a somewhat neglected textual focus for this issue, I will offer a brief analysis of past representative studies of nationalism and universalism in the book of Isaiah.[7]

Denial of the existence of a theological tension or of the need to resolve it. For Norman Snaith and R. N. Whybray, nationalism swallows up universalism. Israel is the elect nation with no missionary task, and the nations will be abased, submitting to Yahweh's universal assertions of sovereignty.[8] For Sigmund Mowinckel and Norman Gottwald, universalism swallows up nationalism. Israel's election and entire history are merely the preparatory means for its missionary responsibility.[9] For G. I. Davies, no effort need be

---

5. D. B. Sandy, *Plowshares and Pruning Hooks: Rethinking the Language of Biblical Prophecy and Apocalyptic* (Downers Grove: IVP, 2002), offers the most thorough treatment of this issue.

6. J. F. A. Sawyer, *Semantics in Biblical Research: New Methods of Defining Hebrew Words for Salvation*, SBT 2nd Series 24 (Naperville: Allenson, 1972), p. 46.

7. The following analysis draws extensively on the survey of past literature by A. Kebede, 'How Can the Concepts of Universalism and Nationalism in the Book of Isaiah be Reconciled?' (PhD diss., New Orleans Baptist Theological Seminary, 2002), pp. 1–46, although the categorization of approaches is mine. In the following comments I will use the designation 'Isaiah' simply to refer to the prophet/author as a label of convenience to avoid explaining each summarized scholar's understanding of the book's compositional history.

8. N. H. Snaith, 'The Servant of the Lord in Deutero-Isaiah', in H. H. Rowley (ed.), *Studies in Old Testament Prophecy* (New York: Charles Scribner's Sons, 1950), pp. 191–200; R. N. Whybray, *The Second Isaiah*, OTG (Sheffield: Sheffield Academic Press, 1995), pp. 63–65.

9. S. Mowinckel, *He That Cometh*, tr. G. W. Anderson (New York: Abingdon, 1954), pp. 207, 250; N. K. Gottwald, *All the Kingdoms of the Earth: Israelite Prophecy and International Relations in the Ancient Near East* (New York: Harper & Row, 1964), pp. 207–208, 330, 343.

made to present a unified perspective, since the book simply offers a 'bill-board' of viewpoints.[10]

Redaction-critical. C. C. Torrey and Paul Dion attribute problematic nationalist-ic texts to later interpolations or assign these two emphases to separate redac-tional layers, thereby offering an *explanation* of the tension but no *resolution.* Here one employs a *history of religions* approach, which posits a development from nationalism to universalism followed by late resurgent nationalism.[11]

Tradition-critical. According to Joachim Begrich, Isaiah simply inherited nationalistic traditions that he was unable or unwilling to change.[12]

Socio-historical. Joseph Blenkinsopp explains individual texts as reflecting specific developments within the Israelite community. For example, Isaiah 66 merely presents 'the dreams and fantasies' of one segment of post-exilic Judaism. Taking a more author-centred approach, Johannes Lindblom sug-gests that Isaiah changed his mind on this issue in the light of changing his-torical realities.[13]

Rhetorical. Julius Bewer claims that Isaiah's nationalist emphasis is intended to appeal to Israel's pride following their prior negative response to his uni-versalistic promises. According to Deryck Sheriffs, Second Isaiah's nationalist assertions are a polemic against Babylonian nationalism.[14]

Semantic. P. A. H. de Boer takes the promise of *mišpāṭ* as referring to 'judg-ment against' the nations rather than 'justice for' the nations. Mark Long argues that 'Israel' in Isaiah sometimes designates only *true* Israel, while D. E. Hollenberg contends that the term 'nations' also includes Israel. J. Severino Croatto understands 'nations' terms as *geographical* rather than *ethnic/political* designations (i.e. the location of diaspora Jews).[15]

---

10. Davies, 'Destiny', p. 106.

11. C. C. Torrey, *The Second Isaiah: A New Interpretation* (New York: Charles Scribner's Sons, 1928), pp. 120–121; P.-E. Dion, 'L'Universalisme religieux dans les différentes couches rédactionelles d'Is. 40–55', *Bib* 51 (1970), pp. 161–182.

12. J. Begrich, *Studien zu Deuterojesaja*, TB 20 (Munich: Chr. Kaiser, 1963).

13. J. Blenkinsopp, 'Second Isaiah – Prophet of Universalism', *JSOT* 41 (1988), pp. 98–99; J. Lindblom, *The Servant Songs in Deutero-Isaiah: A New Attempt to Solve an Old Problem* (Lund: Gleerup, 1951), pp. 66–67, 73.

14. J. A. Bewer, *The Literature of the Old Testament* (New York: Columbia University Press, 1933), pp. 207–208; D. Sheriffs, '"A Tale of Two Cities": Nationalism in Zion and Babylon', *TynBul* 39 (1988), pp. 19–57.

15. P. A. H. de Boer, *Second Isaiah's Message* (Leiden: Brill, 1956), pp. 90–91; M. T. Long, 'The Inclusion of the Nations in Isaiah 40–66', *Theological Educator* 44 (1961),

Intertextual. Hyun Chul Kim views the rich intratextuality of Isaiah as producing 'purposeful ambiguity'. Elmer Martens finds in intertextual and intratextual connections involving central Isaianic texts a warrant for expanding the book's 'missionizing' emphasis.[16]

Redemptive-historical or logical. Some posit a sequence of developments that encompasses both nationalistic and universalistic phases. For example, the nations are first punished, then transformed (Gottwald), or salvation comes only through restored Israel as the nations witness and desire Israel's exaltation (Davidson).[17]

Hermeneutical/theological. Lindblom and Davidson attribute the tension to divine mystery or paradox. D. W. van Winkle and Anthony Gelston identify non-exclusive polarities, such as Israel's unique status *and* the nations' inclusion in salvation, or the salvation *and* submission of the nations. Another claim is that Isaiah announces experiences that will be shared by both Israel *and* the nations: only individuals will be saved (Aschalew Kebede), while all of the wicked will be judged (Roman Halas).[18] Rikk Watts suggests that the judgment and salvation of the nations represent alternative conditional destinies that individual (survivors from the) nations will receive on the basis of their response to Yahweh's self-revelation and their treatment of Israel.[19]

Footnote 15 *(continued)*

    pp. 85–92; D. E. Hollenberg, 'Nationalism and the Nations in Isaiah 40–55', *VT* 19 (1969), pp. 23–36; J. S. Croatto, 'The "Nations" in the Salvific Oracles of Isaiah', *VT* 55 (2005), pp. 143–161.

16. H. C. P. Kim, *Ambiguity, Tension, and Multiplicity in Deutero-Isaiah*, SBL 52 (New York: Peter Lang, 2003), pp. 205–216; E. A. Martens, 'Impulses to Mission in Isaiah: An Intertextual Exploration', *BBR* 17 (2007), p. 215.

17. Gottwald, *All the Kingdoms*, p. 208; R. Davidson, 'Universalism in Second Isaiah', *SJT* 16 (1963), pp. 171–173. Oswalt, 'Nations in Isaiah', pp. 41–42, offers a harmonious ten-step sequence.

18. Lindblom, *Servant Songs*, p. 73; Davidson, 'Universalism in Second Isaiah', pp. 174–175; D. W. van Winkle, 'The Relationship of the Nations to Yahweh and to Israel in Isaiah 40–55', *VT* 35 (1985), pp. 446–458; A. Gelston, 'Universalism in Second Isaiah', *JTS* 43 (1992), pp. 377–398; Kebede, 'How Can the Concepts', p. 250; R. Halas, 'The Universalism of Isaias', *CBQ* 12 (1950), pp. 162–170.

19. R. E. Watts, 'Echoes from the Past: Israel's Ancient Traditions and the Destiny of the Nations in Isaiah 40–55', *JSOT* 28 (2004), pp. 505–508. Watts traces these two alternatives back to the earlier Abrahamic, exodus, conquest and Davidic-Solomonic traditions concerning the relationship between Israel and the nations.

Limitations of past studies and features of the current study

Although the literature examining this issue is extensive and insightful, several common limitations must be noted: (1) a focus on only one section of the book, especially Second Isaiah; (2) a focus on only one dimension of the theme, such as election or missions; (3) readings of individual texts that expand or reduce the universalistic emphasis in Isaiah; (4) a tendency to overlook possible references to distinctive groups within both Israel and the nations; (5) an inadequate effort to resolve the apparent tension between nationalism and universalism, implicitly suggesting that this is impossible or unnecessary.

In an effort to offer a new perspective on this issue, this chapter will feature four elements: (1) an examination of the distribution and confluence of the various terms that make up the semantic field of the 'nations'; (2) a focus on the contextual units in which these terms are concentrated and on the contribution of the interplay between these terms to thematic development within the major sections of the book; (3) a synchronic approach to the book; and (4) a consideration of the significant intertextual links between 'nationalistic' or 'universalistic' texts.

Particular election and the universal offer of salvation

Thesis

Within the canonical book of Isaiah, particular election, which brings Israel divine blessing and restoration following judgment and exile, is presented as the primary – but not exclusive – means of extending a future universal offer of salvation to the nations that unfolds gradually and thus is not within the purview of every section of the book. This thesis is supported by the semantic data related to the 'nations' and thematic development within the book.[20]

The semantic data and their distribution

The four primary terms from the semantic field of 'nations', *'am* (people), *gôy* (nation), *'î* (coastland), and *lĕ'ôm* (population group), occur a total of 230 times within the book of Isaiah (128× in chs. 1–39, 56× in chs. 40–55 and 46× in chs. 56–66). It would be problematic, however, to limit an analysis of the issue of nationalism and universalism in Isaiah to those texts that use one or more

---

20. As summarized in R. L. Schultz, 'Isaiah, Book of', in K. J. Vanhoozer (gen. ed.), *Dictionary for Theological Interpretation of the Bible* (Grand Rapids: Baker, 2005), pp. 338–341.

of these terms. A comprehensive study of this theme must include expressions such as 'the end(s) of the earth', 'the inhabitants of the earth' and 'all flesh', as well as texts that name specific nations and peoples. A number of insights can be derived from an analysis of the use and combination of these terms in Isaiah.[21]

'Am is used more frequently in Isaiah (130×) than the other three terms combined, appearing 25 times in the plural, all with reference to the nations and often in parallelism with *gôyyîm*. Nearly all of the remaining uses refer to Israel or a subset of Israel (28:14; 30:19; 33:24), often occurring with a pronominal suffix (49×), usually denoting Yahweh. Also noteworthy is the pejorative expression 'this people' (10× regarding Israel). *Gôy* (72×) is the preferred term to refer to foreign nations in the book of Isaiah. It usually occurs in the plural but can denote specific foreign nations in the singular (14:32; 18:2, 7); 'all the nations' is a common phrase (12×). Surprisingly, *gôy* clearly refers to Israel at least 7 times, perhaps thereby equating Israel with other nations. Most of the 17 occurrences of *'î* are in chapters 40–66 (12× – all plural). *'î* often appears to refer to the farthest places of the earth (41:5; 49:1; 60:9; 66:19), specifically the coastlands or islands. The *'iyyîm* are distant places from which God will bring back his people (11:11; 60:9; 66:19). They are subject to judgment but also may look forward to a more positive future. Of the four terms, *lĕ'ôm* is used the least frequently in Isaiah (11×, 8 in chs. 40–66). It is always plural, except in 51:4, and always refers to foreign nations, apparently as a poetic complement or as an archaic term.

Although *'am* and *gôy* appear together frequently as parallel, and apparently interchangeable, terms, especially in chapters 1–33, there is sufficient contextual support to understand the former as designating an ethnic-cultural and the latter a political-geographic entity.[22] All four terms can be used to denote foreign nations, typically in the plural. *'am* refers predominantly to Israel, *gôy* does occasionally, *lĕ'ôm* may refer to Israel in 51:4, and *'î* never does.

Thematic development within the canonical book: reading Isaiah in reverse
The striking diversity encountered when tracing the theme of nationalism and universalism through the book of Isaiah calls for a reading strategy. Since such diversity may reflect accidental or intentional ambiguity resulting from

---

21. Most of the following statistics and observations are derived from a comprehensive analysis of the semantic field of 'nations' conducted by my doctoral student Jamie Viands.
22. R. E. Clements, '*gôy*', in *TDOT* 2:427.

the book of Isaiah's complex compositional process, one could simply let it stand.[23] Another possibility is to suggest that the initial ambiguity is progressively clarified as the book unfolds.[24] Accordingly, one can look to the culmination of the thematic development in Isaiah 65 – 66 and then read preceding texts in the light of this resolution, in effect reading Isaiah in 'reverse'. As the French literature scholar Michael Riffaterre describes this 'retroactive' process, 'the meaning of what already has been read is constantly being modified by what one is currently reading'.[25]

Therefore, I begin my examination of the developing relationship between the nation of Israel and the nations within the book of Isaiah with chapters 65–66, before returning to Isaiah 1 and moving synthetically through the book, noting how the employment of the 'nations' terms in particular texts contributes to that development.

Isaiah 65 – 66

Yahweh's lengthy response to the equally lengthy prayer for deliverance (63:15 – 64:12 [Heb. 11]) in Isaiah 65 – 66 brings the book's portrayal of the intertwined futures of Jerusalem and the nations to a dramatic conclusion. In chapter 65 the nations disappear temporarily from view as a final picture of God's people, Israel, is sketched. Striking here is the rather unexpected distinction made between two groups, God's people and his servants,[26] making clear that Israel as a whole is not being extended global assurances of future blessing. The nation as a whole (*góy*) is described as not interested (v. 1), a stubborn people (v. 2) who provoke God's anger (v. 3). Thus his people will face severe divine judgment (vv. 6–7), but not total annihilation, for the sake

---

23. See Kim, *Ambiguity*.

24. Cheryl Exum has argued this with regard to Isa. 28 – 31. See J. C. Exum, '"Whom Will he Teach Knowledge?": A Literary Approach to Isaiah 28', in D. J. A. Clines, D. M. Gunn and A. J. Hauser (eds.), *Art and Meaning: Rhetoric in Biblical Literature*, JSOTSup 19 (Sheffield: JSOT Press, 1982), pp. 108–139.

25. M. Riffaterre, 'Models of the Literary Sentence', in T. Todorov (ed.), R. Carter (tr.), *French Literary Theory Today: A Reader* (Cambridge: Cambridge University Press, 1982), p. 18. For a fuller discussion and illustration of this approach to intertextuality in Isaiah see R. L. Schultz, 'Intertextuality, Canon, and "Undecidability": Understanding Isaiah's "New Heavens and New Earth" (Isa 65:17–25)', *BBR*, forthcoming.

26. The designation 'servants' is introduced in 54:17, but in 63:17–18 the 'servants' appear to be coextensive with 'the tribes of your heritage' and 'your holy people'.

of his servants (v. 8). Accordingly, his future 'people' are now further qualified
as 'my people who have sought me' (v. 10; cf. v. 1), while others are rejected as
abandoners of Yahweh (v. 11). Their destiny will be in sharp contrast with that
of his servants (vv. 13–15). Isaiah 65:18–19 suggests that God ultimately will
create a new people to inhabit a new Jerusalem, a people who will be a source
of divine joy and will experience unending joy. This group will be his chosen
ones (v. 22; cf. 65:9, 15) and will be permanently blessed by Yahweh (v. 23).

Isaiah 66, in turn, offers a final portrait of the nations' future and their
relationship to Israel, which builds on the preceding chapter and is equally
surprising. The distinction within Israel is continued in verses 5–6, with 'your
brothers who hate you' being identified as God's enemies who will be punished
(cf. v. 14). Verse 8 picks up the promise from chapter 65 of the new creation
of both Jerusalem and its people by speaking of a land and a nation coming
into being (being born) instantaneously. Verse 12 echoes the earlier promise
of the nations' 'glory', which certainly includes their wealth (cf. 60:5, 11, 13;
61:6), flowing to Jerusalem. Whereas verse 16 speaks of Yahweh's executing
judgment on 'all flesh', with many being slain, verses 23–24 describe 'all flesh'
as coming to bow down before Yahweh and being repulsed by the worm-eaten
corpses of the slain rebels. These rebels are presumably Israelites, in the light
of the thematic use of the Hebrew *pš'* at key points throughout the book to
designate God's rebellious people.

According to Childs, 66:18–23 [24] is 'a succinct summary of eschatological
themes that occur throughout the entire book'.[27] The striking verbal parallels
between 66:17–18a and 65:2–5 in their descriptions of abominable cultic acts
indicate that it is a judgment against rebellious Israelites that is the occasion for
Yahweh's gathering 'all nations and tongues' to behold his glory in punishing
his own people. Some of the Israelites who survive this judgment will, in turn,
be sent back to the nations, including the distant coastlands, which have not
been gathered by Yahweh (v. 19; cf. v. 18), in order to declare his glory among
them. The nations will return the favour, bringing back 'Israelite brothers'
from all the nations to the Jerusalem temple and offering them, as it were, as an
accompanying grain offering (v. 20). This will be a fitting action, since Yahweh
will select some of these foreigners to serve him as cultic personnel (v. 21).
Thus 'all flesh' who still remain alive in that day will willingly and continuously
worship God. The concluding chapters of Isaiah indicate that Israel's election
also entails its judgment for rebellion, which will serve as a catalyst for the
gathering of the nations.

---

27. B. S. Childs, *Isaiah*, OTL (Louisville: Westminster John Knox, 2001), p. 542.

Isaiah 1 – 5

As the book begins, Israel is described initially as rebellious sons (1:2) and 'my people', expressing possession and pathos (1:3). Isaiah 1:4 labels God's elect 'people' as just another sinning nation (*gôy*) that is equally worthy of divine judgment. Jerusalem is indicted for spiritual harlotry (vv. 21–23), leading to the announcement of the city's purgative and redemptive judgment (vv. 24–31). The juxtaposition of the future Jerusalem as 'the righteous and faithful city' (v. 26; my tr.) with the exaltation of the mountain of the Lord's house in 2:1–5 in the more distant future suggests a redemptive-historical sequence. The latter text also introduces, rather unexpectedly, the theme of the nations in the book: 'all nations', 'many peoples', presumably not including Israel, will come to Jerusalem (vv. 2a–3a; cf. v. 4a) to seek Torah instruction and the resolution of their disputes. What is striking here is the non-role of Jerusalem, which is reduced to the locus of divine action. The description of the nations offers clear 'evidence of relational, attitudinal, and moral-behavioural transform-ation' (my definition of salvation suggested above), as they not only cease making preparations for war but also desire to 'walk in [God's] paths' (v. 3a). This future transformation of the nations prompts the prophet's concluding charge to Israel to 'walk in the light of the LORD' (v. 5). To view 2:1–4 primar-ily in terms of 'the restoration of Zion'[28] is to overlook its almost exclusive focus on the nations; Mount Zion's elevation increase is at most a means to that end. Interestingly, Isaiah 1:2 – 2:4 parallels Isaiah 65 – 66 in contrasting the judgment of idolatrous Jerusalem with the pure worship offered there by the nations, offering an interpretative framework for understanding the relationship between Israel and the nations in the book as a whole.

The prophet's admonition in 2:5 is warranted by the people's current conduct and resulting abandonment by the Lord (2:6–7). The sequence in 3:12–15 is noteworthy: the Lord is about to take his stand (part.) and judge the guilty 'peoples' (v. 13),[29] but enters (impf.) specifically into judgment against the elders of 'his people' (v. 14), who are 'crushing my people' (v. 15), since the destroyers of his 'vineyard' are insiders. God announces his intention to allow

---

28. See e.g. C. R. Seitz, 'Isaiah 1–66: Making Sense of the Whole', in C. R. Seitz (ed.), *Reading and Preaching the Book of Isaiah* (Philadelphia: Fortress, 1988), p. 116.

29. H. G. M. Williamson, *Isaiah 1–5*, ICC (London: T. & T. Clark, 2006), p. 265, explains the plural as implying that 'God's anticipated judgment of the foreign nations is turned against his own people', but prefers to emend it to 'his people', supported by LXX and Syr, in which case all occurrences of *'am* in 3:12–15 would have a pronominal suffix.

his 'vineyard' to be trampled and filled with briers and thorns (5:5–6), this vague reference to foreign invaders being made explicit in verse 26 as distant nations are summoned from the end of the earth.

Isaiah 6 – 12

The prophet's self-identification with 'a people of unclean lips' (6:5) is confirmed by the shift in the divine designation to the pejorative-accusatory 'this people' (6:9–10; also 8:6, 11–12; 9:16 [15]; cf. King Ahaz's 'people': vv. 2, 17). Despite the threat of impending punitive invasion by the King of Assyria, the prophet boldly defies the 'peoples' (vocative address), 'all you distant lands', who set their sights on Israel. They will be shattered because 'God is with us' (8:9–10).

'*Am* occurs five times in chapter 9 with the definite article, here describing those in the northern kingdom who, in the future, will see 'a great light' (v. 3 [2]) after first experiencing the darkness of divine judgment (vv. 9, 13, 16, 19 [8, 12, 15, 18]). Since 'the oppressed of my people' are being deprived of justice (10:2), God will send Assyria as the rod of his anger against 'a godless nation . . . a people who anger me' (10:5–6, an intensification over 1:4).

The coming of a righteous Davidic ruler and the restoration of animal harmony (11:1–9) have consequences both for the peoples and for Israel in the future messianic era ('in that day'; 11:10–16; cf. 10:21–22). Whereas the motif of the banner (*nēs*) in 5:26 summons the distant nations to deport God's sinful people (5:29), here the nations will seek or consult the 'messianic' ruler like a 'banner' and enjoy his rest (cf. 28:12). This image of the transformation of the peoples is as rich (and as unexpected in the context) as in 2:1–4. Oswalt's limitation of verse 10 to 'God's people . . . the historical nation of Israel . . . the remnant'[30] is questionable. There is an integral (causal or temporal) relationship between the restoration and transformation of Israel and the transformation of the nations. At that time (v. 11) Yahweh will extend his hand to gather 'the remnant of his people' (my tr.) from all directions, including the 'islands of the sea'.[31] Verse 12 appears to summarize the two 'in that day' promises: Yahweh will both raise a banner for the nations (v. 10) and 'assemble the scattered people of Judah' (v. 11). Verses 13–14 offer a jarring picture of newly allied Ephraim and Judah despoiling and subjugating their named neighbours. Young seeks to explain this away as consisting of the 'blessed task of making

---

30. J. N. Oswalt, *The Book of Isaiah Chapters 1–39*, NICOT (Grand Rapids: Eerdmans, 1986), pp. 286–287.

31. This is the first occurrence of '*ī*.

the saving power of God known', while Motyer reduces these actions 'to fidelity to a [warrior] metaphor'.[32] But presumably these actions do *not* involve the same 'nations' that consult the ruler (v. 10) but rather those who remain 'Judah's enemies' (v. 13). Furthermore, the exact nature of their relationship to their neighbours hinges on the meaning of the Hebrew *mišma'at*, translated elsewhere as 'bodyguard' (1 Sam. 22:14; 2 Sam. 23:23; 1 Chr. 11:25), and thus does not necessarily indicate a servile duty. Israel's response of praise in Isaiah 12 is editorially linked to Isaiah 11 by the twofold repetition of 'in that day' (vv. 1, 4). The second 'stanza' gives a charge to make Yahweh's deeds known 'among the peoples' (vv. 4–5; my tr.), probably emphasizing ethnic groups rather than political units, in order to call them to recognize that his name is exalted (cf. 2:11, 17; 33:5). The purpose of the proclamation of verse 4a remains unclear, since no response is indicated.

Isaiah 13 – 23
Despite the scholarly convention of referring to Isaiah 13 – 23 as the 'oracles against the foreign nations', this section also contains oracles directed toward Jerusalem and promises of future restoration and blessing for the nations. These chapters thus assert Yahweh's sovereign control over the national history of all peoples and not just his own people, Israel.

As the section opens, an army is amassed to be an agent of divine wrath against human arrogance, 'a great people … kingdoms, nations … from a distant land, from the end of the heavens' (13:4–5; my tr.). The King of Babylon, like Assyria previously, is a 'rod' that subdues peoples and nations (14:5–6, 12; cf. 10:5–7, 13–15, 24), only to be smashed, in turn, by God. The climax of the Babylon oracle is the description of Israel's restoration following the Babylonian exile (14:1–2). This portrayal contains features that will recur in the course of the book: foreigners uniting with Israel (v. 1, *haggēr*) and other 'peoples' (my tr.) assisting the exiles in their return to the land and also serving Israel (v. 2). This reversal is strikingly summarized as 'they will take their captors captive and rule over their oppressors' (my tr.). Duhm calls this expression of 'nationalism' a 'repulsive arrogant expectation first expressed by Trito-Isaiah'.[33] The real tension, however, is posed

32. E. J. Young, *The Book of Isaiah*. Vol. 1: *Chapters 1–18*, NICOT (Grand Rapids: Eerdmans, 1965), p. 399; J. A. Motyer, *The Prophecy of Isaiah* (Leicester: IVP, 1993), p. 126.

33. B. Duhm, *Das Buch Jesaia*, 5th ed. (Göttingen: Vandenhoeck & Ruprecht, 1968), pp. 116–117.

by the juxtaposition of verses 1 and 2, with the former sounding much more favourable toward the nations than the latter (cf. Isa. 56:3, 6). Goldingay sees here a second, better occupation than under Joshua, in which aliens are welcomed, their territory remaining 'the land of Yahweh',[34] though it remains unclear why those who assist in Israel's resettlement should subsequently become their slaves. It is helpful to note that the actions of 14:1–2 are attributed to the Lord's compassion toward his people, Israel, rather than to their warlike actions.

The remarkable oracle regarding Egypt in Isaiah 19 has been much discussed.[35] In a reversal of roles the Egyptians will be subjected to harsh bondage and plagues and will cry out to God because of their oppressors (vv. 4, 20, 22; cf. Exod. 1:14; 7:27; 3:9). The description of Egypt's subsequent transformation in verses 18–25 is as marked as any in the book: five cities swearing by the Lord of the hosts; an altar to Yahweh; the Lord sending a saviour and legal defender; the self-revelation and acknowledgment of Yahweh; worship through sacrifices, offerings and vows; a turning to Yahweh (*wĕšābû 'ad-yhwh*); worship alongside Assyria; and a recipient (or source) of blessing, culminating in a divine election that rivals that of Israel ('Blessed be Egypt my people', v. 25; cf. 60:21; 64:7). What is most striking here is not simply that two world powers and Israel's dreaded enemies, Egypt and Assyria, are portrayed as blessed by and fervently worshipping Yahweh, but that this occurs far away from Mount Zion and without a mediating role being played by Israel. Simply dismissing this text as an aberrant, late, anti-nationalistic tradition is too easy a solution; one also must account for its inclusion in the book of Isaiah in the light of its resultant impact on reading so-called 'nationalistic' texts in the same section of the book. It is a bold affirmation of God's ultimate salvific purposes on behalf of all nations. By contrast, the oracle regarding Tyre that concludes this section illustrates divine judgment against human pride (23:9) with no promise of future restoration.

Isaiah 24 – 27
In Isaiah 24 – 27 the focus shifts from the immediate future of the neighbouring nations and world powers that either tempt or terrify God's people to a more general portrayal of God's sovereign control over the earth and all of its

---

34. J. Goldingay, *Isaiah*, NIBCOT (Carlisle: Paternoster, 2001), p. 102.

35. A recent article that focuses on the theological significance of the chapter is H. Hagelia, 'A Crescendo of Universalism: An Exegesis of Isa 19:16–25', *SEÅ* 70 (2005), pp. 73–88.

inhabitants,[36] which has clear implications for his people. The response of joy in 24:14–16a, presumably to the ruination of the unidentified city (vv. 10, 12), is universal (from the west and east, the islands of the sea, and the ends of the earth), and there is no compelling reason to limit it to exiles from Israel. Nor should this rich description of worship, which has parallels in the Psalms (cf. Ps. 22:23 [24]; 50:15, 23; 86:9, 12), be viewed as a mere acknowledgment of Yahweh's victory over Israel's foes (cf. the similar sequence in 25:2–3).

The high point of this section is found in 25:6–8, which describes a universal banquet on Mount Zion for *all* peoples, following the termination of death and the end of sorrow, marking this text as pointing further into the eschatological future than any other text in Isaiah. In the midst of this rich enjoyment of the fruits of salvation by all peoples, special attention is still directed toward 'his people' (v. 8b) and divine judgment against Moab's pride is not excluded (vv. 10–12).

Isaiah 28 – 39

In Isaiah 28 – 39 the future salvation of the nations fades temporarily from view. In chapters 28–31 and 36–39 the focus shifts back to eighth-century political developments and the temptation for Judah's leaders to rely on a military alliance with Egypt as a protection against Assyrian military domination. The pejorative designation 'this people' occurs here (28:11, 14; 29:13–14), as does the intimate 'his/my people' (28:5; 30:26; 32:13, 18). Mighty Egypt is denigrated as a useless people (30:5–6), and Assyria is described now as an 'arrogant people' with 'incomprehensible' speech who will be seen no more (33:19). Instead, God's people will gaze on the eschatological reign of the messianic king, the expansive land and tranquil Jerusalem in a festival mood (33:17, 20), free of both illness and guilt for their past sins (33:24). Isaiah 34 – 35 serves to introduce the major themes of judgment and salvation illustrated concretely in the imminent deliverance of Jerusalem from Sennacherib (chs. 36–39) that will be developed more fully in Isaiah 40 – 66.

Isaiah 40 – 48

In Isaiah 40 – 48 the emphasis shifts to Israel's imminent restoration to the land and to their God. 'Nations' terminology becomes more common, while references to concrete historical events become infrequent and often vague. The first verse sets the tone: 'Comfort, comfort *my people*, says your God'

---

36. The word 'earth' (*'ere*s) occurs 29 times in these chapters, and the related word *tēbēl* 4×.

(my italics; cf. 43:20; 47:6). The nations, including the distant coastlands, are summoned to witness and bear witness to God's actions upon the world stage (41:1; 45:20–21): his deliverance of the nations and their kings into his agent's hands (41:2; 45:1) and his restoration of his people to their land (43:5–9).

The place of the nations within God's salvific plans is especially prominent within the so-called 'servant songs',[37] which introduce a second, contrasting agent whose saving actions will be distinctly non-military in nature. This servant will not evoke fear; instead, the nations will respond in amazement and with the expectation that his actions to 'bring justice to the nations' will benefit them as well (42:1, 4). The mention of the coastlands hoping in 'his Torah' (42:4; my tr.) recalls 2:3. The key verse is 42:6:

> I have given you as a covenant to the people,
> > a light to the nations.
> (NRSV)

In the light of the manner in which singular and plural terms for 'nations' are normally juxtaposed in the book of Isaiah in order to distinguish *one* nation or people among the many (e.g. 43:8–9), it is most likely that 'people' and 'nations' should not be equated in 42:6 (cf. the expansion of 42:6 in 49:6). The servant is the means of re-establishing Israel's covenantal relationship with God and of bringing the light of his salvation to the nations. Verse 7 explains the promised light as a removal of blindness and release from prison (cf. 9:2).[38]

Equally important is the repeated call to the nations to praise Yahweh for his mighty deeds as well as the assurance that they will do so in the future (cf. 42:10, 12). It is exegetically improbable that the addressees in a verse like 42:10 can be limited to exiled Israelites, but the more difficult question is whether this is simply a public acknowledgment of God's successes or rather a description of worship coming from transformed individuals.

Isaiah 43:1–7 offers a unique promise of God's redemptive intent. Just as Egypt, Cush and Seba served as a 'ransom' for Israel during the exodus event (v. 3), so, in the future, he is prepared to give a person in their place and population groups in exchange for their life (v. 4). It is better to take this claim as a figurative expression of the price that God is willing to pay to redeem

---

37. See R. L. Schultz, 'Servant, Slave', in *NIDOTTE* 4:1194–1196.
38. Since God's people as his servant are described repeatedly as 'blind', they presumably will also receive this light (cf. 42:16, 18–19; 43:8; contrast 44:9) and, as those in exile, are also in need of 'release' (cf. 49:9).

his precious people from exile (vv. 5–7)[39] rather than as a specific historical reference (e.g. to Cyrus).[40]

In Isaiah 45:20–21 Yahweh summons the 'fugitives of the nations' (*pĕlîṭê haggôyyîm*; my tr.), further described as those who pray to a 'non-saving god' (my tr.). This is followed in verse 22 by one of the most universal invitations in the entire book:

> Turn to me and be saved,
>> all you ends of the earth;
>> for I am God, and there is no other.

It is problematic to limit this saving act to temporary deliverance from political oppression, since verses 23–24 describe this 'turning' that will ultimately take place:

> Before me every knee will bow;
>> by me every tongue will swear.
> They will say of me, 'In the LORD alone
>> are righteousness and strength.'

Once again this response looks like genuine worship rather than mere submission. Thus in this section God's actions in history and those of his agent, the 'servant', are directed toward the salvation of both Israel and the nations; these ends are related chronologically but not necessarily causally.

Isaiah 49 – 57

In Isaiah 49 – 57[41] the focus shifts to the spiritual deliverance brought about by Yahweh's servant. Although the identity of this chosen servant remains

---

39. J. Goldingay, *The Message of Isaiah 40–55: A Literary-Theological Commentary* (New York: T. & T. Clark, 2005), p. 194, responds to Snaith's claim that vv. 3–4 express Second Isaiah's 'nationalist, even anti-gentile, stance' by noting that 'they are set in the context of poems that indicate that Yhwh has a positive concern for gentile peoples'.

40. So Duhm, *Jesaia*, p. 322.

41. We begin a new subdivision of the book after ch. 57 rather than after ch. 55, as is typical, primarily on the basis of literary-thematic rather than compositional-redactional considerations, including the 'refrain' in 48:22 and 57:21 that concludes two major sections (cf. 66:24).

ambiguous in chapter 42, with Jacob-Israel or a group within Israel being a potential 'candidate', beginning with Isaiah 49, the servant takes on increasingly individualistic rather than corporate characteristics. In 49:1 the servant himself addresses the distant coastlands and population groups, proclaiming his commission on their behalf. Isaiah 49:6 parallels 42:6 in setting forth his twofold task: (1) as God's servant, to restore Jacob-Israel (cf. 49:5), and (2) as the nations' light, to extend God's salvation to the end of the earth (cf. 51:4, *lĕ'ôr 'ammîm*). In verses 8–13 Yahweh, in turn, addresses his servant, repeating the commission from 42:6:

> I will keep you and will make you
> to be a covenant for the people.
> (v. 8b)

Though initially despised by a nation (probably a generic sg.), the nations will someday recognize him as God's elect one, by bowing down to him (v. 7).

It is unclear in chapter 49 whether the liberated captives who 'come from afar' (vv. 9, 12) are the same group as 'your sons' (and daughters) who 'hasten back' (vv. 17, 22); that is, exiled Israelites (vv. 13, 19). This equation appears justified, due to the verbal links between the respective subunits, namely the repetition of 'compassion' (vv. 10, 13, 15), the obeisance of the foreign rulers (vv. 7, 23), and God as 'redeemer' (vv. 7, 26). Verses 14–23 describe how the peoples/nations respond to the raised hand and banner of God by bringing the exiled sons and daughters back (v. 22; cf. 11:10). The nations' role here appears 'subservient': carrying the exiles, the rulers serving as 'foster fathers' and 'nursing mothers' (v. 23; cf. 60:16; 66:11–12), licking the dust at their feet, even forced to eat their own flesh and blood (v. 26)! Before citing this text as evidence of the irresolvable polarity in the book of Isaiah between nationalism and universalism, one should notice the purpose of these events, as indicated by the 'divine recognition formula' used in verse 23 with respect to Israel and in verse 26 with respect to 'all flesh' (NRSV). The emphasis in Isaiah 49 is not on the subjugation of the nations (note v. 6) but on the unambiguous demonstration of 'who's in charge here'; that is, Israel's saviour and redeemer, the mighty one of Jacob (v. 26).

As Isaiah 51 begins, God announces to his elect *people* and population group (v. 4a, *ûlĕ'ûmmî*, sg. only here) his saving purposes for the *peoples* and coastlands who will benefit from his instruction, just rule, light, righteousness and salvation, which will continue for ever (vv. 4b–8). The establishment of justice will also involve curtailing evil oppression (v. 5; cf. vv. 13, 23), but the events described may include, but should not be limited to, the exiles' return from Babylon (v. 11; cf. 35:10). In the distant future (note the parallels with 2:1–4), God's oft-oppressed people will pursue righteousness, seek the Lord and internalize his Torah-instruction (vv. 1, 7), and will experience not only his redemption, deliverance and just rule, but also the removal of their sins through the servant's sacrificial death (cf. 'my/his people' in 51:4, 16, 22; 52:4–6, 9; 53:8; 56:3; 57:14). The 'new exodus' will be the occasion of this universal revelation of Yahweh's saving arm to all the nations and the ends of the earth (vv. 10–12). This bold announcement is followed immediately by the fourth 'servant song', which describes the profound impact that the servant's death will have on *many* nations and kings (52:14–15),[42] suggesting that the *many* (*rabbîm*, 53:11–12) whose sins will be borne and who will consequently be accounted righteous will also include (some from) the nations and kings. Thus Isaiah 51 – 53 makes it clear that the nations' place within God's plan is not limited to their actions related to Israel's restoration, as described in chapter 49.

Due to its expanding population, Zion's offspring will inherit (or displace) nations (54:2–3; cf. 49:19–21, perhaps an allusion to Gen. 24:60), occupying their 'desolate cities'. This sounds like a 'nationalistic' grab for more *Lebensraum* (living space) if one chooses not to spiritualize or historicize the text.[43] Once again the focus is not on imperialistic expansion but on God's renewed compassion (54:7–8, 10; cf. 55:5) and covenantal loyalty (54:8, 10; cf. 53:3) toward his previously barren and abandoned 'wife' (vv. 1, 6–7), now described as the 'servants of Yahweh' (54:17; my tr.). These servants' outstanding hereditary possession (v. 17) is not more real estate but a restored relationship, not bejewelled walls but divine instruction and abundant well-being (vv. 11–13).

Isaiah 55 then strikes a clearly more 'universal' tone, extending the offer of free – but priceless – fare, further described as the provisions (*ḥasdê*) of the enduring covenant with David, to all who come, seek Yahweh and (re)turn to

---

42. Despite the wide consensus that *yazzeh* should be translated as 'startled', due to the gesture 'shut their mouths' in the adjoining clause, 'sprinkle' is linguistically and contextually more likely, given the repeated use of sacrificial terminology in this text. This position has been defended recently by Goldingay, *Message*, pp. 492–493.

43. For the former option see E. J. Young, *The Book of Isaiah*. Vol. 3: *Chapters 40–66*, NICOT (Grand Rapids: Eerdmans, 1972), pp. 362–363, who relates this to 'the great spiritual conquest of the nations through the worldwide preaching of the Gospel'. For the latter see J. N. Oswalt, *The Book of Isaiah Chapters 40–66*, NICOT (Grand Rapids: Eerdmans, 1998), p. 417, who sees here a description of the returnees reclaiming 'property seized by the non-Jewish people who had been transported into the land during the exile'.

him (vv. 1, 6–7). This presumably includes those from an 'unfamiliar nation' (v. 5; my tr.; probably a generic rather than specific use of the singular), which will respond eagerly to the Davidic agent's summons.[44] The emphasis here on a restored relationship with God and on the effective word that 'goes out' from his mouth (v. 11) indicates that 'going out' (my tr.) in joy (v. 12) should not be limited to the return from exile but viewed rather as enjoying the covenantal blessings.

If Isaiah 55 is understood as an offer of salvation extended to all God-seekers (Israelites and non-Israelites), then chapters 56–57 serve to confirm the breadth of this offer and set forth the demands of salvation. This is the most dramatic universalistic text in the book of Isaiah. The opening call is now to *maintain* rather than to *await* justice (56:1). Neither the foreigner nor the eunuch is to be excluded from God's people or from temple worship (v. 3), despite the earlier Mosaic cultic restrictions concerning them (cf. Deut. 23:1–8). Both can demonstrate their loving loyalty by serving and worshipping God (vv. 3–6; cf. 14:1). They will know the joy of offering acceptable sacrifices and of free access to the temple as a place of prayer for all nations (vv. 7–8; cf. 1 Kgs 8:41–43). The ultimate intent of the God who gathers the 'scattered' Israelites is to gather 'still others' (v. 8).[45]

Isaiah 58 – 66

The final section of the book of Isaiah focuses on the future glorification of Zion through the actions of both Yahweh and the nations, culminating in the 'new heavens and new earth' (my tr.). The section commences, however, by indicting 'my people' for rebellion (58:1–2; also designated as a *gōy*). Following a further indictment by the prophet (59:1–8), the people confess their sins (59:9–15a), leading to the Divine Warrior's establishment of justice (59:15b–19), as he displays his wrath against his enemies, including the 'coastlands' (my tr.) that elsewhere are described as longing for divine *mišpāṭ*. This act of judgment will evoke fear/reverence toward Yahweh from west (the coastlands) to

---

44. Goldingay, *Message*, p. 549, reduces the gift extended by Yahweh in vv. 1–2 to Israel's 'acknowledgment' by Cyrus' Persia. More likely, the gift consists of the offer of abundant pardon that lies at the heart of Isa. 55.

45. Kebede, 'How Can the Concepts', pp. 181–211, understands the 'individualism' in 56:1–8 as offering the hermeneutical key for resolving the tension between nationalism and universalism. It is unclear, however, that the concept of individualism can justifiably be read into 'universalistic' texts that occur earlier in the book of Isaiah.

east (v. 19), probably not an expression of transformation or worship, since verse 20 speaks, contrastingly, of those in Jacob 'who repent of their sins'.

Isaiah 60 introduces the theme of Zion's 'glorification' (vv. 1–2, 7, 9, 13, 19–20) in this section and also exhibits the highest concentration of 'nations' terminology in the entire book, once again with a more nationalistic tone. Verse 2 describes global darkness, but when the light of God's glory shines forth, nations and kings will be drawn to it (v. 3). The nations will facilitate the return of Israel's exiled sons and daughters, even bringing them by ships from the coastlands, along with treasures and sacrificial animals presented by the nations. The kings of the nations will lead the procession and join in serving Israel and rebuilding Jerusalem (vv. 4–11). What initially looks like sincere worship (e.g. broadcasting Yahweh's praiseworthy deeds, v. 6), however, is coerced. Any nation or kingdom that refuses to serve Israel will perish (v. 12a), so that even those who *despise* them will bow down before them (v. 14; cf. 45:14; contrast 49:7). Israel will be nourished by nations and kings (v. 16, expanding 49:23; cf. 66:11–12). The ancestral promises once again will be fulfilled and even surpassed (vv. 21–22), with God's entire people being (declared) righteous (cf. Gen. 15:6), taking possession of the land for ever (cf. Gen. 15:7; 28:4), and multiplying into a mighty nation (cf. Gen. 18:18; 24:60).

Isaiah 61 continues this description: foreigners take over agrarian duties in the land and sustain God's people with their own wealth, freeing them up to serve God as 'a kingdom of priests' and temple ministers (61:5–7; cf. Exod. 19:6). Their descendants will be acknowledged by the nations/peoples, which, observing the prosperity of Israel's descendants, will recognize this blessing as coming from Yahweh (v. 9).[46] Isaiah 62:1–2 offers a similar description; here as well righteousness is portrayed as distinctly Israel's, rather than a shared, possession (cf. 60:17; 61:3, 10–11; 62:1–2). The subsection focusing on Zion's glorification ends in 62:10–12 with a final mention of a banner being raised for 'the peoples' (my tr.),[47] who are carefully distinguished from 'the people' (v. 10). Yahweh makes a universal proclamation that the latter alone constitute 'the holy people' (vv. 11–12). The use of the singular and plural forms of 'people' in verse 10 militates against interpreting the highway as being prepared so that all nations can 'return to God'.[48] It is difficult to know how to understand this strong 'nationalistic' emphasis at this point in the book,

---

46. It probably is too much to see in this description (or in v. 11) an 'element of witness', as Oswalt, *Isaiah 40–66*, p. 573, claims.

47. Or 'over the peoples' (Heb. *'al*; cf. *'el* in 49:22).

48. Contra Motyer, *Prophecy of Isaiah*, p. 508.

especially the sharp distinction between Israel and the nations. In part it can be explained as the culmination of the dominant Zion theme within the book.[49] The nations' subservient role as portrayed here may pertain merely to the transitional time of Israel's final restoration to the land, leading to the establishment of a final age of security, righteousness, joy and divine presence (60:17b–22; cf. 65:17–25).

Isaiah 63:1–6 describes the Divine Warrior as coming to take revenge on behalf of his people, *trampling* down 'peoples' (my tr.) by himself (i.e. using no agents, vv. 3, 6), despite his people's (cf. vv. 8, 11, 14, 18)[50] disappointing history of rebellion (63:7–14), which has led to God's sanctuary being *trampled* as well. This action appears to anticipate the lengthy prayer for deliverance (63:15 – 64:12 [11]) in which the petitioners address God as 'father', requesting special attention as his people (64:8–9 [7–8]). They call for his intervention because Jerusalem and the temple have been devastated (64:10–12 [9–11]) and because the nations are also *his* enemies (64:1–2 [63:19 – 64:1]; also 59:18). As previously summarized, in Isaiah 65 – 66 God responds to this fervent prayer, describing the ultimate intertwined futures of Israel and the nations. According to these concluding chapters, the glorification of Zion (chs. 60–62) neither entails the ultimate salvation of the entire nation nor occurs to the exclusion of the nations. In the end all rebels will be condemned and all nations, including Israel, will serve God alone.

Conclusions

Summary of findings
Having followed the long and sometimes twisting thematic highway through the book of Isaiah, we are in a position to draw some observations about the relationship between nationalism and universalism in Isaiah:

1. Both 'nationalistic' and 'universalistic' emphases are found in all major sections of Isaiah, sometimes even in adjoining texts. All of the major perspectives have been introduced by chapter 27, some rather abruptly, and no clear, ordered sequence of events emerges as one progresses

---

49. See B. G. Webb, 'Zion in Transformation: A Literary Approach to Isaiah', in D. J. A. Clines (ed.), *The Bible in Three Dimensions* (Sheffield: JSOT, 1990), pp. 65–84.
50. Despite a few textual variants in 63:11, *'ammô* should be preferred as the more difficult reading.

through the major sections of the book.[51] Rather, this apparent tension is preserved or even highlighted in the book read as a whole.

2. Nevertheless, a consistent pattern emerges that Israel's punishment and exile as well as its restoration and salvation as God's elect people both involve and ultimately transform the nations.

3. Within the final canonical shaping of the prophetic book, however, a more universalistic reading is indicated by the frame of the book (Isa. 1 – 2 and 65 – 66), which describes the ongoing rebellion and subsequent punishment of all but a remnant within Israel and the unhindered access of Gentiles from many nations to divine instruction and to the worship of Yahweh in the temple.

4. Efforts to resolve the tension can lead one to overinterpret or ignore textual details or to spiritualize (or 'materialize') them.

5. Rather than viewing divergent emphases as indicative of theological tensions or compositional complexity, it is more helpful to consider how a 'nationalistic' or 'universalistic' emphasis functions in a particular text and context in the light of the primary theme or emphasis of that text.

6. Rather than viewing contrasting emphases within the book of Isaiah as alternative options between which both Israel and the Gentiles can choose, it is legitimate to understand the book as presenting the various (non-conflicting) ways in which God is pursuing his salvific purposes for both groups, both through and apart from human or national agents.

The initial goal of this chapter was to survey various approaches to the 'so-called' tension between nationalism and universalism in the book of Isaiah and take a different approach in hope of arriving at a more satisfying solution. Goldingay may be correct, however, in claiming that this tension represents 'a false antithesis' and that these two emphases are better understood as complementary.[52] In some respects the world envisioned in Isaiah parallels our own, where most people are unwilling to serve and worship God alone, even if 'his glory' has been declared to them, where oppression and persecution are common, and where sincere and genuine believers coexist with nominal and

51. Cf. Oswalt's reconstructed sequence, n. 17 above. Richard Hays offers a seven-event synthesis of 'Isaiah's story' according to Paul in which the alleged tension vanishes. See R. B. Hays, *The Conversion of the Imagination: Paul as Interpreter of Israel's Scripture* (Grand Rapids: Eerdmans, 2005), pp. 45–47.

52. Goldingay, *Isaiah*, pp. 143, 264.

presumptuous ones. Above all, the 'nationalistic' and 'universalistic' emphases in Isaiah vividly illustrate how the creator God and Lord over all the nations is willing to use all possible means to draw people and peoples to himself in saving faith, a task in which we can participate as his 'servants'.

7. WISDOM IN ISAIAH

Lindsay Wilson

Why explore wisdom and Isaiah?

In a seminal article on wisdom and Isaiah, Fichtner proposed that 'there are few so completely antithetical phenomena as prophecy and *ḥokmâ* (wisdom). Two worlds stand in total opposition.'[1] However, a number of scholars have debated whether 'Isaiah might have drunk from wisdom's stream'.[2] There are at least three reasons for looking at the possible connections between Isaiah and wisdom.

First, a connection between Isaiah and wisdom would not be surprising given Proverbs 25:1, which introduces a collection of proverbs edited or copied in the time of Hezekiah. Indeed, King Hezekiah specifically interacts with the prophet Isaiah in Isaiah 37:1–7, 21; 38:1–8; 39:3–8. If wisdom flourished in the time of Hezekiah, then it would be striking if Isaiah showed no awareness and made no use of wisdom ideas, forms and words.[3] Morgan

1. J. Fichtner, 'Isaiah among the Wise', in J. L. Crenshaw (ed.), *Studies in Ancient Israelite Wisdom* (New York: KTAV, 1976 [orig. 1949]), p. 429.
2. This expression is used by H. Wildberger, *Isaiah 28–39*, tr. T. H. Trapp, CC (Minneapolis: Fortress, 2002), p. 597.
3. D. F. Morgan, *Wisdom in the Old Testament Traditions* (Oxford: Basil Blackwell, 1981), pp. 76–77.

suggests that the real issue with Isaiah and wisdom is not whether there is wisdom influence (that, he argues, is clear), but rather about how to interpret wisdom in the book. His conclusion is that 'the use of wisdom by Isaiah is an important and positive aspect of the prophet's message'.[4]

Secondly, prophecy and wisdom are two key elements of the Old Testament corpus. If we want to develop an Old Testament theology (and ultimately a biblical theology), it is a helpful question to ask how these important strands of Old Testament thought relate in this key prophetic book.

Thirdly, the place of wisdom in non-wisdom books has been a fruitful pathway towards discovering a more balanced biblical theology. Too often Old Testament and biblical theologies have tried to read down the wisdom distinctives to make them appear more like the covenant or salvation-history strands. Such an approach is reductionistic, and needs to be supplemented by studies that observe how wisdom's distinctive features have a legitimate place in other traditions and in the Old Testament as a whole.

A sampling of previous studies of wisdom and Isaiah

A number of previous studies have explored the connections between Isaiah of Jerusalem and wisdom, or alternatively Deutero-Isaiah and wisdom.

In a pioneering study Fichtner suggests that Isaiah was a member of the wise before he became a prophet. It makes sense that he would use his familiarity with wisdom forms and vocabulary to make his message more telling and effective to his intended audience. However, while Fichtner argued that Isaiah used wisdom forms, motifs and terminology, he also observes that he criticized the sages (e.g. Isa. 5:21; 19:11–15; 29:14). His conclusion was that Isaiah used to stand within the wisdom tradition, but he had turned against those who misused their wisdom for political ends, or who too-confidently set out their plans, especially after his prophetic call.[5] However, Whedbee has rightly argued that it rests on a flimsy assumption that Isaiah's use of wisdom terms and forms meant that he must have belonged to a particular institutional setting.[6] It may just be that his proximity to the court and his level of literacy

---

4. Ibid., p. 82.

5. Fichtner, 'Isaiah among the Wise', pp. 434, 437. M. O'Kane, 'Wisdom Influence in First Isaiah', *PIBA* 14 (1991), p. 69, responds that the mere use of wisdom terms establishes neither Isaiah's prior role nor his intended goal in using them.

6. J. W. Whedbee, *Isaiah and Wisdom* (Nashville: Abingdon, 1971), p. 19. Whedbee

(Isa. 8:1, 16; 30:8) made him informed about the offices and messages of the wisdom tradition.[7]

Whedbee has undertaken the most comprehensive study of the links between the eighth-century prophet Isaiah and the wisdom circles of the Jerusalem court. He views the parables of Isaiah 1:2–3, 5:1–7 and 28:23–29 as being in the wisdom style. Building on the work of Brevard Childs, he also refers to 'summary appraisal formulas' which he finds in Proverbs 1:19 and Isaiah 14:26, 17:14b and 28:29. One useful insight from Whedbee is that he explores why Isaiah might have used wisdom. He suggests that it enabled him to speak more effectively to the Jerusalem court, since wisdom patterns were common there.[8] However, even his argument was based on identifying which parts of Isaiah 1 – 39 were not from the hand of Isaiah of Jerusalem (e.g. Isa. 3:10–11; 32:1–8).[9]

Vermeylen has, in contrast, argued that one cannot see any influence from the wisdom tradition in Isaiah. Instead, he suggests that the parallels pointed out can be explained by the prophet's educated background and the fact that he is addressing a cultured audience.[10] He admits that wisdom elements might include the allegory of the vine (ch. 5), the parable of the farmer (ch. 28), the wonderful counsellor (ch. 9), the figure of chapter 11 endowed with the spirit of wisdom and understanding and the common use of terms like 'wise', 'know', 'counsel' and 'understanding'.[11] However, Isaiah's attack on

---

comments that you could equally mount an argument that he was a former priest since he has a similarly ambivalent attitude to the cult.

7. A similar criticism could be levelled against J. Lindblom, 'Wisdom in the Old Testament Prophets', in M. Noth and D. W. Thomas (eds.), *Wisdom in Israel and in the Ancient Near East*, VTSup 3 (Leiden: Brill, 1955), pp. 201, 204, who argues that whenever the prophets used figurative language, this showed wisdom influence. Whedbee, *Isaiah and Wisdom*, p. 24, rightly responds, 'It would be arbitrary and artificial – not to say foolish – to put a wisdom brand on all comparison speech in the prophets.'

8. Whedbee, *Isaiah and Wisdom*, p. 152.

9. Ibid., p. 25. O'Kane, 'Wisdom Influence', p. 70, rightly argues that 'Whedbee's approach suffers from the disadvantage that he limits his iniquity [*sic*; inquiry?] to the so-called "authentic" Isaianic material.'

10. J. Vermeylen, 'Le Proto-Isaïe et la sagesse d'Israël', in M. Gilbert (ed.), *La Sagesse de l'Ancien Testament*, BETL 51 (Leuven: Leuven University Press, 1990), p. 57. This essay was written in 1979.

11. Ibid., pp. 53–57. He suggests that he is often addressing the court sages in terms they frequently use (e.g. Isa. 3:1–3; 5:19; 7:5; 14:24; 29:15; 30:1).

empty wise advisors in 29:14 reveals his true attitude to the sages and their wisdom. His approach was to look for links between Isaiah and the sages at each redactional layer in Isaiah 1 – 39, based on a hypothetical reconstruction of the (largely post-exilic) redactional process.[12]

The connection between Torah and wisdom has been most exhaustively explored by Jensen, who argues that the word *tôrâ* is used by Isaiah to refer to the teaching of the whole wisdom tradition rather than the prophetic or legal traditions. He proposes that Isaiah is carrying on a debate with the wisdom leaders of his day, trying to show them that they have neglected Yahweh and his wisdom, and so not lived up to the expectations of their own tradition.[13]

More recently, Jensen has noted the importance of the wisdom tradition in the book of Isaiah.[14] He comments that 'Isaiah's relation to the wisdom tradition is not a key to unlock all the mysteries of his book, but it does help to explain a lot and appears to provide important elements of the content of his ethical teaching.'[15] His view also is based on identifying what are authentic and inauthentic materials.[16]

Wildberger has a useful outline of apparent overlaps with wisdom in chapters 1–39, arguing that wisdom was evidently a significant influence on Isaiah of Jerusalem. He points to the widespread use of wisdom forms, vocabulary and themes, and argues from Proverbs 25:1 that there was a strong home for wisdom traditions at Hezekiah's court in the time of Isaiah. Wildberger concludes that Isaiah is rebuking those among the leaders who claimed to be wise but were not (e.g. Isa. 29:14).[17] He further suggests that Isaiah uses the wisdom ethos as the basis for evaluating the actions of the people and its leaders.[18]

As well as an interesting survey of past discussion, O'Kane also provides some suggestions about how Isaiah of Jerusalem uses wisdom, and for what goal. He concludes that in Isaiah wisdom has a literary function of assessing

---

12. Ibid., p. 408. This is in his supplementary note to the revised 1990 ed.

13. J. Jensen, *The Use of* tôrâ *by Isaiah: His Debate with the Wisdom Tradition*, CBQMS 3 (Washington: Catholic Biblical Association, 1973).

14. J. Jensen, *Ethical Dimensions of the Prophets* (Collegeville: Michael Glazier / Liturgical, 2006), p. 112.

15. Ibid., p. 113.

16. Thus, in ibid., pp. 111–112, he says that 'In the authentic oracles of Isaiah there is no reference to covenant, to Sinai, to Moses, to Mosaic law, and only one (indirect) reference to the Exodus tradition.'

17. Wildberger, *Isaiah 28–39*, pp. 614–615.

18. Ibid., pp. 607–608.

and evaluating material so as to instruct the reader on how to read and apply the book. Indeed, he suggests that the fifth-century redactor's 'aim was to present all 66 chapters as a guide to the righteous life'.[19]

Williamson has written a useful review article, which outlines the major discussions of Isaiah 1 – 39 and wisdom up to the 1990s. He suggests two areas that need further exploration. The first is the issue of epistemology, or how Isaiah came to know God's will for Israel. The second is whether Isaiah's relationship with the king's political advisers implies that he is rejecting wisdom itself.[20] These issues will be picked up below.

The broadest survey is still that of Morgan, who deals separately with the three putative sections of Isaiah.[21] Unfortunately, he does not synthesize these into the book of Isaiah as a canonical whole. He points out that the prophets were aware of the wise in foreign countries (e.g. Isa. 10:13; 19:11–15; 44:25) and of the different offices or functions held there (e.g. Isa. 19:1; 44:25). He sees parallels of forms, vocabulary and themes between the various parts of Isaiah and the wisdom tradition, and regards Isaiah of Jerusalem and Second Isaiah as two of the four prophets most influenced by wisdom.[22]

In an earlier article Morgan helpfully sets out four areas where scholars have found wisdom influence in Isaiah:[23]

A. Form/style: 1:2–3, 23; 2:22; 3:10–11, 24; 5:1–7, 8–24; 7:9; 10:1–5, 15; 14:4, 26; 17:6, 14; 23:20–21; 28:23–29; 29:15–16; 32:6a; 40:12–17; 45:9; 49:24; 55:8, 13; 61:11; 65:8.

---

19. O'Kane, 'Wisdom Influence', pp. 76–77. He builds on the proposal of G. T. Sheppard, *Wisdom as a Hermeneutical Construct: A Study in the Sapientializing of the Old Testament*, BZAW 151 (Berlin: de Gruyter, 1980), that wisdom was a redactional category used to shape the prophetic books, and seeks to apply this to Isa. 28 – 33 in particular.

20. H. G. M. Williamson, 'Isaiah and the Wise', in J. Day et al. (eds.), *Wisdom in Ancient Israel* (Cambridge: Cambridge University Press, 1995), pp. 133–141.

21. Morgan, *Old Testament Traditions*, pp. 63–83, 90–93, 114–119.

22. Ibid., pp. 212–216. At p. 212 he observes that the prophets 'may utilize vocabulary, forms, and themes from the wisdom tradition, but they have changed and adapted it for their own purposes'. At p. 216, however, he too suggests that some passages which appear to be the result of wisdom influence (e.g. Isa. 2:22; 3:10–11) are often regarded as late editorial glosses.

23. D. F. Morgan, 'Wisdom and the Prophets', in E. A. Livingstone (ed.), *Studia Biblica 1978*, JSOTSup 11 (Sheffield: JSOT, 1979), pp. 229–231. This chart is a slightly modified conflation of two separate charts given by Morgan.

B. Theme/motif: 1:2–3, 10, 21–26; 2:2–4; 3:9–11; 5:1–7, 11–12, 21–24b; 8:1, 16,
18, 20; 9:1–6; 10:1–4; 11:1–9; 19:14; 26:7–10; 28:13, 23–29; 29:13–15; 30:1, 8–9; 31:2;
40:12ff.; 41:1; 42:5; 43:5, 13; 44:13, 24b–25; 45:9, 11, 15; 48:13, 19; 50:9–10; 51:8–9, 15,
17; 53:2–4, 9; 61:9; 65:23.

C. Vocabulary: 1:3, 26; 3:3; 5:19–24; 6:9–10; 9:5; 10:13ff.; 11:2; 14:24–27; 17:14;
19:1–3, 11–13; 27:11; 28:23–29; 29:14–16, 20, 24; 30:1–5; 31:1–3; 33:19; 40:12–17,
28–31; 43:10.

D. References to the wise: 1:26; 3:1–3; 5:8–14, 18–19, 21; 7:5; 8:9–10; 10:5–15;
11:1–5; 14:24–27; 19:1–4, 11–15; 29:13–16; 30:1–5; 31:1–3; 44:25; 47:10; 50:4.

A number of scholars have also seen significant links between God's challenging questions in Isaiah 40 – 55 and the Yahweh speeches of Job 38 – 39.[24]
These and other links will be brought out in the discussion of possible wisdom
forms, vocabulary and themes in the whole book of Isaiah.

Methodology and terminology

Terminology
The question of wisdom influence in non-wisdom texts is complicated by the
variety of terms used by scholars. While some may appear interchangeable,
the specific terms need to be carefully distinguished. There are no right and
wrong terms, but it is vital that they are not regarded as interchangeable, and
that writers articulate the nuances of the terms they choose to use.

At one end of the spectrum, terms like 'wisdom literature' or 'wisdom text'
generally imply that a text not only reflects ideas found in the wisdom books,
but that the corpus of literature thought to come from a wisdom setting
should be expanded to include this text as well. The 'wisdom setting' is often
understood to be a royal court setting, commonly a wisdom school for training
courtiers, but others would argue for the setting of wisdom literature to be in
the clan or family, either in addition to or instead of a royal court.

---

24. See e.g. S. Terrien, 'Quelques remarques sur les affinités de Job avec le Deutéro-
    Isaïe', in *Volume du Congrès. Genève 1965*, VTSup 15 (Leiden: Brill, 1966), pp. 295–310;
    also H. L. Rowold, 'The Theology of Creation in the Yahweh Speeches of the
    Book of Job as a Solution to the Problem Posed by the Book of Job' (ThD thesis,
    Concordia Seminary in Exile, St. Louis, 1977), pp. 60–65; 'Yahweh's Challenge to
    Rival: The Form and Function of the Yahweh-Speech in Job 38–39', *CBQ* 47
    (1985), pp. 199–211.

Further along the continuum is the term 'wisdom influence', which is usually a claim that wisdom forms or ideas (or a redactor who belongs to a 'wisdom setting') are one part of a given text, and that these wisdom aspects have mingled with, and influenced, the other traditions and material in the text. Sometimes what is meant is that wisdom is the major influence. At other times it may mean only that there is some wisdom influence among a variety of other factors. The imprecision of such a term makes it somewhat unsatisfactory.

Still further along is the term 'wisdom element', 'wisdom echo', 'wisdom parallel' or, clearer still, 'wisdom-like element'. This is more a minimal claim that aspects of a text (ideas, motifs, forms, vocabulary etc.) appear to mirror or remind the reader of similar features found in wisdom books. There is not necessarily any assertion that they have come from a wisdom setting, or been added by wisdom writers. All that is being claimed is that particular aspects are prominent in (typical of) and distinctive (not necessarily exclusive) to other texts that are clearly wisdom literature. Such terms leave open the question of the setting of the text, and the way in which these 'wisdom-like elements' relate to other parts of the text.[25]

Often the lack of precision has served to cloud the debate. While some advocate the minimal position of 'wisdom echoes' in the text, others have mounted arguments against the maximal position of the passage as a whole being viewed as wisdom literature. In this chapter the first stage will be identifying any wisdom-like elements, before trying to account for their significance in Isaiah.

Methodology

Recent scholarship on Isaiah has moved towards reading the canonical book of Isaiah as a whole book, even if its component parts may have been written in different centuries. Some connections with a wisdom setting or theme can be made by reading the 'authentic' parts of Isaiah against their putative eighth-century setting, but additional insights may emerge from reading the literary work as a whole. This shift in approach invites a re-examination of the connection of wisdom to the entire book, and not simply to its component parts.

Few scholars factor in a canonical approach when considering the connection between Isaiah and wisdom. Even O'Kane, who mentions the existence of canonical approaches to the book, argues from the ambiguous attitude

---

25. For a wider discussion of these terminological issues see L. Wilson, *Joseph Wise and Otherwise: The Intersection of Wisdom and Covenant in Genesis 37–50*, PBM (Carlisle: Paternoster, 2004), pp. 28–30.

to Assyria, the displacement of passages like 10:1–4 and the positioning of 6:9–10 that even within chapters 1–39 there has been editorial activity subsequent to the eighth century BC. The presence or otherwise of wisdom ideas is thus more than whether Isaiah of Jerusalem was influenced by them. It includes whether subsequent editors could use and adapt wisdom categories to promote their later agendas.[26]

This chapter proposes moving the debate away from the question of whether Isaiah of Jerusalem was or was not a wisdom figure, or whether he was subject to wisdom influence. It invites us instead to explore first whether wisdom-like elements are present in the book of Isaiah as a whole. It then encourages us to explain the effect of these wisdom-like elements on the book as we have had it handed down to us. O'Kane offers a note of caution here:

> It is one thing to recognize vocabulary, literary genres and forms which have parallels in the Wisdom books especially Job and Proverbs: it is quite another to determine their function within the Old Testament book in which they occur: this is especially true of the book of Isaiah.[27]

This is not the only possible approach, but it is worth testing to see if it is useful. It will focus on the final form of the book rather than the 'authentic' parts of each section.

Wisdom-like elements in the book of Isaiah

Even though the book of Isaiah is a major prophetic book, connections between it and wisdom are claimed in three main ways. First, several 'wisdom forms' are claimed to be present in Isaiah. Secondly, it is suggested that certain distinctive wisdom words are evident. Finally, it is proposed that some wisdom themes are found in the book. Morgan observes that 'Virtually all commentators have recognized the presence of wisdom forms, themes, and vocabulary in the teaching of Isaiah of Jerusalem.'[28] As we will see, there is also evidence of them in the book as a whole.

In each of these three areas I will outline those aspects of the book of Isaiah that are seen to be wisdom-like and will then evaluate their significance.

---

26. O'Kane, 'Wisdom Influence', pp. 64–67.
27. Ibid., p. 68.
28. Morgan, *Old Testament Traditions*, p. 76.

Wisdom forms

Teaching formulae

The first suggested example of a wisdom form is found in the opening verses (Isa. 1:2–3) which are sometimes labelled as a teacher's opening formula. Here we see comparisons with animals, father–son language, wisdom terms ('to know', 'to understand'), and parallels with other proverbs. However, there is a clear covenant framework of God acting in history that is central here, which suggests that even if this is a wisdom form, it is not making a wisdom conclusion. However, the learning from the created world (ox, donkey) is worth noting.

Woe oracles

The next passages are the woe oracles, which are most clearly found in Isaiah 5:8–24; 10:1–4; 29:15–16; 30:1–5; 45:9–10. Gerstenberger, and later Whedbee, argue that these are largely connected with wisdom forms.[29] Clearly, these oracles are characterized by social concerns and imagery parallel to that of Proverbs. However, the woe oracle is said to have a provenance or origin in the life of the clan (Gerstenberger's home for wisdom), whereas Isaiah's 'wisdom-like elements' are generally otherwise linked with royal or court wisdom.

Wildberger agrees that the woe oracle does not find its home in palace wisdom, but suggests it is rooted instead in the non-wisdom form of the lament for the dead.[30] He suggests that some wisdom details have been used to supplement the prophetic woe oracles. The intertextual connections are fairly evident. The woe oracle of Isaiah 5:18–20 has clear overlap with Proverbs 5:22. This does not mean Isaiah knew the exact proverb, but he appears to be quite familiar with such thinking. Isaiah 5:22 connects with the wisdom theme of strong wine and drink (e.g. Prov. 31:3b–7). Isaiah uses *dîn* (justice) in 10:2 but nowhere else. It occurs in this sense in Proverbs 20:8; 29:7; 31:5, 8–9. Wildberger suggests the woe oracle of Isaiah 30:1–5 may be reflecting thematically on 1:2–3, and so evidences wisdom concerns.[31] The woe oracles of Isaiah 45:9–10 also use comparisons from the worlds of nature and experience, but seem to echo Job 38 – 39 rather than the book of Proverbs.

---

29. E. R. Gerstenberger, 'The Woe Oracles of the Prophets', *JBL* 81 (1962), pp. 256–258, 261–262; Whedbee, *Isaiah and Wisdom*, pp. 80–110.

30. Wildberger, *Isaiah 28–39*, pp. 604–605.

31. See the discussion of these and other examples in ibid., pp. 605–606.

Summary-appraisals

Childs has identified as a wisdom genre the summary-appraisal form, which
he locates in Isaiah 17:14b; 28:29; 14:26–27.[32] This comprises a demonstra-
tive pronoun introducing a summary followed by an appraisal towards the
end of the unit. Childs suggests that both the form and the content in these
Isaianic examples come from wisdom.[33] This is based on the dissimilarity
from other prophets, the non-cultic character of the form, its didactic function and parallels in wisdom literature (e.g. Prov. 1:19; Ps. 49:13; Job 8:13;
Eccl. 2:26).

Parables

Another form is that of the parable, such as that of the farmer in Isaiah
28:23–29, the ox and donkey in 1:2–3 and the vineyard in 5:1–7. In each case
the prophet appeals to natural experience and examples to make his point.
However, this may not be as clear cut as it might seem, since the parable form
is probably also used by Nathan in 2 Samuel 12. Yet, while Wildberger concedes
that Isaiah 5:1–7 is form-critically an accusation speech, he argues that there
are 'wisdom facets' (e.g. a vineyard as an allegory of a woman, Song 8:11). He
concludes that there is evidence of Isaiah's familiarity with and use of wisdom
material, but that 'the transmitted material is once again turned into something
quite different in his hand'.[34]

Challenge to rival

Rowold has argued that there is a remarkable similarity between the Yahweh
speeches in Job 38 – 39, and the disputations with the idols/gods of the
nations in Isaiah 40 – 55 (e.g. Isa. 40:12–26). He notes that both include
the challenging question as a crucial element. In Isaiah the antagonists are
those who are rivals for the loyalty of God's people, and the function of the
speeches is the same in each book – declaring God's unbridled kingship over
the world. Rowold designates these as a 'challenge to rival' genre. As opposed
to a covenant lawsuit, it is one where Yahweh challenges his antagonists to
duplicate the deeds which are the basis for his authority. He notes that there
is one difference – there is a purpose/result clause in Job not present in Isaiah
40 – 55. While the purpose of this section of Isaiah is to expose any rival
claims to Israel's allegiance, and to establish Yahweh as Lord of all, the aim in

---

32. B. S. Childs, *Isaiah and the Assyrian Crisis*, SBT (London: SCM, 1967), pp. 128–136.

33. Ibid., p. 130. See also Whedbee, *Isaiah and Wisdom*, pp. 75–79.

34. Wildberger, *Isaiah 28–39*, pp. 603–604. The quotation is from p. 604.

Job is to move beyond submission to a restoration of a proper relationship with Job.[35]

Other forms

The book of Isaiah also includes proverbial sayings (Isa. 1:3; 2:22; 3:10–11; 10:15; 29:16; 49:24; 55:8, 13), rhetorical questions and comparative sayings. However, these are probably not confined to the wisdom tradition – though certainly found there – and may be present in popular speech.

Significance

Clearly, these examples establish some interconnection between wisdom and Isaiah. However, although the exact nature of this interrelationship is unclear, two observations can be made. First, the specific overlapping forms are not the central ones in either the wisdom or prophetic traditions. The most common wisdom forms are not the ones found in Isaiah. Nor are the key prophetic forms derived from wisdom. Secondly, the location of these wisdom-like forms is suggestive. While these forms occur throughout the book of Isaiah, they are more common in chapters 1–39, where most of the comparisons are with the book of Proverbs. Where these wisdom-like forms are evident in the latter part of Isaiah, the connections seem to be rather with the book of Job.

Wisdom vocabulary

In Isaiah the identification of wisdom-like words appears less fruitful than elsewhere. One of the difficulties of using vocabulary to discern the presence of wisdom is that there is no agreed list of wisdom or predominantly wisdom words.

Examples

However, there are several interesting examples in Isaiah. For example, the phrase 'wise in one's own eyes' occurs in Isaiah 5:21 and elsewhere only in Proverbs (Prov. 26:5, 12, 16; 28:11; 3:7, though with different pronominal suffixes).[36] The paired imperatives 'hear and understand' and 'see and per-ceive' are found in Isaiah 1:2, but are common in wisdom (Prov. 4:1, 10; 23:19; Job 13:6; 34:2).[37] Isaiah 11:2 overflows with wisdom words, and the

---

35. Rowold, 'Theology of Creation', pp. 60–65.

36. Fichtner, 'Isaiah among the Wise', p. 434.

37. So R. B. Y. Scott, *The Way of Wisdom* (New York: Macmillan, 1971), p. 125.

pairing of wisdom and understanding is reminiscent of Proverbs 14:33. This overlap between Isaiah 11:2 and wisdom is surprising because of wisdom's comparative lack of interest in Yahweh's spirit.[38]

Wisdom terms are also used in the second part of Isaiah. There is, for example, an unusual concentration of terms for knowing, learning and understanding in Isaiah 40:13–14. Other key wisdom words are used in Isaiah 40:21; 41:20; 44:18–19, 25, while terms like justice and righteousness are jointly used in both wisdom and prophetic texts.

Isaiah 55:8–9 makes a similar point to Proverbs 16:1–3 (see also Prov. 3:5–6; 21:2; Job 38 – 39), with both passages using the same words for 'ways' and 'thoughts'.

Significance
While the number of examples is small, some of the specific instances establish a clear connection. The speakers have heard of, and use, particular wisdom-like words and phrases, which seems to reflect some intersection of wisdom and Isaiah.

Wisdom themes
As well as wisdom forms and vocabulary, certain wisdom themes and concerns have also been noted in the book, such as references to nature and knowledge discerned from nature (e.g. Isa. 1:2–3). The following material will deal with a number of these themes, and those parts of the book of Isaiah where they seem to be concentrated.

True and false wisdom
Indeed, some of the explicit statements in Isaiah imply that the book is opposing wisdom practitioners. For example, the wisdom and counsel of Yahweh is contrasted with those who consider themselves wise (Isa. 3:2–3; 5:21; 8:9–10; 10:5–15; 14:24–27; 19:1–4; 29:13–16). Some of these were Israelites and some foreigners, but it is likely that many of these passages were directed at the professional counsellors of the king for their ungodly wisdom. The withdrawal of wisdom from the wise is one of the threats Isaiah makes in Isaiah 29:14.

Footnote 37 (*continued*)
   Wildberger, *Isaiah 28–39*, pp. 600–601, argues that, in contrast to Amos and Hosea,
   Isaiah uses terms like 'wisdom' and 'know' in a wisdom sense.
38. J. Goldingay, *Isaiah*, NIBCOT (Peabody: Hendrickson, 2001), p. 84.

Isaiah 29:14 is sometimes used to argue that Isaiah could not be sympathetic to wisdom, as it predicts the end to the wisdom and discernment of the sages. However, this passage is entirely consistent with a high view of wisdom. Job conflicts with the wise men as well, yet is undoubtedly part of the wisdom movement. What Isaiah opposes here is not the wisdom enterprise itself, but rather false wisdom. This is entirely consistent with the book of Proverbs, which describes wisdom in the hands of a fool as useless (Prov. 26:7) and dangerous (Prov. 26:9). Indeed, whenever wisdom is separated from the fear of the Lord, it becomes false wisdom or folly (e.g. 1 Kgs 11). The rebuke in 29:13–14 is not of all wisdom or all cultic worship; it is a critique of both cult and wisdom gone wrong.[39] Incidentally, this is further testimony that the sages were a recognized feature of the court at this time. While many (e.g. Childs, Sweeney) link Isaiah 29:15–16 with verses 17–21, it does flow on nicely from verse 14.[40] The creation theology of verse 16 provides a restorative balance.

This contrast between true and false wisdom is also found in Isaiah 40 – 66. In Isaiah 47:10 the false wisdom of the Babylonians is condemned, just like the earlier wisdom figures of Egypt (Isa. 19:11–13). While this wisdom was perhaps mantic (in the light of vv. 9, 11–13), it was at least wisdom and knowledge mixed with pride (vv. 7–8, 10). This is a warning to Israel about a certain kind of wisdom that does not honour God (Isa. 44:25). Again this is not a rejection of wisdom, but of wisdom no longer serving its intended purpose.

The use of tôrâ

Another key area is the way *tôrâ* is used by the prophet. In contrast to Hosea, who assumes a more cultic conception of *tôrâ*, it is claimed that Isaiah has a wisdom understanding. Yahweh is thus the imparter of wise instruction, based on the parallel with the (assumed) wisdom schools. On this view *tôrâ* (Isa. 1:10; 2:3; 5:24b; 8:16, 20; 30:9) is meant to be understood in a wisdom sense of instruction. The connection between *tôrâ* and wisdom has been most exhaustively explored by Jensen, who argues that the word is used by Isaiah to refer to the teaching of the whole wisdom tradition rather than the pro-phetic or legal traditions. He proposes that Isaiah is carrying on a debate with the wisdom leaders of his day, trying to show them that they have not lived

---

39. See Wildberger, *Isaiah 28–39*, p. 598.

40. B. S. Childs, *Isaiah*, OTL (Louisville: Westminster John Knox, 2001), pp. 214–217; M. A. Sweeney, *Isaiah 1–39 with an Introduction to Prophetic Literature*, FOTL 16 (Grand Rapids: Eerdmans, 1996), pp. 373–378.

up to the demands and expectations of their own tradition, in that they have neglected Yahweh and his wisdom.

In relation to 5:8–24 he writes:

> Those here addressed, i.e., the royal officials, function both as advisers to the king and as administrators of justice. As men who have been educated in the school which undoubtedly existed in Jerusalem for the training of scribes for the royal court and of children of the upper classes, those who were destined for careers at court, they had been introduced into all the riches of the wisdom tradition and could lay claim to belonging to the circle of the wise. Isaiah accuses them of being poor advisers, of being corrupt judges, and of neglecting the ideals of their training, the value of which he does not question.[41]

There is explicit mention of offices and groups associated with the wise (Isa. 1:26; 3:1–3; 7:5; 10:1–4 etc.). At the very least this suggests that Isaiah was aware of a tradition that stressed an experiential method of learning and was to some extent influenced by it.

Isaiah 28 – 33

The large number of wisdom-like features in chapters 28–33 leads Seitz to conclude that they are riddled with the theme of proper wisdom and knowledge (Isa. 28:7–13, 23–29; 29:13–16, 22–24; 31:1–3; 32:1–8; 33:6).[42]

The best-known passage is the parable of the farmer in Isaiah 28:23–29. The farmer illustrates and embodies a practical wisdom as he discerns how and when to farm. This practical skill is at the heart of the Hebrew understanding of wisdom, like the skill of the navigator or craftsman (Exod. 31:1–5; 35:10, 25–26, 30–35; Ezek. 27:8–9). What is striking is that there is no word from Yahweh here (cf. Isa. 28:14 in the previous unit). There is only the voice of instruction.[43] O'Kane thinks that this parable is a fifth-century redactional addition designed to assure the post-exilic community that God acts with wisdom.[44] Its role is to interpret the preceding verses as it moves from drunk-

---

41. J. Jensen, *Isaiah 1–39* (Wilmington: Michael Glazier, 1984), p. 79. There is, however, considerable debate over the extent of schools in Israel.

42. C. R. Seitz, *Isaiah 1–39*, Interpretation (Louisville: John Knox, 1989), p. 208.

43. Wildberger, *Isaiah 28–39*, p. 603. Scott, *Way of Wisdom*, p. 125, notes that there are both 'clear marks of the wisdom style' yet 'the concluding words identify it as a prophetic oracle'.

44. O'Kane, 'Wisdom Influence', pp. 74–76.

enness, confusion and foolishness, through to clarity and wisdom. Whether or not he is correct in his proposed setting, he does make a convincing case that the purpose is clearly educational: 'the reader is urged to learn from the farmer who prospers because he learns from the wisdom of Yahweh'.[45]

Indeed, O'Kane argues that 'Wisdom themes are used in chs 28–33 to interpret a wide corpus of material . . . within the consistent perspective of Yahweh's wise plan.'[46] He suggests that the emphasis in chapters 28–33 on the wisdom of Yahweh binds this section together: the wicked act foolishly and the righteous act wisely. He sees themes such as listening to the words of Yahweh bringing security and peace (Isa. 28:12, 16; 29:18, 24; 30:15, 18, 20); instruction is offered even to the wicked (Isa. 29:24; 32:3–4); God's plans are superior to those of humans (Isa. 28:21; 29:14); the parable of the farmer (Isa. 28:23–29) emphasizes that God's wise actions are carried out in justice. In wisdom terms the reader is summoned to attention (e.g. Isa. 28:23).

Isaiah 40 – 55

Morgan argues that the only wisdom writer connected to the exile (Job) shares many of the concerns of Isaiah 40 – 55. Parallels with proverbial wisdom have been more prominent in chapters 1–39, which are largely connected to more settled times (compared to the exile) of the eighth century. In an exilic setting, which appears presupposed in chapters 40–55 (e.g. Isa. 40:1–2), we would expect wisdom more like Job's questioning and reworking of faith.[47] Terrien notes a number of connections between Job and Isaiah 40 – 55, in particular, the three motifs of divine transcendence (Job 9:4 and Isa. 40:26; Job 9:8 and Isa. 44:24b), existence of being (Job 4:19 and Isa. 45:9, 11) and the servant of God (Job 3:23 and Isa. 40:27a). He argues that the similarity of language, style and fundamental themes suggests that Isaiah 40 – 55 responds to existential questions raised by Job.[48]

---

45. Ibid., p. 76.

46. Ibid., p. 73. He builds on Sheppard's notion of wisdom as a canonical hermeneutical construct, suggesting that, as in Ps. 2, the nations of Egypt, Assyria, Ephraim and Judah are evaluated in terms of whether they have behaved foolishly in ignoring the wise plans of Yahweh.

47. Morgan, *Old Testament Traditions*, p. 119.

48. Terrien, 'Quelques remarques', pp. 297–299. He thinks that the borrowing works that way, since if Isa. 40 – 55 were written first, he would expect that Job would also have picked up Isaiah's notions of vicarious suffering and use of the verb 'to create' (pp. 309–310).

Creation theology

It is often observed that the theology undergirding the wisdom enterprise is creation theology. There is a strong emphasis on God as creator in Isaiah (Isa. 42:5; 44:24; 45:7, 12; 48:13), and the language of restoration uses the image of new creation (e.g. Isa. 65:17–25). The doctrine of creation is usually seen as less prominent in Isaiah 1 – 39, but is clearly present there as well (e.g. the parables in Isa. 5:1–7; 28:23–29; also 2:2; 4:5; 5:12; 17:7–8; 27:11; 29:16; 37:16).[49] While creation theology may not be sufficiently distinctive from wisdom to establish 'wisdom influence', it does show the compatibility between wisdom and the book of Isaiah.

The fear of the Lord

Another prominent wisdom idea central to Isaiah is the concept of the fear of the Lord. Schultz has proposed that the idea is found in Isaiah 7:4; 8:12–13; 10:24; 11:2–3; 12:2; 19:16; 33:6; 35:4; 37:6; 40:9; 41:10, 13–14; 43:1, 5; 44:2, 8; 50:10; 51:7, 12; 54:4, 14; 57:11; 59:19.[50]

A key passage here is Isaiah 8:11–17 (esp. vv. 12–13). The poetic parallelism of verses 12–13 is very significant. In verse 11 Isaiah is urged not to follow the way of the people, which is filled out in verse 12 by 'do not fear what they fear, / and do not dread it' NIV. That parallel between fear and dread is picked up and given a new twist in verse 13. Here there are three terms in parallel:

> The LORD Almighty is the one you are to regard as holy,
>> he is the one you are to fear,
>> he is the one you are to dread.
>
> (NIV)

---

49. S. Paas, *Creation and Judgement: Creation Texts in Some Eighth Century Prophets*, OTS 47 (Leiden: Brill, 2003), pp. 363–419. He makes a distinction between 'creation texts' (Isa. 1:2; 5:12b; 14:32b; 17:7–8; 22:11b; 29:16) and 'creation motifs' (Isa. 1:24; 2:22; 5:1–7; 6:1; 9:6a–b; 28:23–29). He also identifies other passages where creation can be found but does not regard them as being authentically from Isaiah of Jerusalem (Isa. 2:2; 4:5a; 11:11; 16:5; 19:25b; 26:19; 27:1, 11b; 37:16). Paas, at pp. 418–419, concludes that creation theology is important to Isaiah of Jerusalem, and that he uses it to emphasize both Yahweh's kingship and his administration of justice and order.

50. R. L. Schultz, 'Isaiah, Book of', in K. J. Vanhoozer (ed.), *Dictionary for Theological Interpretation of the Bible* (London: SPCK; Grand Rapids: Baker, 2005), p. 344.

They are no longer to be in dread of nations like Assyria, who make a claim to be in charge and able to determine the destiny of Israel. Instead, they are to be in dread of God, which means in its context that they are to make sure that their actions align with his purposes. The notion of the fear of God is transformed in this verse by being in parallel with regarding the Lord Almighty as holy. In other words, the fear of God is regarding God as holy, or even treating or respecting God as God.

Similar ideas can also be found in Isaiah 50:10, where fearing the Lord is in parallel with those who trust and rely on God, and Isaiah 51:7. These examples of the use of the fear of the Lord concept are compatible with the wisdom tradition.

Some false trails

There are, however, some false trails. Sometimes the same topic is under consideration, but the theme is dealt with differently in Isaiah. For example, a prominent motif in the book of Proverbs is the warning against the adulteress or loose woman. This issue is also in view in Isaiah 57, but this passage does *not* seem to have the same flavour as Proverbs 5 – 7. The focus in Isaiah 57 is rather on spiritual adultery coupled with idolatry (vv. 5–8). There is an intersection of topic, but wisdom ways of thinking do not inform the discussion.

Indeed, it is often worth checking how wisdom ways of thinking are actually used in Isaiah. Sometimes there is a wisdom-like set of observations (e.g. the observations about the metalworkers and their skill in Isa. 41:7) but the prophet proceeds to make a non-wisdom point (a word of comfort to his elect people in Isa. 41:8–10). This suggests that here wisdom does not set the agenda for Isaiah – there is no suggestion of any wisdom goals in view. However, the use of the wisdom-like examples does imply that wisdom is more part of society's way of speaking and thinking than some believe. Wisdom is not a 'no-go zone' for the book of Isaiah, but neither is it what drives the writers. It appears to be simply part of the intellectual and literary world in which they live.

A similar example can be found in Isaiah 11:2, where a cluster of wisdom terms (wisdom, understanding, counsel, knowledge, fear of the Lord) is used to describe the future king. However, it too leads on to the topic of judgment for breaches of the covenant (Isa. 11:4–5) and a picture of the eschatological future (Isa. 11:6–9). These concerns are not customarily part of wisdom texts, so it appears that these wisdom terms have been incorporated into the book for a different purpose.

Significance

The prevalence of these themes in all parts of the book, as well as the centrality of the ideas to both Isaiah and the sages, indicates a strong intersection between wisdom and the book of Isaiah. Yet Isaiah does not appear to be promoting either a wisdom or an anti-wisdom agenda. His concerns for righteousness and justice, for the honouring of Israel's covenant, and for the holiness and majesty of God remain crucial prophetic concerns. The book uses wisdom ideas because they are understood and accepted by the readers, even when the aim is not (as in Isa. 11:2; 41:7; 57:3–8) to effect a sapiential goal. The most compelling reason for this overlap with wisdom is that these wisdom ideas are adopted and adapted because they are seen to be consistent with the prophetic agenda of the book.

Drawing the threads together

Some general observations

It is evident that some of these supposed parallels between wisdom and Isaiah are overdrawn, or at least they need more substantial support than what has been given. In general the parallels between Proverbs and Isaiah 1 – 39 are more persuasive than those between Job and Isaiah 40 – 55. Job, of course, could have had a long literary history, and may include older wisdom ideas.

It is also apparent that a variety of wisdoms have been suggested as backgrounds to the book of Isaiah: the wise in the court, clan wisdom, scribal wisdom in schools. This implies that wisdom itself must be recognized as a diverse movement.

Yet many wisdom ideas and expressions appear to have been adopted into the book of Isaiah, but not uncritically. The views of the wise (especially the wise of the court) are often qualified or critiqued. Just as the later wisdom books of Job and Ecclesiastes qualify fossilized views of wisdom derived from Proverbs, so the prophets qualified the views of those who had misunderstood the teaching of the sages. The wisdom that is part of Old Testament theology is not a wisdom left unchanged by the other strands. It must be adapted as it is adopted into the mainstream of Old Testament thought. Throughout the canon, the wise in Judah, and their counsel, are often subject to criticism in the historical and prophetic writings (e.g. Isa. 29:14; Exod. 7:8–13; 2 Sam. 13:3–5; 14:1–21; 16:23 – 17:23; 20; 1 Kgs 1 – 2; Gen. 3). This is best understood as a correction to those among the wise who overstepped the limits of true wisdom. This is not a rejection of wisdom, but a correction of wisdom wrongly applied.

Hubbard has suggested that 'What the prophets oppose, especially Isaiah, is a wisdom from which the fear of God has been drained, a paganized kind of political understanding that distorts the true ideal of wisdom.'[51]

Wisdom as part of everyday life

The wise counsellors or sages were common figures in leadership in the Israelite monarchy. There were wisdom advisors to David and Absalom; the wise women of 2 Samuel 14, 20; the wise as a group in Jeremiah 8:8–9; 18:18.[52] Thus it would not be a surprise for them as leaders and educators in Israel to have had some influence on the writer(s) of the book of Isaiah. A useful question to ask is 'Why were wisdom or wisdom-like elements able to be incorporated so easily into the book of Isaiah without standing out as foreign?' The obvious answer is that wisdom observations resonated with the Israelites who knew that both wisdom and the wise were genuine parts of Israelite society. It is not a matter of whether Isaiah has drunk from wisdom's stream. Rather, wisdom's stream flows as part of a mixed water supply in Israel.

Wisdom, and its exponents, the sages, were important components of Israelite society, both in contributing to it and learning from it. In particular, wisdom shows a way forward in many situations of everyday life (e.g. Isa. 28:23–29) not explicitly covered by the law or by a direct word from God.[53] Wisdom forms and vocabulary are thus unsurprising in a prophetic book like Isaiah. Since wisdom is a crucial player in Israelite society, wisdom forms, themes and interests are part of the toolbox of society in Israel from before the time of Isaiah. As Morgan expresses it, 'the wisdom tradition is an integral part of Israelite religion and society, accessible to priest and prophet, counsellor and king'.[54]

Scott also notes a number of common elements between prophets and the sages, such as a common inheritance and shared social experience. Both

---

51. D. A. Hubbard, 'The Wisdom Movement and Israel's Covenant Faith', *TynBul* 17 (1966), p. 19.

52. Contra S. Weeks, *Early Israelite Wisdom* (Oxford: Clarendon, 1994), p. 90, who argues against Jer. 8:8–9 and 18:18 as providing any evidence of 'a class of wise men representative of the secular or political establishment'. He seems to be trying to argue away a lot of evidence.

53. Scott, *Way of Wisdom*, p. 114, puts it like this: 'The prophet calls on men to hear, decide, and obey. The wise man summons them to understand and to learn. He does not demand, but seeks to persuade and instruct.'

54. Morgan, 'Wisdom and the Prophets', p. 220.

groups were intellectual and articulate, used to the skilful use of language, and referred to moral teachings as part of the common stock of that community.[55] Jensen looks at the sources of Isaiah's moral teaching, and argues that Isaiah was almost certainly educated at the same school in Jerusalem responsible for the training of the leaders and rulers in his day. This suggests a society where wisdom had an integral place.[56]

Wisdom as part of Israelite theology

It is not just that the wise were part of Israelite society. Wisdom itself is a key component of Israelite theology. Many distinctively wisdom themes and concerns are part of the common stock of traditions in the Old Testament. If these wisdom ideas had permeated the common cultural stock, this highlights that wisdom is already woven into the way of thinking of the prophets. This seems to confirm Murphy's view that 'the sages' understanding of reality is not to be judged as an esoteric view of a given class. Their understanding of reality, as this emerges from the wisdom literature, is the Israelite understanding of reality. Priest and prophet and sage shared in this common understanding.'[57] Wisdom ideas are part of 'orthodox Israelite theology' and so are not foreign bodies needing to be excised from the prophetic traditions. Wisdom, it seems, was one strand of thinking that became progressively interwoven with the other theological strands to form the core theology of the Old Testament.

Thus a commitment to social justice evident in Isaiah (e.g. Isa. 1:2–20; 5:8–23; 58:1–14; 61:1–11) is also a feature of wisdom (e.g. Job 31) and indeed of the law (e.g. Deut. 15). There is a high degree of overlap between the teachings of the book of Proverbs on the poor (Prov. 14:31; 19:17; 21:13; 22:16; 22:22–23), sacrifice (Prov. 15:8), justice and sobriety in judgment (Prov. 17:15; 19:5; 31:4–5) and the accusations of the prophets.[58] Fichtner suggests that this ethical instruction is part of the common property of every Israelite, and points out the parallel views of displacing boundaries, false weights, corruption and so on and a common critical stance to the cult (e.g. Isa. 1:10–17; Prov.

---

55. Scott, *Way of Wisdom*, pp. 122–125.

56. Jensen, *Ethical Dimensions*, p. 113. See also Wildberger, *Isaiah 28–39*, p. 599.

57. R. E. Murphy, 'Wisdom Theses', in J. Armenti (ed.), *Wisdom and Knowledge*, 2 vols. (Philadelphia: Villanova University, 1976), p. 190, quoted in Morgan, 'Wisdom and the Prophets', p. 228. See also R. E. Murphy, *The Tree of Life: An Exploration of Biblical Wisdom Literature*, 3rd ed. (Grand Rapids: Eerdmans, 1990), p. 113.

58. Jensen, *Ethical Dimensions*, pp. 115–116.

15:8, 29; 20:25; 21:3, 27; 28:9; 30:12).[59] Furthermore, in Isaiah 1:2–3, 5:11–13 and 6:9–10 it is the basic wisdom concept of failure to know or inability to understand that is Israel's fundamental problem.

This suggests that Isaiah's critique of the wise in passages like 29:14 is not a rejection of the wisdom enterprise, but of its excesses and wrong applications. Weeks, however, argues that in 31:2 the wisdom of God is set against human wisdom, not only the 'false' wisdom of the nation's leaders, and that in 44:25 'wise men', alongside diviners, stand in contrast to the prophets.[60] A better reading of these passages is that Isaiah is simply rebuking those who have used wisdom wrongly. Jensen suggests that when Isaiah criticizes the wise, it is related either to their administration of justice or their advice to the king.[61] Scott puts it well: 'The calculating politicians whom Isaiah denounces as self-styled wise men are no more typical of wisdom as a whole than the false prophets who opposed Jeremiah are typical of prophecy.'[62]

In the broader context of the Old Testament, Goldingay's twin poles of creation and redemption provide the undergirding for much Old Testament theology.[63] In relation to Isaiah 40 – 55, Stephen Lee has argued that both creation and redemption are aspects of an even more fundamental theme – that of God's absolute sovereignty, or his active kingly rule.[64] In other words, God can actively rule as king in the time of Isaiah both by raising up nations to fight against Israel (and, of course, to intervene to deliver a king like Hezekiah), but also by actively promoting his goals in everyday life, or in the created world.[65] If Israelite or Old Testament theology is essentially about God's active kingly rule (both in creation and in Israel, both in his mighty acts and in his daily sustaining of his creation, both for the Israelites and for humanity at large), then wisdom is a significant part of God's broader concerns. The book of Isaiah, with a strong creation theology and a firm belief in God's redemptive plans, testifies to a God who is actively ruling as king in all spheres of life.

---

59. Fichtner, 'Isaiah among the Wise', p. 430.

60. Weeks, *Early Israelite Wisdom*, p. 85.

61. Jensen, *Ethical Dimensions*, p. 114.

62. Scott, *Way of Wisdom*, p. 103.

63. J. Goldingay, *Theological Diversity and the Authority of the Old Testament* (Grand Rapids: Eerdmans, 1987).

64. S. Lee, *Creation and Redemption in Isaiah 40–55*, JDDS 2 (Hong Kong: Alliance Biblical Seminary, 1995), pp. 192–198.

65. On this duality in the Joseph narrative see Wilson, *Joseph Wise and Otherwise*, ch. 11. It could equally be argued in the time of Isaiah.

Wisdom is a home for additional resources that may be useful in addressing dilemmas arising among God's people. In particular, it can cover those areas of life not regulated by the law, and on which the prophets have received no specific revelation – but which are important areas for them to address. Thus there is in the book of Isaiah an appreciative but still discerning adoption of some crucial wisdom concepts, analogies and expressions, since they fit well in this Isaianic framework.

Bibliography

Childs, B. S., *Isaiah*, OTL (Louisville: Westminster John Knox, 2001).

—, *Isaiah and the Assyrian Crisis*, SBT (London: SCM, 1967).

Fichtner, J., 'Isaiah among the Wise', in J. L. Crenshaw (ed.), *Studies in Ancient Israelite Wisdom* (New York: KTAV, 1976 [orig. 1949]), pp. 429–438.

Gerstenberger, E. R., 'The Woe Oracles of the Prophets', *JBL* 81 (1962), pp. 249–263.

Goldingay, J., *Isaiah*, NIBCOT (Peabody: Hendrickson, 2001).

—, *Theological Diversity and the Authority of the Old Testament* (Grand Rapids: Eerdmans, 1987).

Hubbard, D. A., 'The Wisdom Movement and Israel's Covenant Faith', *TynBul* 17 (1966), pp. 3–33.

Jensen, J., *Ethical Dimensions of the Prophets* (Collegeville: Michael Glazier / Liturgical, 2006).

—, *Isaiah 1–39* (Wilmington: Michael Glazier, 1984).

—, *The Use of* tôrâ *by Isaiah: His Debate with the Wisdom Tradition*, CBQMS 3 (Washington: Catholic Biblical Association, 1973).

Lee, S., *Creation and Redemption in Isaiah 40–55*, JDDS 2 (Hong Kong: Alliance Biblical Seminary, 1995).

Lindblom, J., 'Wisdom in the Old Testament Prophets', in M. Noth and D. W. Thomas (eds.), *Wisdom in Israel and in the Ancient Near East*, VTSup3 (Leiden: Brill, 1955), pp. 192–204.

Morgan, D. F., 'Wisdom and the Prophets', in E. A. Livingstone (ed.), *Studia Biblica 1978*, JSOTSup 11 (Sheffield: JSOT, 1979), pp. 209–244.

—, *Wisdom in the Old Testament Traditions* (Oxford: Basil Blackwell, 1981).

Murphy, R. E., *The Tree of Life: An Exploration of Biblical Wisdom Literature*, 3rd ed. (Grand Rapids: Eerdmans, 1990).

—, 'Wisdom Theses', in J. Armenti (ed.), *Wisdom and Knowledge*, 2 vols. (Philadelphia: Villanova University, 1976), 2:187–200.

O'Kane, M., 'Wisdom Influence in First Isaiah', *PIBA* 14 (1991), pp. 64–78.

Paas, S., *Creation and Judgement: Creation Texts in Some Eighth Century Prophets*, OTS 47 (Leiden: Brill, 2003).

Rowold, H. L., 'The Theology of Creation in the Yahweh Speeches of the Book of Job as a Solution to the Problem Posed by the Book of Job' (ThD thesis, Concordia Seminary in Exile, St. Louis, 1977).

—, 'Yahweh's Challenge to Rival: The Form and Function of the Yahweh-Speech in Job 38–39', *CBQ* 47 (1985), pp. 199–211.

Schultz, R. L., 'Isaiah, Book of', in K. J. Vanhoozer (ed.), *Dictionary for Theological Interpretation of the Bible* (London: SPCK; Grand Rapids: Baker, 2005), pp. 336–344.

Scott, R. B. Y., *The Way of Wisdom in the Old Testament* (New York: Macmillan, 1971).

Seitz, C. R., *Isaiah 1–39*, Interpretation (Louisville: John Knox, 1989).

Sheppard, G. T., *Wisdom as a Hermeneutical Construct: A Study in the Sapientializing of the Old Testament*, BZAW 151 (Berlin: de Gruyter, 1980).

Sweeney, M. A., *Isaiah 1–39 with an Introduction to Prophetic Literature*, FOTL 16 (Grand Rapids: Eerdmans, 1996).

Terrien, S., 'Quelques remarques sur les affinités de Job avec le Deutéro-Isaïe', in *Volume du Congrès. Genève 1965*, VTSup 15 (Leiden: Brill, 1966), pp. 295–310.

Vermeylen, J., 'Le Proto-Isaïe et la sagesse d'Israël', in M. Gilbert (ed.), *La Sagesse de l'Ancien Testament*, BETL 51 (Leuven: Leuven University Press, 1990), pp. 39–58.

Weeks, S., *Early Israelite Wisdom* (Oxford: Clarendon, 1994).

Whedbee, J. W., *Isaiah and Wisdom* (Nashville, Abingdon, 1971).

Wildberger, H., *Isaiah 28–39*, tr. T. H. Trapp, CC (Minneapolis: Fortress, 2002).

Williamson, H. G. M., 'Isaiah and the Wise', in J. Day et al. (eds.), *Wisdom in Ancient Israel* (Cambridge: Cambridge University Press, 1995), pp. 133–141.

Wilson, L., *Joseph Wise and Otherwise: The Intersection of Wisdom and Covenant in Genesis 37–50*, PBM (Carlisle: Paternoster, 2004).

8. THE THEOLOGY OF ISAIAH

John Goldingay

I find seven dominant theological themes emerging from Isaiah:[1]

1. Revelation via divine initiative and the mediation of a prophet, and the ongoing significance of Yhwh's words.
2. Yhwh as Israel's holy one, upright and merciful.
3. Israel as Yhwh's people and Jerusalem as Yhwh's city, both rebellious but chosen.
4. The remnant of Israel, surviving by Yhwh's grace and challenged now to be responsive.
5. The destiny of nations, empires and their kings.

---

1. The exegetical basis for positions assumed here may be found in J. Goldingay, 'The Compound Name in Isaiah 9.5 [6]', *CBQ* 61 (1999), pp. 239–244; '"If Your Sins Are Like Scarlet . . . " (Isaiah 1:18)', *ST* 35 (1981), pp. 137–144; *Isaiah* (Peabody: Hendrickson; Carlisle: Paternoster, 2001); 'Isaiah i l; ii 1', *VT* 48 (1998), pp. 326–332; *The Message of Isaiah 40 – 55* (London: T. & T. Clark, 2005); J. Goldingay and D. Payne, *Isaiah 40 – 55*, ICC (London: T. & T. Clark, 2006). A longer version of the chapter appears at <http://documents.fuller.edu/sot/faculty/goldingay>, accessed 29 Dec. 2008.

6. Divine sovereignty and human responsibility.
7. The day of Yhwh and the David to come.

Revelation

Isaiah 1 begins, 'The vision (*ḥāzôn*) of Isaiah ben Amoz' (1:1).[2] What we read in Isaiah 1 is something Isaiah saw that not everyone could see; more literally or more usually, he heard God speak (1:2, 10–11, 18, 20, 24). Slightly paradoxically, the chapter's colophon similarly describes it as 'the word that Isaiah ben Amoz saw (*ḥāzâ*)'. Isaiah 1, and more broadly the book that this chapter introduces, is not something Isaiah thought up but something that presented itself to him. He heard Yhwh speaking to him or externalizing an inner reflection or making a declaration to the court in the heavens. Subsequently, Isaiah speaks like a messenger repeating his master's words, 'the Lord Yhwh has said this' (e.g. 7:7; 10:24). He comes with the great king's authority and speaks with the 'I' of the great king (cf. 36:4, 14, 16). Isaiah 1 uses the less common *yiqtol*, 'Yhwh says' (1:11, 18), which may be even more worrying. Yhwh not merely says this once but continues to aver it. Other formulations underline the matter's seriousness. Isaiah speaks 'Yhwh's word', something 'the mouth of Yhwh spoke', 'the declaration (*nĕ'um*) of the Lord Yhwh Armies' (1:10, 20, 24). This is a revelation with the authenticity and demand of divine dictation. 'Yhwh Armies revealed himself in my ears' (22:14).

Yet Isaiah 1 is not 'Yhwh's vision' but 'Isaiah's vision'. To the scene opening up before him, Isaiah ben Amoz brings an angle of vision differing from one Jeremiah or Ezekiel would bring. Revelation comes via human words. The Rabshakeh may sometimes pass on Sennacherib's actual words (36:4–10, 13–20), but also dialogues with Hezekiah's staff, and continues then to speak as if relating the king's words. Even when himself devising the words, he uses the king's 'I': his words are still the king's words, with the king's authority. So it is with Isaiah.

Isaiah's person brings Yhwh's revelation. He and his children are signs and portents from Yhwh (8:18). His name, 'Yhwh-is-deliverance', embodies his message; more explicitly, his children's names do so (7:3 with 10:21–22; 8:1–4; perhaps also 7:14). Isaiah walks around Jerusalem stripped, as a sign of the coming fate of Egypt and Nubia, on whom Judah would therefore be unwise to rely (20:1–6). And as Yhwh's representative, he gets treated as people treat Yhwh (28:7–10).

---

2. All Bible translations in this chapter are my own.

In Isaiah 40 – 55 being a prophet also means being identified with Israel in order to fulfil a ministry:

Yhwh summoned me from the womb . . .
And said to me, 'You are my servant,
    Israel, in whom I will display my attractiveness.'
(49:1–3)

The prophet is to embody the service of Yhwh that Israel is called to and still destined for, and thus

to turn Jacob back to him,
    to stop Israel withdrawing.
(49:5)

This means listening to Yhwh like a disciple, doing what the teacher says, and being tough enough to face the concomitant shame and persecution (50:4–9).

There is much more to the toughness of the task, and to the identification with the community. In 52:13 – 53:12 the prophet is on the way to death. The community assumes that this confirms its convictions about the prophet, but eventually realizes that actually this servant of Yhwh suffers for the sake of ministering to them, turning the undeserved suffering that this ministry entails into an offering to Yhwh that might compensate for the community's own wilfulness. And Yhwh is behind all that; Yhwh's own promise is that this suffering will not be the end. The self-offering will be effective. Horrific affliction will be succeeded by a spectacular anointing. And the prophet will be the means whereby cleansing comes to nations and kings.

A prophet speaks further in 61:1–3. Anointing is the rite whereby a priest consecrates a king or priest. Here Yhwh anoints a prophet; the declaration takes up the promise in 52:14. The prophet continues the ministry exercised by the one who speaks in Isaiah 40 – 55, as the community still experiences weakness, hurt, servitude and abandonment.

There is another facet of Isaiah that relates to traditional discussion of revelation and its relationship to Scripture. Isaiah 1 – 39 and 40 – 55 incorporate material explicitly addressing the eighth century BC and the 540s. Isaiah 56 – 66 incorporates material implicitly addressing a subsequent context, perhaps the latter part of the sixth century BC; the book may also include other material that implicitly addresses other contexts. Sometimes a message in one part of the book becomes the text on which a later message is based. Earlier material has become the recognized Word of God on which later material preaches. So 2:2–4 is taken up and nuanced in 42:1–4 (if the second passage is actually earlier than the first, the flow from text to exposition is the reverse, but this does not affect the principle). Motifs recur in the book, such as blindness (6:9–10; 29:9–10; 32:3; 35:5; 42:7; 43:8), potter and clay (29:16; 45:9; 64:8 [7]) or the preparing of Yhwh's way (40:3; 57:14). The 'sermons' take up their texts in varying ways: they may nuance them, say 'Yes, but/and now . . . ', riff on them or reapply them. In each case they assume that ongoing significance attaches to Yhwh's earlier words. Prophetic revelation has become authoritative tradition and eventually written text that can be illuminating for subsequent generations, and can invite them to consider what Yhwh is doing with them in the light of it.

The God of Israel: the holy one, Yhwh armies, upright and merciful

The description of Yhwh as 'Israel's holy one' runs through all three main parts of Isaiah (e.g. 1:4; 17:7; 29:19; 37:23; 41:14; 55:5; 60:9). The vision described in 6:1–13 may have led to Isaiah's adopting or devising the title. There, Yhwh is not merely once holy, or twice holy, but thrice holy; not merely holy, or very holy, but utterly holy. The accompaniments and reactions to the scene point to the significance of holiness. It is not a moral category but a metaphysical one. Beings such as gods and angels are holy whether or not they are very moral. 'Holy' means belonging to the heavenly realm, the supernatural world, not the everyday, worldly, human, created, this-worldly one. As the thrice-holy one, Yhwh is the ultimate in the supernatural, extraordinary, uncreated, heavenly.

The associated epithet 'Yhwh Armies', *yhwh ṣĕbā'ôt* (6:3), also characteristic of Isaiah 1 – 55 (e.g. 1:9; 13:4; 24:23; 28:5; 37:16; 44:6; 54:5), underlines that. While somewhat enigmatic, its general implication is clear. It points to Yhwh's power as warrior (cf. 13:4; 24:21; 31:4; 42:13–14). Yhwh controls or embodies all forceful might, all strength and power. While this title does not occur in Isaiah 56 – 66, these chapters incorporate further powerful expositions of the image of Yhwh the warrior (59:15b–19; 63:1–6).

So warfare is not left to earthly powers. Sennacherib reckons he is the only military power in the Middle East and that no alleged gods can frustrate him. Hezekiah therefore bids Yhwh to act 'so that all earth's kingdoms may acknowledge that you alone are Yhwh' (37:18–20). This might seem not a very profound acknowledgment, but it involves a recurring ellipse. To say Yhwh is *the* holy one is in effect to say that Yhwh is the only God. This is not merely an assertion of monotheism; it is a bigger declaration than that. Isaiah does not start from the question how many gods there are or whether there is a principle of unity behind reality but from the question of who is God and from the unrivalled holiness of Yhwh. There is such a difference between Yhwh and other gods that only Yhwh deserves the description 'God'. The terms 'Yhwh' and 'God' have different meaning but the same reference; both refer to only one reality.

So to 'acknowledge that you alone are Yhwh' is to acknowledge that you alone are God. That is evidenced by the story of Yhwh's activity over the centuries, embodied in Abraham and Cyrus, and by the associated record of Yhwh's speaking over the centuries about events that were to take place then and are taking place now (41:1–7, 21–29; 43:9–13). Yhwh is 'first and last', creator and able to declare an intention in contemporary history and fulfil it (44:6–8; 48:12–16a). As creator, Yhwh is greater than the nations that seem to control Israel's destiny, than the images that the nations construct, than the kings who are much more impressive than Judah's, and than that heavenly army itself (40:12–26). As sovereign in history, Yhwh brings about the good and the bad things that happen, Israel's flourishing and its calamities, the victories and the defeats. No one else is involved (45:6–7).

Yhwh therefore contrasts with the images that people take seriously. The process of their manufacture shows they are stupid, or rather that people who take them seriously are stupid (44:9–20). They obviously cannot do anything. In theory, people do not identify images with the gods they represent, but in practice, people do so. And the images do represent their gods very well. They can neither speak nor act; neither can the gods. Their needing to be carried contrasts with Yhwh's being the God who carries people: you cry out to images, and they do not answer; they cannot save you from your distress (46:1–7). Yhwh alone is God. Israel has no business turning to traditional supernatural and spiritual resources, as the book emphasizes at its opening and closing (1:29–31; 65:1–12).

For Yhwh to be the thrice holy, almighty God can be good news or bad news. Both implications are worked out in Isaiah, in a way that gives moral content to the metaphysical epithet 'holy'.

The powerful people in Judah are characterized by self-indulgence, confidence and refusal to think about Yhwh's intentions (5:8–14). In Isaiah's vision they become the humiliated. Yhwh has demonstrated where real authority lies:

> Yhwh Armies has become majestic in exercising authority,
>   as the holy God he has made himself holy in doing right.
>
> (5:15–16)

The powerful are the people who should have been exercising authority and doing right, exercising *mišpāṭ ûṣĕdāqâ* (cf. 56:1). This latter phrase is conventionally translated by expressions such as 'justice and righteousness', but neither word means either 'justice' or 'righteousness'. We do not have words in English to correspond to them, but *mišpāṭ* means something like 'exercising authority', while *ṣĕdāqâ* suggests 'doing what is right' by people, in particular people with whom you have a relationship; the closest English word is 'faithfulness'. Whereas Yhwh looked in Judah for *mišpāṭ ûṣĕdāqâ*, instead he found *mišpāḥ ûṣĕ'āqâ*, 'pouring [of blood] and crying out' (5:1–7). Yhwh has therefore intervened to exercise *mišpāṭ ûṣĕdāqâ* against the powerful and for the ordinary people. In this way Yhwh has 'made himself holy' or manifested holiness. The positive aspect to this manifestation of holiness means acting on behalf of people who are abused. But Isaiah here focuses on its negative aspect, necessary if the positive is to be achieved. Isaiah emphasizes the great anger Yhwh can generate in this connection. The phrase 'for all this his anger has not turned; / his hand is still extended' recurs (e.g. 5:25), suggesting how vast is the reservoir of Yhwh's anger at people's misuse of their intelligence and their power, their self-assertiveness and their self-indulgence.

Yhwh's holiness and majesty appropriately inspire trust and confidence and also respect and awe (7:1–17; 8:1–13). Their encouragement becomes explicit in a surprising way in Isaiah 40 – 55. Here 'Israel's holy one is your restorer' (e.g. 41:14), 'your deliverer' (43:3). As restorer (*gō'ēl*), Yhwh behaves like the member of an extended family with the resources to rescue another family member in trouble. Yet the people to whom the holy God acts as restorer are essentially the same people as Isaiah's earlier addressees, or at least their descendants; they have the same personality profile. Yhwh could reasonably continue to 'make himself holy in doing right' by leaving them to their own devices. Instead, the holy one is acting as their restorer, relating to this mob of rebels on the basis of their being part of the holy one's family.

The relationship between Yhwh and Israel can be described in historical/ covenantal terms as well as familial ones. The holy one created, shaped, chose Israel (43:15; 45:11; 49:7). Israel became Yhwh's people and Yhwh became Israel's God, became Israel's holy one. But people enter into covenants historically and voluntarily and can get out of them. They cannot choose whether to belong to their family. Family imposes obligations whether we like it or not; evading them brings terrible shame. Isaiah 40 – 55 mostly utilizes family imagery rather than covenant imagery. Jacob-Israel has no moral claim on Yhwh ('children I reared, brought up, / and they – they rebelled against me!' [1:2]), but Yhwh accepts family obligations to Jacob-Israel, acting like a prodigal father reaching out to his son before he even takes a step towards home. And it is as the holy one that Yhwh does so.

So Yhwh's being the holy one is solemn news and encouraging news. If you do wrong, you should expect the holy one to act against you. Yet there is no formula here; being committed to you, the holy one may be merciful. Yhwh is the high and lofty one, the eternal and holy one, who dwells on high; Yhwh also dwells with the crushed and humbled in spirit (57:15–19), people who have been crushed and humbled by Yhwh because of their waywardness. Yhwh gets angry, confronts, withdraws and hits, yet Yhwh does not stay angry, but heals, comforts and brings well-being. 'The heavens are my throne / and the earth is my footstool' (66:1); where could you build him a house?

> But to this person I pay attention,
>> to the weak and broken-spirited,
>> to the person who trembles at my word.
> (66:2)

Yhwh dwells with them, reviving their hearts and spirits, even when they do not deserve it.

The use of *mišpāṭ* (authority) and *ṣĕdāqâ* (doing the right thing) parallels the talk of holiness. Yhwh's exercise of *mišpāṭ* can be good news (e.g. 42:1, 3–4; 51:4); it means taking decisive action on Israel's behalf. Yhwh's doing *ṣĕdāqâ* can be good news (e.g. 45:8, 23–24; cf. *ṣedeq* in 41:2, 10). Doing *ṣĕdāqâ* has relational implications; it implies not merely acting in the light of a principle of justice, but doing the right thing in the light of relationships in your community. So there can be a tension for Yhwh as for parents or elders in a community about taking action against wrongdoers or being merciful. Letting Jerusalem fall implemented *ṣĕdāqâ*; restoring Jerusalem implemented *ṣĕdāqâ*. Justice would mean leaving Judeans in exile and the temple in ruins; *ṣĕdāqâ* means Yhwh's returning and bringing exiled Judeans home.

Yet there is something odd about Yhwh's acting violently against Judah. It is a 'strange' deed, one 'foreign' to Yhwh (28:21–22). It does not come naturally. Yhwh can summon up the resources to undertake this alien deed; people must listen and not scoff at the prospect. But it remains an alien deed. Faithfulness, mercy and protection are more natural to Yhwh than wrath and punishment.

In origin, then, holiness is a metaphysical rather than a moral term; it denotes Yhwh as the supernatural God. But this particular majestic God is characterized by *mišpāṭ ûṣĕdāqâ*, the exercise of authority in a way that reflects what is right, not least in the light of relationships with the community. Yhwh thus redefines the meaning of holiness.

Israel and Judah, Jerusalem and Zion

Isaiah's vision concerns 'Judah and Jerusalem'. It begins with Yhwh's expostulation

> Israel does not acknowledge,
>   my people does not pay attention.
> (1:3)

Judah is identified with Israel. Politically, Israel is Judah's northern neighbour's name (7:1), but Isaiah usually calls the northern kingdom 'Ephraim' (e.g. 7:2–9, 17) and uses 'Israel' more as a theological term than a political one. It denotes 'my people'. Judah therefore *is* Israel.

That could imply that Judah rather than Ephraim is the real Israel; likewise Isaiah 40 – 55 in addressing 'Jacob-Israel' might imply that its addressees are the real Israel (and other groups are not). But the contexts point in another direction. The addressees are people who can hardly believe that they are Yhwh's people or that this designation now means anything. The prophet's point is not 'they are not Jacob-Israel; it is you who are' but 'you are not nothing; you are Jacob-Israel'.

> You as Israel are my servant,
>   as Jacob you are the one I chose,
>   as Abraham's offspring you are my friend.
> (41:8)

So you need not share other peoples' fear as Cyrus advances, even though you feel as feeble as a worm. As Yhwh's servant, Jacob-Israel then has a vocation to fulfil as the means of Yhwh's governance becoming known to the world (42:1–4). Its very existence is designed to show the world what Yhwh's covenant means, and thus to bring light to nations (42:5–9).

But it cannot fulfil that vocation. This servant is deaf and blind (42:18–25). That does not mean Yhwh abandons it. Yhwh intends to bring Israelites back from all over the world, doing something that makes it simultaneously possible both to remember the great events of the past and to forget them, because the new event eclipses them for this generation (43:5–7, 16–21). Blind and deaf as Israel is, Yhwh still intends it to witness to Yhwh's words and acts. Indeed, this puts them in an even better position so to witness. They enjoy the lasting commitment and covenant promised to David, and corporately now play David's role (54:17b – 55:5). They will be called 'the holy people, the ones restored by

Yhwh' (62:11). Yhwh's insistence on staying committed will at last turn them from disbelief to trust, from rebellion to acknowledgment, from blindness to sight (43:8–13). Yhwh will raise Jacob's clans, turn Israel's shoots (49:6): 'clans' indicates reference to the whole people, and the language suggests a restoration that is both religious and material.

> They rebelled
>   and hurt his holy spirit,
> and he changed into their enemy.
> (63:10)

Abraham or Israel would hardly recognize them. Yet on the basis of Yhwh's earlier acts they can still call on Yhwh to act as father and restorer (63:7 – 64:11).

As well as underscoring their status, designating them 'Israel' underscores the seriousness of their rebellion (1:2–3). Judah is not any old people living a wayward life; it is Israel, 'Yhwh's vineyard' (5:7). Yet Yhwh has a servant in a position to intercede with Yhwh on its behalf (53:1–12). Yhwh wipes out its rebellion and declines to think about its failures, 'for my own sake' (43:25), because of my identity as one who carries people's wrongdoing and of my desire to safeguard my good name. It is on this basis that the prophecy urges people to turn back to Yhwh (44:22).

Isaiah also has Jerusalem-Zion as a central focus. The expression 'holy city' first comes here (48:2; 52:1). Zion is uniquely described as 'my people' (51:16).

Jerusalem-Zion (like 'servant') is a tensive symbol, capable of having more than one referent. It can denote a location, a physical city, the people who live in the city, the corporate personality of the city, even that corporate personality as a metaphysical entity that in some sense exists independently of its population, and perhaps even the city's people living elsewhere but identified with it.

After Sennacherib's desolating of Judah, 'Maiden Zion has survived / like a shelter in a vineyard, / like a hut in a melon field,' almost as devastated as Sodom and Gomorrah (1:8–9). Its Sodom-like experience matches its Sodom-like behaviour (1:10–23). Jerusalem-Zion is significant because the temple is there, and the people have been faithful in their worship there. But there is a mismatch between their fervent worship and the city's life outside worship (cf. 29:13; 58:1–7). When their hands were raised in praise and prayer, what Yhwh saw was the blood on them (cf. 5:1–25). 'Truthful town', where 'faithfulness used to stay', has become immoral in its unfaithfulness to Yhwh, the place where murderers live (1:21).

Does Yhwh's commitment to Jerusalem mean it can always be sure of pardon? Or does Yhwh's commitment to righteousness mean it is bound to be abandoned and destroyed?

Isaiah 1 suggests an interim answer. Yhwh has exacted redress (1:24), but the city has been preserved; the parallel with Sodom breaks down. Yhwh has fulfilled a promise: 'I will protect this city and deliver it for my sake and for the sake of David my servant' (37:35), not because its present occupants deserve it. Hezekiah fills out the argument behind that (e.g. 37:15–20). In the light of its wrongdoing Yhwh camped against Jerusalem (29:1–4). It looked doomed to fall as it once fell to David, but in a great reversal Yhwh 'attends' to Jerusalem in a positive way; suddenly the strangers attacking the city disappear (29:5–6). Yhwh descended on Zion like a lion or vulture pouncing on its prey, but turned up to shield and rescue it (31:4–5).

Jerusalem escaped because of Yhwh's mercy, not because it deserved it. It had regard to its defences and looked to its water supply, 'but you did not have regard to the one who did it, you did not look to the one who shaped it long before' (22:11). 'If this waywardness could be expiated for you before you die . . . ,' Yhwh continues, with the terrible solemnity of an oath, but leaving the consequences unstated. Cleansing and reconciliation are made impossible only by the denial that there is a problem and the consequent refusal to have it dealt with. Therefore you have to turn back to Yhwh (31:6). Then the people of Jerusalem will not continue to weep because Yhwh will show great grace at the sound of their crying out (30:19–26). The city's chastisement is not merely punitive but also restorative (1:21–31). Its silver has become slag but the turning of Yhwh's hand against it is designed to smelt that away.

> I will restore your authorities as at the first,
>   your counsellors as at the beginning.
> Afterwards you will be called
>   faithful city, truthful town.
> Zion will be redeemed with the exercise of authority,
>   those in her who turn with faithfulness.
> (1:26–27)

Jerusalem's destruction in 587 is the more radical answer to the question of whether Yhwh will stay long-tempered for ever. But that catastrophe, too, cannot be the end of the story. After fifty years of devastation and the exile of many of its people, Yhwh declares that its chastisement is over; the time for its comfort has come (40:1–11). Its God has begun to reign and is returning (52:7–10). But meanwhile, Zion says to itself:

Yhwh left me;
   my Lord forgot me
(49:14)

Yhwh here denies the charge and points to the way its exiles are gathering; instead of being short of inhabitants, it will be overwhelmed by them (49:15 – 50:3). Or Yhwh admits having abandoned it but did so only briefly, is now re-establishing it and promises not to abandon it again (54:1–16a). The city will become like a woman bejewelled, its people now Yhwh's disciples, all enjoying well-being and security.

The picture is gloriously developed in Isaiah 60 – 62. The world is in darkness but Yhwh's light has dawned on Zion, so that nations can walk by it. Its children are coming from afar. So is the nations' wealth, for Zion's sake, to declare Yhwh's praise and bring offerings. That benefits the city and glorifies Yhwh. These foreigners will build its walls and it will be splendidly appointed. All nations and kings are to serve it. 'Zion of the Holy One of Israel' will know Yhwh as its deliverer and restorer. It will mean the creation of new heavens and new earth (65:17–25). The context indicates that the prophet portrays not a literal new cosmos but a whole new world for this city. 'The sound of weeping and the sound of a cry will not make itself heard there again' (contrast 5:7). People will live out their lives instead of having them cut off, build houses and live in them, plant vineyards and enjoy their fruit, rather than having enemies destroy them. They will have a relationship of living, instant communication with Yhwh, in which the new-creation vision of 11:6–9 will be realized.

Isaiah 12 lays out songs for Zion to sing so that all the nations can hear 'in that day', the day of Yhwh's restoration. Isaiah 26:1–6 provides another song to sing about Judah's strong city. It lacks literal walls, but 'deliverance is what he makes walls and rampart': who then needs walls? (Cf. Zech. 2:1–5 [5–9].) It has gates, but they are there in order to be opened for

the faithful nation, the one that guards truthfulness.
[Its] intention held firm, you guard it in peace,
   in peace because it is trustful in you.
(26:3)

Yhwh founded Zion;
   in it the weak of his people
   can take refuge.
(14:32)

The moon will know shame, the sun will know disgrace,
    when Yhwh Armies has begun to reign
On Mount Zion and in Jerusalem,
    and before his elders will be splendour.
(24:21–23)

The remains

Thus one way of resolving the tension between the demands of faithfulness and of righteousness means bringing calamity on the people but keeping it in being in a reduced form so that it can blossom again. The idea of a 'remnant' links with that, though the 'remains' of something are just the leftovers, and that is the first connotation of *šě'ār* and *yeter*, emphasizing the scope of the disaster, for Judah (1:8–9; cf. 30:17; 37:4; 49:21), Assyria (10:19), Ephraim (17:4–6) or the whole world (24:6, 11–12). The terms *śārîd* and *pālîṭ*, however, indicate that something has 'survived' or 'escaped' the disaster, hinting that all may not be lost. If there are Judeans who have escaped, they can be recipients of majesty and glory; if there are remains, leftovers, they can be called 'holy' (4:2–3; cf. 28:5; 37:31–32; 46:3; 11:11–16).

The preservation of leftovers is an act of mercy. The remains are not people who deserved to survive but the fortunate beneficiaries of Yhwh's mercy to the people as a whole. They do not survive because they turn to Yhwh; rather, they must turn to Yhwh because they have survived. The surviving remnant must become the faithful remnant, now leaning on Yhwh in truth instead of stupidly leaning on the superpower (10:20–21).

Isaiah often makes this point without using 'remnant' language. Thus 50:10 asks:

Who among you reveres Yhwh,
    listens to his servant's voice?
One who has walked in deep darkness
    and had no brightness
must trust in Yhwh's name
    and lean on his God.

The remnant community must become the faithful remnant. The effect of this challenge may be to constitute a remnant within the remnant, which becomes 'my servants' (65:13–16), people who 'tremble' at Yhwh's word (66:5).

'The remains' is thus a usefully ambiguous expression. The first great ambiguity attaches to 6:9–13. Cities are to lie ruined without inhabitant and houses without anyone in them, so that the land is quite deserted. Does verse 13 then continue the sobriety (NRSV) or turn to promise (NJPS)? Isaiah's meeting with Ahaz raises similar questions. He takes his son *šě'ār yāšûb*, 'Remains-will-turn' (7:3). Is this name a promise that only remains of Assyria will return home? Or a warning that only remains of Judah will survive? Or a promise that remains of Judah will survive? Or a challenge that the remains of Judah must turn to Yhwh?

Then, after describing how more or less nothing will 'remain' of Assyria, Isaiah speaks of 'Israel's remains' (10:20–23), with initially solemn implications. But that initial impression is put in question by the declaration that these 'remains', which are also 'people who have escaped' (putting it more positively), will now 'lean' on Yhwh rather than on Assyria. In Isaiah, hardly anything more impressive could be said; who you lean on or rely on or trust in is a key indicator of who you are and how you relate to God (cf. 30:10; 31:1; 50:10). Thus Isaiah indeed indicates that the remains 'turn' to Yhwh. The surviving remnant has become the faithful remnant. Yet the next sentence returns to the negative connotations of 'remains' and 'turn', or at least reintroduces the expressions' ambiguity as it speaks of devastation overflowing with *şědāqâ*. Is it overflowing with 'retribution' (NJPS), or is the overwhelming moderated by *şědāqâ* with its more positive connotation of God's doing the right thing by Judah (cf. 1:27)?

While some of this ambiguity may reflect diachronic, textual or redactional factors, such hypotheses themselves presuppose that theological issues are involved. Remnant thinking seeks to handle a theological issue. The ambiguity of the eventual form of the text, like the ambiguity of Isaiah's son's name, places questions before the people. They have to decide how to read the ambiguity and how to respond to it.

The nations, the empires and their kings

The 'remnant principle' applies also to the nations. Convulsions in the Middle East can mean there being virtually nothing left of them, too (14:22, 30; 15:9; 16:14; 17:3; 21:17). Yet the people among the nations who have 'escaped' (escaped Cyrus? escaped Babylon?) are urged to let events make them recognize the emptiness of their gods and to recognize Yhwh (45:20–25). Indeed, in due course those escapees will themselves go to proclaim Yhwh's honour among the nations (66:19).

Such invitations to draw near to Yhwh are set in context by the promise in 2:2–4. Metaphorically speaking, the mountain where Yhwh's house stands is to become the highest in the world; its exaltation will draw all the nations, to learn to walk in the ways of Yhwh, who will arbitrate between them and thus make warfare between them cease. Isaiah 1 – 12 closes with a linked declaration that the whole world is to know of Yhwh's deeds in restoring Zion (12:3–6). Isaiah 40 – 55 develops that theme. At the rise of Cyrus, the nations panic (41:1–7); but the object of Yhwh's action is that people in general may see and acknowledge that Yhwh has acted (41:20). They are destined to learn about the way Yhwh exercises authority in the world (42:1–4), to have their eyes opened, their imprisonment ended (42:5–9). They are therefore summoned to give praise to Yhwh (42:10–12). They will bring their wealth to Jerusalem in connection with recognizing that Yhwh, the only God, is there (45:14–17; 60:1–22).

While all this brings good news to the exiles (49:22–26), the fact that 'Yhwh has bared his holy arm in the eyes of the nations' and 'all earth's extremities have seen our God's deliverance' (52:10) is good news for the nations themselves. They are in darkness but Yhwh's light has dawned on Zion, so they can walk by it.

> New moon after new moon,
>   sabbath after sabbath,
> all flesh will come to bow down before me . . .
> (66:23)

Thus this good news relates not merely to their outward circumstances but to their relationship with Yhwh.

> The many were appalled at Yhwh's servant . . .
> but he will sprinkle them,
>   and at him kings will shut their mouths.
> (52:14–15)

> By his acknowledgment my servant shows himself faithful to the many,
>   and carries their waywardness. Therefore I will allocate him many . . .
> He was the one who carried the shortcoming of many,
>   makes intercession for the rebels.
> (53:11–12)

As keeping sabbath now becomes the key marker of keeping the covenant, of attaching yourself and ministering to Yhwh, of loving Yhwh and being Yhwh's servants, it qualifies foreigners to bring their offerings and prayers in Yhwh's house (56:1–8). Foreigners and exiles have the same status; they are all people whom Yhwh is 'gathering'. Foreigners need not feel that just because of their ethnicity they are the victims of the separation (*hibdîl*) that Yhwh expects of the holy from the ordinary or the clean from the taboo. Yhwh's house is a prayer house for all peoples.

The poems about particular nations (Isa. 13 – 23) come at their destiny from a different angle. These are nations that in different ways impact Judah: great powers that oppress Judah or peoples by whom Judah might be impressed, powers that seemed unassailable but are not, peoples with whom Judah might ally against Assyria. The prophecies thus warn Judah, 'Don't even think about it.' Yet the chapters include notes of hope for these peoples (e.g. 14:26–32; 16:1–5). Most spectacularly, in Egypt (of all people!) there will be cities swearing allegiance to Yhwh, an altar to Yhwh, Yhwh's answering people's prayers and healing people, and a highway to Assyria enabling both nations to serve Yhwh as 'my people' and 'my handiwork' alongside Israel as 'my possession' (19:16–25). Even that old whore Tyre after being put in her place can resume her trade and devote her profits to Yhwh (23:17–18).

Isaiah 24 – 27 then mostly lacks such concrete references. Here the earth/world withers and in its midst desolation characterizes 'the city' (24:1–13; cf. 34:1–4) because it

has become profaned
   under its inhabitants,
because they have transgressed teachings,
   overstepped laws,
   broken the ancient covenant.
(24:5)

The whole world lives under Yhwh's covenant, knows Yhwh's expectations, and is thus guilty for ignoring them. As is the case with Israel, such action turns the earth from something holy to something defiled. Moab provides a concrete (and vivid!) illustration of Yhwh's devastating the fortified city (25:11–12).

There is a double contrast between that 'city' (see also 25:1–5) and 'this mountain' (25:6–10a): perhaps Mount Zion, though what will happen here may better fit the mountain land of Canaan (11:9; 57:13; 65:25). Here Yhwh Armies will arrange the ultimate festival banquet, 'for all peoples', bring death to an end for 'all peoples ... all nations', and thus wipe the tears from 'all faces';

no more war, no more death, no more mourning. Whether the mountain is Canaan in general or Zion in particular, Yhwh does not abandon the particularity that characterizes the Scriptures as a whole. Yhwh's plan was to reach the world by relating to Israel in particular; Israel's resistance to Yhwh brought it chastisement and shame; but it is still through Israel that Yhwh fulfils that purpose, and its shame is removed as the strong and terrifying nations have been put down and it is no longer a weak, pathetic, humiliated little people but the host of this great festival!

Is all that destruction necessary?

> As your decisions come about for the earth,
>   the inhabitants of the world learn faithfulness.
> If grace is shown to the faithless,
>   they do not learn faithfulness;
> in the land of uprightness they do wickedness
>   and do not revere the majesty of Yhwh.
> (26:9–10)

> They cannot or will not see Yhwh's hand raised,
>   taking action in passion for Israel
>   and consuming Yhwh's enemies.
> They need to see it in order to be put to shame.
> (26:11)

The nations' destiny in relation to Yhwh is thus not so different from Israel's destiny. Like Israel, they are expected to live in the light of their knowledge of God's expectations of them, in their attitude to God and to one another. Like Israel they are liable to God's 'attending' to them because of the shortcomings in their attitudes. Like Israel, they are liable to be cut down so that little remains. Like Israel's remains, these remains can then turn to Yhwh, and ultimately the nations are indeed destined to turn to the God who lives on Zion and to find their mutual relationships healed there.

The great Middle Eastern empires have a prominent place in Isaiah. Yhwh is involved in the expansionism that turns Assyria into a great empire, drafting its army to fulfil its own instincts so as to implement Yhwh's intention to devastate Judah (5:26–30). Assyria does not know it acts as Yhwh's agent. Its expansionism serves its own agenda. Its king had vast ambitions, achieved them, and thus gained unparalleled respect and esteem in his world, and in his own assessment. He thus had grounds for pride. But he had come to see himself as more important than the one whose unwitting agent he was. So Yhwh will put him in his place (e.g. 10:13–19). He did not see his achievement in the context of Yhwh's purpose but only as his own achievement, scoffing at the idea that Yhwh could deliver Jerusalem (36:18–20; cf. 37:22–29). The centre of the poems about the nations (17:12–14) applies to 'many peoples, that roar like the seas' roaring', language applied to Assyria in 8:7. Yhwh shouts them down and they flee. In the evening they inspired terror; by morning they are gone, like Assyria in 36:1 – 37:37. Assyria becomes a figure for any such threat (Babylon, Persia, Greece, Rome, Turkey, Britain, the USA . . .).

It is through Babylon that Yhwh effects Assyria's final downfall, and also Judah's fall. But then Yhwh will attend to Babylon (13:1). In this connection Yhwh speaks of having summoned sanctified warriors from kingdoms and nations to destroy the whole earth for its waywardness (13:2–16). There is no reference to a specific empire there; it is the context that indicates that Babylon's downfall will be a concretion of this event. Thus the relationship between historical and ultimate is the converse of that in 17:12–14, where the particular gives a way of thinking about the ultimate. Against the background of the generic declaration, 13:17–22 then speaks more concretely about the Medes as the people who will shatter Babylon in its majestic splendour and turn it into something resembling Sodom and Gomorrah. In this context, there is a particular purpose in doing that: 'Because Yhwh will have compassion on Jacob and again choose Israel and settle them on their soil' (14:1–2). The empires' destiny relates in negative and positive ways to Yhwh's involvement with Israel.

When Yhwh gives Israel relief from the pain and turmoil of their oppression, they will be in a position to declaim a mocking poem over Babylon's king (14:4–11). A parallel dyslogy compares the Babylonian king to Venus, the morning star, that rises as if seeking to ascend to glory each morning but is outshone by the rising sun and disappears. In place of an emperor's splendour the king will have an ignominious death without proper burial and thus without proper resting place (14:12–21). His fate is mirrored in the city's fate (14:22–23). It falls like a woman taken down from her position of authority in the household. It had shown no compassion and had assumed it would always be in its position of power, thinking it had all the information resources it needed to cope with any threats or crises, which turns out to be wrong (47:1–15).

So one empire gives way to another and one great king gives way to another. Cyrus no more acknowledges Yhwh than Sennacherib or Nebuchadnezzar had done, yet this no more stops Yhwh giving him victories than was the case with Assyrian and Babylonian kings; indeed, this action is designed (among other things) to lead to such acknowledgment, by Cyrus and by the world from east to west (45:3–6).

Divine sovereignty and human responsibility

Yhwh's relationship with Assyria illustrates the interweaving of divine sovereignty and human responsibility. Yhwh summons the Assyrian army (5:26); its club is the means of Yhwh's anger finding expression (10:4). Yet Assyria is critiqued for its action (10:7–19). Though a means of Yhwh's acting, it is responsible to act in a moral way, recognizing the specialness of Yhwh, and not to become too impressed with itself.

Divine sovereignty and human responsibility interweave in different ways in the relationship between Yhwh and Judah. Here there is direct communication between the two parties. Yet sometimes Yhwh speaks as if making decisions that leave no room for human response. 'Yhwh's mouth has spoken'; so this really will happen. 'The Lord sent a word on Jacob, / it fell on Israel' (9:8 [7]), and meant devastation. Yhwh's word is performative, not merely informative. The past tense verbs Isaiah often uses to describe events that have not yet happened (e.g. 2:9; 3:1) make the same point.

Isaiah 6:9–10 underscores Yhwh's sovereignty. It is quite understandable that Yhwh should commission Isaiah to make people deaf and blind (cf. 29:10–11) as part of punishing them for their intransigence (cf. Mark 4:10–12). Yet taking such words literally introduces an air of unreality into Isaiah's ministry. Sharing such words with the people looks more like one further attempt to shake them to their senses. Again the prophet subsequently declares, 'I have heard annihilation decreed from the Lord Yhwh Armies upon the whole land' (28:22). Yet the context urges people not to scoff at this warning, suggesting that this decree is not final. While Yhwh's speech is thus not only informative but performative, it can be performative in more than one way. It has the intention and may have the effect of making people turn to Yhwh. It has then done its work and need not be implemented in its literal sense.

Divine sovereignty is thus more subtle than it at first seems. A dialectical relationship obtains between divine decision-making and human decision-making. While nothing happens outside Yhwh's control and outside parameters Yhwh lays down, and some things happen because Yhwh makes explicit decisions, many things happen in part because of human beings' response to Yhwh.

Yhwh's promises of restoration from exile also emphasize divine sovereignty. Yet they presuppose that people will respond; there is 'no well-being for the faithless' (48:22). Isaiah 56 – 66 underscores this fact; that warning recurs (57:21). Implicitly, this principle provides some explanation for why the restoration falls short of its promises (cf. 58:6–14). If Yhwh's arm is not raised in action to deliver, this does not mean it cannot do so or that Yhwh's ears are deaf, or only that those ears are deliberately deaf. Whereas nothing separates foreigners from Yhwh, the people's waywardness, deception and bloodshed does so for them, making Yhwh's face turn away. And that is why Yhwh's decisive action in faithfulness (*mišpāṭ ûṣĕdāqâ*) is far away from them (59:1–15a).

It would be a mistake simply to make Yhwh's act of restoration conditional on people's turning. But it does require such turning as a response, otherwise the whole project fails (cf. the argument of Rom. 6:1–14).

Talk in terms of divine and human planning constitutes another way of discussing the divine and human role in history. Yhwh plans like a farmer, sometimes ploughing, sometimes sowing.

> He has made his planning wonderful,
> > made his insight great.
> (28:26)

Isaiah speaks of a royal prince bearing the name 'the-Mighty-God-is-a-wonderful-planner' (9:6 [5]). Like other names in Isaiah, this name is not a description of the child himself, but a statement of what his reign will prove as Yhwh delivers and blesses the people. It makes the political affirmation Isaiah presses on Judah's rulers. Yhwh is the one who makes plans and implements them; politicians need to take account of that.

Yhwh's threat to take away planners along with other leaders (3:3) presupposes that they are in principle legitimate means whereby the community is directed, as does the promise that Yhwh will in due course restore planners to Jerusalem (1:26) and that the shoot from Jesse's stump will have a spirit of planning (11:2). But human planning usually proceeds on the basis of what can be humanly discerned and managed. Syria and Ephraim make such a plan to get Judah to join them in rebelling against Assyria (7:5). When we bring God into the picture, plans like those can be scorned (8:10). All Babylon's planning may get it nowhere (47:13).

The story of Sennacherib's invasion (36:1 – 37:38) discusses these issues with some irony. Sennacherib asks about the basis for the Judeans' trust that they will be able to resist Assyria by means of planning. But with his slurs on Yhwh, Sennacherib digs his grave. Yhwh made a plan to break Assyria, and no one could frustrate that plan (14:24–27). Isaiah urges people to relax, but this simple advice seems ridiculous. They assume they have to take responsibility for their safety, but their action is actually calculated to have the opposite effect (28:11–20; 30:15–17). 'He too is insightful, but he has brought disaster, / and not revoked his word,' and 'the Egyptians are human beings, not God; / their horses are flesh, not spirit'; they will fall (31:3). But the natural temptation of politicians is to scorn alternative alleged plans, such as ones involving God (5:19). Judah's rebellion lies in making plans that do not come from Yhwh, and thus piling wrong on wrong (30:1–7).

Two planners and two sets of plans confront each other; Yhwh is now doing unpleasant wonders in Judah through which 'the insight of the insightful will perish, / the discernment of the discerning will hide itself' (29:14). They are people 'who go deeper than Yhwh to hide their plan, / and whose deed happens in the dark, / and who say "Who sees us? Who recognizes us?"' as if they were clay that could operate independently of its potter (29:15–16). When told that Yhwh is using Cyrus to restore Jerusalem, the prophet imagines people responding, 'You can't do that!', and retorts by asking them to reconsider who is the potter and who is the clay here (45:9–13). 'Your plans are not my plans / and my ways are not your ways,' Yhwh reminds them (EVV 'thoughts' for *maḥăšābôt* is too imprecise) (55:8–11).

The future

A horrific aspect of Judah's ruining is Yhwh's removing its leadership and replacing it by people who are incompetent in that they cannot safeguard moral and social order; yet the reason for this action is that the present leadership is itself oppressive (3:1–15; cf. 9:14–17 [13–16]). A city needs lookouts to guard it and a flock needs shepherds, but this people's lookouts/shepherds are too drunk to see anything (56:9–12). One flawed leader can be replaced by another, but he will fall short of people's hopes, too (22:15–25; cf. 36:3).

Yhwh therefore promises a day when a king will reign and leaders will lead by the faithful exercise of authority (32:1–8). They will thus be protectors for people who need protection, people with insight and a capacity to listen (to God, to the cry of the needy?), thoughtful and articulate in the way they speak (of God?), living by principle. Not much of that was true of Judah's leadership when this promise was given.

That promise is not linked to the position of David, unless implicitly. There arc promises attaching to David's household that its present representative declines to live by. 'Listen, household of David,' Isaiah says to Ahaz (7:13; cf. v. 2). There is no indication that the baby referred to in 7:14 is to be born to the royal family, or, if it is, that this child will eventually sit on the throne. The passage's emphasis lies elsewhere, on the child's significance as a sign that Yhwh can be trusted. In contrast, the vision in 9:2–7 [1–6]) is associated with David. This child's birth promises that the darkness that has afflicted the land will come to an end; permanent peace and the faithful exercise of authority will become realities.

The David passage in 11:1–10 explicitly relates to a future figure and is thus the nearest thing to a messianic prophecy in Isaiah. The Davidic tree has been felled; yet a felled tree can sometimes produce new shoots and grow again. Isaiah promises that this will happen to the Davidic tree, and this David will manifest the best qualities of a king such as Hezekiah (37:1 – 38:1–22) and of the ideal expressed in Psalm 72, ruling with wisdom, reverence for Yhwh, and a decisiveness that protects the weak and poor and sees that the faithless get put down, and draws the nations. In the context, the picture of harmony in the animal world is another promise of people who are by nature inclined to feed off others living in harmony with them.

The Davidic idea appears in a quite different, and scandalous, form in 44:24 – 45:7. The Persian king is 'my shepherd' and 'my anointed'. Yhwh had anointed David to shepherd Israel, and 11:1–10 promises Israel that a Davidic king will shepherd Israel again. Here the pagan king is anointed to do this shepherding. David had commissioned the building of Jerusalem and of the temple; now Cyrus will do so. Yhwh had led David to great victories over foreign nations; now Yhwh will so lead Cyrus. Cyrus is the one Yhwh loves or espouses, and has summoned (48:14–15); the Isaianic Scriptures do not speak of Yhwh's loving David.

Further passages also deconstruct the Davidic idea. The picture of the servant in 52:13 – 53:12 has Davidic resonances, including exalted majesty and a spectacular anointing, though in general it contrasts with the kingly ideal of someone handsome like David, for whom all the girls fall. No one falls for this servant. Yhwh's purpose is achieved through someone who is nothing like David. Then Yhwh promises that Israel as a whole is to have David's role in the world, in accordance with the Abrahamic promise (54:17b – 55:5). Isaiah 56 – 66 develops this emphasis on Israel's drawing power and ignores David; a prophet's testimony to anointing (61:1) underscores the point.

Isaiah thus constitutes a microcosm of the complex scriptural attitude to monarchy and messianism. The Old Testament both accepts and rejects the notion of kingship and works with and sidesteps the notion of a Messiah. Jesus both accepts the idea that he is the Messiah and warns that it is misleading.

In Isaiah, as elsewhere in the Old Testament, the broader notion of the end or of Yhwh's day is more prominent than the promise of a new David.

Much of Isaiah focuses on extraordinary things Yhwh plans to do imminently, and it can speak of this as the coming of Yhwh's day (e.g. 2:12–17; 7:18–25). 'In a little while' Yhwh's wrath will have exhausted itself and renewal will come (10:24–26; 29:17). 'On that day' things will be transformed (10:20; 29:18–21; 31:7). Other victims of Yhwh's army are similarly warned that 'Yhwh's day is near; it will come like destruction from the Destroyer' (13:6; cf. vv. 9–11, 22). Isaiah 40 – 55 does not use 'Yhwh's day' language, unless 'day of deliverance' (49:8) riffs on that expression (Isa. 56 – 66 similarly uses the correlative expression 'day of redress' in 61:2; 63:4). It does declare that Yhwh's *ṣĕdāqâ*, Yhwh's act of faithfulness, is near (51:5).

The ultimate day of Yhwh did not arrive within the temporal framework of Isaiah. What theological understandings of this might then emerge from Isaiah?

One is indicated by the transition from Isaiah 1 – 55 to Isaiah 56 – 66. The latter begins by urging the community to see to the implementing of *mišpāṭ ûṣĕdāqâ*, of faithful decision-making in the community, 'because my deliverance is near to coming, / my *ṣĕdāqâ* [is near] to revealing itself' (56:1–2). Where there is no human *ṣĕdāqâ*, people cannot expect to see divine *ṣĕdāqâ*. Where Judah fails in its relationship with Yhwh, 'therefore Yhwh will wait to show grace to you' (30:18).

Another understanding is suggested by Yhwh's implicit reserving of the right to take a broader set of factors into account in deciding when to act. 'I, Yhwh, will speed it at its time' (60:22). It has a time of its own within Yhwh's purpose.

Yet another understanding is suggested by the non-specific language of some 'Yhwh's day' passages, such as 13:2–16. 'Yhwh's day' is the day when Yhwh's ultimate purpose is fulfilled, which does not come within the book's temporal framework. But that purpose does find periodic partial fulfilment within this age. When Isaiah speaks of that day as imminent, it may not distinguish between ultimate and interim fulfilment; only the event itself and its aftermath will indicate which it is.

Beyond that, many references to 'that day' point away from something imminent and more explicitly suggest the ultimate. (I avoid the terms 'eschatological' and 'apocalyptic', which sound like technical terms but are of unfocused meaning.) The other side of the felling of the Davidic tree and of the exile (and therefore not in the immediate future, from the perspective of Isaiah ben Amoz), 'on that day' Jesse's root will draw the nations and bring about a second exodus (11:10–11); 'on that day' Judah will give praise for this (12:1, 4). Yhwh's ultimate day even affects cosmic or supernatural forces resistant to him (24:21–23; 27:1).

Other visions of earthly transformation do not incorporate any time expression (32:15–20; 35:1–10). They contrast with ones that follow in Isaiah 40 – 55, using similar imagery but relating the vision to a particular time. But the talk of 'that day' commonly implies a time that looks suspiciously far away rather than around the corner. The people of God therefore 'wait' and 'long'; they 'yearn in the night' and then get up early for the morning worship time to pray (*šāḥar*) that Yhwh will implement all that these visions portray (26:8–9).

***

Isaiah is wide-ranging in the complex issues it handles. It indicates that nothing is simple, and in its richness encourages readers to think through the multifacetedness of key theological questions so as to do justice to them and inspire a theology that can be lived with.

© John Goldingay, 2009

9. THE TEXT OF ISAIAH AT QUMRAN

Dwight Swanson

The twenty-one copies of Isaiah found among the Dead Sea Scrolls make it the third most copied biblical book among the corpus, behind the Psalms and Deuteronomy. Compared to the primacy of citation of these same books in the New Testament, this can be considered evidence, at least, that these three books formed something of a canonical core in Judaism in the Second Temple period. Six pesharim[1] on Isaiah make it the most numerous focus of the surviving commentaries. This, together with citations of Isaiah in key sectarian works such as the Community Rule, shows the prominence of this book in the self-understanding of the community that preserved and copied the scrolls.

This chapter will consider afresh two of these three aspects of Isaiah's use among the scrolls just mentioned: the biblical manuscripts and the pesharim. Consideration of explicit citations will have to wait for another time.

---

1. Pesharim are commentaries unique to the Dead Sea Scrolls and sectarian community believed to have inhabited the Qumran settlement. These commentaries are related to prophetic texts, and are recognizable for first citing the prophetic text, then indicating the interpretation by *pishro*, 'its interpretation is . . .'

The biblical manuscripts

An overview of the evidence
The significance of the figure of twenty-one copies of the biblical book of
Isaiah can be grasped with the help of a number of comparisons, as that
above, indicating this is the third-most copied biblical book among the finds.
For example, in Cave 1 two copies of Isaiah were found among sixteen biblical texts, including two each of Deuteronomy and Daniel, and three Psalms
scrolls. One fragmentary manuscript was found in Cave 5. The rest come from
Cave 4, among the 142 biblical manuscripts that represent nearly a quarter of
the estimated 600 manuscripts in the find. From another standpoint, it is at
least curious that no copy was found in Cave 11, which admittedly contained
few biblical manuscripts, except for five Psalms manuscripts (half the MSS).[2]

Outside the eleven Qumran caves only one other manuscript has been
recovered in the wilderness of Judea, in Wadi Muraba'at. It will be taken into
consideration as well.

For our purposes here it is helpful to gather a variety of descriptive details
of the manuscripts to gain a broad sense of the status of the book at Qumran.
We will then consider the status of the text of the book separately.

Texts by palaeographical dating[3]
A first approach is to consider the dating of the manuscripts, for purposes of
comparison of the text. This is an imprecise exercise, because we are largely
dependent on palaeographical dating as given by the editors of each manuscript. Carbon dating might be considered more reliable, but first, of the Isaiah
manuscripts only 1QIsa[a], the Great Isaiah Scroll, has been carbon dated; and,
secondly, the results for those manuscripts that have been carbon dated has a
margin of error which prevents precise conclusions. For the Isaiah Scroll, for
instance, the dates given from the Tucson lab are 341–325 or 202–114 BCE; and
the Zurich lab dating is 201–93 BCE. This essentially corroborates the palaeo-

---

2. These figures are based on data in E. Tov (ed.), *The Texts from the Judaean Desert:
   Indices and an Introduction to the Discoveries in the Judaean Desert Series*, DJD 39 (Oxford:
   Clarendon, 2002). The figure for the total number of MSS may differ from other
   accounts, where as many as 800 are estimated, and around 900 in Qumran overall.
3. Tov, *Texts from the Judaean Desert*, pp. 378–446. The date is that given by the editor(s).
   This is recognizably a general idea of relationship between MSS, since there can be
   overlap of scribal palaeographic styles, as well as some vagueness in the editors'
   dating. When this is the case, Tov's 'mid-point' date is used.

graphical dating of this manuscript (mid- to late second century BCE), but little more. What this means for this discussion is that we may look to palaeography for comparing manuscripts to each other relative to this datum.[4]

The texts are given below in chronological order of dating (Table 1, below). Obviously, when more than one is given the same spread of dates, there is no way of knowing the order of relation between these. This is not a major issue in interpreting the data. Finally, the typification of the scribal era is given according to the ruling monarch. These factors allow a general sense of historical context.

From this table can be seen, first, that the production of Isaiah manuscripts began prior to the habitation of Qumran. If we follow the archaeological dating of the site by Jodi Magness,[5] then the Great Isaiah Scroll was brought to Qumran, having already been copied. Who brought it we can only conjecture, though if we follow Tov's theory of Qumran Scribal Practice,[6] under which he includes this manuscript, it must have been by the very people who established that scribal practice at Qumran. The busiest period of copying of Scrolls, overall, was the Early Herodian period; in comparison, Isaiah is an 'early' text.

Secondly, it can be seen that the most vigorous period of copying was in the first half of the first century BCE, during the Hasmonaean era, coinciding with the reign of Alexander Jannaeus. Half the texts come from this period. Even

---

4. Ibid., p. 365. Interpretation of the carbon dating has been contended by Greg Doudna, 'Dating the Scrolls on the Basis of Radiocarbon Analysis', in P. W. Flint and J. C. VanderKam (eds.), *The Dead Sea Scrolls after Fifty Years: A Comprehensive Assessment*, 2 vols. (Leiden: Brill, 1998), 1:430–471; J. Atwill and S. Braunheim recalculated the Zurich and Tucson data in 'Redating the Radiocarbon Dating of the Dead Sea Scrolls', *DSD* 11.2 (2004), pp. 143–157, arguing that the carbon dating offers no evidence for evaluating the accuracy of the palaeographical dating; this, in turn, has been refuted by Johannes van der Plicht, 'Radiocarbon Dating and the Dead Sea Scrolls: A Comment on "Redating"', *DSD* 14.1 (2007), pp. 77–89, who argues that the carbon dating does corroborate the palaeography. In any case, the Isaiah Scroll remains within the second century BCE frame.

5. J. Magness, *The Archaeology of Qumran and the Dead Sea Scrolls* (Grand Rapids: Eerdmans, 2002), pp. 63–68, dates the beginning of settlement at Qumran at 100 BCE.

6. E. Tov, *Scribal Practices and Approaches Reflected in the Texts Found in the Judean Desert*, STDJ 54 (Leiden: Brill, 2004), pp. 261–273, 277–288.

so, the book continued to be produced until the middle of the first century CE, at least.

Table 1   Biblical manuscripts by palaeographical dating

Text	Date	Scribal era[7]
1QIsa[a]	125–100	Early Hasm.
4QIsa[r]	c. 90	Mid-Hasm.
4QIsa[f]	100–50	
4QIsa[h]	100–50	
4QIsa[i]	100–50	
4QIsa[l]	100–50	
4QIsa[m]	100–50	
4QIsa[n]	100–50	
4QIsa[o]	100–50	
4QpapIsa[p]	100–50	
4QIsa[k]	50	Late Hasm.
1QIsa[b]	50–25	Late Hasm./early Herod.
4QIsa[a]	50–25	
4QIsa[b]	50–25	
4QIsa[j]	50–25	
4QIsa[g]	50–1	Early Herod.
4QIsa[e]	30–1	
4QIsa[q]	30–1	
5QIsa	15–70	'Late'
Mur Isa	20–84	Pre-revolt
4QIsa[c]	30–68	Devel. Herod.
4QIsa[d]	30–68	Late Herod.

We will later consider how these data relate to textual development, as well as how the pesharim relate to the history of the text.

Texts by content

It is easy for someone coming to the Scrolls for the first time to imagine we are speaking of some twenty complete scrolls. The sad truth, of course, is

---

7. The nomenclature for the development of scribal style, or palaeographical dating, is taken from the ruling monarch of the period: Early/Mid/Late Hasmonaean; Early/Late or 'Developed' Herodian. The dates for each period can be seen in the second column.

that apart from the complete Great Isaiah Scroll and 1QIsa[b], we have only fragments of the rest – some relatively sizable, many very small. In order to gain perspective on what *is* in the manuscripts, see the data in Table 2 below.

Table 2   Biblical manuscripts by content

Manuscripts presumably containing the complete Isaiah						
	1 – 12	*13 – 23*	*24 – 33*	*34 – 39*	*40 – 55*	*56 – 66*[8]
1QIsa[a] 1–66	───▶					
1QIsa[b] 7–59	───────────────────────────────────────▶					
4QIsa[b] 1–66	───────────────────────────────────────▶					
4QIsa[c] 9:3 – 66:24	──────────────────────────────▶					
4QIsa[e] 2:1 – 59:16	──────────────────────────────▶					
Manuscripts containing a portion of Isaiah						
4QIsa[a]	1:1 – 33:17 ────────────────▶					
4QIsa[f]	1:10 – 29:8 ──────────▶					
4QIsa[j]	1:1–6					
5QIsa	1:4–14					
4QIsa[p]	5:28–30					
4QIsa[l]	7:14 – 8:14					
4QIsa[o]		14:28 – 15:2				
4QIsa[k]			28:26 – 29:9			
4QIsa[r]			30:23			
4QIsa[h]					42:4–11	
4QIsa[g]					42:14 – 43:24	
4QIsa[d]					45:20 – 58:7 ────────▶	
4QIsa[q]					54:10–13	
4QIsa[i]						56:7 – 57:8
4QIsa[n]						58:13–14
4QIsa[m]						60:20 – 61:6

8. The section divisions are arbitrary, not reflecting sense division so much in the first half, as reflecting the clusters of chapters in the MSS themselves.

Only five manuscripts are complete enough to contain portions covering the whole of our Isaiah. 1QIsa[a], of course, is complete. 1QIsa[b] comprises only fragments for chapters 7–25, with full columns extant beginning at 38:12. The three Cave 4 manuscripts contain at least some fragments from all sections of Isaiah.

The rest of the manuscripts are much less full. That is not to say they are more fragmentary, but that they contain text from more limited sections of Isaiah, which raises the question of how much of Isaiah they may have contained to start with. When discussing other biblical manuscripts at Qumran, it is customary to think of the existence of any number of fragments as representing what was at one time a complete copy of that given book, particularly when speaking of the Torah. But there are clear exceptions to this generalization. First, it appears that some manuscripts of Deuteronomy may contain only an excerpt, for example the poem of Deuteronomy 32.[9] Secondly, copies of some of the Megilloth (e.g. Songs) appear to have been excerpted portions of the books rather than complete copies. And, most notably, the Psalms manuscripts of Cave 11 include manuscripts containing a single psalm (e.g. 119), and a variety of numbers of psalms. The most complete, 11QPs[a], contains no psalm lower in Masoretic Text number than 100.[10]

So it is possible that some of these manuscripts never contained the whole of Isaiah as we have it, but excerpts. George Brooke has drawn attention to what this table shows very clearly: that nine manuscripts contain only the first half of Isaiah; seven contain only the second half.[11] Altogether absent from the fragments is the parallel with 2 Kings, which does not appear anywhere among the Cave 4 manuscripts. We will consider below whether these matters offer insight to the scribal view of the structure of Isaiah, and its implications.

The Great Isaiah Scroll

The first text brought to the attention of scholarship, and to be identified among the manuscripts of Cave 1, was a complete scroll of Isaiah, while

---

9. Tov, *Scribal Practices*, p. 168, identifies 4QDeut[q].

10. See D. Swanson, 'Dead Sea Scrolls', in T. Longman III and P. Enns (eds.), *Dictionary of the Old Testament: Wisdom, Poetry and Writings* (Downers Grove: IVP, 2008), pp. 88–99, for discussion of excerpted texts.

11. G. J. Brooke, 'On Isaiah at Qumran', in C. Mathews McGinnis and P. K. Tull (eds.), *'As Those Who Are Taught': The Interpretation of Isaiah from the LXX to the SBL* (Atlanta: SBL, 2006), pp. 79–80.

a second, partial, scroll was also to be found in that cave. The story of its identification by William Brownlee and John Trever has been recounted in numerous places.[12]

The text of the manuscript

The text-critical analysis of the manuscript in comparison to the Masoretic Text shows the majority of variant readings are orthographic and morphological.[13] It is useful to summarize the textual evidence as it has been described extensively by both Malachi Martin and E. Y. Kutscher:[14]

1. Use of vowel letters, extension of *matres lectionis*.
2. Treatment of gutturals, indicating dialectical peculiarities.
3. Nominal forms (suggesting an older pronunciation than the Tiberian).
4. Personal pronouns and pronoun suffixes lengthened in 2nd and 3rd he (also archaic).
5. Verbal forms in *tiqtōlu* versus Tiberian *tiqtĕlu* (1QIsa[a] being older tradition).

The implications of these features for the textual history of Isaiah led to an early broad consensus that the Isaiah Scroll was of limited value for textual criticism. Moshe Greenberg viewed the Scroll as a 'vulgar', popular type text which existed alongside the shorter, 'standard' texts.[15] Joseph Rosenbloom characterized the Scroll as 'an interpretative copy of the MT'.[16] Kutscher held

---

12. Notably, their own accounts. Cf. W. H Brownlee, *The Meaning of the Qumran Scrolls for the Bible with Special Attention to the Book of Isaiah* (New York: Oxford University Press, 1964); and J. C. Trever, *The Dead Sea Scrolls: A Personal Account* (Old Tappan: Fleming H. Revell, 1965).

13. Tov's characterization of 'Qumran scribal practice', in *Scribal Practices*, pp. 262–263, for whom the Isaiah Scroll is a key witness.

14. M. Martin, *The Scribal Character of the Dead Sea Scrolls*, 2 vols. (Louvain: Publication Universitaires, 1958); E. Y. Kutscher, *The Language and Linguistic Background of the Isaiah Scroll (1QIsa^a)* (Leiden: Brill, 1974); summarized together by J. Høgenhaven, 'The First Isaiah Scroll from Qumran (1QIsa^a) and the Massoretic Text: Some Reflections with Special Regard to Isaiah 1–12', *JSOT* 28 (1984), pp. 17–35. Square brackets indicate Høgenhaven's comments.

15. M. Greenberg, 'The Stabilization of the Text of the Hebrew Bible', *JAOS* 76 (1956), pp. 157–167.

16. J. R. Rosenbloom, *The Dead Sea Isaiah Scroll: A Literary Analysis and Comparison of the Qumran Scroll with the Masoretic Text of Isaiah* (Grand Rapids: Eerdmans, 1970), p. 71.

that the manuscript represented a Judaic dialect, the language of the scribe, which he also contrasted to the 'standard' biblical text, or Masoretic Text.[17] Martin, slightly differently, understood the gutturals and orthography to exhibit the traditional praxis of the time. For him, it was not a 'vulgar' adaptation, but characteristic of the language.

In these analyses the Masoretic Text was accepted as the 'standard' text against which the Isaiah manuscript was to be judged. Martin, following F. M. Cross, however, was leading in the direction of seeing geographic differences of language, in which 1QIsa^a is a genuine ancient linguistic tradition alongside the Masoretic Text. Isaiah represents a Palestinian tradition, Masoretic Text a Babylonian tradition.[18]

What I wish to highlight in this discussion is the need to leave aside the assumption that the Masoretic Text represents a more archaic Hebrew than the Qumran texts, and to place them alongside one another, the Masoretic Text developing out of a proto-Masoretic Text that lies alongside a pluriformity of text forms that represent real textual traditions, even in the pesharim. It is only in the course of the first century BCE that the form of the text becomes increasingly 'standardized' in the direction of the Masoretic Text.[19]

Scribal practice
Scribal features of the manuscript itself give clues to the interpretation of the book. Tov[20] notes that the Great Isaiah Scroll is unique among Dead Sea Scrolls biblical manuscripts in being written by more than one scribe, using

---

17. Kutscher, *Language and Linguistic Background*, pp. 78–79, contrasted with the 'popular' category.
18. See Høgenhaven, 'First Isaiah Scroll', p. 31. More recently, see P. Pulikottil, who views 1QIsa^a's unique readings in terms of scribal practice, *Transmission of Biblical Texts in Qumran: The Case of the Large Isaiah Scroll 1QIsa^a* (Sheffield: Sheffield Academic Press, 2001), not far off Tov's theory of 'Qumran scribal practice'; and O. Steck, who follows Kutscher's view of the scroll as a private study copy, *Die erste Jesajarolle von Qumran (1QIsa^a): Schreibweise als Leseanleitung für ein Prophetenbuch*, SBS 173.1 (Stuttgart: Katholisches Bibelwerk, 1998), pp. 19–20.
19. The term 'pluriformity' is that introduced by Eugene Ulrich in his work on the biblical text at Qumran, which is spelled out in *The Dead Sea Scrolls and the Origins of the Bible* (Grand Rapids: Eerdmans, 1999).
20. Tov, *Scribal Practices*, Table 1, p. 21.

different orthography.[21] Of particular interest is the fact that the change takes place precisely in the middle – between columns 27 and 28, that is, chapters 33 and 34 – following three ruled but uninscribed lines at the bottom of column 27. Tov dismisses the likelihood that two scribes worked concurrently, noting that it would have been impossible to be certain that they would come out just so precisely.[22] He also dismisses the proposal that the orthographic differences between the two halves may be ascribed to two different *Vorlagen*. This is the extent of Tov's discussion of the feature, which he seems to think of as essentially a scribal convention; he does not include this factor in relation to his discussion of Delimitation Criticism, at the point of 'sense divisions'. And, notably, both of these points were made by William Brownlee.

Delimitation criticism
Delimitation Criticism, propounded by Marjo Korpel and Josef Oesch,[23] is a recent addition to the stock of biblical studies which looks at manuscripts as a whole, and not only the text. That is, the very way in which a scribe lays out the text on the page/scroll, as well as marginal notations, is taken into consideration in understanding the history of interpretation of the text. Open spaces, as well as filled space, are noted.

George Brooke raises such issues on precisely this subject by way of Brownlee's proposal to view the literary formation of the book of Isaiah through the lens of the Isaiah Scroll.[24] Brownlee began from the phenomenon of the bisection of the manuscript at midpoint, and argued that the text reflects

---

21. The *Temple Scroll* has two hands involved, but the second is that of the scribe who repaired the first four columns.

22. Tov, *Scribal Practices*, pp. 20–21.

23. M. C. A. Korpel and J. M. Oesch, *Delimitation Criticism: A New Tool for Biblical Scholarship* (Assen: Van Gorcum, 2000); J. M. Oesch, *Petucha und Setuma, Untersuchungen zu einer überlieferten Gliederung im hebräischen Text des Alten Testament* (Freiburg: Vandanhoeck & Ruprecht, 1979). E. Tov's work incorporates much from this approach.

24. Brooke, 'On Isaiah at Qumran', pp. 77–81, citing W. H. Brownlee's little-known 'The Literary Significance of the Bisection of Isaiah in the Ancient Scroll from Qumran', Proceedings of the 25th Congress of Orientalists (Moscow 1962–3), pp. 431–437; and *Meaning of the Qumran Scrolls for the Bible with Special Attention to the Book of Isaiah* (New York: Oxford University Press, 1964), p. 246; C. A. Evans offers additional evidence for Brownlee's case in 'On the Unity and Parallel Structure of Isaiah', *VT* 38.2 (1988), pp. 129–147.

an ancient understanding of the literary structure of the book: as two parallel sections dividing between chapters 33 and 34 (see Table 3).

Table 3   Literary structure of Isaiah

Isaiah 1 – 33	Isaiah 34 – 66
1–5 The ruin and restoration of Judah	34–35 The restoration of Judah and the Davidic kingdom
6–8 Biography	36–40 Biography
9–12 Agents of divine blessing and judgment	41–45 Agents of deliverance and judgment
13–23 Anti-foreign oracles	46–48 Anti-Babylonian oracles
24–27 Universal judgment and the deliverance of God's people	49–54[25] Universal redemption through the Lord's servant; also the glorification of Israel
28–31 Ethical sermons indicting Israel and Judah	56–59 Ethical sermons, the ethical conditions for Israel's redemption
32–33 Paradise lost and regained	60–66 Paradise regained: the glories of the New Jerusalem and the new heavens and the new earth

Whereas Tov's points regarding the scribal practices involving two different scribes, working consecutively, stand as a given, they do not negate the literary aspect of Brownlee's observations. And, as Brooke goes on to note, the evidence of the Cave 4 documents (as noted above with regard to Table 2) strengthens the impression that Isaiah was seen as a work of two parts. Brooke goes on to press the argument from scribal marginal notes in 1QIsa[a] that appear to coincide with Brownlee's divisions – even though Brownlee himself did not note this factor.[26]

For our purposes, this evidence is called into play primarily to draw attention to an aspect of the Qumran manuscripts that has not, heretofore, been given wide consideration in either textual or biblical criticism and exegesis. This manuscript is the oldest evidence we have for grasping how the content

---

25. Ch. 55 is missing in Brownlee's presentation.

26. Brooke, 'On Isaiah at Qumran', p. 79; building on his own article 'The Bisection of Isaiah in the Scrolls from Qumran', in P. S. Alexander et al. (eds.), *Studia Semitica: The Journal of Semitic Studies Jubilee Volume* (Oxford: Oxford University Press, 2005), pp. 73–94.

of the book of Isaiah was understood. Since the nineteenth century, scholarship has thought of the book in terms of First Isaiah, Second Isaiah and Third Isaiah, with divisions between chapters 39 and 40, and 55 and 56. There is no corresponding scribal space after chapter 39, and the fragmentary evidence at the bottom of column 1 of 1QIsa[b] leaves no room for such space either. It could be argued that this scribal evidence requires a reordering of our ideas of the sense divisions of Isaiah.

Sense divisions

This point can be illustrated on a smaller scale by a comparison of paragraph divisions between 1QIsa[a] and Codex Leningradensis.[27] The selection in Table 4 below represents Isaiah 7:1 – 9:6, chosen to coincide with the textual comparisons made below.

Table 4   Sense units in 1QIsa[a] and Codex Leningradensis

Isaiah Scroll	Codex L
7:1–2 = OP	7:1–6 = OP
7:3–9 = OP	7:7–9 = OP
CP at 6; Palaeo-Heb. waw at 8	
7:10–20 = OP, P after 9	7:10–17 = CP
	7:18–20 = OP and full line *vacat*
7:21 = CP	7:21–25 = OP
7:22–25 = OP	
8:1–4 = OP; CP in 3, after 'son'	8:1–4 = OP
8:5–8 = OP and P	8:5–8 = OP and indented
8:9 = CP and P	8:9–10 = OP and indented
8:10 – 9:6 = OP; CP and P at 8:15; CP	8:11–15 = OP and indented
and P at 8:18; CP and P after 9:1	8:16–18 = CP
	8:19 – 9:6 = CP (OP at 9:20)

The sense units in the Isaiah Scroll are 'Open Paragraphs' (OP); that is, the new paragraph starts at the beginning of a line following a line which may have as little as a single word. A 'Closed Paragraph' (CP) indicates a unit division within a line of about the length of a single word. There are scribal marks (commonly called *paragraphos* marks, or 'P') in the margins, which suggest additional sense notations, but their significance and origin can only be guessed at.

27. These are treated at length by O. Steck, *Die erste Jesajarolle*; see the table on pp. 46–51.

Codex Leningradensis, likewise makes use of Open and Closed Paragraph spaces (not always noted consistently in *BHS*, with פ or ס respectively).

These sense units may be further compared to the NRSV paragraphs: 7:1–2; 7:3–9; 7:10–17; 7:18–19, 20, 21–22, 23–25; 8:1–4; 8:5–8; 8:9–10; 8:11–15; 8:16–22; 8:23 – 9:6 (9:2–7, ET).

On one hand, the 1QIsaᵃ division of 7:1–9 (followed by the NRSV) fits the sense of these verses better than Codex L. On the other hand, Codex L's placing of 8:9–10 apart from the surrounding text (placed in poetic form in the NRSV), seems more fitting than 8:9 standing by itself in 1QIsaᵃ. Nevertheless, the fact that the Isaiah Scroll sees this one verse as more significant in some way calls the interpreter to consider why this might be.

The Isaiah manuscripts: sampling the text

The next task is to consider the evidence of the rest of the Isaiah manuscripts in relation to the Masoretic Text. The fragmentary nature of the Cave 4 manuscripts makes this difficult. It happens, however, that there is significant overlap of manuscripts in chapters 8–10. I will therefore illustrate the broader nature of the relationship of the texts with one example where there is an overlap between four Qumran manuscripts. The Masoretic Text[28] is given first, for convenience of comparison; the Qumran manuscripts are placed in their relative chronological order.[29]

MT Isaiah 8:7–8

7 וְלָכֵן הִנֵּה אֲדֹנָי מַעֲלֶה עֲלֵיהֶם אֶת־מֵי הַנָּהָר
הָעֲצוּמִים וְהָרַבִּים אֶת־מֶלֶךְ אַשּׁוּר וְאֶת־כָּל־כְּבוֹדוֹ
וְעָלָה עַל־כָּל־אֲפִיקָיו וְהָלַךְ עַל־כָּל־גְּדוֹתָיו׃
8 וְחָלַף בִּיהוּדָה שָׁטַף וְעָבַר עַד־צַוָּאר יַגִּיעַ
וְהָיָה מֻטּוֹת כְּנָפָיו מְלֹא רֹחַב־אַרְצְךָ עִמָּנוּ אֵל׃

---

28. It needs to be noted that Codex Leningradensis reads עמנואל as one word in v. 8, unlike the *BHS* as given here. It is two words in v. 10. This skews the example somewhat, but highlights the problems in interpretation of ignoring the MS itself.

29. Guide to *sigla* in the Qumran texts, in the order they occur: *black circle* above a letter = only a portion of the letter is visible, but the reading is certain; *raised letters* or words = scribal correction added above the text of the word that follows; *square brackets* = missing text; *open circle* = only a small portion of a letter is visible, the reconstruction by the editor is likely; *double strike-through* = text has been erased by the hand of the correcting scribe, but is still readable.

1QIsaᵃ

ולכן הנה אֲדֹנָי יֹהֹוֹה מעלה עליהם את מי הנהר

[   ]לכ אשור ואת כול כבודו

[   ]גדוותיו

וחלף ביהודה שטף ועבר עד צואר יגיע

והיה מטות כנפיו מלוא רחב ארצך עמנואל

4QpIsaᶜ Fragment 2

[עָלה עליהֹן]ם את מֵֵי הֹנהר [   ]

הֹן[   ]

[עַל כל אפיקו והלך על כל גדֹו]תֹו[ן   ]

[   ]

[יו מטות כנפו מלא רחב ארצכֹ]ה [   ]

4QIsaᶠ Fragment 12 column ii, 14–15

[מעלה עליהם את מי הנהר   ]

הרבים וה]ןעצומים [ואת כל כבדו

ועלה על כל]ן[[לֹ]ן[   ]

[   ] [ף]ן[[שטֹף ועבר עד צואר יֹגֹ]ן[ ]

[רחב ארן] [עמנוֹאֹל   ]

4QIsaᶜ Fragments 4–10

[כֹוֹ]הֹ]ן[[מֹעלה עליהם] הֹן[[

[יֹם את מלך אן]כל כבודו   ]

ועלה עֹן]כֹל אפיקיו והלך על כלן]דיֹוֹהֹ]ן [

[ף ועבר עד צער] [   ]

[הֹ] [מטוֹן [נֹפֹיֹו מלא רחב ארצך עמנואל   ]

Notes on 1QIsaᵃ

- The manuscript is damaged at the bottom of the column, affecting verse 7.
- *'Adonai* is placed directly over *Yhwh*, which is not erased. It would appear in this instance, at least, that the erasure of the Sacred Name was not allowable, so remained in the text.
- This portion of the scroll fairly consistently uses non-final forms in the final position; note the kaph and two pes; the kaph of 'your land' serves as a rare exception.
- The use of *matres lectionis* is inconsistent.
- Note that Emmanuel is written as a single word. This is followed by a

closed paragraph space (following v. 9 there is a full *vacat* – space void of text).

Notes on the pesher (dated 86 BCE)
Inclusion of a pesher may be considered controversial. However, it is useful to place the evidence before us. What is of note with this text is that it is older than almost all the Cave 4 manuscripts of Isaiah, so represents the earlier period of transmission among the Scrolls. It could, conceivably, have an influence on later copies. As such, it can be instructive.

- In line 1,[30] *mēy*, 'waters' (construct), is dotted for correction, and erased.
- Line 3, פיקן), 'channel', is apparently in the singular. Horgan reconstructs the last word of line 3 to agree with 'channel'.[31] The defective plural construct is fairly common among scrolls related to the Qumran scribal tradition.[32] It does not necessarily follow that the pesher would be consistent, but it is a reasonable conjecture.
- In line 5 we have the 3rd pl. suffix (only) for *hayah*, where the other texts have the sg., and then the sg., *his wing*, where the others have *wings*, pl. The question is, what is the subject of the verb? If this referred back to 'waters' (*mey*), it would be a sensible correction. However, 'waters' is erased! (Unless this was done by a later scribe.)

---

30. The line numbers in the comments refer to this layout, and not to the MS fragments themselves.

31. The text here follows M. P. Horgan in *The Dead Sea Scrolls: Hebrew, Aramaic, and Greek Texts with English Translations*. Vol. 6b: *Pesharim, Other Commentaries, and Related Documents*, ed. J. H. Charlesworth et al. (Tübingen: Mohr Siebeck; Louisville: Westminster John Knox, 2002). For J. Strugnell, 'Notes en marge du Volume V des "Discoveries in the Judaean Desert of Jordan"', *RevQ* 7 (1967–9), pp. 183–199.

32. E. Qimron, *The Hebrew of the Dead Sea Scrolls* (Atlanta: Scholars Press, 1985/6), p. 59; cf. G. J. Brooke on this example, 'The Qumran Pesharim and the Text of Isaiah in the Case of Cave 4 Manuscripts', in A. Rapaport-Albert and G. Greenberg (eds.), *Biblical Hebrews, Biblical Texts: Essay in Memory of Michael P. Weitzman* (Sheffield: Sheffield Academic Press, 2001), p. 309; and 'The Biblical Texts in the Qumran Commentaries: Scribal Errors or Exegetical Variants?', in C. A. Evans and W. F. Stinespring (eds.), *Early Jewish and Christian Exegesis: Studies in Memory of William Brownlee* (Atlanta: Scholars Press, 1987), pp. 85–100.

Notes on 4QIsa^d

- In line 2 the word order of 'mighty and many' of MT is reversed. This portion is missing from 1QIsa^a, so we cannot tell if this variant is unique.
- 'His glory' is written without the waw, which even the MT has here.
- Emmanuel is written as a single word.
- Emmanuel is followed by a *vacat*, thus a closed paragraph space, with v. 9 starting the next line.

Notes on 4QIsa^e
- Of the text which remains here, there is not a single variant from MT, other than Emmanuel appearing as a single word.

Overall summary

First, in this snapshot of Isaiah, we can see the orthography changing gradually, but 1QIsa^a is no different from the others in offering 'good' or 'bad' readings. The pesher has the greatest difference from the others, but seems to be wrestling with issues of the text itself, rather than offering interpretative glosses.

In terms of section delimitation, two of the three Qumran manuscripts (1QIsa^a and 4QIsa^f) have divisions following verse 8, that of the Great Isaiah Scroll emphasized by the marginal *paragraphos* mark of a (probably later) scribe. These are the earliest of the manuscripts.

Although it cannot come through too clearly in this single example, there is a noticeable move towards a Masoretic Text text-type in the later manuscripts. By the Late Herodian period the increasing uniformity is almost complete, with some singular exceptions.

What is, perhaps at first glance, most interesting in this example is that in none of the Qumran manuscripts is there a space between עמנו and אל. The same is true at verse 10 in the two Qumran texts which contain that text. Masoretic Text stands alone in spacing them. Is it possible, or likely, that the Masoretic Text reading reflects a Christian-era scribal reaction to messianic interpretation of this word?

Works based on Isaiah

Pesharim

Moving from the Isaiah manuscripts, we turn to the pesharim. For the sake of comparison of the dating of the manuscripts, Table 5 (below) repeats the list of Isaiah manuscripts, with the addition of the pesharim.

Table 5 The pesharim[33]

Text	*Date*	*Scribal era*[34]
1QIsa[a]	125–100	Early Hasm.
4QIsa[r]	c. 90	Mid-Hasm.
4Qpap pIsa[c]	85	
4QIsa[f]	100–50	
4QIsa[h]	100–50	
4QIsa[i]	100–50	
4QIsa[l]	100–50	
4QIsa[m]	100–50	
4QIsa[n]	100–50	
4QIsa[o]	100–50	
4QpapIsa[p]	100–50	
4QIsa[k]	50	Late Hasm.
1QIsa[b]	50–25	Late Hasm./Early Herod.
4QIsa[a]	50–25	
4QIsa[b]	50–25	
4QIsa[j]	50–25	
4QpIsa[d]	50–25	
4QpIsa[b]	50–25	
4QpIsa[a]	50–25	
4QIsa[g]	50–1	Early Herod.
4QIsa[e]	30–1	
4QIsa[q]	30–1	
4QpIsa[e]	30–1	
3QpIsa	c. 20	Herod.
5QIsa	15–70	'Late'
4QIsa[c]	30–68	Devel. Herod.
4QIsa[d]	30–68	Late Herod.

33. Pesharim b and d do not appear in the DJD 39 palaeographical list.

34. See n. 7 above for explanation of abbreviations.

The papyrus pesher c stands alone in the Hasmonaean era, prior to virtually all of the Cave 4 copies of Isaiah. The rest, except for the lone Cave 3
exemplar, are copied (if not written) in the peak period of Qumran scribal
activity. This factor is of interest with regard to the historical setting of the
pesharim which may be gleaned from the interpretations, but for our purposes
we consider the text of Isaiah only.

The cryptic text is dealt with below, but is included in this list for comparison.
It is considered to be the oldest of these texts.[35]

Table 6   Text of Isaiah cited[36]

Pesharim	1 – 12	13 – 23	24 – 33	34 – 39	40 – 55	56 – 66[37]
4QcryptA	11:6–7					
4QpIsa^c	8:8 – 32:6					
4QpIsa^d		→			54:11–12	
4QpIsa^b	5:5–25 (6:9?)					
4QpIsa^a	10:21 – 11:5					
4QpIsa^{e38}	11:11 – 32:7 + 40:12				→	
3QpIsa	1:1–2a					

The papyrus text, the oldest of these manuscripts, is also more extensive
than most. Whether this is because of the accident of decay of the manuscripts is impossible to ascertain. Pesher d is unique in dealing only with the
second half of Isaiah, whereas the others deal only with the first half. The
exception to this is pesher e, a later text, which overlaps the twofold division
of Isaiah only by use of Isaiah 40:11–12, which appears twice. The remainder of the text cited (all from the first half of Isaiah) goes no further than
Isaiah 32. No far-reaching conclusions can be drawn from such fragmentary evidence, but the additional factor of four out of the six manuscripts

---

35. Tov, *Texts from the Judaean Desert*, p. 385, based on S. Pfann, in P. S. Alexander et al.,
    Qumran Cave 4: Cryptic Text, in consultation with J. VanderKam and M. Brady,
    Miscellanea, Part 1, DJD 36 (Oxford: Clarendon, 2000), p. 682, the last quarter of
    the second century BCE.

36. These are listed in chronological order. By the nature of the pesharim, not all of
    the text within these limits given would actually appear.

37. The section divisions are arbitrary, not reflecting sense division so much in the first
    half as reflecting the clusters of chapters in the MSS themselves.

38. Pesher e evidence is deceptive here. It begins with 40:11–12, and returns to it
    midway; but other extant texts are not in canonical order: 14 – 15 – 40 – 21 – 32 – 11.

containing portions of chapters 8–11 allows for some degree of conjecture. The interest in the Emmanuel passages has already been highlighted, but suggests a degree of interest in this same section of Isaiah that the Gospels find interest in.

As noted in the previous section, the cited texts in the pesharim fit within the normal parameters of textual pluriformity among the Scrolls, and do not exhibit evidence of interpretative variants. As such, they should be included in text-critical comparisons.

4Q 250b papyrus cryptA text related to Isaiah 11[39]

Only one other text among the Qumran manuscripts deals with Isaiah, besides the pesharim. It is unique, in being found among the cryptic texts – that is, texts written in a 'code', thus meant to be kept secret from general perusal. The text is problematic for purposes of this study, given the sparse evidence that one fragment with three discernible words offers. We look at it more closely here in order to evaluate its pertinence to understanding the text of Isaiah.

First, the text is reproduced:

ﬡﬦﬡ[יֹחֹדִיו מֹצ   ] 1
נ[ער קטנן   ] 2

1.]together
2. a s]mall boy[

Secondly, Stephen Pfann's summary of the evidence:

1. These two complete words appear in the Hebrew Bible within two lines of each other only in Isaiah 11:6–7.
2. There are three possible ways of viewing the evidence:
   a. The text is a variant of Isaiah 11:6–7.
   b. The text is related to Isaiah 11 as paraphrase, commentary or allusion.
   c. Their relation to each other may be just coincidence

Pfann opts for 2b above.

Before accepting Pfann's identification of the text, it seems wise to consider any other biblical contexts for the words.

---

39. S. Pfann, DJD 36, p. 692: Mus. Inv. 593, 598; PAM 41.984 (verso), 41.985 (recto), 41.990, 43.410, 43.413 (recto), 43.414 (verso).

First, the phrase 'little child'[40] is found three times in 1 and 2 Kings: once used of himself by Solomon, once of Hadad the Edomite and once describing Na'aman's flesh after his healing; and in 1 Samuel 20:25, of David and Jonathan with a small boy. So, outside Isaiah 11, the two words occur together only in the Deuteronomistic History.

The fragmentary letters at the end of the first line are identified by Pfann as מֹצ. There are at least six possible candidates for these letters: (1) אמֹץ = strength; (2) כמֹץ/המֹץ = the chaff/like chaff; (3) חמֹץ = leaven; (4) קמֹץ = fist; (5) שמֹץ = whisper; (6) ימצא = be found.

None of these words, in any of their possible forms, is found in proximity to the Deuteronomic texts. Nor does any of these fit plausibly together with Isaiah 11 and animals being 'together' in some way. Thus it would seem we can rule out any other biblical text besides Isaiah 11:6–7, while simultaneously raising questions over the conjectured reading of the letters of line 1.

Having eliminated other possible readings, we can now go over the text again with Isaiah 11:6–7 in view. There are three ways of aligning the text of Isaiah and the text of this fragment.

Option A places the keywords as close as makes sense within the Masoretic Text:

וְגָר זְאֵב עִם־כֶּבֶשׂ
וְנָמֵר עִם־גְּדִי יִרְבָּץ
וְעֵגֶל וּכְפִיר
וּמְרִיא יַחְדָּו
וְנַעַר קָטֹן נֹהֵג בָּם׃
וּפָרָה וָדֹב
תִּרְעֶינָה יַחְדָּו
יִרְבְּצוּ יַלְדֵיהֶן וְאַרְיֵה
כַּבָּקָר יֹאכַל־תֶּבֶן׃

Here, the 'young child' (underlined) will just about fit directly under 'together'. It is clearly not a perfect alignment. More problematic is the length of the lines that has to be posited for this to 'fit'. One could only imagine an excerpted text with very narrow columns. This is not impossible, but such variation in the length of lines is not seen elsewhere in Qumran manuscripts.

In Option B the approach is to put the 'young child' with the 'together' of verse 7 rather than verse 6:

---

40. No other combinations of קטֹן and נַעַר can be found in the biblical corpus.

וְגָר זְאֵב עִם־כֶּבֶשׁ
וְנָמֵר עִם־גְּדִי יִרְבָּץ וְעֵגֶל וּכְפִיר
וּמְרִיא יַחְדָּו וְנַעַר קָטֹן נֹהֵג בָּם: וּפָרָה
וָדֹב תִּרְעֶינָה יַחְדָּו יִרְבְּצוּ יַלְדֵיהֶן
וְאַרְיֵה כַּבָּקָר יֹאכַל־תֶּבֶן:

The presence of 'will lie down' in Isaiah 11:7 almost fits the two letters Pfann reads at the end of the first line of the text, מֹצ. My observations, based on the photos in DJD, and in the electronic version,[41] can make out the cryptic daleth and yodh, and can imagine that I see the waw of the יחדיו in line 1. But I can see no signs that look like mem or tsade – either of which would easily be mistaken for a beth. If ירבצו were to be considered here, then we might be looking at a text related to, but not precisely, Isaiah.

In Option C we place the words as they appear in the fragment, and try to persuade the text to fit around them, while also attempting to keep the line length as consistent as possible. This is possible by beginning with the last words of 11:5:

אזור חֲלָצָיו וְגָר זְאֵב עִם־כֶּבֶשׁ
וְנָמֵר עִם־גְּדִי יִרְבָּץ וְעֵגֶל וּכְפִיר
וּמְרִיא יַחְדָּו [וירבצו]
[   ] [וְנַעַר קָטֹן נֹהֵג בָּם: וּפָרָה
וָדֹב תִּרְעֶינָה יַחְדָּו יִרְבְּצוּ יַלְדֵיהֶן
וְאַרְיֵה כַּבָּקָר יֹאכַל־תֶּבֶן:

One can see at a glance that several words will have to be found to fill the space required between the Masoretic Text יחדיו and ונער (I place my conjectured reading of the fragments that follow the יחדיו as a starter). If this is Isaiah 11, then it contains either a major variant reading, or, at best, scribal haplography.

Conclusion

If the partial word could be construed as from רבץ, then one could just about make a case for this being a variant of the Isaiah text. This does not, however, seem to be the most likely possibility. Even so, Steven Pfann's conclusion certainly remains open – this is a reference to the text in 'some way'.

---

41. *The Dead Sea Scrolls Electronic Reference Library, 2*, Center for the Preservation of Ancient Religious Texts at Brigham Young University (Leiden: Brill, 1999).

Where does such an ambiguous conclusion leave us? An important question arises as to why Isaiah 11 would be alluded to in a cryptic text. These manuscripts appear to have been written to protect the Yahad teaching from public disclosure, either from novices not yet inducted into the mysteries of the Community, or from falling into the hands of outsiders when members were travelling outside their base.[42] Was there some specific application of their era in a messianic fashion that was to be kept a vital secret?

Although these questions do not add much to our understanding of the text of Isaiah, it does hold out a tantalizing possibility of the significance of messianic interpretation of Isaiah 11 at Qumran.

Summary

This is all the literature among the Dead Sea Scrolls that relates to the book of Isaiah – six commentaries and possibly one enigmatic fragment.[43] It is remarkable, in comparison to the Pentateuch, for its sparsity. There simply is not a great industry in texts expanding or rewriting Isaiah.

Why does the Torah, the basis of Halacha for all of Jewish life, generate such a riot of literature, rewriting and expanding and playing with the text as it does in the Second Temple period, while a prophetic book, Isaiah, achieves a settled text relatively rapidly, and generates few 'spin-offs'?

The answer must lie in 'some aspect of their authority and status',[44] as George Brooke suggests. Conceivably, the pre-eminent authoritative status of the Torah could be enough to explain why so much is written in response to it. On this basis, Isaiah attracts less interpretation or expansion because the prophets hold a lesser degree of authority. But this is not Brooke's argument. With regard to Torah, he suggests, 'Perhaps such rewriting within the Torah was understood as authorizing an ongoing practice of rewriting.'[45] From the inner-biblical exegesis evident within, for example Leviticus and Numbers, to 'rewriting' of Exodus in Deuteronomy, to the pluriformity of the texts found

---

42. Yahad is the self-designation of the sectarian group, ostensibly Essenes, associated with the scrolls found in the Qumran vicinity. Literally meaning something like 'the unity/oneness', it is usually translated 'the Community'.

43. We do not consider the allusions at this point.

44. G. J. Brooke, 'On Isaiah at Qumran', in Mathews McGinnis and Tull, 'As Those Who Are Taught', p. 82.

45. Ibid.

at Qumran, the Rewritten Bible, apocryphons, and rudimentary commentaries, the evidence of the first century BCE is of a dynamic conversation within the boundaries of 'Torah'. Increasingly this pluriformity would frustrate inter-Jewish debate, since arguments relating to correct Halacha could not take place from an agreed authority; whether intentional or not, argument on the meaning of an authority led to the focus on a commonly agreed text – something not complete until well into the Christian era.

For Isaiah, on the other hand, 'something else must be at work', as Brooke says.[46] The fact of a stable text tradition for the Cave 4 Isaiah manuscripts at an earlier stage suggests to Brooke that the text of Isaiah had gained authoritative status at an earlier stage in the Second Temple period. With this in mind, we might consider possible reasons. It seems that the prophet's immediacy of inspiration led to a ready acceptance of its authority. There was no room for questioning the direct word of the Lord.

If we follow this reading of the evidence, then our conception of the nature of the authority of texts, and of the relation of the prophets to Torah, is in need of a reconfiguration. The Torah, as a scribal work, allows for a large degree of fluidity of textual development within its overarching authoritative status; the Prophets, as charismatic bearers of the fresh word of the Lord, attain fixed textual status more quickly and earlier. While the relative authority of the books of Moses is clearly superior, this nevertheless leaves open the possible influence of the Prophets on the Torah with regard to matters of intertextual development.

---

46. Ibid.

10. ISAIAH IN THE NEW TESTAMENT

Rikk E. Watts

Introduction

With almost 100 citations and some 500 allusions, Isaiah is the most frequently referenced single work in the New Testament.[1] Its influence extends from elucidating occasional particulars to providing pervasive themes and much in between. Herein we focus on the citations and more important allusions.[2] But this already raises questions: What constitutes a citation, how does it differ from an allusion, and how does one identify the latter? A formal introduction (e.g. 'as Isaiah says') is useful but honoured more in the breach than the observance. Matters are not helped when the 'citation' frequently differs from its purported source. In the past this led some scholars to seek the particular manuscript tradition that lay behind these unusual forms. It is now recognized that these forms could equally have originated with the New Testament authors themselves who in following standard ancient practice freely adapted

---

1. Only the larger Psalms compilation has more references.
2. See the more detailed and comprehensive works of S. Moyise and M. J. J. Menken (eds.), *Isaiah in the New Testament* (Edinburgh: T. & T. Clark, 2005), and esp. G. K. Beale and D. A. Carson (eds.), *Commentary on the New Testament Use of the Old Testament* (Grand Rapids: Baker; Nottingham: Apollos, 2007).

their citations to bring out what they saw as the meaning as it related to their argument.[3] Determining an allusion is even more difficult since much depends on how attuned the now-inaccessible author's ear was to Isaiah. In this chapter the terms 'citation' and 'allusion' indicate their relative position along a continuum, with a citation having greater congruence of syntax and words than an allusion, which tends to the thematic and conceptual. Key to both however is the criterion that to establish a link between given Old Testament and New Testament passages there must be 'sufficient' uniquely shared features.[4] Lacking the space to argue each case, we will confine ourselves to generally accepted instances.

Equally problematic are questions of whether or not the New Testament authors' readings of Isaiah reflect a coherent perspective, and if so to what degree Isaiah provides an overarching interpretative 'grid'. Motivated solely by immediate concerns do they merely proof-text or, in more recent parlance, engage in rhetorical acts of persuasion through authoritative appeals to Scripture (usually with negative connotations)?[5] Or were matters more complex?

Clearly, their immediate 'present' is important. However, this present includes not only a particular community's circumstances but the overriding conviction that God had intervened eschatologically through Jesus Christ, his Son, to fulfil his long-standing promises to Israel. Furthermore, it now appears that the New Testament authors were, from the very earliest, offering the kind of devotion to Jesus previously reserved for God alone.[6] Monotheists still, they held that not only had God acted through Jesus but Jesus himself was in some mysterious way identified with God. If so, the general rule of thumb that restricts a high Christology to 'late' John will no longer do and we will need to rethink the Christological implications of various Isaiah texts in earlier New Testament documents.

---

3. C. Stanley, *Paul and the Language of Scripture*, SNTSMS 74 (Cambridge: Cambridge University Press, 1992); for details of such changes in each of the instances discussed below see Beale and Carson, *Commentary*.

4. See the chapters in Part 1: Methods and Canons, in C. A. Evans and J. A. Sanders (eds.), *Early Christian Interpretation of the Scriptures of Israel*, JSNTSup 148 (Sheffield: Sheffield Academic Press, 1997), pp. 18–96.

5. See e.g. S. E. Porter (ed.), *Hearing the Old Testament in the New Testament* (Grand Rapids: Eerdmans, 2006), and C. Stanley, *Arguing with Scripture* (London: T. & T. Clark, 2004).

6. L. Hurtado, *Lord Jesus Christ* (Grand Rapids: Eerdmans, 2003); G. D. Fee, *Pauline Christology* (Peabody: Hendrickson, 2007).

At the same time the sheer weight of Scripture in the New Testament testifies to its ongoing authority. Since the Scriptures 'cannot be annulled' (John 10:35)[7] they had to be squared with this new thing God had done, and therein lay the rub. Jesus' manner of life, death and resurrection were unexpected, to say the least. The critical issue, then, for the New Testament authors was how to integrate their views of Scripture with their convictions about Jesus, and particularly in the face of unanticipated large-scale Jewish rejection and equally surprising significant Gentile qua Gentile acceptance. It is precisely in seeking to understand these events that their rereadings of Isaiah, alone and combined with other Old Testament texts, emerge. In this latter respect, attending solely to Isaiah is really just a first step toward appreciating the New Testament authors' sophisticated engagement with Scripture.[8] Furthermore, since they were not writing in a vacuum, a fuller treatment would also need to consider contemporary interpretations of Isaianic texts, clearly beyond the scope of the present chapter.[9]

This chapter, then, constitutes only an initial foray. We will begin with the use of Isaiah in understanding Jesus' life. Given the Synoptic relationship and accepting for sake of argument that Mark wrote first, we begin with Isaiah in that Gospel (parallels in Matthew and Luke are noted in parentheses), followed by the unique contributions of Matthew and Luke-Acts, and then finally John. Turning to the epistles we will begin with the Pauline, disputed Pauline and then the other letters, before, given its uniquely allusive character, considering Revelation. I will then offer some final observations.

The Gospels

Mark

Isaiah 40:3's classic summons to prepare for Yahweh's coming to deliver his exiled people is key to Mark's opening (Mark 1:2; see Matt. 3:3 // Luke 3:4–6).[10]

---

7. Unless stated otherwise, all translations are from the NRSV (and italics in Bible quotations are added).

8. See e.g. J. R. Wagner, *Heralds of the Good News: Isaiah and Paul 'In Concert' in the Letter to the Romans*, NovTSup 101 (Leiden: Brill, 2002).

9. One of the strengths of Beale and Carson, *Commentary*, is its thorough discussion of these interpretations.

10. On Isaiah in Mark see J. Marcus, *The Way of the Lord* (Louisville: Westminster John Knox, 1992); R. E. Watts, *Isaiah's New Exodus in Mark*, WUNT 2.88 (Tübingen: Mohr Siebeck, 1997).

But immediately there are questions. Does Mark, arguably using the Septuagint to emphasize John's desert location, intend solely to identify him? Or does the citation say something about Mark's Gospel as a whole and in particular Jesus? In a sense both are right. John is clearly important but that he is principally a forerunner places the emphasis on who and what he 'foreruns'. If so, then in appealing to Isaiah 40:3 Mark implicitly identifies Jesus with neither a prophet nor a messianic figure but Yahweh's own personal presence, come to effect Israel's eschatological new-exodus deliverance (the same is implied by Mal. 3:1, which Mark combines with Isa. 40:3 in 1:2–3; cf. Matt. 11:10 // Luke 7:27).

The first invocation of Isaiah that directly addresses Jesus occurs during his baptism. In Isaiah, 64:1 (ET) forms the climax of a lament asking God to rend the heavens, come down and repeat the fearful wonders of the exodus in aid of his people. Mark's unusual 'rent heavens' (1:10) suggests that this lament has now been answered in Jesus (cf. Matt. 3:16 // Luke 3:21), who is thereby again closely identified with God's very presence. Only then does the voice from heaven, echoing the famous first 'servant song' (Isa. 42:1; Mark 1:11; cf. Matt. 3:17 // Luke 3:22), designate Jesus also as Isaiah's Spirit-anointed servant who will both deliver 'blind and deaf' captive Israel and bring God's justice to the nations.

Two allusions to Isaiah next indicate the significance of Jesus' activities. The first, Isaiah 43:25 (Yahweh's self-declaration that he alone forgives Israel's transgressions) is echoed in the scribes' hostile rejection of Jesus' forgiveness of the paralytic's sins: 'Who can forgive sins but God alone?' (Mark 2:7; Matt. 9:2–3 // Luke 5:21). Interestingly, the only place in the Old Testament where the lame and forgiveness of sins are explicitly connected is in the restoration text of Isaiah 33:23–24, a collection that also celebrates Yahweh as Israel's sole judge, ruler, king and saviour (33:22). In his corroborative healing of the man, Mark's Jesus not only fulfils the Isaianic hopes of restoration (33:23–24; 35:6) but to the extent that forgiveness of sins was the sine qua non of their deliverance (40:1–2; 44:22) he is revealed to be the one who inaugurates Israel's redemption. Moreover, by having Jesus do what only Yahweh can do, Mark further underlines the implications of his earlier Isaianic citations: God himself is somehow mysteriously present in him.

The second text, Isaiah 49:24, concerns God's promise to do the impossible by binding 'strong man' Babylon and so rescuing his plundered people. In the climactic confrontation over his exorcisms (3:27; Matt. 12:29 // Luke 11:21–22) Jesus declares they testify to his already having bound the 'strong man' (cf. Isa. 49:24). Granted the common intertestamental tradition that Israel's ultimate enemy is Belial (Beelzebul), the Isaiah allusion further presupposes Satan's defeat and, once again, signifies the inauguration of Israel's new-exodus salvation. Consequently, after commanding the sea in a repetition of the exodus, it is not an Egyptian, Babylonian or Roman host that perishes in the deep but a demonic one (Mark 4:35 – 5:20; Matt. 8:23–34 // Luke 8:22–39).

Integral to this confrontation, Isaiah 63:10 in Mark 3:29 underlies Jesus' warning as to the unforgivable sin of blaspheming the Holy Spirit (Matt. 12:31–32 // Luke 12:10). Again part of Isaiah's last lament (see 64:1 in Mark 1:10 above) the prophet recalls how Israel's rebellion in the first exodus grieved Yahweh's 'holy spirit' causing him to become their enemy. As Jesus is indeed God's answer to that lament (Mark 1:11), the implication is that in attributing his work to Satan his opponents are likewise rebelling against the Holy Spirit, thus making God their enemy.

In the face of this hostility, Isaiah 6:9–10 then informs the Markan Jesus' understanding of his preaching and particularly his use of parables (Mark 4:12; Matt. 13:13–15 // Luke 8:10). In Isaiah's day the prophet's offer of salvation with its summons to repentance had likewise been rejected and resulted in the pronouncement of judgment (5:1–30). Isaiah's idolatrous and self-reliant hearers were to be 'created' in the image of the blind and deaf gods they worshipped (6:9–10; cf. Pss 115, 135) and their cities laid waste (6:11). This was subsequently effected through Isaiah's 'parable-name' preaching (7:1 – 8:8). So too with Jesus. His offer of salvation on the basis of repentance (Mark 1:15 // Matt. 4:17) had also been rejected by the Jerusalem leadership (3:22) and he too responds by speaking in parables (3:23). Just as Isaiah's parable names revealed the true character of Ahaz's insincere piety, so Jesus' parables reveal the true nature of the soil-hearts of his hearers (4:1–25), similarly effecting God's blinding and deafening judgment (4:10–12) on those hard or shallow hearted who do not listen aright (4:3, 9, 23–24). It is often remarked that Matthew's version softens the judgment by making the hearers' obstinacy the cause: '*because* they see but do not perceive . . .' (13:13b; my tr. and italics). But in Isaiah the hearers' idolatrous blindness is both the cause and the *lex talionis* judgment. Mark and Matthew simply note either side of the one reality.

This theme continues in Mark's second and most extended account of Jesus' conflict with his Jerusalem opponents (7:1–23). Here he cites Isaiah 29:13 (Mark 7:6b–7; Matt. 15:7–8), a passage which describes a national leadership already exhibiting the judicial blinding of the previously cited Isaiah 6 (cf. Isa. 29:9–10). Although Isaiah's immediate concern is the nation's self-reliant wisdom, whereas Jesus attacks his censuring opponents' hypocritical aspirations to exaggerated purity, the underlying issues are identical. Both Isaiah and Jesus confront a leadership who belies a professed loyalty to Yahweh by refusing to obey the present word of his agent. Jesus' 'Well did Isaiah prophesy concerning you' (my tr.) is probably less an assertion that Isaiah had the present leadership in mind than an affirmation that the prophet's critique suits them to a tee.

The eschatological gravity of Jesus' teaching is underlined in Mark 9:48 where Isaiah 66:24 is invoked as the destiny of those who stumble one of his little ones. Concluding the entire work and in stark contrast to the blessings enjoyed by God's servants (65:8–26; 66:1–3, 10–14, 18–21), 66:24's undying worm and unquenched fire constitutes the fate of arrogant and elitist rebels for ever excluded from the newly recreated Jerusalem (e.g. 65:1–7). Strikingly, however, the warning is given not to Jesus' opponents but his followers. Reconstituted Israel though they might be, their lives are to be marked by a cross-bearing repudiation of status; and so, remarkably, it is not sinning against Torah or temple but one of Jesus' little ones that disqualifies from salvation.

Having already been designated Isaiah 42's servant (Mark 1:11) whose call included restoring Israel to be a light to the nations,[11] it is unsurprising that Jesus cites Isaiah 56:7's vision of the temple as a house of prayer for all nations as part of his critique of the present establishment (Mark 11:17; Matt. 21:13 // Luke 19:46). In Isaiah the restored temple was to be a place where foreigners who had embraced Yahweh could serve him – this was after all the point of his glory being seen among the nations. But in Jesus' day the presence of commercial activities in the one place reserved for Gentile worship showed utter disregard for them and any prayer offered therein. Israel had fallen culpably short of their Isaianic calling.

In the light of all the foregoing it is both tragic and inevitable that, as in Isaiah, Jerusalem and its temple come under judgment. First, Jesus' parable of the tenants (Mark 12:1–9; Matt. 21:33–41 // Luke 20:9–16) closely echoes Isaiah 5:1–10's juridical parable. There Jerusalem and Judah are likened to a useless vineyard upon which their inhabitants themselves pass judgment. In Mark, however, it is the Jerusalem hierarchy 'tenants' who, having refused to give the 'owner' Yahweh his due, even to murdering his son and heir, are to be destroyed. God's vineyard will be given to others: Jesus' followers. This ominous story is followed by Jesus' extended announcement of the temple's coming destruction, wherein two Isaianic texts, 13:10 and 34:4, play a central role (Mark 13:24–25; Matt. 24:29 // Luke 21:26). Both employ the imagery

---

11. W. A. M. Beuken, 'The Main Theme of Trito-Isaiah "The Servants of Yahweh"', *JSOT* 47 (1990), pp. 67–87.

of cosmic dislocation characteristic of the baleful Day of the Lord. Tellingly, Isaiah 13 describes the fall of arrogant Babylon, the archetypal anti-God human city, and Isaiah 34 that of Edom, the great betrayer – both destructions being closely linked with Israel's new-exodus salvation. Jesus' shocking invocation of these two texts to describe the destruction of the temple suggests that Jerusalem in its murderous rejection of him has now taken on the character, and thus the fate, of both.

But this is not the end of the story. Although much debated (largely because of the allusive nature of the language), it now seems likely that Jesus' understanding of his suffering and death was fundamentally shaped by the career of the 'suffering servant', namely Isaiah 50:6 (Mark 10:33–34; Matt. 20:18–19 // Luke 18:31–33) and especially 53:3–12 (Mark 8:31; 9:31; 10:45; Matt. 16:21; 17:22–23; 20:28 // Luke 9:22). Too detailed to develop here, three lines of evidence constitute a formidable case: (1) there is no other figure in Israel's Scriptures whose suffering is so clearly connected with eschatological salvation, (2) the sheer weight of Isaianic materials throughout strongly suggests that Isaiah is indeed the primary horizon within which Jesus' understanding of his sufferings is to be understood, and (3) linguistically and conceptually all the evidence points to an Isaianic origin.[12] In Isaiah, and echoing the exilic curses of Deuteronomy (28:59–61; cf. Isa. 53:4–5),[13] the servant's abuse and death is accepted by Yahweh as atonement (53:10–12) for disobedient Israel's infidelity (e.g. 48:1, 8). Consequently, against all expectation the faithful servant's suffering is shown to be Yahweh's mighty arm (53:1) by which he will effect Israel's new-exodus redemption. So too, then, Mark's messianic Son of Man, in scandalously laying down his life in service to God and for others, becomes the means by which many will be ransomed (Mark 10:45).

Thus at the last Supper, fittingly given Passover's exodus connotations, an allusion to Isaiah 53:11–12 ('poured out for many') reiterates the significance of Jesus' death (Mark 14:24; cf. 10:45, 'a ransom for many'). Just as the servant's suffering facilitated Israel's redemption from exile, so Jesus' death marks the institution of a new Passover and a new covenant around which God's reconstituted people will gather. Given the foregoing, it might even be that Mark intends the concluding confession of the centurion (Mark 15:39; Matt. 27:54 // Luke 23:47) to represent the first fruits of the Isaianic servant's bringing God's justice to the nations (Isa. 42:4–6; 49:6–7; 52:15).

---

12. See Watts, *Isaiah's New Exodus*, pp. 257–287.

13. A. R. Ceresko, 'The Rhetorical Strategy of the Fourth Servant Song (Isaiah 52:13–53:12)', *CBQ* 56 (1994), pp. 42–55.

Matthew

Matthew adds several important Isaianic texts to the first half of his Gospel.[14] In 1:23 his claim that the virgin birth fulfils Isaiah 7:14 is generally seen as an idiosyncratic attempt to legitimate Jesus' dubious origins, with the Emmanuel reference implying God's presence in him.[15] The problem, however, is that as far as we know no one ever read Isaiah 7 either as a messianic text or as describing a virginal conception. Alternatively, if we consider Isaiah's context, then the name Emmanuel takes on a very different association, namely the ensuing judgment when God's potentially saving presence encounters idolatrous unbelief. Jesus' two names, then, indicate his ultimate significance. Jesus ('he will save his people from their sins', 1:21) describes the redemption that results from trust, while Emmanuel (1:23) presages the awful consequences of unbelief. Isaiah 7:14 can, then, be said to be fulfilled in Jesus since in him we encounter the final expression of God's coming in judgment on a nation that rejects his definitive offer of salvation (cf. e.g. 8:11–12; 23:1–38).[16]

Only Matthew explains Jesus' transition to public ministry in Galilee as the fulfilment of the messianic hopes associated with the return from exile: in Jesus the long-awaited great light has begun to dawn (Isa. 9:1–2 ET in Matt. 4:12–17). Later, citing Isaiah 53:4, Matthew 8:16–17 implies that Jesus' 'removal' of Israel's illnesses both testifies to Israel's inaugurated new-exodus liberation and identifies him as the servant whose suffering will eventually complete it. Thus, in responding to the imprisoned Baptist's question (Matt. 11:2–5), Matthew's Jesus implies that his healings are the fulfilment of Isaiah's promised restoration (35:5–6; 29:18–19; 61:1). The servant theme is also uniquely emphasized in Matthew 12:18–21, where he picks up Isaiah 42, already alluded to in the baptism (v. 1 in Matt. 3:17) but now cited at much greater length (vv. 1–4). Over against the punctilious criticisms of the Pharisees and their burdensome view of the Law (Matt. 12:1–14), the Isaiah text is invoked to show that it is Jesus'

---

14. See J. Blenkinsopp, *Opening the Sealed Book* (Grand Rapids: Eerdmans, 2006), pp. 147–168.

15. D. Kupp, *Matthew's Emmanuel*, SNTSMS 90 (Cambridge: Cambridge University Press, 1996).

16. R. E. Watts, 'Immanuel: Virgin Birth Proof Text or Programmatic Warning of Things to Come (Isa 7:14 in Matt 1:23)?', in C. A. Evans (ed.), *From Prophecy to Testament* (Peabody: Hendrickson, 2004), pp. 92–113; for another approach, W. Carter, 'Evoking Isaiah: Matthean Soteriology and an Intertextual Reading of Isaiah 7–9 and Matthew 1:23 and 4:15–16', *JBL* 119 (2000), pp. 503–520.

merciful reading of Torah that is in keeping with Yahweh's Spirit and hence reflects the justice for which the nations hope.[17]

Luke-Acts

Also highlighting the Isaianic character of Jesus' healings (Luke 7:20–22), Luke alone draws on Isaiah to stress the international scope of Jesus' salvation. Simeon's designation of the child Jesus as a light of revelation for the Gentiles echoes Isaiah 49:6 (Luke 2:32). In Isaiah Yahweh responded to the failure of blind and deaf 'servant' Israel in the preceding chapters (e.g. 42:18–25; ch. 48) by appointing a new servant to both restore Israel and be a light to the nations (Isa. 49:1–6). That new servant's calling is now fulfilled in Jesus. Similarly, when introducing John (3:1–20), Luke extends the Isaiah 40 citation to include the all-important purpose clause: that all flesh might see the glory of God (3:6), a major Isaianic new-exodus motif.

Luke also employs Isaiah to elucidate the character of Jesus' ministry. Whereas Mark and Matthew use summary statements to transition to Jesus' public ministry, Luke reports the extended Nazareth sermon. Its centrepiece, Isaiah 61:1–2 combined with 58:6, designates Jesus as the servant-like prophet who announces Yahweh's eschatological Jubilee and so sets the agenda for much of Luke's subsequent material (see also Acts 10:35–38). The servant theme is picked up once more in Luke 22:37, where Isaiah 53:12 is invoked to explain the necessity of Jesus' own and the disciples' consequent marginalization as outlaws. While alone insufficient to establish that Isaiah 53 influenced the Lukan Jesus' self-understanding of his suffering, a reading in concert with the Isaiah materials that Luke retains from Mark's three Passion predictions (see above) suggests otherwise.

Isaiah also features prominently in Acts.[18] In its original setting Isaiah 66:1–2's 'the heavens are my throne . . . what house will you build for me?' (my tr.), addressed to a post-exilic Israel awaiting redemption, relativizes the temple by emphasizing the centrality of the worshipper's humble obedience particularly over against the abominable practices of apostate Israelites. Luke's Stephen makes the same point in Acts 7:49–50. But now, with obedience and apostasy defined by one's stance toward Jesus (v. 52), to reject him is to oppose the Holy Spirit. Isaiah 53 (vv. 7–8) reappears in 8:32–33 when

---

17. R. Beaton, *Isaiah's Christ in Matthew's Gospel*, SNTSMS 123 (Cambridge: Cambridge University Press, 2002).

18. Esp. D. W. Pao, *Acts and the Isaianic New Exodus*, WUNT 130 (Tübingen: Mohr Siebeck, 2000).

Philip explains to the Ethiopian that it applies to Jesus, confirming our earlier hunch that Luke understands Jesus' death in terms of that poem's 'suffering servant'.

Paul's two sermons in Pisidian Antioch occasion two further citations. In his first, Luke's Paul invokes the climactic Isaiah 55:3 ('I will give to you [pl.] the holy promises made to David', Acts 13:34), a text of invitation that concludes the new-exodus message of Isaiah 40 – 55. In typically compressed rabbinic fashion he argues that since Jesus' resurrection shows him to be David's true heir (Acts 13:32, 35), it also means the beginning of Isaiah's good news 'to us' whereby all of God's people can now enjoy David's promised mercies (Acts 13:32–34). In the second, after Paul's preaching is rejected by the local Jewish community he cites Isaiah 49:6 ('I have set you [sg.] to be a light to the nations'; my tr.) to justify his and Barnabas' turning to the Gentiles (Acts 13:47). In so doing he identifies their role with that of the Isaianic servant, whom Luke earlier declared to be Jesus (Luke 2:32). This is in keeping with Isaiah, where the servant's task included restoring other Israelites to their servant call.[19] Restored by the Lord Jesus, Paul and Barnabas continue Jesus' and reconstituted Israel's servant mission to be a light to the nations. Finally, in the concluding division over Jesus among the Jews in Rome, Paul cites Septuagint Isaiah 6:9–10 (Acts 28:23–28), a text already prominent in the Synoptics. Although recognizing that Isaiah spoke to their ancestors, Paul's clear implication is that his present disputants are no different and, as in Matthew, the Septuagint form attributes their refusal to believe to an idolatrous hardness of heart.

John

In common with the Synoptics John's Gospel is equally concerned to identify the Baptist as the one who prepares for the Isaianic coming of Yahweh himself to save his people (Isa. 40:3 in John 1:23). But aside from this, and perhaps not surprisingly given its distinctive character, John takes a different tack in its use of Isaiah. Even though present in other Old Testament texts, a number of John's symbols and metaphors are widely seen as drawn from Isaiah, and particularly those associated with new-exodus hopes: the vine (Isa. 5:1–6), living water (Isa. 55:1), good shepherd (Isa. 40:11), light (Isa. 9:1; 42:6; 49:6; 51:4; 60:1), glory (Isa. 35:2; 40:5; 48:11; 58:8; 59:19; 60:1) and the absolute use of 'I am' (41:4; 43:10, 13; 46:4; 48:12; 51:12; 52:6), the latter in its evocation of the divine self-predication being well-suited to the above-noted citation of

---

19. Beuken, 'Main Theme'.

Isaiah 40:3.[20] In keeping with John's characteristic melding of scriptural images and allusions, it might well be that in his hands the Baptist's declaration 'Behold the Lamb of God who takes away the sin of the world' (1:29 RSV) also alludes to Isaiah 53's oracle concerning the servant who is 'like a lamb' (v. 7), 'bears our sins' (v. 4 LXX), and indeed 'bore the sin of many' (v. 12). Likewise, the possibly original 'my Chosen one' (John 1:34) in the context of the descent of the Spirit (vv. 32–33) constitutes the Johannine parallel to the Synoptics' voice from heaven whereby Jesus is identified as the servant of Isaiah 42:1. If so, then as in the Synoptics both servant 'songs' are applied to Jesus. Isaiah 54:13's promise that in the eschatologically restored new Jerusalem God would be Israel's teacher appears in John 6:45. It seems fitting in a Gospel whose structure is built around feasts in Jerusalem that having just claimed that no one can come to him unless the Father draws them, Jesus implies that if they wish to participate in this promise they must listen to him, since he alone is now the source and agent of God's eschatological instruction.

At the end of Jesus' public ministry John cites two Isaianic texts to address the question of Jewish unbelief. In the first, the question 'Lord, who has believed our message and to whom has the arm of the Lord been revealed?' (Isa. 53:1 in John 12:38) not only speaks to the significance of Jesus' rejection but suggests, given the exodus/new-exodus imagery throughout the Gospel, that in Jesus' signs Yahweh has bared his mighty delivering arm (John 12:37; cf. Matt. 8:16–17). Moreover, if John has more of Isaiah 53 in view, as was suggested above concerning his earlier identification of Jesus as the sin-bearing lamb, then Jesus is also Isaiah 53's suffering servant whose death as the Passover lamb will decisively accomplish Israel's new-exodus deliverance. It might also be that Jesus' exultation wherein his lifting up will draw all people to himself (prompted by the inquiry of some Greeks [John 20:20–21; cf. v. 19]) echoes the servant's exaltation even before nations and kings who will see what they had not been told (Isa. 52:13–15).[21] In the second, John 12:40, Isaiah 6:10 is once again cited but this time with the emphasis on the divine activity in hardening: 'He has blinded their eyes . . . ' John immediately follows the citation with the statement that Isaiah said this because he 'saw his glory and spoke about him'. If by this John intends a reference to Isaiah's temple vision, then the glory that Isaiah saw was, according to John, none other than the glory of Jesus. To have seen his glory in John is to have seen the Father's glory (cf. 14:9–11). How could it be otherwise given that Jesus' glorious signs

---

20. C. H. Williams, 'Isaiah in John's Gospel', in Moyise and Menken, *Isaiah*, p. 101.

21. J. Beutler, 'Greeks Come to See Jesus (John 12,20f)', *Bib* 71 (1990), pp. 333–347.

(e.g. John 2:11) are none other than Yahweh's bared delivering arm? Just as John's account of Jesus' public ministry began with the implication that Jesus was somehow the visible manifestation of God's personal presence (Isa. 40:3 in 1:23; cf. 1:14), so too, as he embraces the cross, it concludes.

The epistles

Introduction
In turning to the epistles one immediately notes the great diversity in density of citations, ranging from a massive concentration in Romans 9 – 11 to almost none in Philippians. Moreover, at the risk of stating the obvious, whereas the Gospels' use of Isaiah is structured around the life of Jesus, the epistles are driven by their particular occasional concerns. This means that any unifying rubric if present will be more implicit. We begin with the generally accepted Paulines, followed by the disputed epistles, and conclude with the remainder.

Pauline epistles
In terms of sheer weight of citations (fifteen) and allusions (around twelve) as well as five explicit mentions of Isaiah, Romans must take pride of place. Paul apparently seeks to persuade his audience that his gospel, especially in the face of Israel's generally negative response, is not only the eschatological fulfilment of but also entirely consistent with God's dealings with his people. One would expect, then, to find numerous references to precisely those dealings. The first two Isaiah texts are marshalled to establish Israel's present needy condition in spite of having the Law. While Isaiah 52:5 concerns the dishonour Israel's exilic humiliation brings on Yahweh, in Romans 2:22 Paul's citation gets to the heart of the matter: Israel's sinfulness. It caused the exile in the first place, and continues to cause Yahweh's name to be blasphemed. Hence in 3:15–17 it is Isaiah 59:7–8's list of Israel's post-exilic iniquities that demonstrates that with or without the Law both Jew and Gentile presently stand under God's righteous judgment. The next Isaiah reference, an allusion, appears much later in Romans 8:33–34. Echoing the rhetorical questions of the third servant song wherein the servant expresses his assurance of final vindication (Isa. 50:8–9b), Paul encourages the same confidence among his hearers. If God has vindicated his Christ, presumably Isaiah 50's servant, from whose love we can never be separated, then surely as his 'chosen ones' we too need fear nothing.

The overwhelming majority of Romans' Isaiah materials occurs in chapters 9–11. Here Paul finally responds to perhaps the most serious challenge to the validity of his gospel: if this is God's doing, why have most of Israel rejected it?[22] In an earnest and complex argument Isaiah is first cited in Romans 9:27–29 to show that as in the past (Isa. 1:9) so also in the eschatological present (Isa. 10:29) only a remnant of Israel would be saved. The hostility of most is, then, not to be wondered at. The reason, historically and in the present, is Israel's proclivity to self-reliance. In Isaiah God purposed to place a stone in Zion that would cause the self-reliant wise to stumble (8:14), while providing a sure foundation for those who believed (28:16). This Paul says is precisely what has happened in Jesus (Rom. 9:33). Those who seek righteousness apart from Christ, namely by doing what the Law requires, stumble over him, while whoever believes in him will not be put to shame (cf. Rom. 1:16–17). As we saw in Stephen's speech in Acts 7, the issue is no longer obedience to Torah but rather faith in what God has done in Jesus (Rom. 10:2–4). Interestingly, since in Isaiah 8:14 it is God himself who is the stone, Paul's combination of the two texts might suggest that he identifies the two stones and hence identifies Jesus with Yahweh. Be that as it may, his point is that God's righteous dealings have not changed either in undermining human self-confidence or in his desire for trust. Thus in Romans 10:13 Paul again appeals to Isaiah 28:16, this time to emphasize that now as then the critical issue is faith.

And it is not as if Israel has not heard. In this day of eschatological salvation, God has sent Isaiah 52:7's heralds among whose number is Paul himself (Rom. 10:15). Presumably, this was to announce God's saving intervention, reversing the blasphemies uttered against him among the nations (see Isa. 52:5 in Rom. 2:22 above) and even now bearing fruit in the conversion of the Gentiles. Nevertheless, as Isaiah's witnesses lamented concerning their confession of the equally offensive suffering servant (Isa. 53:1), not all have believed Paul's good news about a suffering Messiah (Rom. 10:16). In typically compressed form Paul explains what has happened (Rom. 10:20–21). Isaiah 65:1–2 describes God's willingness to be found by post-exilic idolatrous and self-willed Israel even though they did not call on him. The remarkable thing says Paul is that it is idolatrous Gentiles, who similarly did not call on God's name, who have responded to his presence in Christ (Isa. 65:1 in Rom. 10:20; cf. 'Here I am', Isa. 65:1b), while Israel remains disobedient (Isa. 65:2 in Rom. 10:21). So while the elect have attained the goal, the rest of wilful Israel have been hardened, just as they were in Isaiah's day (Isa. 29:10; 6:9–10 in Rom. 11:8).

But again this is not the whole story. In Isaiah 59:20–21 when God found none to save, he himself came as Warrior to redeem. Whereas the Masoretic

---

22. Esp. Wagner, *Heralds*.

Text has him coming to those who turn from transgression, the Septuagint, followed by Paul, has him turning transgression from Jacob (Rom. 11:26). The two are not so much divergent views as different ways of expressing the same reality. Both the Masoretic Text and the Septuagint are well aware that the wicked in Israel will be judged (e.g. Isa. 65 – 66) and that the end result is the restoration of a contrite and humble people who tremble at God's word (Isa. 66:2). The Septuagint simply expresses what the Masoretic Text implies: there will no longer be transgression among God's (remnant) people. As God had promised earlier in Isaiah 27:9, he has removed his people's sins (Rom. 11:27). Where Paul differs is that while the Masoretic Text has the Lord coming to Zion and the Septuagint for the sake of Zion, Paul says the Deliverer will come from Zion. While this may be a diaspora perspective, it may also be a Christian one in which Jesus, having already come to Zion, now in resurrected glory comes from it to those among the nations. It is in and through Jesus that God will accomplish his purposes and thus all Israel will be saved.

Given all this and because as Isaiah 45:23 declares every knee will bow before God, Gentile and Jewish Christians ought not judge one another since they together will appear before his judgment seat (Rom. 14:11). In Paul's concluding instructions on mutual acceptance he again reminds his readers that the inclusion of Gentiles was always part of God's messianic plan (Isa. 11:10 LXX in Rom. 15:12). This finally is why Paul seeks their help for his proposed missionary ventures in Spain (Rom. 15:24). God had intended that his exalted suffering servant would be recognized by those who had never been told of him (Isa. 52:15). Paul's call was that they might do so through his preaching (Rom. 15:22). One last observation. Throughout all of this Paul's fundamental assumption appears to be that the great restorational promises of Isaiah had not earlier been fulfilled and that only now in Christ has the 'righteousness of God been revealed . . . from heaven' (Rom. 1:16–18). If so, then it seems he too believes that to some extent Israel is still in exile.

Similar themes are found elsewhere. Paul's famous allegory of unbelieving Israel being likened to Hagar, and Gentile believers to Sarah (Gal. 4:27), claims that Isaiah 54:1's hope of the abundant children of restored Daughter Zion is fulfilled in the Galatian converts themselves (Gal. 4:28–30),[23] whom he later designates the Israel of God (6:16). Appropriately, the latter's 'peace be upon them and mercy' seems also to reflect God's promise a few verses later of

---

23. M. C. De Boer, 'Paul's Quotation of Isaiah 54.1 in Galatians 4.27', *NTS* 50 (2004), pp. 370–389.

eternal loving kindness and peace to Zion (Isa. 54:10 LXX).[24] In 1 Corinthians
15:54 Christ's resurrection has put in train Isaiah 25:7's great eschatological
promise that death itself will finally be swallowed up for ever. Thus when Paul
speaks of those in Christ as a new creation in which the old has gone and all
has become new (2 Cor. 5:16–17), he probably has in mind Isaiah's new creation (Isa. 43:18–19; 42:9; 48:3, 6–7). In Isaiah this was largely the result of the
servant's suffering as implied by the account of his humiliation and death (Isa.
52:13 – 53:12) being the middle term between the summons to leave Babylon
(52:1–12) and the hope of a restored New Jerusalem (Isa. 54). It was God's
will (Isa. 53:10a) that, although innocent (53:9b), the servant bore 'our sins'
(53:5a, 11b, 12b) that many might be 'made righteous' (53:11–12; my tr.). Paul
apparently sees Jesus fulfilling this role when he goes on in the next few verses
(2 Cor. 5:18–21) to state that (1) God was in Christ reconciling the world to
himself (2) by making him who knew no sin to be sin that (3) we might become
the righteousness of God (cf. Isa. 61:3). Likewise the 'hymn' of Philippians
2:7–11, where God highly exalted Christ because he 'emptied himself', taking
on the form of a servant even to death on a cross, probably reflects the servant
of Isaiah 53, who is also 'highly exalted' (Isa. 52:13) because in great humiliation (53:2b–3) he 'poured out' (my tr.) himself to death (53:8–9). Indeed, just
as the Isaianic servant's great exaltation (52:13) echoes that of Yahweh (6:1) so
Isaiah 45:23's every knee which was to bow to God (cf. Rom. 14:11–12 above)
will now bow to Jesus (Phil. 2:10). Given this reality (that through Christ's
servant death Gentile believers are also the new-creational offspring of the
New Jerusalem) the Corinthians are then exhorted, as were the redeemed
exiles of Isaiah 52:11, 'to come out . . . and be separate . . . and touch nothing
unclean' (2 Cor. 6:17).

Paul's call again echoes that of the Isaianic servant. His statement that he
was set apart from his mother's womb to preach to the nations (Gal. 1:15–16)
seems to reflect both Jeremiah 1:5 and Isaiah 49:1–6, but perhaps particularly
the latter given the eschatological cast of Paul's ministry. His appeal to the
Corinthians that they not take hold of Isaiah 49:8's day of salvation 'in vain'
(2 Cor. 6:2) likewise suggests that he sees his mission, as Christ's ambassador,
in terms of the servant of Isaiah 49:1–6, who was concerned that he had
laboured 'in vain'.[25] Paul's brief declaration that he was sent to preach but not

---

24. G. K. Beale, 'Peace and Mercy Upon the Israel of God: The Old Testament
    Background of Galatians 6,16b', *Bib* 80 (1999), pp. 204–223.

25. M. Gignilliat, 'A Servant Follower of the Servant: Paul's Eschatological Reading
    of Isaiah 40–66 in 2 Corinthians 5:14–6:10', *HBT* 26 (2004), pp. 98–124.

with eloquent wisdom (1 Cor. 1:16) suggests to some an identification with the servant-like figure of Isaiah 61:1, who was 'sent' 'to preach' to the poor (implying not to the rich with their desire for eloquence).[26] Similarly, Paul's participation in Christ's sufferings where his daily being given up to death that life might come to the Corinthians (2 Cor. 4:10–12) could recall the servant's pouring his life out unto death (Isa. 53:8–9), whereby Paul's being in Christ means he follows in Christ's 'suffering servant' footsteps (cf. Isa. 49:6 in Acts 13:47). At the same time the Warrior motif of Isaiah 59 (cf. Rom. 11:26) is again picked up but with believers themselves exhorted to take up verse 17's armour (1 Thess. 5:8; cf. Eph. below).

Finally, as we saw in Romans, there is also God's 'unintelligible' eschatological act in Jesus (Isa. 29:14 LXX in 1 Cor. 1:19). In Isaiah the unintelligibility of the invading Assyrian speech was God's judgment on the self-reliant wise ones' rejection of the prophet's clear message. In 1 Corinthians this unintelligibility lies in the apparent 'folly and weakness' of the cross, which is now the means by which God judges both the Jewish desire for signs and the Greek love of wisdom. By the same token, when it comes to worship, uninterpreted tongues being unintelligible to outsiders effectively condemn them before they have had a chance to hear clearly (Isa. 28:11–12 in 1 Cor. 14:21–23). Christian gatherings where God's salvation is still on offer are therefore to be characterized by intelligibility and hence no tongues without interpretation (14:14–25).

Disputed Paulines

Although containing no explicit citations of Isaiah, Ephesians 2:13–17's account of those who were far off being made near through the proclamation of peace 'to those both far and near' (v. 17; my tr.) employs the language of the post-exilic promise of the eschatological return from exile (Isa. 57:14–19, itself echoing the earlier 'proclamation' to Zion of the exiles' soon return, Isa. 52:7).[27] For the writer these texts apparently find their fulfilment in the unity of believing Jews and Gentiles in Christ. This being so Ephesians 4:30's injunction 'do not grieve the Holy Spirit of God', who signifies their redemption, is an appropriate evocation of Isaiah 63:10 (cf. Mark 3:29 above). As God's newly created people the letter's recipients are warned not to repeat the sins of the first exodus whereby that recently redeemed but cantankerous and complaining people grieved God's Holy Spirit (cf. Eph. 4:31). Although debated,

---

26. F. Wilk, 'Isaiah in 1 and 2 Corinthians', in Moyise and Menken, *Isaiah*, p. 135.

27. T. Moritz, *A Profound Mystery: The Use of the Old Testament in Ephesians*, NovTSup 85 (Leiden: Brill, 1996), pp. 25–55.

there are also strong linguistic and conceptual correspondences between the description of the believers' armour (Eph. 6:10, 14–17; cf. 1 Thess. 5:8) and the panoply of Yahweh (59:17–18; cf. 52:17) and his messiah (Isa. 11:4–5).[28] The implication is that believers, already reigning in the heavenlies with the victorious Christ (Eph. 2:6), continue God's work in him on earth by effecting his Warrior-like restoration of all things through prayer and the proclamation of the gospel. In other words, God's own people, being 'in Christ' and indwelt by his Spirit (Eph. 4:1–7), are now themselves the earthly embodiment of Isaiah's Yahweh-Warrior. Turning to Colossians and in a similarly triumphal context (2:15) there is one possible allusion again to the anti-wisdom polemics of Isaiah 28 – 29. This time various regulations concerning food and festivals are dismissed as merely 'human commands and teachings' and antithetical to genuine Christian life (Col. 2:22; cf. Isa. 29:13; see Mark 7:6b–7 above).

Other epistles

For all of Hebrews' appeal to the Old Testament, Isaiah rarely features and the rationale behind the one clear citation (Isaiah 8:17–18 in 2:13b) is not immediately obvious. The basic point is the superiority of Jesus to other Jewish forerunners as demonstrated in his suffering identification with his people. The author, placing Isaiah's words on Jesus' lips, apparently puts Jesus and the letter's addressees in a similar situation to that confronted by the prophet and his children. Faced with rejection, as was Isaiah, Jesus also clearly put his trust in God and, as did Isaiah, takes his unashamed stand with his children as they await their vindication. Presumably, if this was true of Isaiah how much more of the one who fulfilled his prophecies? Later, Hebrews 9:28's reference to the sacrificial language of Jesus' being 'offered' to 'bear the sins of many' seems to have Isaiah 53:12 in mind. Finally, that Jesus' description as the source of 'eternal salvation' (Heb. 5:9) is found only in God's promise of the same in Isaiah 45:17 suggests that Jesus is its fulfilment.

1 Peter, on the other hand, is rich with Isaianic materials. In 1:24–25 he exhorts his hearers to give themselves to the gospel since it is the eternal Word of God beside which all that is merely human perishes like grass (Isa. 40:6–8). Then, as we saw in Paul (Rom. 9:33), 2:6–8 appeals to a combination of Isaiah 28:16 and 8:14, whereby Christ is the promised stone, a sure foundation for those who believe and a rock of offence for those who do not. Those who believe are therefore a 'chosen race, a royal priesthood, a holy nation, God's

---

28. T. R. Neufeld, *Put on the Armour of God: The Divine Warrior from Isaiah to Ephesians*, JSOTSup 140 (Sheffield: Sheffield Academic Press, 1997).

own people, in order that you may proclaim the mighty acts of him who called you out of darkness into his marvellous light' (1 Pet. 2:9). Originally deriving from Exodus 19:5–6, this description is picked up in Isaiah 43:20b–21's promise of the new exodus in which God's people will walk in his glorious light (42:16; 51:4; 58:8, 10; 60:1, 19). That all of this is in fulfilment of Isaiah's hopes is confirmed by perhaps the New Testament's clearest identification, in 2:22–25, of Jesus with the suffering servant of Isaiah 53 (vv. 4–7, 9, 12). His suffering redeemed them and they are urged to follow his example. The subsequent encouragement not to fear what others fear but instead to sanctify the Lord in their hearts (3:14–15) again reflects God's word to the prophet Isaiah (Isa. 8:12–13). For Peter's hearers, similarly confronted by a surrounding hostility, this gospel, the word of the same God, can also be trusted, and indeed to do so is to honour his holiness. Finally, 4:14's partial citation of the description of the Spirit-anointed Messiah, now applied to believers, reflects a deeper underlying theology. Just as in Isaiah the servant gave rise to many similar servants who as God's redeemed people would enjoy David's promised mercies, so in 1 Peter, where Jesus combines both servant and messianic roles, his people likewise share both in his servant sufferings and his messianic anointing of the Spirit.

Revelation

As is often noted, Revelation stands alone in the New Testament for its unmatched frequency and highly allusive use of Old Testament texts.[29] Our treatment, then, must perforce be more general and thematic. Central to all is the vision of the exalted Lord of creation, surrounded by his six-winged attendants, whose holiness stands over against a sinful earth soon to come under judgment (Isa. 6:2–3 in Rev. 4:8). The fundamental concern, however, in keeping with John's opening vision of the glorious resurrected Christ is Christological. Having received the keys of the house of David (Isa. 22:22 in Rev. 3:7) Jesus is the promised root of Jesse (11:10 in 5:5; 22:16) who makes war on the nations with the rod of his mouth (11:4 in 19:11). At the same time, Jesus' designation as 'the first and the last' identifies him with God (Isa. 44:6; 41:4; 48:12 in Rev. 1:8, 17; 21:6; 22:13) and it is he who judges the earth in the

---

29. J. Fekkes, *Isaiah and Prophetic Traditions in the Book of Revelation*, JSNTSup 93 (Sheffield: JSOT: 1994); G. K. Beale, *The Book of Revelation* (Grand Rapids: Eerdmans; Carlisle: Paternoster, 1999).

eschatological Day of the Lord (Isa. 34:4, 12, 2:10, 18–20 in Rev. 6:12–17; and Isa. 63:1–3 in Rev. 14:19–20). By the same token, Isaiah's oracles against Edom (34:10, 11–14), Tyre (23:8, 17) and Babylon (47:7–9; 21:9) inform the judgments against the nations and Rome (Rev. 14:8–11; 17:2; 18:2–23). But as in Isaiah the final goal is a restored Jerusalem to which the nations stream. Thus John's closing account of the heavenly bride-city come to earth is awash with Isaianic imagery (Isa. 25:8, 43:19, 51:9–10, 52:1, 61:10, 62:5 and 65:17–20 in Rev. 21:1–8; 54:11–12 in Rev. 21:18–21; and 60:3–16, 2:2–5 in Rev. 21:22–27).

Final remarks

The hermeneutical significance of Isaiah for the New Testament can hardly be doubted. Even so, not every New Testament book makes use of the prophet (Isaiah features most prominently in the Synoptics' interpretation of Jesus and Paul's treatment of Israel and God's righteousness in Rom. 9 – 11), nor is every section of Isaiah evoked by those that do. Further, in contrast to the explicit, and even apologetic, appeals of the Gospels, in the epistles and Revelation Isaianic salvation seems more the natural presupposition. This suggests that although the Gospels are later, their thoroughgoing Isaianic outlook reflects earlier tradition going back in essence probably to Jesus himself,[30] which Paul and the other New Testament authors seem naturally to assume. At least in this respect Paul is not the inventor but rather the subsequent interpreter of early Christianity.

Drawing together the various threads from the foregoing suggests the following Isaianic 'narrative'. The salvation Jesus' inaugurated is that new-exodus new-creational reconciliation (42:9; 43:18–19; 48:3, 6–7) which Isaiah proclaimed (40:3; 61:1). Through the long-awaited rent heavens (64:1–3) Jesus himself is identified as Isaiah's messianic servant (42:1) who, as the eschatological herald, announces salvation to Zion (61:1) bringing light both to oppressed Israel (8:23 – 9:1) and the nations (49:6). He effects God's promised forgiveness of sin (43:25), deliverance from exilic bondage (49:24), and healing (35:1–6; 26:14; 29:18–19; 53:4; 61:1). Jesus is thus mysteriously God's presence among us (40:3; 43:25; 7:14), the 'I am' (e.g. 41:4; 43:10, 13; 46:4; 48:12; 51:12; 52:6) and the first and the last (41:4; 44:6; 48:12) whose glory Isaiah saw (6:10) and who is thus Israel's eschatological divine teacher (54:13). At the same time, through his servant-suffering (50:6; 53:3–12) Jesus inaugurates a new covenant

---

30. Blenkinsopp, *Opening*, p. 137.

(53:12) and engenders 'offspring', other servants, including Paul and Barnabas, who in imitating his sufferings continue his work both to Israel and the nations (49:1–8; 53:12; 61:1).

As Isaiah had foretold (11:10), the Gentiles who had not previously heard now believe (65:1–2). But, as of old, present-day Israel's worship is hypocritical (29:13) and hence they have failed to be a light to the nations (56:7). Torah has not brought Israel righteousness (59:7–8) and so, along with the world, they stand under judgment (52:5). Deliberately undermining human wisdom (29:14; 40:6–8), what God requires is faith in Christ, Zion's new cornerstone (28:16). But Israel have not believed the message (53:1; 52:7) and in rejecting the Spirit of God's work in Jesus have made him their enemy (63:10). Consequently, as in Isaiah's day the word of God, whether through Jesus' parables or Paul's preaching, effects judicial blinding on their idolatrous hearts (6:9–10). Jesus thus 'fulfils' Isaiah's Emmanuel (7:14) and unbelieving Jerusalem comes under the same judgment as the idolatrous nations (13:10; 34:4). Nevertheless, although only a remnant will be saved (1:29; 10:22–23), self-reliant Israel's stumbling over Jesus (8:14; 28:16) and subsequent hardening (29:10) is not the last word. When the full number of Gentiles has come in, God will yet fulfil his promises and remove unrighteousness from Zion (59:20–21; 27:9).

In the meantime, as newly restored Zion (54:1) and the one reconciled people of the one God (43:20–21; 52:11; 57:19) before whom every knee will bow (45:23), believing Jews and Gentiles must not judge one another but work together as his 'warrior' people to establish his righteousness (11:4–5; 59:17). As Jesus' family (8:17–18) they need not fear (8:12–13) but as partakers of his glorious Spirit (11:2) imitate his sufferings (53:4–12). As this one new humanity, they must avoid Israel's past errors: reliance on merely human instruction (29:13) and grieving the Spirit through dissension (63:10), since causing one another to stumble will lead to eschatological destruction (66:24). Because unintelligibility is a sign of judgment (28:11–12), Christian worship should be characterized by intelligible proclamation as they await the eschatological defeat of the final enemy, death (25:8). Although the eschatological conflict with Satan continues, nevertheless Jesus, as both Isaiah's Davidic scion (11:4–10; 22:22) and the 'First and Last' (44:6 etc.), will defeat the hostile nations (21:9; 23:8, 17; 30:10–14; 47:7–9) and establish for ever the new Jerusalem (2:2–5; 25:8; 43:19; 51:9–10; 52:1; 54:11–12; 60:3–16; 61:10; 62:5; 65:17–20).

This kind of coherence is unlikely to be the product of isolated and near-sighted proof-texting. Instead, Isaiah's narrative of God's dealings with his people provides a, perhaps even the, dominant conceptual framework by which Jesus and his later interpreters conceived their self-identity.[31] Eschatologically speaking, the salvation Jesus brings is that of which Isaiah spoke, being drawn largely though not exclusively from his messianic (chs. 9, 11) and return-from-exile (chs. 35, 40–66) hopes of a gloriously renewed Zion. There death is finally defeated and, ecclesiologically, a remnant of faithful Israel and many believing Gentiles are drawn to be reconciled to God and one another. The city, however, is no longer to be identified with earthly Jerusalem but is instead the new people of God 'in Christ'. The New Testament interprets Jesus (thus Christologically) by drawing on various characteristics of these Isaianic figures; that is, the servant, the Davidic scion/prince, Isaiah 61's eschatological herald, and even Isaianic descriptions/attributions of God himself. Once one takes this view, then with a kind of inevitable logic the classic texts of Isaiah's pre-exilic wisdom debate (where the self-reliant wise ones reject the scandal of Yahweh's 'foolish' plan to restore Jerusalem) are invoked to explain present-day Israel's and the world's opposition to the apparent 'folly' of a crucified Messiah and his law-free and faith-dependent gospel. In rejecting Jesus, however, 'faith'-less Jerusalem and oppressive Rome are with a similar inevitability identified with idolatrous Jerusalem of old and God's paradigmatic city-enemies, Babylon and Edom, coming naturally under the same judgment (chs. 6–7, 28–29, 63, 66 and 13, 34 respectively). The New Testament hermeneutic is as clear as it is fundamental: Jesus, as God's suffering but vindicated agent and indeed his very presence, now constitutes his true messianic servant-Israel Son. Israel and the nations are now redefined around him. It is in him and his 'servant' descendents, Jew and Gentile together, that Isaiah's several agents of salvation and his many and varied promises to Israel and Zion necessarily find their locus and fulfilment. Similarly, to oppose this new thing God has done is to stand with Isaiah's apostate Israel and idolatrous nations, whether past or future, and hence to suffer their fate.

One last observation as we scurry to conclude. Because world views are the presupposition of interpretation, they rarely appear on the surface of thought. It is only when they are themselves challenged that their underlying structures are revealed.[32] That Isaiah plays such a major role in engaging two critical world view issues – the identity of Jesus and thus his followers, and the meaning of Israel's rejection and Gentile acceptance of him – further confirms its foundational role in New Testament self-understanding.

© Rikk E. Watts, 2009

---

31. Cf. ibid., p. 136 and below, who shows that a similar approach was taken by Qumran.
32. See discussion in Watts, *Isaiah's New Exodus*, pp. 45–47.

PART 3: STUDIES IN SELECTED TEXTS

11. WHAT'S NEW IN ISAIAH 9:1–7?

Paul D. Wegner

Isaiah 9:1–7 is a fascinating passage loaded with controversy and giving rise to a variety of opinions regarding its interpretation and date. A chapter this size can only touch on the most important issues regarding the passage's interpretation. First, however, a word about a proper hermeneutic is in order. At present, there is little consensus concerning the best model for interpreting this book. Therefore a wide range of diachronic and synchronic readings abound. I prefer a mixture of these approaches, which may properly be called a 'developmental approach'[1] that mixes the best features of both. After examining the various levels of the text (diachronic approach) and how the text has been formed, we will attempt to understand the final shape of the text (synchronic approach) and to see what the text means in its present form. There will certainly be a significant difference concerning the text's date, but there should be significantly more agreement on its present meaning.

---

1. A name first suggested by H. G. M. Williamson, but I have probably taken it in ways he never expected.

History of interpretation

Traditionally, Isaiah 9:1–7 was thought to contain authentic Isaianic material with a clear messianic intent,[2] a view that continues to have a consistent following today. However, near the turn of the twentieth century, Bernard Duhm,[3] Karl Marti[4] and Gustav Hölscher[5] strongly challenged this consensus by suggesting the passage was a post-exilic messianic oracle, a view still held by many modern scholars.[6] Then, about the middle of the twentieth century, an interesting shift began to take place with the seminal work of Albrecht Alt,[7] followed by a host of others. These scholars argued this passage was an authentic accession oracle for a Judean king (often thought to be Hezekiah). Alt's view still has a strong following, even though some have questioned whether it is indeed an accession oracle or whether it employs the structure of a fivefold, Egyptian throne name. Both of these issues significantly affect the interpretation of the passage. Nevertheless, Brevard Childs correctly points out that even if parts of this passage originally came from different contexts and dates, they must be read in the light of its present context to determine its meaning. He concludes:

> The description of his reign makes it absolutely clear that his role is messianic.
> There is no end to his rule upon the throne of David, and he will reign with justice

2. See Matt. 4:15–16; J. Calvin, *Commentary on the Book of the Prophet Isaiah*, tr. W. Pringle, 4 vols. (Edinburgh: T. Constable, 1850), 1:307; M. Luther, *Luther's Works: Lectures on Isaiah, Chapters 1–39*, eds. J. Pelikan and H. C. Oswald, 55 vols. (St. Louis: Concordia, 1969), 16:100.

3. *Das Buch Jesaja*, GHAT, 4th ed. (Göttingen: Vandenhoeck & Ruprecht, 1922), p. 88.

4. *Das Buch Jesaja*, KHAT 10 (Tübingen: Mohr Siebeck, 1900), p. 91.

5. *Die Profeten: Untersuchungen zur Religionsgeschichte Israels* (Leipzig: J. C. Hinrichs'sche Buchhandlung, 1914), p. 348.

6. S. Mowinckel, *He That Cometh*, tr. G. W. Anderson (Oxford: Basil Blackwell, 1956), pp. 102–110; G. Fohrer, *Das Buch Jesaja*, ZBK, 3 vols. (Zurich: Zwingli, 1966), 1:138; W. Werner, *Eschatologische Texte in Jesaja 1–39: Messias, Heiliger Rest, Völker*, FB 46 (Würzburg: Echter Verlag, 1982), pp. 15–16, 202; O. Kaiser, *Isaiah 1–12: A Commentary*, tr. J. Bowden, OTL, 2nd ed. (London: SCM, 1983), pp. 204–206.

7. 'Jesaja 8,23–9,6. Befreiungsnacht und Krönungstag', in W. Baumgartner (ed.), *Festschrift A. Bertholet zum 80. Geburtstag* (Tübingen: Mohr Siebeck, 1950), pp. 29–49; repr. in *Kleine Schriften zur Geschichte des Volkes Israel*, 3 vols. (Munich: C. H. Beck'sche Verlagsbuchhandlung, 1953), 2:206–225.

and righteousness forever. Moreover, it is the ardor of the Lord of Hosts who will bring this eschatological purpose to fulfillment. The language is not just of a wishful thinking for a better time, but the confession of Israel's belief in a divine ruler who will replace once and for all the unfaithful reign of kings like Ahaz.[8]

Even if Childs overstates the case, the passage at least refers to a coming deliverer who will reign for ever on the Davidic throne with peace and justice. In many ways, therefore, the passage's interpretation has come full circle, except that modern scholars are significantly more cautious and nuanced in their interpretations.

Larger literary structure

In chapter 8 God speaks three times (vv. 1, 5, 11), followed by Isaiah's statement that he will wait for the Lord, who is hiding his face from Israel (v. 16). The next section, verses 19–22, describes a picture of gloom and darkness, which ends with Israel being exiled, most likely referring to the Assyrian deportations between 732 and 722 BCE that occurred during the lifetime of the eighth-century prophet. This picture of gloom and destruction is then reversed in verse 23 [ET 9:1], and even employs similar wording for effect. The message of reversal from judgment to restoration is a recurring theme throughout the book of Isaiah.

Examining the passage

Isaiah 8:23 [ET 9:1][9]

This verse appears to be the connecting link between the earlier passage and the poem of deliverance that follows, providing significant evidence for its background and setting. Just when it appears that the times could get no darker, Isaiah 8:23 [9:1] pictures a stark reversal of the situation. While verse 22 describes a time of distress, darkness and gloom (*mě'úp*) of anguish (*sûqâ*), by contrast verse 23 declares a time when there will be no more gloom (*mû'āp*) for her who was in anguish (*mûṣāq*). The words for 'gloom' and 'anguish' are rare

---

8. B. S. Childs, *Isaiah*, OTL (Louisville: Westminster John Knox, 2001), p. 81.

9. The translation of the NRSV will be assumed except in places where my translation is significantly different from theirs.

in the Old Testament – *mĕ'ûp* and *mû'āp* (gloom) are hapax legomena, and *ṣûqâ* (Prov. 1:27; Isa. 8:22; 30:2; always used with *ṣārâ*, 'distress') and *mûṣāq* ('anguish'; Job 36:16; 37:10; Isa. 9:1) are used only three times each. The *kî* beginning verse 23 is a strong adversative (GKC §163a, b), contrasting a former time to a latter time described in the rest of verse 23. Some scholars have questioned this adversative;[10] however, the present structure of the Masoretic Text makes good sense and has strong textual support from the ancient versions.[11] The phrase 'her who was in anguish' most likely refers to 'the land' (*'ereṣ* [v. 22]) since countries are commonly referred to in the feminine in Hebrew (GKC §122 h, i).

Several possible interpretations have been suggested for 8:23b [ET 9:1]: (1) most believe it contrasts two time periods, (2) some that it contrasts two rulers, and (3) others two leaders, but containing a split merismus.[12] In its present context a contrast between a time of punishment (God turns his face from the nation) versus a time of restoration (God turns his face back toward the nation) makes good sense. The hiphil forms of *qālal* are consistently used as 'to treat with contempt' when referring to countries or people. Thus the rendering 'to treat leniently' for verse 8:23b, as some scholars have suggested,[13] is extremely unlikely. The latter idea is generally expressed with such idioms as 'he caused his hand to be light' (1 Sam. 6:5) or 'his yoke was made lighter' (1 Kgs 12:4, 9–10; 2 Chr. 10:4, 9–10).

Zebulun and Naphtali (v. 23b) refer to tribal lands in the northern kingdom, but the other three designations are significantly more difficult. In 1950 Albrecht Alt[14] suggested these names referred to regions that Tiglath-pileser III brought under his leadership.[15] In 734 BCE Tiglath-pileser annexed the coastal area and

---

10. *lō* (*BHS*; 1QIsᵃ) and *lû* (H. L. Ginsburg, 'Pekah and Hoshea of Israel (Isa. 8:23)', *ErIsr* 5 [1958], p. 64).

11. LXX (*ouk*); Tg (varies from the MT, yet contains a negative particle); Vg (*non poterit avolare*); Peshitta (*l'*).

12. J. A. Emerton, 'Some Linguistic and Historical Problems in Isaiah VIII.23', *JSS* 14 (1969), pp. 168–169; R. E. Clements, *Isaiah 1–39*, NCBC (London: Marshall, Morgan & Scott, 1982), p. 104.

13. Emerton, 'Isaiah VIII.23', p. 165; Clements, *Isaiah 1–39*, p. 106; J. H. Hayes and S. A. Irvine, *Isaiah the Eighth Century Prophet: His Times and His Preaching* (New York: Abingdon, 1987), pp. 176–177.

14. 'Jesaja 8,23–9,6'.

15. A. Alt, 'Tiglathpilesers III. erster Feldzug nach Palästina', *Kleine Schriften zur Geschichte des Volkes Israel*, 3 vols. (Munich: C. H. Beck'sche Verlagsbuchhandlung, 1953), 2:157, 209–212.

changed its name to Du'ru after its capital city, Dor. Similarly, in 732 BCE Jezreel and Galilee were included in the area of Magidū, with Megiddo as its capital; and the area on the other side of the Jordan River, formerly Gilead, became known as the province of Gal'azu. Alt's suggestion that these geographical designations refer to the northern kingdom around 734–722 BCE corresponds well to the events Israel suffered, but the 'glorification' of this area as indicated in verse 23b poses significant difficulties. In 722 BCE the Assyrians took the northern kingdom into captivity. While little is known about the region following this time period, it could hardly be considered a time of glorification. Isaiah 8:23a appears to have been used intentionally to join these two very different passages; thus a time of glorification must have seemed plausible to the person joining them.

Overview (Isa. 9:1–6)

Isaiah 9:1–6 [ET 9:2–7] contains a poem further describing Israel's restoration. Scholars have significantly disagreed concerning the form of this poem; some suggest a thanksgiving hymn (*Danklied*), others an accession oracle and still others a birth announcement. While the passage contains elements of each, its primary purpose appears to be a birth announcement (cf. Gen. 16:11–12; Judg. 13:3–5), with the declaration of the birth and announcement of the name in verse 5 [6]), and a further prophecy/promise in verse 6 [7]. If so, then it corresponds closely in form to Isaiah 7:14–17 and is even somewhat similar to Isaiah 8:1–4.

Isaiah 9:1 [ET 9:2][16]

This metaphorical darkness appears to represent the period of punishment described in Isaiah 8:21–22. Thus verse 1 [2] describes a country (or people) in dire straits experiencing God's delivering power. Neither parallel unit in verse 1 specifically identifies the people (*hā'ām*) walking in darkness. If verse 23b was not originally part of the poem, it would seem reasonable to assume that 'the people' refers to Judah, since verse 6 [7] speaks of a child sitting on David's throne. However, given its present context and the geographical designations

---

16. Most likely these verbs are prophetic perfects – the events are so certain in the author's mind that they are recorded in past tense (GKC §106 n; B. K. Waltke and M. O'Connor, *An Introduction to Biblical Hebrew Syntax* [Winona Lake: Eisenbrauns, 1990], p. 490, para. 30.5.1e). See H. G. M. Williamson's succinct argumentation, *Variations on a Theme: King, Messiah and Servant in the Book of Isaiah* (Carlisle: Paternoster, 1998), p. 44.

in verse 23b [ET 9:1], it more likely refers to the northern kingdom and a time when it will be made glorious. It is possible that the ambiguity intentionally refers to the whole nation. If this verse is intended to relate to Isaiah 8:16–18, then the time when God hid his face from Israel is finally over.

Isaiah 9:2 [ET 9:3]

This verse poses a significant textual problem. The negative particle usually precedes the word it negates and would result in the translation 'you will not make great the joy', which contrasts with the parallel phrase that follows. It is more reasonable to argue that a scribal error resulted from the two similar-sounding words, *lō'* (not) and *lô* (to itself), giving rise to the textual reading *haggōy lô*. Alternatively, *BHS* suggests, combining the words as *haggîlâ*, 'you will multiply the joy'. The former reading has strong support from about twenty later Hebrew manuscripts and from the ancient versions (LXX, Tg, Vg) – the Targum even specifies Israel as the nation. The latter reading is favoured by the parallel units in the verse. Either reading is still very similar, for God (most likely the 'you') will bring great joy to replace the darkness the nation was experiencing. To help the reader understand the immensity of this joy, it is likened to other times of great rejoicing: (1) when the harvest is brought in, and (2) when plunder is divided among victorious soldiers. Thus this verse prepares the reader for an equally amazing joy and the reasons for it are described in the following verses.

Isaiah 9:3 [ET 9:4][17]

Three reasons are given for the great joy mentioned in the previous verse and each begins with *kî* (vv. 3–5). The first reason (v. 3) is because the nation will be released from its bondage. The metaphor in verse 3 [4] describes the subjugation and oppression of an ox to his owner. Other Old Testament passages use the image of 'yoke' to portray domination (Isa. 10:24–27; 14:24–25; 47:6; etc.), particularly by Assyria or Babylon (Isa. 10:24–27; 14:25; 47:6; Jer. 27:8, 11–12; etc.). The term 'burden' (*subbōl*) is used only three other times in the Masoretic Text, all in Isaiah (9:13; 10:27; 14:25) and each referring to Assyrian oppression. A similar cluster of terms is found in Isaiah 10:24–27 and 14:25–27, also in reference to Assyrian oppression. The last phrase, 'as in the day of Midian', probably refers to God's deliverance through Gideon in Judges 7, thus suggesting an equally miraculous divine intervention.

---

17. The LXX (*Madiam*) and 1QIsaᵃ (*mdym*) contain variant forms, but *mdyn* is confirmed by the majority of MSS and versions.

Isaiah 9:4 [ET 9:5]

The second reason (*kî*) for the great joy mentioned in verse 2 is the destruction of battle gear. Boots[18] and clothing were generally taken as spoil and reused,[19] but in this case the military equipment is destroyed (cf. Ezek. 39:9–10). Bloodstained clothing might reasonably be burned, but why destroy valuable boots that can easily be cleaned unless they were no longer needed? The accession of a new king could inspire hopes for peace, but destroying valuable military equipment suggests either highly figurative language or a time of peace and safety hitherto unknown.

If this poem refers to liberation from Assyria and destruction of its army, when could this have taken place? The historical destruction of Assyria occurred at the end of the seventh century BCE, but this verse does not appear to describe this period for two reasons: (1) the Assyrian destruction was gradual, not a grand display of Yahweh's deliverance like at Midian; and (2) neither Israel nor Judah experienced a significant degree of liberation, for the Babylonians merely assumed domination over them. Some scholars[20] have suggested this poem was part of a later redaction of the Immanuel passage near the end of the seventh century BCE, since (1) by this time Assyria was showing signs of weakening, and (2) Josiah was a righteous king who might have engendered hopes of restoration. But if Miller and Hayes are correct that the Egyptian domination began for Judah as early as 627 BCE, then an anti-Assyrian redaction (rather than an anti-Egyptian one) at the end of the seventh century BCE seems unlikely. However, the biblical text describes a divine punishment that Assyria experienced in 701 BCE (2 Kgs 19:35–37; Isa. 37:36–38), which would be a more feasible time for engendering the hopes mentioned in the poem of Isaiah 9. Still, the actual historical events at that time fell far short of the hopes recorded in this poem.

---

18. *Sĕ'ôn* is a hapax legomenon possibly meaning 'boot' or 'shoe' (*AHw* 3:1213–1214; BDB, p. 684b; *HALOT* 3:738). The more typical word for sandal (*na'al*) occurs in other places in Isaiah (e.g. 5:27; 11:15; 20:2), suggesting that this unique term may have been chosen because of its relevance to the Assyrian army, especially if it derives from the Akkadian *šēnu*.

19. Judg. 14:19; 2 Sam. 2:21; *ANET*, pp. 245–247, 257, 278–280.

20. H. Barth, *Die Jesaja-Worte in der Josiazeit: Israel und Assur als Thema einer produktiven Neuinterpretation der Jesajaüberlieferung*, WMANT 48 (Neukirchen-Vluyn: Neukirchener Verlag, 1977), esp. pp. 176–177; J. Vermeylen, *Du Prophète Isaïe à l'apocalyptique, Isaïe I–XXXV, miroir d'un demi-millénaire d'expérience religieuse en Israël*, *EBib*, 2 vols. (Paris: Librairie Lecoffre, J. Gabalda, 1977–8), 1:245–249.

Isaiah 9:5 [ET 9:6][21]

The third reason (*kî*) for this great joy is the birth of a son. The child is not clearly identified, but the next verse says he will sit upon David's throne and thus continue the Davidic promises. However, this passage is complicated by the fact that while the child is said to have a physical birth and is born 'for us' (*lānô*)[22] (or possibly 'to us'), his name appears to go beyond human capabilities. We learn two things about this child.

1. *He will rule over the nation of Israel.* *hammiśrâ* is used only twice in the Masoretic Text and both occurrences are in this passage (vv. 5–6 [ET 6–7]). It is probably related to *śar*, 'prince', or 'leader', and may be a purposeful play on the word to distinguish between God's role as king of the nation of Israel (cf. Isa. 6:5; 33:17) and this person's role. The child is never called a king in the passage, though he is said to rule on David's throne (v. 6 [ET 7]). But since Isaiah in particular sees Yahweh as the king of Israel (cf. 6:5), this term may imply this child will rule in proper relationship to God.

2. *His name suggests a wish or expectation associated with this child.* There has been great variation in the translation and interpretation of this name. It could be lengthy like Mahershalalhashbaz, or it may be a composite of individual titles (similar to those for David in 2 Sam. 23:1). Scholars typically divide the name into four pairs, but this is unnecessary. Some have attempted to derive five titles similar to Egyptian throne names, but this is problematic.[23] This child is born and yet has a name that suggests divinity; see Isaiah 10:21, where *'El gibbôr* is used of Yahweh.

W. L. Holladay endeavoured to resolve this difficulty, suggesting the middle two titles were theophoric names referring to God.[24] While Holladay's suggestion is plausible, it seems more reasonable that the whole name should be divided into two parallel units, each containing one theophoric element. This clearer chiastic pattern fits the context well and would render the name as

---

21. Although *BHS* suggests some minor emendations, they do not significantly affect the meaning of the verse. Also the niphal form for the word *wayyiqrā'* is unnecessary; see GKC §144d.

22. Lamed of interest (R. J. Williams, *Williams' Hebrew Syntax*, rev. J. C. Beckman, 3rd ed. [Toronto: University of Toronto Press, 2007], p. 48, para. 271) or lamed of direct object (Williams, *Hebrew Syntax*, p. 48, para. 269).

23. Alt among others.

24. W. L. Holladay, *Isaiah: Scroll of a Prophetic Heritage* (Grand Rapids: Eerdmans, 1978), pp. 108–109.

'a wonderful planner (or counsellor) [is] the mighty God, the Father of eternity [is] a prince of peace'.[25]

God will demonstrate his 'awesomeness' (*pele'*) by bringing about this amazing deliverance. He demonstrates that he is 'a prince of peace' in the following verse by bringing about a peace that will have no end. Both *yō'ēṣ* and *śar* may be intentionally used to draw a contrast between the 'counsellors' and 'rulers' of Israel, who are leading the nation into shame and defeat (Isa. 30:1–5; 31:1–3), and Yahweh who will lead the nation wisely and in ways of true peace.

Isaiah 9:6 [ET 9:7][26]

The verse clearly indicates that this future deliverer will advance the Davidic kingdom and bring peace to the troubled nation. He will rule in righteousness and justice from then and into the unforeseeable future.[27] This verse pulls together many of the themes of Isaiah (e.g. Davidic ruler, justice// injustice, righteousness//unrighteousness, peace // no peace) and appears to bring them to the ultimate climax. The final phrase, 'the zeal of the LORD will accomplish this', acts as a colophon to the oracle and confirms the restoration's certainty. It occurs only three other times, each dealing with the Assyrian defeat in 701 BCE (2 Kgs 19:31; Isa. 9:6 [7]; 37:32).

Summary

This passage describes an amazing, divine deliverance of Israel from the Assyrians and the establishment of a kingdom of peace and righteousness extending without end into the future, ruled by a Davidic king. In the present context it initially refers to the northern kingdom, but ends with the child sitting on David's throne – a probable reference to the whole nation. According to 2 Kings 19, Isaiah 10 and 37, during Sennacherib's invasion of 701 BCE there was a supernatural intervention that devastated the Assyrian

---

25. P. D. Wegner, 'A Reexamination of Isaiah ix 1–6', *VT* 42 (1992), pp. 103–112. See also J. Goldingay, 'The Compound Name in Isaiah 9:5 (6)', *CBQ* 61 (1999), pp. 239–244; Williamson, *Variations*, pp. 43–44.

26. The MT contains a final mem in the middle of the word *lmrbh*, but the Q reading (without the final mem) is found in approximately twenty-five MSS (*BHK* 621) and 1QIsaᵃ.

27. See Williamson's excellent discussion of this verse, *Variations*, pp. 35–42.

army. Even though indirect evidence corroborates this destruction,[28] the events of 701 BCE undoubtedly fell far short of the deliverance described in this passage. What is more amazing is that the eighth-century prophets Hosea and Micah also pictured a deliverance culminating with a ruler reigning over Israel into the unforeseeable future. Micah also pictures this great deliverance after a defeat of the Assyrians (cf. Mic. 5:5b–6).

Generally it is argued that Isaiah 8:23 – 9:6 [9:1–7] cannot both be early and refer to the Messiah, since (1) the eschatological elements associated with the Messiah did not originate until after the exile, and (2) the expectation of a Messiah would most likely have arisen after the exile with the cessation of the Davidic dynasty.[29] However, I suggest this passage may have been combined with royal ideology, thereby giving rise to the concept of a 'future deliverer/ruler' who would release the nation from Assyrian bondage and would later develop into the traditional understanding of the Messiah. At this point in the development of messianic expectation, (1) the future deliverer is not the restorer of the Davidic dynasty since it had not yet been destroyed, (2) the hope of deliverance only included the deliverance of Israel from the Assyrians and did not extend to the whole world, and (3) the deliverance was clearly within the present age. Thus the expectation had a teleological intent without being encumbered with all the eschatological elements it later developed.

But why did these prophets picture God's deliverance during the time of the Assyrians? I suggest the prophets understood their prophecies against the backdrop of their time. As they looked into the future they pictured all the events correctly, but did not know how much time intervened between them. Walter C. Kaiser calls this the 'prophetic perspective':

---

28. The Annals of Sennacherib mention the plunder and number of captives taken from Jerusalem, and that Hezekiah was caught like a 'bird in a cage'; however, it falls short of saying that Jerusalem was sacked and destroyed. It is also interesting that Sennacherib's palace in Nineveh contains rock reliefs of the capture of Lachish rather than Jerusalem. Jerusalem was the capital city and a much more impressive victory to depict if indeed it had been captured.

29. J. Lindblom, 'Gibt es eine Eschatologie bei den alttestamentlichen Propheten?', *ST* 6 (1952), pp. 80–82; Mowinkel, *He That Cometh*, pp. 3–4, 125–126; J. Becker, *Messianic Expectation in the Old Testament*, tr. D. E. Green (Philadelphia: Fortress, 1980), pp. 83–92.

'Prophetic perspective' occurs quite frequently in the Old Testament prophets. It is the phenomenon of blending together both the near and the distant aspects of the prediction in one and the same vision. . . . Some have referred to this same phenomenon as prophetic foreshortening. The common illustration is that of two distant mountain peaks that give little hint to the viewer as to how much distance lies between the two. In the same way, interpreters looking across the corridor of time tend to see later events connected with the original context.[30]

The picture of two separate mountain peaks may not be the best way to picture this idea, since it may miss the organic unity between the ideas, but the 'prophetic perspective' may help explain why the eighth-century prophets pictured their coming deliverance in the context of an Assyrian defeat that ushers in an unending divine kingdom.

In conclusion, is there anything new in Isaiah 9:1−7? As the saying goes, 'The more things change, the more they stay the same.' While there have been significant advances in the study of this passage since the mid-1800s, in some senses our interpretation of Isaiah 9:1−7 is still very much the same. We have certainly gained more clarity and precision as to how the concepts in Isaiah 9:1−7 fit into an eighth-century context. We have a better understanding of how passages from different contexts and dates have been interwoven into a new structure. We can better explain why an author or editor described this deliverance against a background of destruction of the Assyrian Empire. We even have a better grasp on how to understand this child's name. But by and large the interpretation of this passage is quite similar to what it was at the start of the eighteenth century. It speaks of a coming deliverer (though not necessarily with all the later elements associated with 'the Messiah') who will sit upon the throne of David and bring great deliverance and joy to the nation of Israel. His kingdom will be one of peace and justice that will not end. It is hard to improve upon this amazing message unless we look at the end of the book of Revelation and see the ultimate conclusion of God's deliverance.

---

30. W. C. Kaiser and M. Silva, *An Introduction to Biblical Hermeneutics: The Search for Meaning* (Grand Rapids: Zondervan, 1994), pp. 143−144. See also T. N. Sterrett, *How to Understand Your Bible* (Downers Grove: IVP, 1974), pp. 140−142; W. W. Klein, C. L. Blomberg and R. L. Hubbard, *Introduction to Biblical Interpretation* (Dallas: Word, 1993), pp. 304ff.

Bibliography

Alt, A., 'Jesaja 8,23–9,6. Befreiungsnacht und Krönungstag', in W. Baumgartner (ed.), *Festschrift A. Bertholet zum 80. Geburtstag* (Tübingen: Mohr Siebeck, 1950), pp. 29–49; repr. in *Kleine Schriften zur Geschichte des Volkes Israel*, 3 vols. (Munich: C. H. Beck'sche Verlagsbuchhandlung, 1953), 2:206–225.

—, 'Tiglathpilesers III. erster Feldzug nach Palästina', *Kleine Schriften zur Geschichte des Volkes Israel*, 3 vols. (Munich: C. H. Beck'sche Verlagsbuchhandlung, 1953), 2:150–162.

Barth, H., *Die Jesaja-Worte in der Josiazeit: Israel und Assur als Thema einer producktiven Neuinterpretation der Jesajaüberlieferung*, WMANT 48 (Neukirchen-Vluyn: Neukirchener Verlag, 1977).

Becker, J., *Messianic Expectation in the Old Testament*, tr. D. E. Green (Philadelphia: Fortress, 1980).

Calvin, J., *Commentary on the Book of the Prophet Isaiah*, tr. W. Pringle, 4 vols. (Edinburgh: T. Constable, 1850).

Childs, B., *Isaiah*, OTL (Louisville: Westminster John Knox, 2001).

Clements, R. E. *Isaiah 1–39*, NCBC (London: Marshall, Morgan & Scott, 1982).

Duhm, B., *Das Buch Jesaja*, GHAT 4th ed. (Göttingen: Vandenhoeck & Ruprecht, 1922).

Emerton, J. A., 'Some Linguistic and Historical Problems in Isaiah VIII.23', *JSS* 14 (1969), pp. 168–169.

Fohrer, G., *Das Buch Jesaja*, ZBK, 3 vols. (Zurich: Zwingli, 1966).

Ginsburg, H. L., 'Pekah and Hoshea of Israel [Isa. 8:23]', *ErIsr* 5 (1958), p. 64.

Goldingay, J., 'The Compound Name in Isaiah 9:5 (6)', *CBQ* 61 (1999), pp. 239–244.

Hayes, J. H., and S. A. Irvine, *Isaiah the Eighth Century Prophet: His Times and His Preaching* (New York: Abingdon, 1987).

Holladay, W. L., *Isaiah: Scroll of a Prophetic Heritage* (Grand Rapids: Eerdmans, 1978).

Hölscher, G., *Die Profeten: Untersuchungen zur Religionsgeschichte Israel* (Leipzig: J. C. Hinrichs'sche Buchhandlung, 1914).

Kaiser, O., *Isaiah 1–12: A Commentary*, tr. J. Bowden, OTL, 2nd ed. (London: SCM, 1983).

Kaiser, W. C., and M. Silva, *An Introduction to Biblical Hermeneutics: The Search for Meaning* (Grand Rapids: Zondervan, 1994).

Klein, W. W., C. L. Blomberg and R. L. Hubbard, *Introduction to Biblical Interpretation* (Dallas: Word, 1993).

Lindblom, J., 'Gibt es eine Eschatologie bei den alttestamentlichen Propheten?', *ST* 6 (1952), pp. 80–82.

Luther, M., *Luther's Works: Lectures on Isaiah, Chapters 1–39*, 55 vols., ed. J. Pelikan and H. C. Oswald (St. Louis: Concordia, 1969), 16:100.

Marti, K., *Das Buch Jesaja*, KHAT 10 (Tübingen: Mohr Siebeck, 1900).

Mowinckel, S., *He That Cometh*, tr. G. W. Anderson (Oxford: Basil Blackwell, 1956).

Sterrett, T. N., *How to Understand Your Bible* (Downers Grove: IVP, 1974).

Vermeylen, J., *Du Prophète Isaïe à l'apocalyptique, Isaïe I-XXXV, mirior d'n demi-millénaire d'expérience religieuse en Israël*, EBib, 2 vols. (Paris: Librairie Lecoffre, J. Gabalda et Cie Éditeurs, 1977—8).

Waltke, B. K., and M. O'Connor, *An Introduction to Biblical Hebrew Syntax* (Winona Lake: Eisenbrauns, 1990).

Wegner, P. D., 'A Reexamination of Isaiah ix 1—6', *VT* 42 (1992), pp. 103—112.

Werner, W., *Eschatologische Texte in Jesaja 1—39: Messias, Heiliger Rest, Völker*, FB 46 (Würzburg: Echter, 1982).

Williams, R. J., *Williams' Hebrew Syntax*, rev. J. C. Beckman, 3rd ed. (Toronto: University of Toronto Press, 2007).

Williamson, H. G. M., *Variations on a Theme: King, Messiah and Servant in the Book of Isaiah* (Carlisle: Paternoster, 1998).

12. A STRUCTURAL-HISTORICAL EXEGESIS OF ISAIAH 42:1–9

S. D. (Fanie) Snyman

Introduction

In this contribution Isaiah 42:1–9 is investigated following a structural-historical approach to the exegesis of the Old Testament.[1] Isaiah 42:1–9 is an inspiring passage and the first of the so-called servant songs (Isa. 49:1–6; 50:4–9; 52:13 – 53:12).

A structural-historical investigation of Isaiah 42:1–9

Demarcating the text
Where does the first servant song begin and where does it end? That Isaiah 42:1 should be seen as the start of a new unit is fairly certain. The previous part (Isa. 41:21–29) has a court scene (v. 21) as its setting, unlike that of Isaiah 42. Furthermore, the prominent 'look'/'see' (*hēn*) as the first word of this verse

---

1. S. D. Snyman, 'A Structural-Historical Approach to the Exegesis of the Old Testament', in D. G. Firth and J. A. Grant (eds.), *Words and the Word: Explorations in Biblical Interpretation and Literary Theory* (Nottingham: Apollos; Downers Grove: IVP, 2008), pp. 51–73.

suggests a new unit with a new point about to be made.[2] The word 'look'/'see' occurs also at the end of Isaiah 41:29, strengthening the argument that a new unit commences at Isaiah 42:1. The elaborate way in which the servant is introduced together with a description of his mission also suggests a new beginning.

The issue of where this new unit comes to an end is a far more difficult question to answer.

Isaiah 42:1–4 taken as a pericope

There are scholars who think that the extent of the pericope stretches only to verse 4.[3] Arguments in favour of this point of view are that verse 5 begins with the well-known messenger-formula that normally indicates a new beginning and that verses 1–4 form a coherent unity apart from either the former unit or the one following it in verses 5–9. The perashim[4] added at the end of verse 4 and again at the end of verse 9 in the Masoretic Text is another argument in favour of viewing verses 1–9 as two separate pericopes. According to Westermann[5] the first servant song comprises only verses 1–4. He regarded verses 5–9 as a later expansion and continuation of the servant song contained in the first four verses because the way of speaking of the servant is quite different. Beuken[6] is also of the opinion that verses 1–4 and verses 5–9 represent two different units. He bases his conviction on form-critical grounds. Verses 1–4 are an installation word as a king introduces his servant to other authorities. Verses 5–9 cannot be seen as representing only one specific literary genre, but verse 5 characterizes the next unit as something different from the previous one. Whybray[7] is also convinced that Isaiah 42:1–4 should be regarded as a unit

2. W. A. M. Beuken, *Jesaja deel II A*, POut (Nijkerk: Callanbach, 1986), p. 108; J. Goldingay, *The Message of Isaiah 40–55: A Literary-Theological Commentary* (London: T. & T. Clark International, 2005), p. 149.

3. J. Renkema, 'De Verkondiging van het eerste lied van de Knecht (Jes 42:1–4)', in *De Knecht, Studies rondom Deutero-Jesaja door collega's en oud-leerlingen aangeboden aan prof dr J L Koole* (Kampen: Kok, 1978), pp. 178–187; G. A. F. Knight, *Servant Theology: A Commentary on the Book of Isaiah 40–55*, ITC (Edinburgh: Handsel, 1984), p. 3; K. Elliger, *Deuterojesaja 1. Teilband Jesaja 40,1–45,7* (Neukirchen-Vluyn: Neukirchener Verlag, 1978), pp. 223–224.

4. These serve to divide segments of the text in the Hebrew Bible.

5. C. Westermann, *Isaiah 40–66: A Commentary* (London: SCM, 1969), p. 101.

6. Beuken, *Jesaja*, pp. 106, 119.

7. R. N. Whybray, *Isaiah 40–66* (Grand Rapids: Eerdmans, 1975), p. 71.

due to 'content, form, structure and metre'. According to Smillie[8] verses 1–4 form a separate unit because verses 1–4 describe the servant in the third person while verses 5–7 address the servant by using the second person. However, the change of person in connection with the servant need not be used as a conclusive argument for separating verses 1–9 into two distinctive pericopes. The addressees are indicated in the last word of verse 9 as 'you' in the plural. This means that both the exiled people of Judah as well as the servant are addressed. The people are addressed to inform them of the new initiative from Yahweh in presenting them with a servant. At the same time the task and responsibilities of the servant are communicated to both the people and the servant.[9]

There are also scholars who are of the opinion that Isaiah 42:1–9 should be divided into three distinctive pericopes consisting of verses 1–4, 5–7 and 8–9.[10]

Isaiah 42:1–9 taken as a pericope

Other scholars are of the opinion that Isaiah 42:1–9 should be seen as a unit in its own right. Lindsey[11] views verses 1–9 as a unit in close relationship with the previous part comprising Isaiah 41:25–29. Zehnder[12] takes Isaiah 42:1–9 to be a unit as well as Koole[13] and Motyer[14] who see 42:1–9 as a unity but in two parts consisting of verses 1–4 and 5–9. Koole[15] makes the interesting distinction between the two parts by saying that verses 1–4 deal with the servant of the Lord while verses 5–9 deal with the Lord of the servant. Goldingay[16] also treats Isaiah 42:1–9 as a unit, although he does not argue the point at any length. However, in an earlier publication[17] it seems as if he draws a sharper

8. G. R. Smillie, 'Isaiah 42:1–4 in its Rhetorical Context', *BSac* 162 (2005), p. 52.

9. Elliger, *Deuterojesaja*, p. 239; Beuken, *Jesaja*, pp. 107, 130; J. L. Koole, *Jesaja II*, COut (Kampen: Kok, 1985), p. 146.

10. O. Kaiser, *Der Königliche Knecht: Eine traditionsgeschichtlich-exegetische Studie über die Ebed-Jahwe-Lieder bei Deuterojesaja* (Göttingen: Vandenhoeck & Ruprecht, 1959), pp. 15–44.

11. F. D. Lindsey, 'The Call of the Servant in Isaiah 42:1–9', *BSac* 139 (1982), p. 13.

12. M. Zehnder, 'Phonological Subtext: A Short Note on Isa 42,1–9', *BN* 123 (2004), p. 35.

13. Koole, *Jesaja*, p. 141.

14. J. A. Motyer, *The Prophecy of Isaiah* (Leicester: IVP, 1993), p. 318.

15. Koole, *Jesaja*, p. 142.

16. Goldingay, *Isaiah*, p. 149.

17. J. Goldingay, *God's Prophet, God's Servant: A Study in Jeremiah and Isaiah 40–55* (Greenwood, S. C.: Attic, 1984), p. 92.

distinction between 42:1–4 and 42:5–9. It is clear that the subject matter of Isaiah 42:1–9 is about Yahweh and the one described as his servant. Blenkinsopp[18] makes the remark that 'the two statements (vv. 1–4, 5–9) belong together even if the second was added later, an opinion often expressed but impossible to prove'.

There are at least three arguments in favour of taking verses 1–9 as a unit. Verse 9 concludes with 'look'/'see' (*hinnê*) repeating the first word of the unit, 'look'/'see' (*hēn*), and thereby creating an inclusio. Verse 10 commences with an imperative calling for the praise of the Lord with a new song, setting a completely new tone and thereby introducing a new unit in the book. Secondly, verses 1–4 and 5–9 share the same vocabulary. Terms such as nations/gentiles (*goŷim*) in verses 1 and 6, 'spirit' (*rûaḥ*) in verses 1 and 5, 'earth' (*'ereṣ*) in verses 4–5 and the verbs 'bring forth' (*yṣ'*) in verses 1, 3 and 7 and 'give' (*ntn*) in verses 1, 5–6 and 8 occur throughout verses 1–9, adding to the unity of the pericope. Furthermore, the way in which 'nations' and 'people' alternate (v. 1, 'nations'; v. 5, 'people'; v. 6, 'people'; v. 6 'nations'/Gentiles) creates a chiastic pattern. Thirdly, it is noteworthy that there is no indication as to who the speaker is in verses 1–4. It is only by logic that we simply take it for granted and assume that Yahweh is indeed the speaker in verses 1–4. Only in verse 5, introducing a messenger formula, is there some indication of who the speaker is. The formula can be literally translated as 'thus the God Yahweh said'.[19] If translated this way, the formula may refer either to the previous saying in verses 1–4 or to the one following in verses 5–9, or even to both the sayings in verses 1–4 and verses 5–9. Verse 5 is therefore taken not only as an indication of who is speaking in verses 5–9, but also as an indication of who is speaking in verses 1–4, as this is the only place where some indication is given as to the identity of the speaker. Beuken[20] argues in this regard that the messenger formula divides the two parts consisting of verses 1–4 and verses 5–9 respectively, but also makes it clear that it is Yahweh speaking in both parts. According to Koole,[21] both parts may be distinguished from one another, but at the same time they also belong to one another. Verses 1–9 are therefore taken as a unit.

18. J. Blenkinsopp, *Isaiah 40–55: A New Translation with Introduction and Commentary*, AB 19A (New York: Doubleday, 2000), p. 209.

19. Goldingay, *Isaiah*, p. 161.

20. Beuken, *Jesaja*, p. 121.

21. Koole, *Jesaja*, p. 141.

Investigating the literary and structural features of the text

An investigation of the literary features and overall structure of the text reveals some interesting insights. The inclusio bracketing the beginning and end of the pericope has already been mentioned. It is furthermore noteworthy to see how first person singular forms dominate in verse 1, as is the case in verses 8–9, strengthening the inclusio.

Verses 1–4 clearly belong together. Verse 1 introduces the servant. What separates verse 1 from verses 2–4 is the fact that the verbs in verse 1 are arranged to form a chiastic pattern. An imperfect verb is followed by two verbs in the perfect form, and then again one finds an imperfect.[22] Verses 2–4 are characterized by the use of the negative particle 'no' (*lō'*) no fewer than seven times. Verses 3 and 4 are also linked by a chiasm:

A a *crushed* reed he will not break
   B and a *dim* wick he will not extinguish . . .
   B he will not grow *dim* and
A he will not be *crushed*.

Verses 1–4 are also linked by the prominent term 'justice' (*mišpāṭ*), which occurs three times. That the servant has a responsibility to bring forth justice is said in verse 1 to be his first (and, considering the negatives that follow, apparently primary) task. It is mentioned again at the centre of the chiasm referred to in verses 3 and 4 and is reiterated at the end of verse 4. To repeat the same concept three times within the space of only four verses, and that at crucial points in the passage, is a sure indication of the importance of the concept.

Verses 1–4 form a unit that consists of two parts, verse 1 (A) followed by verses 2–4 (B). Verse 1 is dominated by first person singular forms, while verses 2–4 are characterized by third person singular forms. In verse 1 the emphasis is on Yahweh, who introduces his servant, while in verses 2–4 the focus is on the servant and what he will and will not do. The structure proposed here is somewhat different from the one proposed by Motyer,[23] who detected an A1 'The servant's ministry of the truth' (v. 1), B 'The servant's ministry to people' (vv. 2–3b), and A2 'The servant's ministry of the truth' (vv. 3c–4), structure. Earlier Koole[24] and Beuken[25] also detected a tripartite

---

22. Ibid., p. 147.

23. Motyer, *Isaiah*, p. 319.

24. Koole, *Jesaja*, p. 146.

25. Beuken, *Jesaja*, p. 107.

division consisting of appointment, equipment and task of the servant (v. 1), correction of complaint motives: no crying out and the languishing does still count (vv. 2–3a) and a guarantee that the servant will not whither and that he will fulfil his mission, with the islands waiting (vv. 3b–4).

Although verses 1–4 and 5–9 may be divided into two distinct parts, they are nevertheless also closely linked to one another. In verse 5 'earth' (*hā'āreṣ*) is taken up after it has occurred in verse 4. The occurrence of 'earth' (*hā'āreṣ*) in verse 5 creates a link with the preceding part of the pericope, adding weight to an earlier argument that verses 1–9, rather than verses 1–4, should be seen as a pericope. As mentioned earlier, the messenger formula in verse 5 may be taken as referring to verses 1–4 and 5–9.

Verse 5 commences with a messenger formula consisting of a doxological statement on Yahweh as creator of the heavens and the earth, who gives life to all earth's human inhabitants. The verb 'give' (*ntn*) used in verse 1 surfaces again in verse 5 in a way reminiscent of verse 1. While Yahweh 'gives' his spirit upon the servant in verse 1, Yahweh also gives breath to the people and spirit to those who walk on earth in verse 5. Verse 5 distinguishes itself from the rest of the pericope by the prominent occurrence of participial forms.

Verse 6 continues with Yahweh still in the focus, opening with an emphatic 'I, the Lord' (*'ănî yhwh*). Verse 6 follows very much the same pattern as verse 1, where the focus is on Yahweh, especially in the use of first person singular forms. The verb 'give' (*ntn*) is used again. In verse 6 Yahweh will give the servant as a covenant of/for a people. The nations mentioned in verse 1 are picked up again in verse 6.

In verse 7 the focus is on the task and duties of the servant – as in verses 2–4. The verb 'bring forth' (*yṣ'*) used twice in verses 1–4, where justice (*mišpāṭ*) is to go forth, occurs again in verse 7, where former prisoners will go forth from a prison or dungeon. What is notable in verse 7 is the use of infinitive forms of the verbs, thereby distinguishing it from the participial forms used in verse 6.

In verses 8–9 the focus shifts back to Yahweh in the same way as in verse 6 with an emphatic 'I, the Lord' (*'ănî yhwh*). The verb 'give' (*ntn*), already referred to in verses 1, 5 and 6, occurs again. This verb occurs no fewer than four times in the pericope and is used every time in connection with Yahweh. As is the case in verses 1 and 6, first person forms dominate verse 8.

Looking at verses 5–9 as a whole, the following structure emerges: verse 5 (C) consists of a messenger formula followed by a doxology in praise of Yahweh. It is followed by verse 6 (A1), where the focus is on Yahweh, characterized by first person singular forms. Verse 7 (B1) focuses on the role of the servant and the pericope comes to a close in verses 8–9 (A2), once again with a focus on Yahweh with first person singular forms dominating. The structure detected here differs from the one proposed by Motyer.[26] According to Motyer, the passage consists of A 'The Lord of creation' (v. 5), B 'The Lord of the servant' (vv. 6–7), and, finally, C 'The Lord of the false gods' (vv. 8–9). Beuken[27] has the same structure but with a difference. Verse 5 provides the reader with a messenger formula, followed by verses 6–7 as an address to the servant in the form of a call oracle, while verses 8–9 are directed to Israel with an appeal for uniqueness.

When the different pieces of this analysis of verses 1–9 are put together, the following picture emerges:

V. 1 Yahweh	A
Vv. 2–4 The servant	B
V. 5 Doxology	C
V. 6 Yahweh	A1
V. 7 The servant	B1
Vv. 8–9 Yahweh	A2

Although the unity of verses 1–9 is argued, the division in two parts as held by many scholars is also maintained.

Investigating the genre (Gattung) and life setting (Sitz im Leben)

Duhm himself did not give a precise description of the genre used in the servant songs other than 'songs' or 'poems'.[28] There are no clear indications from the text giving us an exact description of the genre or *Gattung* employed in verses 1–4. As an initial and broad definition the pericope as a whole can be seen as an *Ich-Rede Jahwes*.[29] Recent literature reveals that there is a scholarly consensus that the genre of a royal designation[30] or installation[31] oracle is used in verses 1–4. Although the *Gattung* is named differently by various scholars, it generally refers basically to the same idea. Westermann[32] calls it the designation

---

26. Motyer, *Isaiah*, p. 321.

27. Beuken, *Jesaja*, p. 121.

28. H. Haag, *Der Gottesknecht bei Deuterojesaja*, EdF 233 (Darmstadt: Wissenschaftliche Buchgesellschaft, 1985), p. 28.

29. I.e. a first person speech by Yahweh. Cf. H. J. Kraus, *Das Evangelium der unbekannten Propheten: Jesaja 40–66* (Neukirchen-Vluyn: Neukirchener Verlag, 1990), pp. 38, 41.

30. Lindsey, 'Call of the Servant', p. 3.

31. H. R. Minn, *The Servant Songs: Excerpts from Isaiah 42–53. Introduction, Translation and Commentary* (Christchurch, Auckland: Presbyterian Room, 1966), p. 2.

32. Westermann, *Isaiah 40–66*, p. 92.

of God's Servant. According to Elliger,[33] Koole,[34] Beuken[35] and Jeremias[36] the *Gattung* used here is that of the presentation of an agent[37] used in a royal context where a king would present a servant upon whom he wants to bestow the highest authority. The servant is made known together with a declaration of his task. The emphasis on justice as the servant's primary task strengthens the idea of a royal setting of this pericope. The plural form 'you' in verse 9 is an indication that the audience meant is not the heavenly court of Yahweh, but rather earthly people currently in need of the services of the servant.

The genre employed in the second part of the pericope is more difficult to determine. The best way seems to be to acknowledge that not one single genre is used but rather a mixture of different genres. In verse 5 there is a messenger formula followed by a hymnlike doxology.[38] Verses 6–7 resemble a call narrative of a prophet but can also be viewed as an 'assistance formula', an 'encouragement formula' or a description of a task. Verses 8–9 make one think of a polemic against the veneration of other gods that can also be called a dispute oracle,[39] which is perhaps the best term to describe the genre of the whole of the pericope. It is assumed that the text is at home in an exilic situation where the Babylonian Empire was replaced by the Persian Empire under the leadership of Cyrus.

Traditional material

The most prominent tradition employed in this pericope is the creation by Yahweh, a well-known tradition used in Isaiah 40 – 55. Yahweh is portrayed as the creator, the one who stretches out the heavens, who spread out the earth and all that comes out of it. Yahweh gives breath to the people and spirit/life to those who walk on it (v. 5). It is notable that the same order of creation as Genesis 1 is followed (heaven–earth–humanity). The majesty of Yahweh's creative power is highlighted in order to relate it to the redemptive initiatives he is about to perform through the servant. Yahweh's creative actions serve to establish Yahweh's claim to control the events of history.[40] The participles

33. Elliger, *Deuterojesaja*, p. 224.

34. Koole, *Jesaja*, p. 145.

35. Beuken, *Jesaja*, p. 146.

36. J. Jeremias, 'Mispat im ersten Gottesknechtslied (Jes XLII 1–4)', *VT* 22 (1972), p. 32.

37. Goldingay, *Isaiah*, p. 149.

38. Elliger, *Deuterojesaja*, p. 224.

39. Koole, *Jesaja*, pp. 145–146.

40. Whybray, *Isaiah 40–66*, p. 74.

used suggest that the creative power of Yahweh was not just unleashed in the past but is still at work now. It is significant that the task of the servant is to establish *mišpāṭ* on earth, as was said in verses 4 and 5, and the creative action of Yahweh on earth is praised.

The verb 'to bring forth' (*yṣ'*), occurring no fewer than three times to describe the task of the servant, is the same verb used to describe the deliverance from Egypt. This observation leads one to the exodus tradition, where the same form of the verb is used in Exodus 6:13 and 27 in connection with the deliverance of Israel from Egypt (c.f. also Exod. 13:3; 12:41; 14:8; Deut. 16:3, 6). Brueggemann[41] calls this verb one of the three decisive 'Exodus verbs'. Just as Israel was once delivered from the bondage of Egypt, they will now again be delivered, but this time from exile, like captives from a prison. The 'I, the Lord' phrase makes one think of Exodus 3 and Exodus 6, where Yahweh revealed his name.

The reference to *tôrâ* in verse 4 and the mention of a covenant in verse 6 reminds one of the Sinai-tradition. *Tôrâ* may be taken as the total of all Yahweh's stipulations, admonitions and instructions to his people given to them at Sinai. Verse 8 may also be interpreted as alluding to the Sinai events. The honour of Yahweh's (name) and the reference to idols is also reminiscent of what is expected from the covenant people in the Decalogue (Exod. 20:4). The covenant is still intact and the stipulations of the covenant are still relevant and applicable even in the difficult times of the exile, where serious doubts were raised about the validity of the covenant. The reference to the exodus serves the purpose of reminding the exiled people of Yahweh's great act of deliverance once performed in the history of the people.

Although the *Gattung* employed in the opening verses of Isaiah 42 suggests a royal designation, the pericope carefully avoids any direct allusion to the Davidic kingship and hence a revival of the David/Zion tradition prominent in the years before the exile.

Redactional material

Redactional matters focus on larger units in a book or even a corpus of literature[42] and therefore little attention will be given to redactional matters here. It is assumed that the so-called servant songs form an independent collection that was incorporated into the composition of Isaiah 40 – 55. Within the

---

41. W. Brueggemann, *Theology of the Old Testament: Testimony, Dispute, Advocacy* (Minneapolis: Fortress, 1997), p. 174.

42. Haag, *Gottesknecht*, pp. 26–27.

immediate context of Isaiah 42:1–9, verses 8–9 seem to refer back to the challenge put to the idols in the previous pericope (Isa. 41:21–29) to foretell what the future holds. The idols are incapable of doing so while the announcement and imminent appearance of the servant together with the accomplishment of his mission prove Yahweh as the One who has the power to make the future known, which will demonstrate him as the true and only God.

Theological reflection

This reading of Isaiah 42:1–9 shows that the pericope is far more about Yahweh and what he did and intends to do than about the unidentified servant. An investigation of the structural features of the text showed how the pericope commences with Yahweh's introducing his servant. The pericope comes to a close with a statement on Yahweh's name, honour and praise. The middle part of the pericope contains a doxology on Yahweh as the creator.

Yahweh is praised as the one and only God, known by the name of Yahweh, creator of heaven and earth and of all humanity. Yahweh as creator of all humanity means that he not only gives human beings the breath of life but also provides them with spiritual capabilities[43] because he is both creator and sustainer and is also in control of world history. He has made things known in the past and will make new things known – even before they happen. He announces these things to the people so that they will realize the power of Yahweh over against the powerless idols. Yahweh is indeed the one and only universal God, a message that would have been particularly comforting to the people of Judah, who had to face the harsh reality of exile as well as the confrontation with foreign gods. Yahweh is not only the universal God; he is also the God who performed wonderful acts in the history of his people. The people are reminded of this by subtle references to the redemption from Egypt and the events that took place at Sinai. Yahweh as the One who has been active in the history of his people will continue to act in times to come. This time his acts will become known through somebody new – his servant.

Yahweh is portrayed as the One who provides his servant – a servant who enjoys Yahweh's support and who is called Yahweh's chosen one and the one in whom he delights. The servant can therefore be assured of Yahweh's care and protection. In fact, the servant is bound to be a covenant for the people and a light to the nations.

---

43. Koole, *Jesaja*, p. 157.

What picture of the servant is painted? What the servant will not do is revealed in seven clauses where the negative particle 'no' (*lō'*) is used. The servant will not do his work in a spectacular way for anyone to hear (v. 2). He will also not crush the downhearted exiles who have lost all hope of a reversal of their fortunes. What he will do is said emphatically: his task is to bring forth justice (*mišpāṭ*) to the nations in a way that will be visible and real for anybody to see. He will endure until his mission is accomplished. What exactly the mission of the servant entails is given in verse 7: he will open the eyes of the blind and release captives from prison. When this happens, Yahweh's justice will be seen by the nations.

It is therefore not the wishes of the exiled people that are primarily attended to; rather, Yahweh's name, honour and praise are at stake. This is the ultimate reason why he demonstrates his power by making known events yet to happen. This was the case in the past, but it is also true for the exile, where the end of the exile is foretold.

Conclusion

An investigation of this kind proves once again that it is a worthwhile exercise to re-examine even a well-known text. The main results of this investigation may be summarized in the following points:

- The first servant song extends indeed to include verses 1–9.
- The text reveals several interesting literary features, which are aids to a better understanding of the text.
- The text makes use of several of the well-known traditions in Israel.
- The theological emphasis of the text is more on Yahweh than on the servant or the people.
- The task and responsibility of the servant is given more attention than his identity.
- The glory and honour of Yahweh is the ultimate aim of the mission of the servant.

What is offered here is not an exhaustive investigation of either the exegetical issues of the text or the questions surrounding the servant of Yahweh. But at least some insights have been gained via this reading of a familiar yet difficult text of the Old Testament.

13. AN INNER-ISAIANIC READING OF ISAIAH 61:1–3

Jacob Stromberg

Isaiah 61:1–3 is perhaps best known from its interpretation at Qumran and in the New Testament, where it was understood in the light of the events and historical context of late Second Temple times. The aim of the present chapter is to read this passage in a very different context, the literary context of Isaiah as a whole. To say the book in some sense forms a meaningful whole is not to say it was written all at one time by a single individual. In fact, most scholars now agree that Isaiah is composite, with different parts stemming from different authors who lived at different times. Breaking with earlier views, scholars now also recognize that these parts did not develop in isolation from one another, but that the later stages presuppose and develop the earlier, creating a complex network of internal links.[1]

Given this history of development, two different approaches have emerged from recent discussion as to how the book (or any passage in it) might be read.[2] Adherents of the two usually agree that the book developed in this way, but differ over the significance this has for reading it. The first reads the book *in the light of* this history, and is called the diachronic approach. The second reads the

---

1. On all of this, see Williamson's chapter (1) in the present volume.
2. See e.g. J. C. de Moor (ed.), *Synchronic or Diachronic? A Debate on Method in Old Testament Exegesis*, OTS 34 (Leiden: Brill, 1995), p. 425.

book without reference to this history, and is called the synchronic approach. Both are valid and can yield valuable insights.

This chapter illustrates a diachronic approach to reading Isaiah 61:1–3 within the book as a whole. It will first show that the post-exilic Isaiah 61:1–3 draws from the earlier exilic Deutero-Isaiah (DI), to portray its speaker in terms of various figures announcing salvation there. It will be seen that this portrayal served the important purpose of recasting earlier unfulfilled prophecies for a new day. The chapter will then show how 61:1–3 was taken up by even later material in Trito-Isaiah (TI). Here it will be seen that this later material limits and expands in various ways the good news announced in Isaiah 61.

Deutero-Isaianic influence on Isaiah 61:1–3

It is widely agreed that both the speaker of Isaiah 61:1–3 and his message are portrayed in terms drawn from DI, so that it comprises a pastiche of earlier texts.[3] This claim is consistent with the immediate and broader contexts of 61:1–3. Scholars agree that the broader context in Isaiah 60 – 62 borrowed heavily from DI.[4] For example, Isaiah 60:9 cites 55:5b almost verbatim, the only difference being that the former begins with 'for the name of'. The immediate context in Isaiah 61:4–11 also alludes to DI. For example, Isaiah 61:8b reads:

> I will give their reward (*pĕʿulātām*) in faithfulness,
>   and I will make an eternal covenant with them (*bĕrît ʿôlām ʾekrôt lāhem*).[5]

---

3. W. A. M. Beuken, 'Servant and Herald of Good Tidings: Isaiah 61 as an Interpretation of Isaiah 40–55', in J. Vermeylen (ed.), *The Book of Isaiah*, BETL 81 (Leuven: Leuven University Press, 1989), pp. 411–440. For further studies on this see B. C. Gregory, 'The Postexilic Exile in Third Isaiah: Isaiah 61:1–3 in Light of Second Temple Hermeneutics', *JBL* 126 (2007), pp. 475–496.

4. Cf. the following: 60:4 / 49:18, 22; 60:9 / 55:5; 60:11 / 45:1; 60:13 / 41:19; 60:16 / 49:26; 62:10 / 40:3; 62:11 / 48:20. On this see e.g. J. Blenkinsopp, *Isaiah 56–66*, AB 19B (New York: Doubleday, 2003), pp. 203–245; B. Childs, *Isaiah*, OTL (Louisville: Westminster, 2000), pp. 493–500; W. Lau, *Schriftgelehrte Prophetie in Jes 56–66*, BZAW 225 (Berlin: de Gruyter, 1994), pp. 22–66; W. Zimmerli, 'Zur Sprache Tritojesajas', in *Gottes Offenbarung: Gesammelte Aufsätze* (Munich: Chr. Kaiser, 1969), pp. 221–225. For 61:1–3 as an integral part of 60–62 see P. A. Smith, *Rhetoric and Redaction in Trito-Isaiah*, VTSup 62 (Leiden: Brill, 1995), pp. 22–49.

5. Unless stated otherwise, all Bible translations in this chapter are my own.

Here, Beuken rightly discerns a textual blend of 40:10b and 55:3b, verses from the prologue and epilogue of DI.[6]

> I will make an eternal covenant with you (*'ekrĕtāh lākem bĕrît 'ôlām*),
>   the sure mercies of David.
> (55:3b)

> Behold his wage is with him,
>   and his reward (*pĕ'ulātô*) before him.
> (40:10b)

The latter passage is also cited verbatim in 62:11b.

If the broader context in 60 – 62 and more immediate context in 61:4–11 borrow from DI, then we can reasonably expect the same to be true of 61:1–3. Therefore, it seems appropriate to consider as instances of influence those cases where a particular word or phrase in 61:1–3 appears to echo an element from DI. It is necessary to stress this cumulative aspect of the argument only because such words and phrases that echo DI might be regarded, when viewed in isolation from one another, as mere coincidence. However, coincidence is a poor explanation when examples of such influence can be multiplied within 60 – 62.[7]

With this in mind, we may now analyse specific examples of such influence in Isaiah 61:1–3.[8] It reads:

> The spirit of the Lord GOD is upon me,
>   because the LORD has anointed me;
> he has sent me to bring good news to the oppressed,
>   to bind up the broken-hearted,
> to proclaim liberty to the captives,

---

6. Beuken, 'Isaiah 61', pp. 430–431.

7. Heskett e.g. overlooks this in his recent study *Messianism within the Scriptural Scrolls of Isaiah*, LIIB/OTS 456 (London: T. & T. Clark International, 2007), pp. 246–247. In my opinion his exclusive focus on the frequency of individual words in 61:1–3 leads to a skewed assessment of the text.

8. This analysis is based on Beuken, 'Isaiah 61', pp. 415–424; Childs, *Isaiah*, pp. 502–506; Smith, *Rhetoric*, pp. 22–26, R. N. Whybray, *Isaiah 40–66*, NCBC (Grand Rapids: Eerdmans, 1975), pp. 239–243; H. G. M. Williamson, *Variations on a Theme: King, Messiah and Servant in the Book of Isaiah* (Carlisle: Paternoster, 1998), pp. 174–188.

and release to the prisoners;
to proclaim the year of the Lord's favour,
    and the day of vengeance of our God;
to comfort all who mourn;
to provide for all the mourners of Zion –
    to give to them a turban in place of ashes,
the oil of gladness in place of mourning,
    the mantle of praise in place of a faint spirit.

Scholars have identified the role described here with a number of offices,[9] the most common perhaps being that of a prophet. However, as will be seen, attention to the DI background of this passage cautions against too quickly assigning everything said here to one particular office. For the sake of convenience, we may distinguish in what follows between those statements related to the speaker's role and those related to his task, keeping in mind that the two are really inseparable.

The speaker's role

The speaker claims the role of DI's servant. In 61:1 'the spirit of the Lord GOD is upon me' immediately recalls Isaiah 42:1, where God says of his servant, 'I have placed my spirit upon him.' By recalling the servant of 42, Isaiah 61 may have wanted to give the speaker a royal role. Many would argue Isaiah 42 depicts the servant in royal terms.[10] For example, Isaiah 42:1 is probably based on the royal figure of 11:1, which says, 'the spirit of the LORD will rest upon him [the Davidic king]'.[11] Also, royal features may be present in 61 when it continues with 'a description of part of the royal task of defending the cause of the poor and disadvantaged'.[12] Thus Isaiah 61:1 may strike a royal note, as it alludes to the spirit-endowed servant of 42:1.

Alternatively, spirit endowment in 61:1 may suggest a prophetic office, an impression reinforced by the task given the figure: to 'proclaim' his message

---

9. See the brief survey in J. Bergsma, *The Jubilee from Leviticus to Qumran*, VTSup 115 (Leiden: Brill, 2007), p. 199.

10. See, with further literature, J. Goldingay and D. Payne, *Isaiah 40–55*, vol. 1, ICC (London: T. & T. Clark International, 2006), pp. 208–211; B. Sommer, *A Prophet Reads Scripture: Allusion in Isaiah 40–66* (Stanford: Stanford University Press, 1998), pp. 84–88; Williamson, *Variations*, pp. 130–148.

11. With further points of contact see e.g. Sommer, *Prophet*, pp. 84–88.

12. Williamson, *Variations*, p. 175.

(vv. 1b–2). Elsewhere, spirit endowment is associated with prophecy (Mic. 3:8). Furthermore, Isaiah 61:1 underscores a prophetic role, claiming that 'the Lord has sent me'. Prophets are often 'sent' by the Lord. In Isaiah 6:8 God asks, 'Whom will I send,' and the prophet Isaiah answers, 'Send me.' A prophetic role perhaps need not exclude from 61 all vestiges of royal language, since the author may have synthesized different portraits from various sources.[13] In either case the speaker in 61:1 claims the role of the servant in 42, when he announces his spirit endowment.

An allusion may be cast back to DI's portrait of Cyrus, when the speaker of 61 reports that the Lord has 'anointed me' (v. 1). Within Isaiah, the 'anointing' of an individual occurs only one other time, at 45:1, where it is applied to the Persian king Cyrus, whom the Lord calls to restore his people. The Old Testament mentions 'anointing' most often in connection with kingship, sometimes even alongside spirit endowment (1 Sam. 16:23; 2 Sam. 23:1–2). While these traits are not exclusively used of a royal role, their predominant association with it and combined use in 61:1 certainly suggest that this text echoes such a role, opening up the possibility that DI's portrayal of the anointed king Cyrus stands in the background.

According to Williamson, the speaker, 'is here claiming to take over those parts of Cyrus' role which still remained to be fulfilled'.[14] In support of this and the allusion in general, Isaiah 61 implies that aspects of DI's restoration originally connected with Cyrus remain unfulfilled, so that the speaker views it as his duty to announce their immanent fulfilment. In Isaiah 61:4 he alludes to DI's restoration, promising:

> They will build up ancient devastations,
> > they will raise up former desolations;
> they will renew ruined cities,
> > the devastations of many generations.

By contrasting 'former (*rîšōnîm*) desolations' with 'renewal' (*ḥidēšû*), this verse recalls the 'former' (*rîšōnôt*) and 'new' (*ḥadāšôt*) things of DI, which are situated around the impending restoration under Cyrus (e.g. Isa. 41:22, 27; 42:9; 43:9,

---

13. See e.g. W. Ma, *Until the Spirit Comes: The Spirit of God in the Book of Isaiah*, JSOTSup 271 (Sheffield: Sheffield Academic Press, 1999), pp. 120–125; Williamson, *Variations*, p. 179. Also note 1 Sam. 10, 16, where Saul and David are anointed and endowed with the spirit of the Lord.

14. Williamson, *Variations*, p. 176.

18; 44:6).[15] For example, Isaiah 48 mentions the 'former' and 'new' things in connection with Cyrus' defeat of Babylon and freeing of captive Israelites (see 48:3–6, 14, 20). Also other phrases in 61:4 recall DI's awaited restoration. To 'raise up' (*qwm*) 'desolations' (*šōměmôt*) recalls 49:8, where God takes the servant 'to raise up (*qwm*) the land and apportion desolate (*šōměmôt*) heritages' (Isa. 61:2 is also thought to borrow from 49:8[16]). The 'desolations' and 'devastations' (*ḥorbôt*) of 61:4 also reflect DI's description of Judah's desolation in the exile (44:26; 49:19; 54:3). Isaiah 44:26 seems especially to have influenced 61:4, describing how God vowed to Jerusalem that in connection with Cyrus, 'I will raise up (*qwm*) her devastations (*ḥorbôteyha*)' (cf. 44:28).

Thus virtually all the terms in 61:4 are taken over from the description of restoration hoped for in DI, a restoration initiated by Cyrus, king of Persia, the 'anointed' of the Lord. That the figure behind 61 is likewise 'anointed' and reports that this restoration will soon be fulfilled suggests strongly that he is claiming to take over those aspects of Cyrus' role thought to remain unfulfilled.

If this is correct, then we may agree with Smith who notes that 'the speaker in 61:1–3 takes upon himself many of the terms and epithets used in chs 40–55 to refer to figures who announce or initiate salvation'.[17] So far we have seen that the speaker has adopted the roles of the servant and Cyrus as they are described in DI.

But why did the speaker associate the role of Cyrus with that of the servant? Such a move certainly required synthetic reflection on these texts. As Whybray observes, divine anointing 'finds no echo in the Servant Songs' of DI.[18] I would suggest the answer lies in a detail noted above, namely the royal description of the servant in 42:1–4. This description would have provided a natural association with that feature taken up by 61 from DI's description of the Persian king Cyrus, namely anointing – a feature most often associated with kings. If this was his logic, then the suggestion has merit that those royal

---

15. For a helpful survey of this theme, see C. R. North, 'The "Former Things" and the "New Things" in Deutero-Isaiah', in H. H. Rowley (ed.), *Studies in Old Testament Prophecy Presented to Professor Theodore H. Robinson* (New York: Scribner's, 1950), pp. 111–126.

16. Where 49:8 promises restoration in 'the time of favour' and 'day of salvation', Isa. 61:2 promises it in 'the year of favour / the day of vengeance': see Beuken, 'Isaiah 61', p. 425.

17. Smith, *Rhetoric*, p. 25.

18. Whybray, *Isaiah 40–66*, p. 240.

aspects of Isaiah 42 (and perhaps also Isa. 11) were not entirely forgotten, as the author of Isaiah 61 drew from these texts.[19]

The speaker's task

Up to this point we have concentrated on the role, or office, of the speaker, and have touched on a few aspects of his task that were influenced by DI. Turning now more directly to the tasks assigned the speaker of chapter 61, we may begin by noting that these are given in a string of infinitives, including 'to bring good news . . . to proclaim . . . to comfort'. As Beuken notes, this string of infinitives recalls an identical stylistic pattern used to describe the task of the servant in DI (e.g. 49:5–6, 8–9; 50:4).[20] One instance of this that also seems to be taken up in 61:1 comes in Isaiah 42:6–7. Here God says to the servant, 'I take you by the hand . . . to open (*lipqōaḥ*) blind eyes and to bring forth the prisoner (*'asîr*) from jail.' This task is adopted by the speaker of 61:1, who proclaims '*pĕqaḥ-qôaḥ* to the prisoners (*'ăsîrîm*)'. While the precise meaning of *pĕqaḥ-qôaḥ* is unclear, it probably derives from the root *pqḥ* (to open), so that it recalls 'to open' in 42:7. Reinforcing a DI background for 61:1, Isaiah 49:9 also speaks of a release of 'prisoners' (*'ăsîrîm*) in connection with the servant. Thus it is clear at the outset that DI influenced both the linguistic form of 61:1–3 as well as the tasks embodied in its infinitives. We may mention three further tasks adopted from DI.

　1. In 61:1 the commission 'to bring good news' (*bśr*) alludes to the repeated use of this verb in DI (40:9 [2×; 41:27; 52:7 [2×]). It does so, however, in development. Where passages in DI announce the good news to Zion (Isa. 41:27; 52:7),[21] the speaker of 61:1 announces it to the 'oppressed' (*'ănāwîm*), probably recalling DI's description of the exiles as 'the oppressed' (*'ăniyîm*; Isa. 41:17; 49:13).[22] Moreover, in 61:1–3 the good news is to be given to those who 'mourn' over Zion, a verb characteristic of TI, but that never occurs in DI.[23]

19. Cf. Bergsma, *Jubilee*, p. 200.

20. Beuken, 'Isaiah 61', pp. 416–417.

21. The two instances in 40:9 could be translated as in the NIV ('you who bring good tidings *to* Zion'): see Goldingay and Payne, *Isaiah 40–55*, pp. 86–87. Others translate it as the NRSV does ('O Zion, herald of good tidings'): see n. 24.

22. Note also DI's description of Zion as the 'oppressed one' (*'ăniyāh*) in Isa. 51:21 and 54:11. Since the messenger bringing good news (*bśr*) is sent to Zion in 41:27 and 52:7, a close association is made in DI between the good news and the oppressed, possibly explaining why the two were combined in 61:1–3.

23. Beuken, 'Isaiah 61', p. 420.

Also in development Isaiah 61 blends aspects of the one who preaches good news in DI with aspects of the servant and Cyrus. And this despite the fact that all three appear as distinct and separate figures in DI. Indeed, Isaiah 40:9 uses the verb *bsr* twice to mean 'herald of good news' and probably refers it *to Zion* ('O Zion, herald of good tidings').[24] In sum the speaker of Isaiah 61:1–3 takes up the task of preaching good news, and thus another role from DI – that of the herald of good news.

2. In 61:1–2 the speaker is twice told 'to proclaim', a command that might have been inspired by the fourfold repetition of this verb in 40:2–6. While the verb itself is not particularly rare, we have already seen that the content of the proclamation in 61:1–2 is drawn from DI. Without repeating what was said earlier, I would simply add the possibility that the call to proclaim 'to captives' (61:1) echoes DI's use of this term twice for Babylonian exiles (49:24–25) and once for the daughter of Zion (52:2).

There are indications here of development. If the proclamation is derived from DI, it is clear that 61:1–2 applies it to a new situation. The speaker of 61:2 proclaims 'liberty' (*dĕrôr*), a word referring to the law of jubilee prescribing emancipation from slavery every fiftieth year (Lev. 25).[25] This expression does not occur in DI, but it does fit the new post-exilic situation reflected in TI, where the people had returned to life in the land. If based on the fourfold use of the verb 'to proclaim' in 40:2–6, then 61:1–2 takes over for its speaker a role originally assigned to someone else. That the voices of 40:2–6 were open to interpretation at a very early stage is clear from the Septuagint and Targum: the Septuagint refers the voices to 'priests' (v. 2) and the Targum to 'prophets' (v. 1). Now Isaiah 40:2–6 is generally thought to be a scene from the divine council. Scholars assign the voices speaking to heavenly beings, including the imperative in verse 2 to 'proclaim' to Jerusalem that her hard service is over (cf. 1 Kgs 22:19–23; Job 1, 2).[26] If 40:2–6 influenced 61:1–2 (it is difficult to be sure), then the speaker adopted yet another role from DI.

3. Finally, and confirming a close relationship with Isaiah 40, the speaker of 61 is commissioned 'to comfort' (v. 2). Immediately this recalls the command of Isaiah 40:1 to 'comfort, comfort my people', a command that is part of the dialogue in the divine council just discussed. 'To comfort' (*nḥm*) occurs several further times in DI, reinforcing its special status in this part of the book (49:13; 51:3, 12, 19; 52:9; 54:11). Since scholars are generally agreed over this point

---

24. Whybray, *Isaiah 40–66*, p. 52; Williamson, *Variations*, p. 148, n. 60.

25. On this topic, see further Bergsma, *Jubilee*.

26. On this see Whybray, *Isaiah 40–66*, p. 48.

of influence, we may note that the speaker is to offer this comfort to those described in 61:3 as the 'faint (*kēhāh*) of spirit'. This perhaps echoes the 'faint (*kēhāh*) wick' of 42:3, those to whom the servant was to minister. This word occurs nowhere else in Isaiah.

We have now examined three infinitives describing the task of the speaker: 'to bring good news ... to proclaim ... to comfort'. To conclude this part of our discussion, we may note that all three are derived from DI, but that none is applied to the servant in DI, whose portrait also influenced 61:1–3. Thus Williamson rightly claims that the speaker

> takes to himself the task of proclaiming the future fulfilment of all the as yet unrealized tasks entrusted to a variety of figures in Deutero-Isaiah: Cyrus, the servant, the herald of good news, God's ministers in the heavenly court and the prophet himself.[27]

From the resulting textual blend in 61:1–3 emerges a composite character who single-handedly takes up God's plan where a host of earlier figures had left it off.

Isaiah 61:1–3 and Third-Isaiah's latest layer

It is widely thought that Isaiah 60 – 62 forms the earliest core of TI, around which much of the rest of this part of the book was written in later development (chapters 56–59 and 65–66).[28] This suggests that the inner-Isaianic reading proposed here remains incomplete if it fails to move beyond the recognition that DI influenced 61:1–3. It is also necessary to consider whether this later textual development might not have taken 61:1–3 itself in a new direction. Several scholars argue this,[29] and three of the main examples will illustrate the point.

1. When Isaiah 66:10 addresses 'those who mourn (*mt'blym*) over her [Jerusalem]', it clearly echoes texts from 60 – 62 promising that Zion's mourning (*'bl*) will end (60:20), and that those who mourn over Zion (*'bly s'ywn*) will receive comfort (61:2–3). Isaiah 66:10 develops these passages. Here, the mourners now appear on the positive side of a division between the righteous

---

27. Williamson, *Variations*, p. 187.

28. See, with further literature, Smith, *Rhetoric*, pp. 22–186.

29. See, with further literature, ibid., pp. 50–172.

and the wicked within the community (e.g. 66:5–6, 14), a division not found in 60 – 62.[30]

2. Taking up 61, Isaiah 58 – 59 reflects the prerequisite for falling on the positive side of this division. Here it is widely agreed that the immanent salvation of 60 – 62 was seen to be delayed by 58 – 59 because of sin, and that any fulfilment of it was made to depend on a change in behaviour. Hence where 60:1 proclaims, 'Arise, shine (*'órî*) because your light (*'ór*) has come', Isaiah 59:9 explains, 'we expect light (*'ór*) but, look, darkness', because of sin (59:1–8). Conversely, obedience to the conditions of 58 brings salvation: 'then your light (*'ór*) will shine in the darkness' (58:10). The passage continues in 58:12, with what is generally recognized as an allusion to 61:3b–4:

> And from you they will rebuild ancient devastations,
>   you will raise up foundations of many generations;
> and you will be called (*wĕqōrā' lĕkā*) repairer of the breach . . .
> (58:12)

> And they will be called (*wĕqōrā' lāhem*) oaks of righteousness . . . ;
> and they will rebuild ancient devastations,
>   they will raise up former desolations;
> and they will renew ruined cities,
>   the desolations of many generations.
> (61:3b–4)

Thus the unconditional promise of 61 receives a condition for fulfilment in the later 58.

3. Several convincingly argue that 56:1–8 takes up and develops 60 – 62 along lines significantly more inclusive with respect to the non-Israelite.[31] This is no less the case for chapter 61. So when 56:6 speaks of the foreigner (*bny hnkr*) who would serve (*lšrtw*) the Lord, there seems to be a clear development of 61:5–6, which speaks of how the foreigner (*bny nkr*) would serve the Israelites who are called 'servants (*mšrty*) of our God'. In support of this allusion we may note that the expression *bny nkr* occurs several times in 60 – 62,

---

30. Ibid., pp. 25–26.

31. Ibid., p. 59; L.-S. Tiemeyer, *Priestly Rites and Prophetic Rage: Post-Exilic Prophetic Critique of the Priesthood*, FAT 2.19 (Tübingen: Mohr Siebeck, 2006), pp. 274–281.

but apart from 56:1–8 is found nowhere else in the book (Isa. 56:3, 6; 60:10; 61:5; 62:8). However, in contrast to 56:1–8, all occurrences in 60 – 62 depict the foreigner as an outsider who will be subservient to Zion and her population on the day of salvation. The same may be said of the verb *šrt* (to serve). Apart from 56:1–8, it is only otherwise found in 60 – 62 within the book, and in the references there foreigners and their wealth are subject to Zion (Isa. 56:6; 60:7, 10; 61:6). Thus Isaiah 56:1–8 develops the vision of 61 in a more inclusive direction. And since 61:5–6 flows immediately out of, and is of a piece with, 61:1–3,[32] we may allow this conclusion to further illustrate the point at hand: that the message of 61:1–3 (which is not to be separated from 61:5–6) receives a new hearing in this latter layer.

From these examples it emerges that the new direction taken by 56 – 59 and 65 – 66 may be described paradoxically as both a qualification and expansion of the salvation announced in 61: it is a qualification because the promise is now conditional and only the righteous will enjoy it; it is an expansion because those considered eligible now include the Gentiles.

Clearly, it has not been possible to give a full argument for every case of Isaianic influence mentioned here. Nor have I been able to treat the many exegetical aspects of the Hebrew. It is hoped, however, that this study will give the student a clearer sense of what it may mean to read Isaiah 61:1–3 diachronically and within Isaiah as a whole. Reading this way, moreover, the student may gain a new appreciation for aspects of its interpretation that emerged into full view in the exegetical practices seen at Qumran and reflected in the New Testament.[33]

Bibliography

Bergsma, J., *The Jubilee from Leviticus to Qumran*, VTSup 115 (Leiden: Brill, 2007).

Beuken, W. A. M., 'Servant and Herald of Good Tidings: Isaiah 61 as an Interpretation of Isaiah 40–55', in J. Vermeylen (ed.), *The Book of Isaiah*, BETL 81 (Leuven: Leuven University Press, 1989), pp. 411–440.

Blenkinsopp, J., *Isaiah 56–66*, AB 19B (New York: Doubleday, 2003).

Childs, B., *Isaiah*, OTL (Louisville: Westminster, 2000).

Goldingay, J., and D. Payne, *Isaiah 40–55*, vol. 1, ICC (London: T. & T. Clark International, 2006).

---

32. Smith, *Rhetoric*, pp. 26–38.

33. See e.g. Gregory, 'Exile', pp. 475–496.

Gregory, B. C., 'The Postexilic Exile in Third Isaiah: Isaiah 61:1–3 in Light of Second
   Temple Hermeneutics', *JBL* 126 (2007), pp. 475–496.

Heskett, R., *Messianism within the Scriptural Scrolls of Isaiah*, LHB/OTS 456 (London:
   T. & T. Clark International, 2007).

Lau, W., *Schriftgelehrte Prophetie in Jes 56–66*, BZAW 225 (Berlin: de Gruyter, 1994).

Ma, W., *Until the Spirit Comes: The Spirit of God in the Book of Isaiah*, JSOTSup 271
   (Sheffield: Sheffield Academic Press, 1999).

Moor, J. C. de (ed.), *Synchronic or Diachronic? A Debate on Method in Old Testament Exegesis*,
   OTS 34 (Leiden: Brill, 1995).

North, C. R., 'The "Former Things" and the "New Things" in Deutero-Isaiah', in H. H.
   Rowley (ed.), *Studies in Old Testament Prophecy Presented to Professor Theodore H. Robinson*
   (New York: Scribner's, 1950), pp. 111–126.

Smith, P. A., *Rhetoric and Redaction in Trito-Isaiah*, VTSup 62 (Leiden: Brill, 1995).

Sommer, B., *A Prophet Reads Scripture: Allusion in Isaiah 40–66* (Stanford: Stanford
   University Press, 1998).

Tiemeyer, L.-S., *Priestly Rites and Prophetic Rage: Post-Exilic Prophetic Critique of the Priesthood*,
   FAT 2.19 (Tübingen: Mohr Siebeck, 2006).

Whybray, R. N., *Isaiah 40–66*, NCBC (Grand Rapids: Eerdmans, 1975).

Williamson, H. G. M., *Variations on a Theme: King, Messiah and Servant in the Book of Isaiah*
   (Carlisle: Paternoster, 1998).

Zimmerli, W., 'Zur Sprache Tritojesajas', in *Gottes Offenbarung: Gesammelte Aufsätze*
   (Munich: Chr. Kaiser, 1969), pp. 221–225.

INDEX OF NAMES

INDEX OF SCRIPTURE REFERENCES

INDEX OF QUMRAN LITERATURE REFERENCES